THE DUCHESS OF DINO

Philip Ziegler is one of Britain's leading historians and biographers. Born in 1929, he was educated at Eton and New College, Oxford, where he gained first class honours in Jurisprudence. He then joined the Diplomatic Service and served in Vientiane, Paris, Pretoria and Bogotá before joining the publishers William Collins, where he was editorial director for fifteen years. His books have included a study of the Black Death, and biographies of William IV, Melbourne, Lady Diana Cooper, and the acclaimed *Mountbatten, King Edward VIII* and *Wilson: The Authorised Life*. He lives in London with his wife.

Also by Philip Ziegler

Addington
The Black Death
King William IV
Melbourne
Diana Cooper
Mountbatten
King Edward VIII
Wilson: The Authorised Life
Osbert Sitwell
Soldiers

THE DUCHESS OF DINO

Chatelaine of Europe

Philip Ziegler

PHOENIX

A PHOENIX PRESS PAPERBACK

First published in Great Britain
by William Collins Sons and Co Ltd in 1962
This paperback edition published in 2003
by Phoenix Press,
a division of The Orion Publishing Group Ltd,
Orion House, 5 Upper St Martin's Lane,
London WC2H 9EA
Phoenix Press
Sterling Publishing Co Inc
387 Park Avenue South
New York
NY 10016-8810
USA

A CIP catalogue record for this book is
available from the British Library.

Printed and bound in Great Britain by
Butler & Tanner Ltd, Frome and London

ISBN 1 84212 586 9

To Sarah

Preface

I had often wished that I could write a book about Prince Talleyrand but knew too well that I lacked both the time and the qualifications required to make any fresh contribution to the copious literature which already existed. I came therefore to his niece, the Duchess of Dino, as something of a second best, a means of writing about Talleyrand without appearing to have done so. It did not take me long to discover that she was a figure of high distinction in her own right but I did not realise until I had almost finished my work that, as a subject for a biography, she was a very acceptable substitute for her uncle.

Except in the interpretation of motives I have eschewed flights of fancy. All the incidents described in this book either took place or, at least, are recorded as having done so in some reasonably reputable history or memoir. The occasional dialogues were transcribed either by the Duchess or by some other witness. So far as possible I have indicated the source in the text but where it seemed necessary I have given details in notes at the end of the book.

The only previous full-length study of the Duchess of Dino was that by Mlle Françoise de Bernardy. It has not been published in an English translation. I have seen a very different Duchess from that portrayed by Mlle de Bernardy—the book, indeed, would hardly have been worth writing if I had not. I am most aware, however, that I owe her all the gratitude which a biographer must always owe to anyone who has already treated his subject with insight and skill.

I am most grateful for the permission to reproduce their pictures given me by the Duke of Talleyrand and of Dino, Duke Jean Sagan-Valençay, Graf Georg Clam-Martinitz, the Travellers' Club and Monsieur Emile Terry, former

Preface

owner of the chateau of Rochecotte, who restored it with a taste and skill that places in his debt all those who care to see the past invoked and cherished. The Duke of Talleyrand and Prince Clary and Aldringen gave me advice and kind encouragement. Lady Diana Cooper generously allowed me to consult Lord Norwich's library at Chantilly. I owe many thanks to Lady Gladwyn who constantly helped and advised me in my efforts to secure material. The staffs of the Bibliothèque de l'Arsenal and of the Bibliothèque Nationale were invariably patient and well-informed. Finally, the help of my wife has been of inestimable value. Without her, it seems certain that an unwieldy mass of manuscript would never have evolved into something which, for all its faults, is indubitably a book.

I

Peter Biren, last reigning Duke of Courland, had done little to deserve his people's love. Under the rule of his family progress had barely touched his remote and gloomy Baltic duchy. So long as his reign continued, there seemed no reason to think that it ever would.

Even before he had succeeded as duke, Peter had acquired a reputation for stubbornness, arrogance and spite. His sudden fits of fury were notorious; less conspicuous though hardly more agreeable were his long bouts of black gloom in which he spoke to no one and suffered no one to speak to him. His first wife, Caroline-Louise, Princess of Waldeck, was driven almost distraught by his brutality and bad manners. She divorced him after seven years. His second wife, Princess Jessupow, lasted only four. In 1779 the duke decided to marry again for what was to be the third and final time; this time, however, he had found a wife who could tame his rages and was to conduct his life to a tranquil and comparatively well-ordered end.

Anne Charlotte Dorothea of Medem had been born in 1761 into one of the richest and most cosmopolitan of the families of Courland. " Seven centuries of noble lineage, an attractive face and a reputation for goodness established from her youth, distinguished my mother . . ." wrote Dorothea of Dino thirty years later and nobody has ever challenged the beauty, charm or intelligence of the new Duchess of Courland. Only nineteen when she married, she seems to have been trustful and equable by disposition; in more sympathetic hands she might have become loving and loyal. As it was, she did not find in her marriage any intimacy beyond the carnal or any relationship warmer than a sullen and suspicious neutrality. She derived from her marriage no satisfaction other than that of being rich, powerful and a duchess. In circumventing and controlling her ageing husband's bouts of fury she learnt cunning and acquired a strange, cold strength. In the battle she lost what she had never more than half possessed ; true sensibility and a heart.

The duchess was popular in Courland but not even she could reconcile the people to their ruler. Peter Biren was always preparing for the day when he would be chased into exile. Like every nervous ruler his attention turned to the possibilities of investment abroad. In 1786, after a protracted tour of Italy and Germany, he had bought the vast estate of Sagan about a hundred miles south-east of Berlin. This property, which had once been a fief of Wallenstein's, carried with it the hereditary title of Duke of Sagan. Frederick II of Prussia, anxious to encourage this rich and resplendent foreigner to live among his subjects, obligingly altered the terms of the fief so that it could descend by the female line as well as by the male. This meant much to Duke Peter, whose first three children had all been daughters. He still hoped for a son but now he knew that at least some part of his glory would pass on.

The purchase of Sagan, undertaken for fear that the Courlanders and, in particular, their recalcitrant Diet, might get completely out of hand, in its turn served to alienate the members of the Diet still more completely from their wandering duke. His absence indeed irritated them hardly less than his presence. The only chance for the duke to restore his position seemed to be to enlist on his side King Stanislas Augustus of Poland, nominally the feudal overlord of Courland. It was decided that the duchess herself should go to Warsaw to see what could be done.

Seventeen-ninety, the year in which the duchess went off alone on her embassy, marked, in a sense, the end of her married life. Duke Peter was only sixty-six but in spirit he was far older. The hectic tempo of his life had burned out his energy, his political disasters sucked away his faith in his own strength. With the decision that his wife should go to

Warsaw to fight his battles for him he virtually abdicated all that was left of his responsibilities and rights. During the last ten years of his life the duchess enjoyed almost complete independence, paying due attention to the proprieties, remembering her husband's existence whenever it suited her, but in reality adopting the habits and the manners of an exceedingly merry widow.

Negotiations in Warsaw dragged on till well into 1791. To win her cause the duchess had to win the support of the Diet and for that she soon decided she would have to win the sympathy of a certain Alexander Batowski. She found the task congenial.

Batowski was then in the early thirties. His slight, dapper figure, deep-set eyes and flowing black hair produced an impression of romantic gloom which he intently fostered by refusing to defer to the normal fetishes of polite society. He came from a Galician family, respectable but without particular distinction, and owed his pre-eminence to his skill in propounding the liberal ideas which he had picked up in France and his good fortune in professing them before a public which found them both novel and attractive.

The concept of a solitary woman battling alone for her family's fortune stirred his romantic enthusiasm and he soon became her devoted champion. When at last the Diet decided in favour of the duchess his efforts were rewarded by more than the mere pleasure of victory. " Her gratitude," Baron Vitrolles wrote dryly, " was as lively as it was natural. She gave to Count Batowski all the evidence of an affection so keen that nothing could efface it."

Duke Peter only enjoyed for a few months the fruits of his wife's triumph. In May, 1792, Russian troops attacked Lithuania and a short time later Courland also was invaded. The duke did not stay to argue but bundled a few pet possessions into his velvet-lined carriage and fled to Prussia. There, a few months later, Batowski followed him. The duchess greeted him with enthusiasm, the duke with, it seems, decent resignation. He was installed in the palace as a more or less permanent guest and settled down to cultivate his friendship with the duchess. Princess Dorothea of Courland was born on the 21st August, 1793.

* * * * *

It is, of course, impossible to state with certainty that Batowski was the father of Dorothea. Most of the available evidence, however, suggests he was. For at least a year before Dorothea's birth Batowski had lived under the same roof as her mother and was everywhere assumed to be her lover. Duke Peter was sixty-nine in 1793 and had crumbled into a premature senility. Portraits of Batowski are too few and inadequate for any real or imagined likeness between him and Dorothea to have more than trifling importance ; certainly, however, it is more easy to detect in Dorothea traces of her mother's dark and slender lover than of her heavy coarse and highly-coloured husband. The only evidence suggesting that Duke Peter was in fact as well as title the father of Dorothea lies in the apparent complaisance with which he accepted her into his family. Even in this, it is easier to see the apathy of the old and tired than the proud enthusiasm of a father.

Whichever of them may have been the true father of Dorothea, it is certain that Batowski played the larger part in the first few years of her life. Shortly after the birth of Dorothea, the Duchess of Courland installed Batowski at Löbikau, her estate in Saxony. From now on she divided her time more or less equally between Sagan and Löbikau ; wintering at the first with her husband and all the four surviving daughters, spending the summers at the second alone with Dorothea and Batowski.

Some of Dorothea's earliest memories were of life at Sagan. She seems to have relished its grandeur and solemnity. Later, to her regret, its architecture was to be curbed to Italianate regularity but in the days when she knew it first Sagan flourished in pell-mell Gothic extravagance above the fast-flowing waters of the River Bober. The castle, grandiose, gloomy and spectacularly uncomfortable, was haunted by the ghost of the great Wallenstein who had built it when his glory was at its zenith but had suffered betrayal and murder before he had been able to enjoy it for more than a few fleeting visits.

Life was run on almost regal lines. Duke Peter, especially after he had sold his duchy to its conqueror, the Empress Catherine, had far more money available to give substance to his grandeur than was the case at most of the more genuinely " royal " courts of Europe. Sagan was always filled with guests, not only the nobility of the provinces but drawn from all the capitals of Europe. The great hunting parties were legendary, the banquets formidable and magnificent, and, after they had ridden all day in the forests and stuffed themselves for two hours in the evening, such of the guests as were still awake would be entertained by the resident team of actors or by the latest singer from Italy or musician from Berlin.

Dorothea had small part to play in this rich if somewhat tedious splendour. She saw little of her father though the old man seems to have been amiable enough whenever he was conscious of her existence. He had always been fond of children and animals and reserved his malice mainly for those more able to appreciate it. Dorothea admired his dignity and found his senile gentleness an agreeable change after the acerbity of her mother. In his old age Duke Peter seems to have lost the capacity and even the desire to injure and with it most of his zest for life. Certainly the tamed and quiescent figure whom Dorothea knew bore little resemblance to the Bluebeard whom the Duchess of Courland had taken on some twenty years before.

In summer Duke Peter and his three eldest daughters would go off to the duke's estate at Nachod while Dorothea and her mother went their way to the rustic idylls of Löbikau. For Batowski indeed, cut off as he was from all the intrigues and publicity which had filled his life in Warsaw, it must have been a little too idyllic to be agreeable.

Batowski was one of those unhappy creatures who are romantic without being capable of any profound or enduring affection and therefore find themselves continually propelled into situations which they have little inclination to sustain. To be in love was a necessity of living with all the occasions that it gave for flamboyant gestures, tears and triumphs, quarrels and reconciliations; but the affair was all and consummation never so exciting as the preceding conflict. The more temperate satisfactions of love in a cottage, even when the cottage had all the appurtenances of Löbikau, were little to his taste.

The Duchess of Courland was ill-equipped to understand her unpredictable and brooding lover. She tried to overcome his rising discontent by pandering to all his whims and merely made him more and more disgruntled. He asked for books ; the finest and richest editions were ordered for him from all over Europe. He announced that the atmosphere of the big house oppressed him and that he must have a refuge where he could be alone. The duchess hired an Italian architect to build him a little lodge in the woods about a mile from Löbikau. To make its surroundings still more delectable a score or so of hundred-year-old oak trees were rooted out and replanted at enormous expense outside his windows. He took it all as his right and sulked as frequently as ever.

It was typical of Batowski and of his whole attitude towards life that he should only have realised how much he loved and needed the duchess when she fell in love with another man. By then it was too late. His petulance and tepid passion had fatally undermined the duchess's affection for him. Her wealth and beauty, her virtual independence from her husband, made her a tempting prey for the adventurers of Europe and in 1798, in Carlsbad, she fell into the company of one whose determination, energy and ruthlessness was to make short shrift of the tears and tantrums of her established lover.

*   *   *   *   *

Gustave Maurice, Baron d'Armfeld was a soldier by profession, born of Finnish parents in 1757. The patronage, first of an elderly field-marshal, then of King Gustavus III, had protected him from the troubles in which his cynicism, insolence and immorality would otherwise have involved him. But when the king died he ran foul of the regent, the Duke of Suderman, was tried for treason, condemned to death *in absentia* and solemnly burnt in effigy.

Now began the period of Armfeld's wandering from court

to court, taking any odd and probably disreputable job that might be offered him and otherwise living off the favours of wealthy female admirers. When the Duchess of Courland met him at Carlsbad he was forty-two. " Monsieur d'Armfeld was remarkably good-looking," wrote the Duchess d'Abrantès. " He was tall with an imposing air and hid, under an appearance of calm and even coolness, the most tempestuous of passions." All reports agree on the strange, almost sinister fascination which was felt by every woman who met him and the force of his personality which imposed itself ruthlessly on anyone who once accepted him as a friend or lover.

The following year they met again at Carlsbad and the duchess's tentative approval warmed quickly into passionate love. They returned together to Löbikau where Batowski still lingered mournfully in his Italianate summer-house. The duchess had no wish to quarrel with him or to hurt his feelings but was in considerable doubt how best to maintain her two lovers in something near harmony. The problem, however, was not yet to come to a head for Duke Peter chose this moment to drift into the illness which was to draw him peacefully to his death. The duchess, escorted by Armfeld, left for the death-bed of her husband.

Duke Peter of Courland died on 13th January, 1800. To his eldest daughter Wilhelmina he bequeathed the fief of Sagan with the title of Duchess, but there was enough left from his enormous personal fortune to ensure that all his daughters were numbered amongst the richest heiresses of Europe. Included in the share of Dorothea was the vast baroque palace in the Unter den Linden which was eventually to become the Russian Embassy at Berlin. The death of her father, this shadowy figure who had treated her with a kindness as occasional as it was remote, made no very vivid impression on the mind of the seven-year-old child. She had a vague understanding that some catastrophe had occurred but her grief was little more intense than it would have been for an earthquake in Mexico or famine in China. There was little in her mother's bearing to suggest that the event had any more personal significance.

The Duchess of Courland could, of course, be relied on to

B

avoid any action which would have been too obviously indecorous. Her first step after the funeral was to retreat with Armfeld to contemplate her future. It promised to be a little complicated. At the moment when her passion for Batowski had been at its most violent she had undertaken to marry him within a year of the death of her husband. A mere verbal promise might not have disturbed the duchess very deeply but, with a business-like thoroughness which to-day seems slightly out of place but was by no means uncommon at the period, she had affirmed the agreement by a contract, formally drawn up and signed, in which she promised in case of default to pay a penalty of a hundred and fifty thousand florins.

She disliked the idea of buying off her former lover at such a price. What was more, though she was cold and selfish enough, she had loved Batowski for too long to discard him without a qualm. But the thought of actually marrying him now seemed to her positively repugnant. Quite apart from her new enthusiasm for Armfeld, once the romantic dust had settled she had realised that Batowski was socially impossible as a husband. How could she, Duchess of Courland, intimate friend of Prussia's royal family, herself of semi-royal status, ally herself with a liberal politician from a petty family of Poland ? And even if she herself was prepared to sacrifice her position how could she inflict such damage upon the prospects of her children ?

The Duchess of Courland was not slow to reconcile her duty with her inclinations. Taking Armfeld along with her to act as a second in the expected battle, she set out to meet and discard her former lover. In the heart-rending and passionately protracted scenes which followed, it is impossible to believe that Batowski did not find some compensation for the years of apathetic luxury at Löbikau. Tears, protestations, invective, oaths of eternal affection : for twenty-four hours without a break the discussions went on. Batowski tried everything : indignant reproaches, supplication, threats of suicide. At last he despaired. Seizing the contract by which the duchess pledged herself to marry him, he flung it into the fire and thus released his mistress simultaneously from her marital obligations and her potential debt of a hundred and fifty thousand florins.

Armfeld, Batowski and the duchess then dined amicably together and the two men left next morning for Löbikau ; on the best of terms, according to Vitrolles. At Löbikau this bizarre *ménage à trois* lingered on for a little while ; Armfeld and the duchess installed in the big house and Batowski in his little lodge. Even for Batowski, however, the emotional atmosphere proved a little turgid and the Pole decided to set out on his travels again. He said an affectionate good-bye to his duchess and departed in search of somebody else with whom he could fall hopelessly in love.

*   *   *   *   *

Armfeld, left master of the field, now proceeded to consolidate his position. " My whole family," wrote Dorothea, " was under the spell of this Baron d'Armfeld ; so fatal to the tranquillity of all those whom he called his friends. He ruled our domestic life despotically . . ." His first interest lay in the marriages of the three elder Princesses of Courland : in 1800 aged nineteen, eighteen, and seventeen respectively. All three were to marry noblemen of great name ; not one of them was to find in their marriage any real affection or even a shred of amicable companionship.

At the death of her father, the eldest daughter Wilhelmina had inherited the title of Duchess of Sagan. It is probably true to say that her wealth, position and undoubted talents made her the most desirable wife in Europe. At one time it was proposed that she should marry Louis Ferdinand, Prince of Prussia, gallant, handsome and impetuous, " a meteor blazing in a heaven of military stars " as Von der Goltz described him. But the king was over-persuaded by his ministers and reluctantly ruled that the marriage should not be.

Profoundly disappointed, Wilhelmina launched herself upon the career of excess and intrigue which was to make her the scandal of Europe. As a first step she showed her pique by marrying a French *émigré* serving with the Austrian army. It is difficult to find for her decision any other motive than that of scoring off the Prussian court. Prince Louis de Rohan certainly bore a great name but otherwise had no claim to such a prize. " He had," wrote Dorothea coldly, " a handsome face in which I never found either nobility or intelligence." He was virtually penniless, his future to say the least was uncertain. One thing at least is certain ; that Wilhelmina never loved him.

Pauline, second of the Courland sisters, was quite as eager as Wilhelmina to leave the chill and stifling discipline of the family home. She snatched gratefully at the first suitor who came along ; Frederick Hermann, Prince of Hohenzollern-Hechingen, from 1810 to be head of the older branch of the house of Brandenburg. From a worldly point of view, Pauline did considerably better for herself than her elder sister. As a happy marriage, however, the match was quite as pitiful a failure. Prince Hohenzollern made as bad an impression on the young Dorothea as had her other brother-in-law : " a great nobleman, no doubt, of whom the only criticism I can make is that there was absolutely nothing in him which one could find to praise except the distinction of his birth."

Alone among the three elder sisters, it seems to have occurred to Jeanne that there might be something else to look for in marriage beyond worldly position and a merciful deliverance from her family. At the age of sixteen she eloped with the music-master, a young German named Arnold. Arnold got Princess Jeanne safely away to Erfurt but there made the mistake of depositing her with some friends while he went on to Hamburg to sell her jewels and arrange their passage to America. During his absence, Prussian troops tracked down the errant princess and carried her, protesting, back to her in-dignant family.

Duke Peter, already moribund, still had just enough spirit left in him to refuse to greet the daughter who had been driven into her folly by his own harshness and her mother's cold indifference. Brooding, he skulked away to Prague. He left as tutor to his daughter, Count Wratislaw, an amateur poet of some repute whose usual and more appropriate occupation was that of Chief of Police. Naturally the latter intercepted all letters to Princess Jeanne and it was not long before he came across one from the music-master who was lurking in the neighbourhood in an effort to persuade the young princess to try her luck again. Count Wratislaw did not fail to profit by this rashness. Arnold was lured to a rendezvous where he expected to find his princess and was arrested on arrival. Here operetta turned to tragedy ; the unfortunate music-master was thrown into prison and, it seems most probable, executed or murdered a few days later.

With a resilience which reflected her upbringing, Jeanne too was shortly looking for a husband and, in fact, achieved her object before either of her elder sisters. In March, 1801, Jeanne married Francis Pignatelli of Belmonte, Duke of Acerenza. Dorothea found quite as little to rejoice at in this match as in those of her other sisters and attributed it to the pressure of the family which, not surprisingly, thought that Jeanne had better find a husband before some fresh escapade finally destroyed her stock in the marriage-market. " It was to these differing motives," she went on sadly, summing up the experiences of her three sisters, " so inadequate as a basis for a decision in the only great problem which arises in the life of a woman, that must be attributed the total lack of happiness which my sisters have found in their marriages and the alacrity with which they have profited from the opportunities offered by the Protestant faith and the customs of their country to escape from their alliances, as ill-matched as they were frivolously arranged."

Wilhelmina set the pattern by breaking up her marriage almost before it had been consummated. Armfeld, now besottedly in love with her, seems to have been responsible. But he could not maintain his position for long. A dangerous, international adventurer and a renowned lover he might have been, but in trying to maintain his grip on the Courland family, simultaneously living with the daughter and retaining his formal status as lover of the mother, he had taken on a task which would have tested a compound of Casanova and Machiavelli.

The Duchess of Courland treated him with ever greater indifference and, according to Nesselrode, seems to have transferred her favours to Maximilien d'Alopeus, Russian Minister in Berlin and, like Armfeld, a Finn. Wilhelmina in her turn soon tired of him, never answered his letters, scoffed at his devotion. Saddened and discouraged, Armfeld wrote in the summer of 1802 to his friend La Tour. " She has some great and some noble qualities ; she has, too, vices which I recognise as clearly. I have cherished her more as my child than as my lover. I do not blind myself to the difference of our ages, to the need which her young heart feels to attach itself to some being who, for a thousand reasons, might please and suit her better than a sorrowful old man . . . I do not ask ever to see her again." At the end of the year he was offered and gladly accepted the post of Swedish Minister at Vienna ; beaten and dejected he crept from the picture while Wilhelmina and her mother continued care-free down the course along which he had done so much to encourage them.

*　　*　　*　　*　　*

It was against this back-cloth of lies and plots, passions and hatreds, selfishness, disloyalty and insincerity, that Dorothea of Courland lived the first years of her life. The fact that she was ten years younger than her nearest sister and the somewhat uncertain circumstances of her birth set her aside from the main life of the family. She was too much of a child to share the pleasures or the work of her sisters and her mother at first showed not the slightest interest in her happiness or her education. The Duchess of Courland was never actively unkind ; merely she found nothing in Dorothea to distract her from her lovers and her salon. She handed over the problems of her daughter's physical, spiritual and intellectual advancement to a half-crazed English governess and thankfully forgot her responsibilities in the pleasures of society. The governess had no doubts as to how to bring up her charge ; if the flesh were sufficiently mortified then the spirit could look after itself. Dorothea was treated with insensate brutality, savagely whipped for any or even no provocation, forced to run naked in the icy cold of a Prussian winter. Of education proper she had none ; discipline was all, discipliue and a ruthless denial of anything which might have softened or made more interesting her existence.

Naturally a nervous and sensitive child, Dorothea under this treatment became sulky, reserved and suspicious of everyone around her. Her body almost broke under the strain but her tenacious spirit clung on to some shreds of self-respect. She varied her usual cowed acceptance of the pains and humiliations which afflicted her with sudden bursts of fierce resistance which sometimes won her a little respite from her torment but earned her also a reputation for obstinacy and ill-will. Dorothea was later to find excuses and explanations for all the misery which came to her through her mother's disinterest and neglect but she was never quite to forget or to feel for the duchess the trust and love which she knew should exist between mother and child.

Dorothea was not a particularly prepossessing child ; if she had been she would have stood a better chance of being occasionally rescued from the nursery to serve as an ornament in her mother's salon :

" Small, skinny, yellow in complexion," she described herself, " always ill from the moment of my birth. My eyes were so dark and huge that they were out of all proportion to the rest of my face and seemed to dwarf the other features. I would have been decidedly ugly if it had not been for my constant ardour and animation which made people forget my almost cadaverous features and suspect the existence of the force which lay underneath. I had a sullen nature and only in my sulkiness did there seem to be anything which properly belonged to childhood. Sad almost to the point of melancholia, I remember perfectly how I longed to die . . . ."

It was those huge, dark eyes which are first to be mentioned in almost every description of Dorothea. Called sometimes deep-blue, sometimes grey, sometimes black, they seem in fact to have been of a blue so dark that save from a few inches away it was impossible to detect that they were not black ; " burning with an infernal fire which turned night into day," as Sainte-Beuve was later to write. There is nothing of an infernal fire in the eyes of Dorothea as they shine from Grassi's portrait of her painted when she was seven years old ; only gaiety and intelligence. Looking at that picture, it is uncomfortable to think how often in the first years of her life those same eyes must have been filled with tears and have shone with pain, fear and anger.

It was Armfeld, in most ways so malign an influence, who delivered Dorothea from this old witch of an English governess. Talking one day to the child he was dismayed to discover that she could neither read or write ; her only intellectual attainment in fact being a knowledge of drawing-room French, servant-quarters' German and a modicum of nursery English. It is much to Armfeld's credit that he did not let himself be put off by the hostility which he met in this haggard little waif but recognised it for what it was—the fear and suspicion of a naturally warm-hearted child who, in all her life, had met little but brutality and cold indifference. He persevered and insisted that Dorothea must at once be taught to read. He suspected, at first, that the child might be naturally stupid, even, so awkward was her manner, mentally deficient. The first few lessons showed him how wrong he was. Within a week she was reading fluently ; like a starved kitten before a bowl of cream she gulped down all that was offered her and asked for more. The Duchess of Courland was informed that, far from being a feeble-minded savage, her daughter was bidding fair to show herself a prodigy. With sudden though short-lived enthusiasm she realised that, after all, this ungainly, moody child might be transformed into a social asset. She began to take an exaggerated interest in her daughter's intellectual advancement :

" A good governess," Dorothea wrote dryly in her *Souvenirs* " who would have been perfectly sufficient for such a child, would not have seemed to give enough lustre to this education which was now being launched with such pomp. To the governess was therefore added a tutor and . . . I found myself subject to two rival powers who were soon in a state of war with each other ; for the abbé Piattoli and Mademoiselle Hoffmann, who began by liking each other too well, finished by disliking each other heartily."

The abbé Piattoli and Mlle Hoffmann ; it would have been difficult to have found for a child's education two people more understanding, conscientious or well-meaning. How happy Dorothea might have been with either, how confused her life was to become when she had the benefit of them both. Each of them was in his own way a remarkable personality and each exercised a profound influence on their young and ductile charge.

Scipione Piattoli, Florentine by origin, began life as a monk but was laicized in 1774 when he was twenty-five years old. He found his way to Poland and became tutor to Prince Adam Czartoryski who was later to become famous as leader of the liberals and hero of the Polish fight for independence. A convinced Voltairean, supporter of any progressive theory, Piattoli did nothing to check Prince Adam's leanings. He himself, by his learning and political activity, soon gained the attention of King Stanislas of Poland. He became secretary to the king and played a large part in the drafting of the liberal constitution of 1791 which did so much to provoke the Russians to attack his country of adoption. It was at this period, when he was a power in Warsaw, that he met the Duchess of Courland and gave her help in her battle against the Diet of Mittau. He was to be repaid many times over, for in 1792 followed the occupation of Poland by the Russians. Piattoli was thrown into prison by the invaders and it is unlikely that he would ever have emerged but for the intervention of the duchess and of his former pupil, Adam Czartoryski, who had now become a close friend of the young Tsar Alexander. Though freed he was not allowed to stay in Poland and, after many wanderings, arrived in Berlin in the spring of 1802. The Duchess of Courland welcomed him enthusiastically and charged him with the education of her daughter. He was hardly an impressive figure, small, thin, balding, whose constant nervous agitation betrayed itself in a host of restless and uneasy gestures. Dorothea, however, took to him at once ; he was sympathetic, highly intelligent, above all, he showed from the start that he cared deeply for the little princess and would think no effort too great if it would lead to her happiness or her improvement.

If Piattoli was a laicized monk, Regina Hoffmann was not far from being a renegade nun. Born German, she had followed a young man to Paris and had been on the point of marrying him when he abruptly died. Abandoned so unkindly almost at the altar, Mlle Hoffmann took refuge in religion, became a Roman Catholic and retired into a convent. A few days before she took her final vows she suddenly had second thoughts about her so recently discovered faith and emerged from the convent a convinced free-thinker. From Paris she found her way to Poland where she became governess to Princess Potocka. For her, as for Piattoli, the Russian invasion meant the disruption of her life. Her pupil's father was thrown into prison and she herself left Poland in search of new occupation. She accepted with alacrity the offer of the Duchess of Courland to take a half share in Dorothea's education.

Piattoli and Mlle Hoffmann should have made a congenial pair. Both were victims of Russian imperialism, both were liberal in idea and relaxed in religious observance, both were sincerely devoted to the little princess. But soon their fundamentally different conceptions of the lines along which they wished their charge to develop and their determination that they alone should be the creative force drove them into bitter and continual dispute. The result might have been fatal to their pupil's advancement but luckily Dorothea, secure in the knowledge that both the combatants wished her nothing but well, surveyed their bickerings with equanimity and even derived a certain entertainment and profit from the ensuing confusion :

" There was nothing in common between them except a passionate affection for me. . . . Their characters . . . were so strongly opposed that I was perpetually perplexed as to how I was to conform to two so contrary wills. My governess, if I wished to act on the advice of the abbé, was immediately struck down by a horrifying attack of nerves ; the abbé, if I did the opposite, railed against the absurd system of education which Mlle Hoffmann had adopted. I ended by becoming well acquainted with the nerves of the one and the furies of the other and accepted from both of them whatever seemed to me reasonable, or, even more, whatever was to my liking. Whatever I did, I was quite sure that one or other of them would approve and rally to my defence."

Regina Hoffmann had more imagination than intelligence, Piattoli more intelligence than imagination ; Regina was a romantic, Piattoli a cynic ; Regina had more warmth and spirit, Piattoli a shrewder and more discerning judgment ; small wonder that their views on education were not in all things harmonious.

Broadly speaking, Mlle Hoffmann was charged with the animal side of Dorothea's education and Piattoli with the spiritual. The rich territory in between was left as a field for guerrilla warfare between the rival pedagogues. A bevy of specialist teachers were, of course, engaged for the more esoteric subjects but these intruders were resented by both parties and given short shrift if they presumed to stray an inch outside their appointed sphere.

Mlle Hoffmann showed herself energetic and by no means unsuccessful in her particular field. She was a devotee of the Emile system[1] and, though the ignorant and ingenuous child of nature whom Rousseau wished to create would not have found much favour in the duchess's drawing-room, Mlle Hoffmann still managed to impose on Dorothea most of the rules which he had laid down for ensuring health and unimpeded growth.

Dorothea, therefore, was dressed in loose, baggy dresses lest the pressure of the clothing might lead to the accumulation of stagnant juices. She never wore a hat so that the bones of her skull might grow harder and less porous. She was made to sleep on a hard bed on the principle that, with such a training, she would never suffer from insomnia and was encouraged to go to bed and to rise with the sun. This régime was varied from time to time with bouts of staying-up late or exceptionally early rising so as to show her that she was above the animal and therefore not subject to the same instinctive discipline. In winter she wore thin clothes ; the death rate was notoriously high in August and it must follow that cold was salutary and heat to be avoided. River water might be drunk at once but well water was allowed to stand for a few hours before serving. Dorothea was not inoculated against smallpox ; the practice was not positively harmful but nature might be relied on to know best what precautionary measures were desirable.

This mixture of enlightened common sense and old wives' tales produced immediate and very beneficial results. Dorothea put on weight, lost the worst of her sallow colouring and began to take an interest in the usual pleasures of little girls. She despised walks and would certainly have deplored lawn-tennis if the game had been then in vogue but she would happily spend hours in climbing trees. Companionship of other children seemed unnecessary ; she devised solitary and ferociously energetic games from which she would return with the skin peeled from her arms and legs and her loose Emilesque dresses reduced to ribbons.

In spite of her mother's exhortations Dorothea took little interest in drawing-room accomplishments. She never learnt a step from her dancing-master, drove her music-master to weary complaints about her indolence and lack of interest, showed some liking for drawing, which she was to take up again in later life but which was not encouraged in her childhood because it was feared the work might strain her eyes. On the other hand she made astonishing progress in arithmetic, was far advanced in algebra by the age of ten and spent many evenings in the observatory at Berlin with Bode, the Astronomer Royal, who had been summoned to Prussia by Frederick the Great and was considered one of the outstanding scholars of the eighteenth century.

Above all, Dorothea read. She read anything on which she could lay her hands : good, bad, sacred, profane, in English, French or German. The abbé Piattoli had assembled a large and discursive library in the Courland palace at Berlin and here Dorothea would willingly have passed every hour of the day, crouched precariously on the top rung of the library steps, poring over whatever volume had come to hand and, as soon as it was finished, thrusting it back into the shelf and plunging on into the next. Regina Hoffmann, alarmed for the success of her system, would come to recapture her pupil and take her into the fresh air where health was to be found. She would begin by pleading, resort to threats and finally herself begin to climb the ladder. Like a frightened spider, the skinny little girl would take to the shelves and scramble upwards until she found a perch among the busts of the philosophers which lined the ledge along the top of the book-cases. From this retreat Dorothea would negotiate the terms of her descent. She felt that she had done badly if she was not granted at least an extra hour with her books.

A final quirk in the education of Dorothea was the almost complete absence of any kind of religious instruction. Mlle Hoffmann, having tried two religions, now found herself without any at all. Piattoli was a follower of the abbé Condillac, himself a friend of Rousseau and Diderot, whose metaphysical studies were not likely to lead his disciple into any serious effort at imprinting religious dogma in the mind of a child. Dorothea was technically a Lutheran. She never said her prayers because she had never been taught any. She went to church for a time and then, having been bored by a particularly lengthy sermon, refused ever to go again. The acute and searching mind of the little girl grappled willingly with the exact sciences but, though she must have come across many religious works in the course of her voracious reading, she was to remain completely bored by all theological argument until long after she had been married and had tumbled into the lap of Rome.

*   *   *   *   *

Since the dismissal of Armfeld, the Duchess of Courland had come to spend most of her year at Berlin where she enjoyed an almost royal status. Her closest friend was Princess Louise of Prussia who had been so daring as to marry Prince Antoine Radziwill, head of a family which boasted great antiquity and distinction but quarterings insufficient to justify a royal match. The princess, however, was never dropped by her royal relations and indeed became the most trusted confidante of her namesake Queen Louise. The children of Princess Louise of Prussia and Prince Antoine Radziwill, as the ill-matched couple had always to be styled, were brought up with the children of the royal house, and the family of the Duchess of Courland joined in the same intimate and exclusive circle.

The Duchess of Courland, however, was too intelligent to be content only with a niche in the starchy barracks-life of the Prussian court. She set out to create a salon which would be the centre of all that was gayest and most stimulating in the life of Berlin. She had few rivals. In 1804 Madame de Staël visited Berlin and found it wanting. " The two classes of society—the scholars and the courtiers—" she wrote " are completely divorced from each other. As a result, the scholars do not cultivate conversation, and mundane society is absolutely incapable of thought."[2] The Duchess of Courland made it her business to break down this barrier and force the courtiers and the scholars to lie down together in mutually profitable, if not always congenial, comradeship.[3]

From time to time Dorothea would venture into her mother's salon but rarely came back satisfied by her expedition. Though interested only in the society of adults and of intelligent adults at that, she was not content unless she was a participant in as well as an audience to their conversation. Precocious though she was, at the age of twelve she found that the pace of the society around her mother was a little more than she could manage. Inhibited by her age from really joining in, disinclined by temperament to accept anything except a leading role, she withdrew and, with the help and encouragement of Mlle Hoffmann, arranged her life elsewhere to a pattern which she found more congenial.

Dorothea was well aware, " too well aware " as she herself admitted, that the palace in which she was living with her mother was in fact her own property. The duchess realised it too and made no opposition when her daughter and Mlle Hoffmann set up what was virtually a separate household. On the contrary, she was rather relieved ; the presence of a child was on the whole an encumbrance in her own worldly life. If Dorothea and her governess longed for independence, then the duchess was quite ready to wish them joy of it. Each morning Dorothea would come to kiss her mother's hand, from time to time the duchess would dine in her daughter's part of the palace ; otherwise each went her own way and Mlle Hoffmann was able to run affairs according to her own ideas.

In this isolation, Dorothea maintained her own rival salon where she could be sure of more attention and appreciation than she found among her mother's friends. Piattoli had now left on a visit to St. Petersburg to try to sort out some of the problems which were arising over the payments still due from the Emperor of Russia out of the purchase price of the Duchy of Courland. The field was thus left clear for Mlle Hoffmann to surround her charge with friends of her own choice. It was a cosy, bourgeois circle, verydifferent from the brilliant society which gathered around the duchess but nevertheless including in it men and women of great talent. Among the regulars were Jean-Pierre Ancillon, a French Huguenot in exile, author, tutor of the Crown Prince and later President of the Prussian Council of Ministers, Madame Unzelmann, greatest of the German actresses of the period, Jean de Müller, the historian, Iffland, the Director of the Royal Theatre. As well as these regular friends, the great Schiller himself made a point of looking in to pay his respects to the little princess whenever he was in Berlin, and occasionally even the duchess would come to cast an eye over her daughter's activities, grimace slightly at what she saw and retire to her own, more worldly gathering.

Dorothea found in her guests interesting argument, talk of things she longed to know and understand, a sympathetic appreciation of her own unformed and tentative ideas. She had a passionate and precocious love of the theatre ; a box was permanently reserved for her at the Royal Theatre and she would spend hours discussing each production with Iffland and Madame Unzelmann. Iffland would teach her how to recite verse and from him she acquired a love of acting which she kept throughout all her life and was to pass on to her children. It is harder to be sure what her guests found to draw them so regularly to her apartments. Certainly there was an element of snobbish satisfaction at being received as friends within the Courland palace but even more there must have been a strange fascination in this solemn, curious, uncertain little girl with her warm affection, her touching gratitude for other people's friendship, her sudden flashes of temper or inconsequence which would remind her companions with a shock that she was still only a child. They came to her drawing-room the first time because of her family, her wealth, the chance that an invitation to the duchess's salon might follow, but they went on coming because they enjoyed it, because it was a pleasure to these sophisticated and clever people to consort with an intelligence uninhibited by fashion, a judgment uncorrupted by prejudice and a capacity for love free from all calculation or prudent holding-back.

*   *   *   *   *

With such a training it is not surprising that, by the time she was twelve or thirteen, Dorothea's education was a crazy patch-work quilt of startling ignorance and precocious knowledge. She worked at what she liked and ignored what bored her. Piattoli, who might have imposed some system on this rebellious mind, was now far away in Russia. Dorothea herself never much regretted the absence of system in her learning :

> " I don't really hold with too much education for women," she wrote nearly fifty years later. " Knowledge has never saved even the most sensible from committing follies and the more gifted one is the smaller a part it plays in one's life. Sluggish and mediocre natures merely become more disagreeable and make themselves ridiculous by what they have been at such pains to learn. There is a kind of spiritual and intellectual wisdom which is drawn from the air one breathes, from the people who surround one and from one's own inherent gifts. At times this wisdom may be difficult to appreciate but, to my mind, it should be perfectly sufficient. A taste for having something to do and a certain self-discipline in one's way of life ; that is what I believe to be the proper basis for the education of a woman. . . ."

Finding her keenest pleasure in books, despising the company of children of her own age but ready to talk to adults if they interested her, accustomed to playing the princess in her own house and drawing-room, always aware of her own rank and wealth : Dorothea at this period was well on the way to becoming an insufferable little prig. Looking at her childhood dispassionately over a gap of twenty years she concluded that, though a trying child, she had nevertheless not been completely intolerable. She advanced in her own defence certain excuses and some compensating virtues. She was proud but never forgot her manners; she admitted few superiors but was always ready to defer to great talents and real goodness; she was generous and hospitable, " finally, one would be judging my very singular education and peculiar position by too conventional standards if one did not find reason to be thankful that I had retained an obliging nature, an unaffected manner and a desire to please . . ."

That Dorothea was more than just a proud and spoiled chit is perhaps most clearly shown in reading the letters which the abbé Piattoli wrote to his " *chère* Dorka " from St. Petersburg in 1804 and 1805.[4] The letters are a model of wisdom, charity and humanity; from time to time Polonius bulks a little obtrusive but never does good advice lose itself altogether in pedantic moralising. The letters to which they are an answer are missing but it is not difficult to reconstruct from Piattoli's replies a detailed impression of their composition and of the author herself; an immensely serious little girl, her solemnity disturbed by sudden flashes of self-ridicule, pouring out to this man who was the nearest thing she had ever had to a father her hopes, fears and confessions. Dorothea had learnt from Piattoli and was never to lose the habit of introspection and of ruthless self-criticism. In these letters she is continually accusing herself of ill-temper, impatience, talkativeness. " The higher the rank, the greater the fortune and the other blessings bestowed by birth or chance . . . the more we must learn gentleness, kindness, patience," replied Piattoli. She learnt how to play piquet; he dryly pointed out that she would never get very far if she did not learn to separate the cards and to put the suits in order—the same lesson could perhaps be applied usefully in other fields of life. The lesson was taken to heart and progress made in other directions since a few weeks later Piattoli was congratulating her on no longer losing her temper when she lost. " That is the most unworthy, the most disagreeable fault in good society, and, since one only plays to amuse oneself, one dreads nothing so much as a player who turns his amusement into an occupation or makes his partner's life a misery."

It is touching to read of the effort which Dorothea put into her hand-writing in the hope of pleasing her abbé, the trouble she took in selecting little presents for him, the naïve pride with which she told him of her achievements, the shame with which she recounted her back-slidings. Ill-brought-up, perverse, moody, obstinate she may have been, but no one could read Piattoli's letters and not construct an image of a child sensitive, intelligent, affectionate and thoroughly good hearted.

2

In the autumn of 1806, King Frederick William of Prussia descended from the fence on which he had so long sat and entered the war against France. On 12th September, the Prussian army entered Saxony; on 4th October, Prince Louis Ferdinand, former aspirant to Wilhelmina's hand and the proudest flower of the royal house was killed at Saalfeld; on 14th October, Napoleon won an overwhelming victory at Jena. The fighting was over almost as soon as it had begun, now all that remained was for the Prussians to taste the full unpleasantness of defeat.

The Duchess of Courland had already left Berlin some months before when she had followed Piattoli to St. Petersburg in an effort to make her business there advance a little more quickly. Dorothea therefore found herself alone with her governess in the midst of a city turbulent with rumour. The French were coming, that much was certain; but no one knew when and whence; no one knew whether in war or in peace. It was reported that Queen Louise of Prussia had fallen into the hands of French irregulars, even that she had been murdered; then there she was, thundering into the city in a carriage drawn by six horses, pausing only an hour to destroy secret papers at the palace, then galloping off again to rejoin the king. The rest of the royal family hustled after her, Princess Louise stopping on the way to urge Dorothea to follow her to Danzig.

Left to themselves, Dorothea and her governess tried hard not to panic. Visions of fire, rape, massacre, clustered into the susceptible imagination of Mlle Hoffmann; the whole basis of existence seemed suddenly destroyed. To stay in Berlin and face the invaders seemed impossible, but where else to go ? The best idea seemed to be to follow the advice of Princess Louise and try to rejoin the court at Danzig. Staying only to throw a few of their more precious belongings into trunks and load them into a carriage, Dorothea and Mlle Hoffmann set off on their journey. Under its heavy burden the carriage creaked ponderously across the Pomeranian plain. The roads were crowded with other refugees ; whole families, without food, without money, without warm clothes, huddled miserably in every coach or cart, with no idea of their destination or real hope of finding shelter but simply intent on getting away before the French arrived. Night fell and the Courland carriage ground slowly on. Every instant the terrified child expected to hear the rattle of bullets which would mean the arrival of the French ; at every stop she imagined that robbers desperate for food were attacking the carriage to loot and to kill. Rarely can the security and luxury of a palace life have been transformed more rapidly into danger and discomfort.

The first thing that Dorothea did on arriving at Danzig was to send an urgent letter to her mother whom she believed to be now in Courland. She had no time to wait for a reply ; the French army was said to be approaching and the weary flight began again, this time to Königsberg which had become the centre of the emigration. Here all the great names of the Prussian aristocracy jostled for possession of the few modest rooms which the town had to offer ; dukes slept in stables and princes of the blood counted themselves fortunate if they had a bed to themselves. There was little to tempt Dorothea to stay, especially since she was now not far from Courland. The duchess might have done little to endear herself to her daughter but at least she stood for security and normality, properties which must then have seemed valuable to the frightened child. Besides, Dorothea was a Princess of Courland and had often planned to visit her family home. The circumstances now might not be ideal but the chance was still not to be missed. Once more the trunks were made up and the unfortunate Mlle Hoffmann and her charge were on their way again.

The Duchess of Dino

A trip along the Baltic coast in mid-winter would hold little for pleasure even in the most luxurious conditions. In an unheated and overladen carriage, constantly fearful of looters or marauding French troops and uncertain what would be found when the destination was reached, it verged continually on the nightmare.

To avoid the quicksands it was necessary to cling to the water's edge, but the weather was so stormy that waves would break over the travellers and even threaten to carry the carriage away. Dorothea had left without stopping to collect any furs, now she found herself continually soaked with icy spray and frozen by the blasts of wind. She counted herself lucky if every few hours the party came across some tumble-down fisherman's shack where she could try temporarily to thaw her unhappy body. It must have seemed that the journey would never end and when, on the evening of the second day, the carriage reached the coast of the Kurisches Haff and she saw the stretch of wind-torn gulf between her and Memel, she felt that she would rather die than venture another yard.

No one was prepared to put to sea in such a storm; even if she were to reach the other side a vista of endless travelling across the drear Baltic plains seemed to be all that the future had to offer. The present was even more unsavoury, offering the choice between a smoky cabin filled with drunken sailors where it seemed quite conceivable that they would both be raped or a night in the carriage where they would certainly be frozen. Sensibly preferring possible dishonour to certain death, Dorothea and Mlle Hoffmann ventured into the cabin and hid as best they could behind the giant stove. To their relief no one assaulted or appeared to notice them and they were beginning to think that even sleep might be possible when there came a still more welcome ending to their evening. A boat had succeeded in crossing the gulf, now the man who had chartered it entered the cabin in search of Dorothea. He was a former servant of the Courland family who the duchess had sent off to meet the fugitives. By good luck he had chanced to find them at this point. He was armed with letters, furs and every kind of provision and it was a warmed and vastly comforted Dorothea who set off next day on the last leg of her journey.

*   *   *   *   *

For the first time, Dorothea now found herself in her ancestral lands. She looked on them with moderate enthusiasm; the poverty and bleakness distressed her and when the peasants threw themselves on to their knees in the snow to kiss the feet of a Princess of Courland she did not know whether she was more sickened or ashamed. At no stage of her life could Dorothea possibly have been described as a democrat or an enemy of privilege but, proud herself, she appreciated pride in others and resented the servility and degradation which she now saw all around her. It was her first glimpse of real poverty and, hesitant though she may have been ever to challenge the social order which produced it, she could never afterwards insulate herself from its miseries with the comfortable ease enjoyed by most of the women of her class.

The aristocracy pleased her little more than the peasants. First stop was the castle of Altautz, belonging to the Duchess of Courland's eldest brother. Here, for the past month, fifty or so noblemen of the province had installed themselves with all their servants, horses and baggage, to hunt elk and eat eight or ten meals a day. This last phenomenon startled Dorothea greatly :

" Never, in all my life," she wrote, " have I seen so much eaten so often as in Courland. They eat if they are hungry, they eat if they are bored, they eat if they are cold ; in short, they never stop eating at all. The lives of the men are entirely filled by farming, hunting and sledge-racing. The women, nearly all of them pretty, are as ignorant as they are boring . . . My aunt, in spite of an income of thirty thousand pounds a year, looks after the kitchens, herself prepares the puddings, collects the butter and eggs from the farmers, darns her husband's stockings and knits clothes for the children. The luxury of living lies only in its abundance ; affability takes the place of culture and all the qualities are as crude as the vices."

It was not to be expected that Dorothea, self-centred, intolerant, used to a sophisticated existence in the centre of her Berlin coterie, would adapt herself very happily to the bucolic lavishness of life at Altautz. She refused to go out because she found the cold too unpleasant. There was not a book to be found in the castle and no one worth talking to except Mlle Hoffmann and her mother. Dorothea's one desire was to get out of Courland altogether. When her mother decided that they should move to Mittau for the rest of the winter she welcomed the move, partly because the life promised to be a little more stimulating but mainly because it seemed a first step on an eventual return to Berlin.

At Mittau, society was far more varied than it had been in the country. In particular, there were the occupants of the former ducal palace. Normally, the Duchess of Courland might have hoped that her husband's old family home might be put at her disposal but as it was she could hardly complain since this bleak northern town had become the place of exile of Louis XVIII of France and the tattered remnants of his court.

If she had been dependent on her mother for her *entrée* into the court, Dorothea would have found herself there but rarely. To the disgust of her daughter, whose instincts were stoutly patriotic and antipathetic to any régime which owed its origin to a revolution, the Duchess of Courland showed a certain sympathy for Napoleon Bonaparte and little interest in the exiled king. As early as 1802 she had tried to arrange meetings with Napoleon, first at Mainz and then at Strasbourg ; now, according to the admittedly hostile and malicious Countess Kielmansegge[1], she was already dreaming of a divorce for the emperor and a share in the imperial crown for herself. Even a suspicion of such sympathies was enough to secure her a chilly reception at the ducal palace ; as a result she went there only as often as minimum courtesy dictated.

Dorothea, however, was frequently received. She owed this devalued honour mainly to the close friendship which existed between her governess, Mlle Hoffmann and the king's current favourite, the Duke of Avaray. Louis XVIII had a fixed affection for this ill, ugly and ambitious little intriguer and, as the pupil of his favourite's friend, Dorothea came in for a share of the royal graciousness. She was invited often to the palace, perched on the king's knee, answered his questions about her studies and was christened by him his *petite italienne* in honour of her dark and flashing eyes. His kindness was more than repaid by the enthusiasm which Dorothea showed for his cause. Exiled monarchs were always to have a keen appeal for Dorothea and this shabby simulacrum of a court playing out its preposterous rituals in the desolation of a Courland winter stirred her pity and stung her to still sharper indignation against their persecutor. She formed a most favourable impression of the royal family of France and looked forward with satisfaction to the day when she might hope to renew her acquaintance with them at the Tuileries.

Mlle Hoffmann and d'Avaray had more to say to each other than court banalities or the trivia of a platonic flirtation. D'Avaray, on behalf of the king, was looking out for a wife sufficiently rich and noble to wed the Duke of Berry, nephew of Louis XVIII and second son of the future Charles X. Dorothea was not yet fourteen years old but in an era when marriages at the age of sixteen or even fifteen were not unusual it was by no means too early for Mlle Hoffmann to dream of suitable matches for her charge. It seems that the king was probably consulted ; the match would have been respectable if not magnificent and he would anyway have been favourably disposed towards a plan put forward by his favourite. The Duke of Berry was in England, it was intended that he should come to Mittau and the question be settled on the spot.

Probably the plan was never pressed very far, certainly not far enough to survive the first discouragement. The confrontation of the duke and his intended schoolgirl bride was never realised ; before he could arrive the king and his court set out on their travels again and, by way of Sweden, found their way to England. It was 1816 before the Duke of Berry was finally to find a wife.

Dorothea herself remained entirely ignorant of this royal alliance which kindly adults were preparing. It might, in fact, have suited her well. The Duke of Berry was certainly the gayest and most intelligent member of his family, probably also the most cultured and genuinely kind. Alone among the *émigrés* he found it quite impossible not to remember that he was a Frenchman as well as a royalist and derived unconcealed if slightly shame-faced delight from Napoleon's victories.

When years later Mlle Hoffmann told her former pupil how near she had been to marrying into the royal family of France, Dorothea decided that she regretted very little the person of the duke. On the other hand she admitted that the political role his wife would have had to play would have suited her very well : " I have often thought that, as my origin does not lie somewhere in the clouds and I don't imagine myself to be exactly an off-spring of the Gods, I could have made myself very useful as a link between these demi-divinities and the rest of mankind."

It is tempting, though largely profitless, to speculate on the difference it might have made to the Bourbons if one of their number had enjoyed good sense, considerable strength of will and enough beauty and charm to ensure that her voice did not go unheard. Could Dorothea have steered her father-in-law into safer courses or would she herself have been corrupted by the obstinate silliness which was to bring the Bourbons to their third expulsion in under fifty years ? It is at any rate certain that, for good or bad, she would have been a force in the royal family and that, whether she had spoken for progress or for reaction, the partisans of that course would have been the more formidable for her support.

*   *   *   *   *

Even with such distractions, life at Mittau was far from pleasing to Dorothea. Her relations with her mother were getting worse and worse. Egged on by Mlle Hoffmann and, to some extent, by Piattoli, Dorothea became steadily more wedded to the cause of Prussia's independence ; the Duchess of Courland, on the other hand, found more and more magnetic the attraction of the heroic young Frenchman who had put Europe at his feet. Dorothea became daily more dogmatic and more truculent, her mother more irritated by her daughter's wrong-headedness. To add to her other frustrations, with the occupation of Prussia by the French Dorothea had lost the greater part of her income. It may not seem much of a hardship for a girl of thirteen to find herself financially dependent on her mother, but Dorothea had had no ordinary upbringing and for her the vexation was very keen. Once independence has been tasted it is painful to lose and it was little consolation for the victim to know that her new-found servitude had always been the lot of other children of her age. Mercifully, in July the treaty of Tilsit came to put a stop to the war and open the road for a return to Prussia. The duchess seemed ready to linger on yet longer in Mittau but Dorothea had had enough and in September she and the faithful Mlle Hoffmann began to retrace their steps to Berlin.

Her anger against the French grew ever more intense as she travelled across the ravaged countryside. Hardly a village, hardly a house had been spared ; everywhere was rubble, ashes, deserted cottages and neglected fields. Plague and famine were now combining to destroy what life the invading armies had left behind. Mlle Hoffmann and Dorothea watched horrified from their carriage, tortured by pity and by fear, living off dry bread and water and, for days at a time, hardly daring to set their feet on the ground. Dorothea had left Berlin a year before, a child of cosmopolitan family who happened to live in Prussia ; she returned, in spite of her fourteen years, a woman, and in spite of her international background, a Prussian patriot.

Dorothea re-entered Berlin by night so as to avoid for as long as possible the sight of the streets she knew so well filled by foreign troops. Saint-Hilaire, the French commander, whose headquarters were installed in the Courland palace on the Unter den Linden, received her politely but made it clear that he was there as a conqueror and that any facilities given to Dorothea were offered as a favour and not in acknowledgment of a right. She was lodged in little rooms on an inner court which were normally used by the upper servants. There she shut herself up for eight days before she could pluck up the courage to venture out into the town ; when she did so, it was only to bemoan the state of all she saw and commiserate with her friends on the pains of life under the occupation. She dressed only in black, went to no parties and, in general, behaved as if she had just lost a favourite parent.

The Duchess of Courland, who had followed her daughter

to Berlin some six weeks later, found this display of gloom a little ridiculous. The war was less painful to her in that her wealth was largely in Russia and therefore unaffected by the presence of the French and, anyway, she did not share her daughter's loyalty to Prussia, found it, indeed, parochial and vulgar. Certainly the royal family were her close friends, certainly the presence of the French troops carried with it inconveniences ; but, on the whole, the duchess did not find the occupation too bad a thing. Indeed, it had an agreeably widening effect on Berlin society. The duchess mixed much with the French and became ever more anxious to visit Paris and see for herself the home of these brilliant and cultivated creatures and their ferociously attractive emperor. Her enthusiasm made her many enemies in the regular society of Berlin and threatened to disrupt her long friendship with the royal family.

One of the few exceptions Dorothea made to her self-imposed solitude was an occasional visit to the theatre. She was there the night that Iffland, defying the orders of the Duke of Belluna, French governor of the city, celebrated with a special prologue the birthday of the exiled Queen Louise. The audience burst into tremendous applause, standing and shouting " Long live the king ! Long live the queen ! " Indignant, the Duke of Belluna sent his officers to arrest the imprudent director of the theatre. Cheering from her box with the rest of the audience, Dorothea saw in the fate of her dear Iffland yet another proof of Prussian virtue and French brutality.

Apart from such excursions there was little to separate one day from another. An exception came on Good Friday, 15th April, 1808, when she was confirmed in the great fourteenth century church of St. Nicolas. In Berlin a confirmation was of social as well as religious significance, possessing some of the magical properties of Queen Charlotte's Ball. Dorothea's was celebrated in the grand manner ; all Berlin, in the snobbish sense of the phrase, was there to watch the young princess receive the sacrament. With characteristic independence she had refused to learn by rote the conventional answers to the catechism but provided her own profession of faith in what seemed to her proper and rational terms. As a result, though the ceremony was technically Lutheran, it was difficult to say into what church, if any, Dorothea had been confirmed. The point worried her little, already she distrusted religious dogmas and formalities. She had, in fact, approached her confirmation with scepticism and was surprised to find herself affected. " The future seemed to unveil itself before me at the moment that the pastor, having invoked for me the blessing of the Most High, declared me a member of the communion of the Faithful. I understood that my entry into adult life meant that I would be called on to fight, to struggle fiercely, rather than to follow the happy and brilliant career which everything seemed to promise me . . ." The impression did not stay with her for long, but it was often to recur in later years.

The day after the ceremony, the Duchess of Courland told her daughter that the time had come to retreat to their property of Löbikau in Saxony. Promised a separate household in the little pavilion which had once sheltered Batowski and freedom to return to Berlin in the winter, Dorothea bowed to convention and agreed to follow her mother. General Saint-Hilaire insisted on providing her with an escort of two of his aides-de-camp. She had reason to be grateful, for the convoy was attacked by marauders when only half a day from Löbikau. The attackers were beaten off but in the fight Monsieur Lafontaine, one of the aides-de-camp, was seriously wounded. For ten weeks he was kept at Löbikau while his wounds healed and it was in tending their saviour, handsome and interestingly pallid, that Dorothea grew out of some of the bitterness towards France which she had acquired so painfully over the preceding years.

*　　*　　*　　*　　*

Dorothea was now almost fifteen years old and her mother was longing to get her off her hands. As a daughter of the Prince of Courland, there were few families indeed which would think themselves too lofty to welcome Dorothea into their midst ; her fortune, it was true, had been considerably reduced of late but, now the war was over, it could be expected rapidly to regain its former sumptuous proportions. It was sure therefore that there would be no lack of suitors, the only difficulty was to pick the one who combined the maximum of breeding and position with the minimum of personal unpleasantness.

Dorothea, as usual, had made up her mind. From the earliest days of his life with Dorothea, the abbé Piattoli had spoken enthusiastically of his brilliant young pupil Prince Adam Czartoryski. During his stay in Russia he had given much news of Prince Adam in the letters he wrote to Dorothea and, on his return to Courland, he found his charge avid for every detail about the habits and prospects of this romantic figure.

Prince Adam was, indeed, well qualified to excite the interest of a young and idealistic girl. He had been born in Warsaw in 1770 and his good looks, intelligence and fiery courage quickly won him a formidable reputation. The Russians paid tribute to his stature when they took him as a hostage to Moscow. Quite apart from his value as a guarantee of the good behaviour of the Poles, it would have been folly on their part to leave him loose in Warsaw to foment trouble and preach the doctrine of independence.

In 1797, as a reward for good behaviour, Prince Czartoryski was appointed aide-de-camp to the young Grand Duke Alexander. He quickly grew to wield great influence over this highly susceptible youth and when Alexander became Emperor in 1801 Adam found himself nominated Minister of Foreign Affairs ; a bizarre position for one who had come to Moscow under duress six years before as a dangerous Polish nationalist. At no moment, however, did he forget that his first responsibility was to set Poland free and in Alexander he imagined that he had found an emperor sufficiently liberal and open-minded. It was not till 1806 that he realised the futility of his hopes and left the service of the Russians. It was at this moment, his occupation gone and his country still in the grasp of foreign troops, that his thoughts turned to marriage as a possible source of spiritual solace and financial reinforcement.

Despite the twenty-three years between their ages and the fact that they had never met, Dorothea had no doubt at all that Adam Czartoryski was the man of her choice. She had been seduced by all that Piattoli had told her of Prince Adam's gallantry, nobility and romantic nature and a part at least of her enthusiasm for her studies arose from the conviction that only by enriching and developing her mind would she make herself worthy of such a match. The Duchess of Courland was by no means so enthusiastic. A minister of the Emperor of Russia was one thing but a Polish nationalist in opposition to the Russians was quite another. The fortune of the duchess was far too dependent on Russian goodwill to allow her to look kindly on any marriage which might annoy the emperor. But she was not inclined to take the threat very seriously. She herself could not have fallen in love with a vision constructed from second-hand reports and she at first dismissed her daughter's feelings as no more than childish sentiment.

In the spring of 1807 Prince Adam appeared at Mittau. Piattoli had not only made propaganda for the match with Dorothea but had often discussed the possibility with Czartoryski while they were together in Moscow. The prince had been non-committal ; as aware as anyone of the financial advantages but doubtful about the wisdom, with middle-age approaching, of saddling himself with an unformed schoolgirl. Besides, this statesman of international standing and indomitable hero of the Polish resistance was firmly under the thumb of his mother and it was well known that old Princess Czartoryski had long planned to marry her son to a young relation whom she had brought up in her own house and trained for the purpose. All in all, Prince Adam was inclined to doubt whether Piattoli's project was really practicable or even desirable but he had no objection to pursuing the matter a little further. Accordingly, he took advantage of the freedom which followed his retirement from the Russian service to visit his old friend and tutor and take a look for himself at this prodigious young princess.

The negotiations at Tilsit which were to open the way for Dorothea's return to Berlin were already in progress when Prince Adam Czartoryski arrived at Mittau. The Duchess of Courland, who owed him much for the benevolent interest which he had shown in her affairs while still in office in St.

Petersburg, could not do other than receive him graciously. All the same, it was with nervousness that she watched the first meeting between her daughter and this putative admirer. She saw little to disquiet her. As she entered her mother's drawing-room to meet the prince, Dorothea relates, " for the first time in my life I felt embarrassment and extreme shyness." Czartoryski evidently found himself in the same plight ; he greeted her coldly, observed her closely but with some suspicion and hardly addressed a word to her during his three weeks' stay in Mittau. A long time later he told Dorothea that he had been pleased with what he saw ; certainly he kept his pleasure well under control and the only sign he gave of any special interest came when he urged her to return to Berlin by way of Warsaw and take the opportunity to pay a visit to his mother.

Dorothea was delighted by this off hand wooing ; it showed, she felt, a serious disposition and a proper disregard for the trivia of social intercourse. She found her sorrowful knight quite as desirable as Piattoli had led her to suppose and, by the end of his stay, was more certain than ever that in him she had found the destiny, harsh but rewarding, which she had seen before her at the moment of her confirmation.

Prince Adam finally left Mittau for St. Petersburg with the Emperor Alexander. The emperor visited the Duchess of Courland on the way back from his negotiations with Napoleon at Tilsit. He took considerable pains to charm all members of the family and Dorothea would have found him altogether perfect if it had not been for the chilly courtesy with which he treated his former minister.

The obvious hostility between Czartoryski and the emperor confirmed the duchess in her belief that the match would be a disaster both for her daughter and, still more, for herself. When Dorothea spoke to her of her projects, she answered with cold indifference and, when her daughter proposed to visit the old Princess Czartoryski in Warsaw, she did not forbid the journey but pointed out the difficulties and discomforts which it would entail. As it happened, the state of Europe made such a visit impossible but Dorothea did not cease to dream of Prince Adam and never doubted that one day he would return to ask her hand in marriage. Meanwhile the prince hesitated in Warsaw, one day writing to Piattoli that he had finally made up his mind to come to Löbikau in search of his bride, the next day succumbing to pressure from his mother and making some fresh excuse for deferring the fatal visit.

Well satisfied by this lack of forcefulness on the part of Dorothea's suitor, the Duchess of Courland took every occasion to commiserate with her daughter on the humiliation which was being inflicted on her and on the whole family. The Czartoryskis, she would argue, by birth and position were hardly eligible to aspire to such a match ; that it should be these insolent Poles who were now the ones to hang back was quite intolerable. Dorothea's vanity was touched by such arguments but she consoled herself with the thought that the delay was certainly quite as painful to Prince Adam as it was to her.

Certainly it was not for lack of alternatives that Dorothea remained constant to her Polish prince. This Prussian Penelope was besieged by suitors, a motley collection with nothing in common except a noble lineage and a burning desire to possess themselves of the fortune which went with the young princess. Prince Augustus of Prussia, the Duke of Coburg, the Duke of Gotha, Prince Florentin of Salm : all these let their interest be known. Prince Mecklenburg and the Prince of Reuss went even further and camped in the duchess's house at Löbikau, hoping by their persistence if not their charms to win in the end a favourable reply. Except in the case of Prince Florentin of Salm, who, she flattered herself, was genuinely in love with her, Dorothea did not imagine that any of her suitors were interested in more than her dowry. " Thin, even skinny with drawn features and a dark, murky complexion," she wrote of herself some ten years later with the objective self-criticism which comes easily to those who have since matured into beauty. Vitrolles knew another aspect of her and wrote with greater charity : " She possessed all the graces and all the charm which could ever be found in a young girl . . . Her capacity for understanding was remarkable and her learning extended over every field in which she found an interest." Such attributes,

however, were of little value to the general run of her suitors ;
a well-rounded chorus girl might have appealed to them, but
apart from such fleshy charms, all they wanted in a wife was
breeding to do them honour and a fortune to replenish their
usually depleted purses.

Dorothea contemplated her crowd of admirers with
indifference and a mild distaste. But they caused her little
trouble. Living as she did about a mile from the main house,
the burden of entertaining this pack of amorous parasites fell
upon her unfortunate mother, and Dorothea usually managed
to time her visits so that she could be sure of finding the house
reasonably empty. The private opinion of the Duchess of
Courland on her importunate visitors was probably very much
the same as that of her daughter ; almost anything however
would be better than Prince Czartoryski and she therefore
treated all comers with civility and gave them such encouragement as she could. She was always careful to say that the
final choice of a husband must rest with Dorothea herself, but
from time to time she would nevertheless pass on a selected
suitor to her daughter's retreat in the hope that the decision
might be favourable. It never was. Dorothea received them,
if not with rudeness, at least with palpable indifference. All
went away discouraged—most to look for a fortune elsewhere ;
a few, like the pertinacious Prince Mecklenburg, to plan the
next assault.

*   *   *   *   *

Despite the growing impatience of the duchess, there was
no reason on the face of it why this state of affairs should not
have dragged on indefinitely ; Dorothea waiting for her prince
to come, while a stream of suitors beat out a path to the summer-
house at Löbikau and then, dejected, back again. Already,
however, the decisions had been taken which were to put an
end to all hesitations. Early in October, 1808, a letter[2] was
received from the Emperor Alexander to say that he would
shortly be leaving Erfurt and proposed to honour the Duchess
of Courland with a visit on his way back to Russia. He would
do no more than stay to dinner and would arrive during the
evening of 16th October.

For such an occasion Dorothea could hardly refuse to emerge from her seclusion. The emperor arrived at five o'clock. Only a small suite accompanied him: notably the French ambassador, the Marquis of Caulaincourt, Duke of Vicenza. A few small fry were also there, among them a handsome young French soldier, aide-de-camp to Caulaincourt, whose name Dorothea understood to be Count Edmond de Talleyrand-Périgord.

3

While Dorothea had been dreaming of her Polish gallant and holding her other suitors at bay, men whom she had never met and whose names were no more to her than a distant legend were making their own decision as to her future. The root of the whole intrigue can be summed up in a sentence : His Serene Highness Charles-Maurice de Talleyrand-Périgord, Prince of Benevento, Vice-Grand Elector, Grand Chamberlain, until recently Minister of Foreign Affairs to the Emperor Napoleon, was looking for a wife for his nephew Edmond.

Though Talleyrand had eventually taken himself a wife— in itself no small achievement for a former bishop of the Roman Catholic Church—he was without any child or at least any that was legitimate. For an heir to his very considerable fortune and various titles he therefore looked to Edmond, the son of his brother Archambaud.

Edmond was a fool and not a particularly pleasant one at that. He was a soldier, now just twenty-one, who owed his rapid promotion to nothing except his name and his uncle's great position. His portrait at Valençay shows him as a dashing slightly effeminate figure in a resplendent uniform, his expression romantic and even a little pensive. It would be rash to assume from this that he was indulging in any sort of intellectual exercise. Edmond thought of only three things : women, horses and gambling ; and the extent of his reflections was limited to speculation as to how he could procure more of the first two and lose slightly less at the third.

To be fair to him, the impression of effeminacy seems also to have been a gloss of the artist's. He was a perfectly adequate regimental officer : limited, courageous, unimaginative, taciturn save when on one of his favourite topics. Given the occasion he would certainly have ridden straight to hounds and provided a fund of salacious anecdotes after the port had gone round. He was occasionally vulgar but never unconventional ; lost money —his own or that of any one foolish enough to lend it to him— with sang-froid and an admirably even temper ; was capable of generosity and, though a libertine, was normally straight and decent in the simpler human relationships. He was, in short, a good man in a regimental mess, a battle and a bed and an intolerable bore anywhere else.

Talleyrand—that pattern of subtlety and finesse—regarded his nephew with dismay and a certain amount of contempt. Edmond was, however, all that there was as heir and his uncle had to make the most of it. Solicitously he pushed him forward in his military career and procured for him a place on the staff of Marshal Berthier. In 1808, Edmond de Périgord came of age and the time had come to find him a suitably rich and noble wife. Relations between the emperor and his Grand Chamberlain were uneasy and it suited Talleyrand well to avoid making any claim on Napoleon's favour by seeking to marry his nephew to one of the heiresses of France. England was, of course, impossible for so long as the war endured ; Italy and Spain were at that time a poor field for matrimonial treasure-hunts. Russian society was an oyster, hard to prise open and jealously guarding for itself such pearls as were hidden within the shell. Prussia, Austria and the lesser German courts seemed therefore to offer the best chance of a suitable match.

Probably Batowski, former lover and still faithful friend of the Duchess of Courland, first hinted to Talleyrand that Dorothea might provide the victim he was seeking. After his eviction by Armfeld from Löbikau and the arms of the duchess, Batowski had gone to Hamburg and thence to the Netherlands[1]. He was known to Talleyrand by the end of 1806 for in November of that year he was recommended by letter to the minister in Warsaw, Hugues Maret, as being an exile from Poland who could profitably be used by the French. " He deserves every confidence on the part of the government to whom he should be able to furnish much accurate information on the people and affairs of Poland." When Talleyrand, then still Minister of Foreign Affairs, spent much time in Warsaw in the course of 1807, Batowski served under him and made himself useful and trusted. No one was better placed to give Talleyrand all the information he needed about the family of Courland.

Batowski must have explained that the more outside support which Talleyrand could rally for his cause the better would be his chances of success. Some powerful arguments were needed. Not only did Talleyrand have to eliminate the minor rivals, overcome scruples which the Duchess of Courland might be expected to feel at marrying her daughter into the race which had treated her friends at the Prussian court so harshly, and prevent Napoleon blocking the match out of pique at his Grand Chamberlain's independence, but he had also to make sure that Dorothea was persuaded out of her loyalty to Prince Czartoryski. This last requirement he could not have taken very seriously. No more than the duchess was he prepared to give much weight to a schoolgirl passion and must have assumed that a few sharp words or a tempting picture of life in Paris would soon put an end to the difficulty.

Most of the difficulties, in fact, did not turn out to be as formidable as Talleyrand had feared : the other suitors, with the exception of Prince Adam, were of negligible importance ; the Duchess of Courland was already well-disposed towards a French alliance and Napoleon, on his side, saw no reason to object. Talleyrand however was taking no risks and found a powerful ally close at hand. In the course of the conference at Erfurt between Napoleon and Alexander of Russia, Talleyrand, finally deciding that the present French policy could lead only to the instability of Europe and perpetual, destructive war, had systematically betrayed his imperial master by passing on to Alexander a full account of Napoleon's thoughts, hopes and weaknesses and virtually writing each night the terms which the Emperor of Russia was to insist on in the negotiations the following morning. For such services as these, the least that Alexander could do was to give Talleyrand all possible help in any enterprise on which he had set his heart. With such support, the way for Edmond seemed easy and assured.

" While in Germany and Poland," wrote Talleyrand in his

memoirs, " I often heard speak of the Duchess of Courland. I knew that she was equally distinguished by her noble sentiments, her high ideals and by every other striking and amiable quality. The youngest of her daughters was still unmarried. Such a match could only give pleasure to Napoleon. It would not deprive him of one of the rich heiresses whom he reserved for his generals and it would flatter the vanity which he felt in attracting to France the great families of other countries ; vanity which had led him, some time before, to marry Marshal Berthier to a Bavarian princess. I therefore made up my mind to ask for my nephew the hand in marriage of Princess Dorothea of Courland and, so as to make quite sure that the Emperor Napoleon should not have any second thoughts or, on a sudden whim, go back on the approval he had once given, I asked the Emperor Alexander, a particular friend of the Duchess of Courland, himself to ask the Duchess to give her daughter as wife to my nephew . . ."

*   *   *   *   *

Though Dorothea did not suspect it at the time, the visit of the Emperor Alexander to Löbikau in October, 1808 was the first shot in a campaign which was to lead her to a most uninviting altar. There were, in fact, a few signs by which she might have suspected something of what was going on. For one thing, the emperor suddenly leant forward and called down the table to ask whether Dorothea had noticed the likeness which he claimed to have discovered between Count Edmond de Périgord and Prince Adam Czartoryski. Dorothea flushed and thought the question most uncalled for.

" Of whom is Your Majesty speaking ? "[2]

" Why, the young man sitting over there. The nephew of the Prince of Benevento . . ."

" I'm sorry, Sire, I hadn't noticed the Duke of Vicenza's aide-de-camp. I'm afraid that I'm so short sighted that I can't even see what he looks like from here."

Temporarily baffled, Alexander pursued the question no further but after dinner took the Duchess of Courland aside. They remained in conclave for fully two hours.

Months afterwards, the Duchess of Courland gave Dorothea

an account of the conversation. Alexander had told her that he had promised Talleyrand that the marriage would take place and that now he counted on her help to ensure that his word did not prove false. The duchess replied that, anxious though she always was to show the devotion and gratitude which she felt for him, she was afraid that this time he had asked for something which it was out of her power to give.

" You know, Sire," she went on, " how full the Germans now are of anti-French ideas. My daughter shares them all. She has a very decisive character, by her position in the world she has a great deal of independence, and her sisters, her relations, her friends, the Prussian court, all Germany will join her in opposing the match. I don't mean to complain of Dorothea but I still must admit that I have very little influence over her and besides, I must tell you frankly, for a long time there has been a question of her marrying an old friend of Your Majesty's. Prince Adam Czartoryski is the man she prefers. I have no valid reason for opposing the match and I don't see any way of stopping it taking place next year."

" Are you in favour of it ? " asked the emperor.

" No, Sire, I've always been against it : partly because of the difference in age ; partly because the old princess has been so difficult and has shown such bad grace over the whole affair."

" Then I don't accept any of your arguments. At the age of fifteen, Dorothea is too young to have any fixed opinions of her own. If you want to avoid all the trouble you speak of, the thing to do is to tell no one about the marriage until the last minute. After that, anyway, both your daughter and you will be living in France and won't have to worry what people are saying in Germany. I am quite sure that your little princess is too well brought up not to pay heed to her mother when it's a matter of choosing a husband. As for Adam Czartoryski, I can assure you that he has no intention at all of getting married. He'll never escape from his mother's apron strings, and she's a dangerous old Pole who never stops plotting. I don't see anything in all that except a child who has let herself get carried away ; for Adam is certainly an excellent fellow but he's become so gloomy and boorish that I don't see he has

55

anything which would attract a girl of fifteen. In short, my dear duchess, I don't accept any excuses. I have given my word and now I ask for yours, and ask for it as a proof of the friendship which you have promised me and which I think I deserve."

It is perhaps not unfair to wonder whether the Duchess of Courland in fact spoke up as staunchly for her daughter's freedom of choice as she would have had Dorothea believe. Certainly, the emperor's last words were altogether too much for her. She knew how completely her prosperity was dependent on the goodwill of the Russians and how easily this goodwill might be forfeited. A French marriage for her daughter was, besides, not at all at variance with her own personal projects. She promised that, when the time came, she would do all she could to persuade Dorothea into the match. Alexander went on his way confident that everything had been successfully arranged. How much Edmond knew of what was intended is uncertain ; he can hardly have failed to guess more or less what was going on. Dorothea perhaps had an uneasy sensation that something was amiss but certainly suspected nothing more precise. It would, indeed have been a source of wonder to her if she had found herself entirely at ease in her mother's house—a faint disquiet was the very least she could expect.

Dorothea was now anxious to return to Berlin : she was bored by her life at Löbikau, was beginning to wonder whether Adam Czartoryski would ever really come and, anyway, felt that she could more profitably await him in town than in the country. She expected however that her mother, who had shown herself very anxious to get Dorothea to Löbikau in the first place, would now show herself equally anxious to keep her there. To her surprise, the duchess saw no objection at all to her daughter wintering in Berlin and sped her on her way with the utmost geniality. On one thing only she insisted ; that Dorothea should come back to Löbikau in time for her mother's birthday in February. So reasonable a request Dorothea could hardly refuse and it was with relief and satisfaction that she set out for Berlin.

*   *   *   *   *

Talleyrand was well satisfied with the results of Alexander's visit to Löbikau ; the support of the mother had been gained and, with it, he felt, nine-tenths of the battle. " I don't know whether we will bring it off," he wrote to Caulaincourt " but what is certain is that I will always be grateful to the Emperor Alexander for his kindness and to you for all the trouble you have taken and the good friend you have been." He was not the man to neglect any precaution which could make the achievement of his wishes still more certain. He had neither the time nor the inclination to descend into the arena himself but he did the next best thing and sent Batowski to make sure that all went well. In the company of Edmond de Périgord, the Duchess of Courland's former lover arrived at Löbikau towards the end of November, 1808. He may have had some qualms about his reception but, if he had, they were soon set at peace ; whether as a tribute to their former relationship or out of enthusiasm for his mission the duchess received him kindly and he found himself invited to pass the winter in her house.

Edmond left for St. Petersburg after the briefest of stays in Saxony to work under Caulaincourt while he awaited the outcome of the negotiations. The journey had been a bore for him but the absence of Dorothea had unexpectedly mitigated his sufferings. It was bad enough that he should be expected to marry this serious and skinny schoolgirl without his being required to be polite to her in the preparatory stages of their wedded bliss.

Edmond and Batowski brought with them a letter to the duchess from Talleyrand. She must have read with the keenest curiosity this first letter from a man of whom she had heard so much and who played so great a part in the country which she was above all anxious to visit and learn to know. It was well calculated to please.

" Madame, Edmond will have the honour of handing this letter to Your Highness. You have been good enough to treat him with kindness ; he is proud of it, has spoken warmly of it to me and would like to devote the rest of his life to proving worthy. I told him that he had undertaken a very considerable task and that, involved as I was in the affairs of Europe, I could not but know to what a degree beauty, grace and high ideals gave Your Highness the right to be exigent. He replied that he knew all this better than I, since I had not had the good fortune to go to Löbikau, but that good nature, gentleness and conduct which had been proved in the most testing circumstances were also worth something . . ." The implication of this highly improbable conversation between Talleyrand and his nephew might seem to be that the chief object of the match was to secure for Edmond a really congenial mother-in-law ; this, however, could hardly displease the duchess who replied reaffirming that she would do everything in her power to ensure that the marriage would take place. She reminded Talleyrand that there was, however, still the matter of her daughter's choice ; this would have to be made freely and without coercion of any kind.

On 16th December, Talleyrand wrote to Caulaincourt and asked him to remind the Emperor Alexander of the state of affairs and seek his help once more. Even with the help that he had given him, he did not trust his nephew to carry through his wooing successfully alone and rightly calculated that imperial pressure was more likely than anything else to keep the duchess firmly on his side.

Caulaincourt duly passed on the request to the emperor who, once more, did what was hoped of him and produced the letter by which Talleyrand set so much store. Armed with this and with a letter from his uncle to the duchess, Edmond set off on his journey. The moment of truth was almost at hand.

Meanwhile Batowski had been busily preparing the ground at Löbikau. If Dorothea were to be brought to accept Count Edmond de Périgord it was essential that Prince Czartoryski should first be eliminated from the scene ; his present cautious tactics advanced his cause very little but left him permanently in the background as an irritating, if evasive menace. It was Piattoli who had first laid the foundations of the affair and Batowski resolved that it should be Piattoli who should finally bring it tumbling to the ground.

The abbé was a dying man. Tired and in continual agonising pain, he had retired to Altenburg so as to be closer to his doctors. During the whole winter he was subjected to pressure from the duchess and Batowski to help rescue Dorothea from her romantic fixation. Piattoli's last months were tormented by this constant struggle. He felt himself too sick and feeble to resist the prayers and importunities of the woman to whom he owed so much ; he had to admit that Prince Czartoryski was, to say the least, a doubtful starter and that he could not feel certain that Dorothea's happiness would really be ensured by the Polish marriage ; and yet how could he bring himself to destroy the hopes which he had cherished so assiduously or to deceive the pupil whom he loved so dearly and who trusted him so implicitly?

His letters to Dorothea were sad, tired, pessimistic. As regards Prince Adam they were evasive but in the last letter which he wrote to her before she left Berlin to return to Löbikau there was nothing which could encourage her. He referred rather obscurely to certain wishes which they had held in common, " Our actions and our efforts are bounded by the laws of propriety and by domestic influences. We have gone as far as we can in this direction. To go further would be against reason ; a useless folly. The dream of my heart has faded and I am the first to admit it. Is it not my duty to admit it to those whose happiness I had hoped could be secured by this very dream . . . ? "

Dorothea did not know quite what to make of this. Presumably Piattoli was intent on telling her that she should no longer yearn for her Polish prince ; in that case, why not say straight out that the marriage was impossible and not talk darkly of laws of propriety and domestic influences ? She had set her heart on Prince Czartoryski and she was far too determined a character to abandon her hopes and plans unless she was given some reason much more cogent than any Piattoli had yet produced. She was due to set out for Löbikau in a few days ; she made up her mind to pass by Altenburg and find out exactly what was going on.

Her visit was a sad one. She was horrified by the state to which her former tutor had been reduced : haggard, emaciated, he seemed so frail that she could hardly bring herself to ask the questions which he was so reluctant to hear and yet to which she was so anxious to have a reply. At last she asked timidly whether he had had any news of Prince Czartoryski.

" Not a word," he replied. " This silence proves, my dear child, that our dreams were no more than chimeras."

" May God not wish it so ! "

" Don't let's speak of it any more ; it is a subject which causes me much pain."

Saddened by the distress of one whom she loved so well and profoundly disturbed by the uncertainty of her own future, Dorothea drove on to Löbikau. Her mother received her with great joy and warmth, insisted that Dorothea's cottage in the woods was uninhabitable in winter and begged her daughter to stay with her in the main house. It is a sad commentary on the usual relationship between mother and daughter that Dorothea was startled by this new and strange welcome and was at once convinced that something was being plotted against her. Especially she was made suspicious by the presence of Batowski ; what could this Parisian Pole be doing in this remote estate, what pleasures could he find here to draw him away from his usual life ?

It might reasonably be thought that talk of plots and suspicions is out of place where the personalities involved were a fifteen-year-old girl in love with a man who showed no visible signs of reciprocation and her mother, anxious to arrange a more suitable match. Certainly the phraseology is dramatic but it is not altogether unjustified. It is impossible to sympathise fully with Dorothea unless it is realised how very much she felt herself alone. Throughout all her childhood she had enjoyed an independence of which the price had been isolation. For her mother she felt neither trust nor deep affection ; she was confident that unless she herself decided her own future then the decisions which would be made would bear little relation to her needs or to her happiness. With her sisters she had never had any relationship beyond the superficial ; the only one for whom she had felt any real liking was the youngest, Jeanne, Duchess of Acerenza and Jeanne was at the moment far from Löbikau. Regina Hoffmann, Dorothea had to some extent outgrown ; she would turn to her governess for comfort but in the secret knowledge that she trusted better her own judg-

ment. Only to the abbé Piattoli would she have listened with
any confidence and now Piattoli was a dying man ; worse still,
even he seemed to be ready to betray her, he spoke reluctantly
and without frankness, he tried to turn her from the aims on
which she had set her heart. Dorothea was left without resource
save in herself ; she was reminded that she was no more than
a child and a child painfully alone, surrounded by those hostile
or indifferent to her happiness. Resolutely, she braced herself
to fight in lonely desperation against all those who sought to
rule her life against her will.

*   *   *   *   *

A few days went by after Dorothea's arrival at Löbikau ;
the duchess's affability was undiminished and, little by little,
the worst of her daughter's fears were quietened. Then
came the eve of the duchess's birthday. Everyone except
Dorothea was upstairs writing letters when she heard the noise
of a carriage arriving at the house. A moment later a footman
looked in and asked whether she had seen the duchess.

" She's in her study. She doesn't want to be disturbed."

" But somebody should tell her that a French officer has
just arrived ; the one who was here recently with the Duke
of Vicenza."

At these words, in a sudden, horrifying flash of clarity,
all the pieces fell into a pattern in Dorothea's mind : her
mother's kindness, the Emperor of Russia's graciousness, the
imagined resemblance between Edmond de Périgord and
Prince Czartoryski, the return of Count Edmond for this
family reunion. She stared blankly at the footman, quite
unable to find any words for him or, still less, to let her mother
know who had arrived. Her first idea was that she must not
be found alone by Count Edmond. In a panic she ran across
the hall, up the staircase and burst breathless into her room.
Mlle Hoffmann, who happened to be there, looked up surprised
at this tempestuous entry.

" He's here ! " cried Dorothea.

" Who ? Prince Adam ? "

" Alas no, the Frenchman," she burst into tears. " I'm sure
he's come to marry me."

" Well, you can always refuse him."

" And what about my mother ? "

" So far she's never tried to force you into anything."

" Because she's never cared a scrap about any of the marriages that I've refused. But you know how much she loves France and how she wants to settle there."

" She can't make you marry against your will. Try to calm down a bit ; otherwise you won't be in a fit state to appear and nothing could be worse than to show everyone what you feel."

Not much fortified by this encouragement, Dorothea dried her tears and went downstairs. She found her mother somewhat embarrassed, yet, at the same time, radiant with satisfaction. She was led over to be introduced to Monsieur de Périgord. This time she looked more carefully at the young French officer and was little pleased with what she saw. He was certainly good-looking in his way but it was not a way which much appealed to her ; the face seemed to lack distinction and intelligence, above all, it was not the face of Adam Czartoryski. Dorothea went off to bed as soon as she decently could but during the night she hardly slept at all.

Next morning Mlle Hoffmann was sent for by the duchess ; she stayed about an hour, then returned, flustered and unhappy. When Dorothea asked what had been said she gave no coherent reply but told her to go at once to her mother. Reluctant as a prisoner on the way to execution Dorothea dragged her feet across the house to her mother's room. The duchess was still in bed, a bundle of letters scattered around her. " The time has come," she announced portentously, " to let you know the real reason for the visit by the Emperor of Russia on his way back from Erfurt." She recounted her interview with the emperor on that October evening four months ago and laid great stress on the emperor's sense of obligation towards the Prince of Benevento and the gratitude which she herself owed towards the emperor.

" You know how in Russia," she did not scruple to say, " the favours of the sovereign are always precarious and everything depends on his whim. I have the greatest possible interest in retaining his goodwill and I promised him to do all I could to arrange this marriage, which he so much desired. I beg you therefore at least not to refuse until you have weighed in the balance all the benefits which will accrue to your family from the match."

Then she handed Dorothea two of the letters which she had at her side and told her to read them. The first was from the emperor at St. Petersburg, the same which Caulaincourt had induced him to write at the request of Talleyrand. " During his stay here, Monsieur de Périgord has increased yet further the good opinion which I have of him. He is a charming young man, filled with excellent qualities and well qualified to make any woman happy. I much hope that Your Highness and the young princess will have the same opinion and that this union, so much hoped for, will come to pass . . ." This letter Dorothea decided to be false, unconvincing, and a revolting abuse of imperial influence ; she put it indignantly aside and turned to the letter from Monsieur de Talleyrand.

" It is unnecessary for me to say," she wrote in her *Souvenirs*, " that it was written with brilliant intelligence, designed as skilfully as possible to reduce the objections which might be maintained against him or against France. He spoke of his nephew Edmond de Périgord as a young man whom he loved as his own son, whom he treated as such and who would one day be his heir. Then he spoke of me in the most flattering terms and finished by a word about his eighty-four year old mother who would be so content to see the happiness of her family ensured before her long life ended. He added some words about the illustrious breeding, the ancient traditions and the undiluted nobility of the great families of Germany. In short, I do not think that the Prince of Benevento ever drafted the most important diplomatic note with greater care than he gave to this letter."

Dorothea folded the two letters and handed them back to her mother. She knew what her answer must be but she dreaded the saying of it. The duchess looked at her expectantly and at last asked whether she had nothing to say.

" Dear mother, if it were not that I felt myself to be already pledged to Prince Adam ; if from the age of twelve I had not considered him as the only man I could ever marry ; if I had not grown profoundly attached to this idea and built on it all my hopes of happiness, then I might have been able to try to forget the past and to overcome all the repugnance which I now feel towards doing this thing which you want so much. But I cannot believe that the delays which have elapsed before Prince Adam's visit stem in any way from his own will, nor can I persuade myself, after all that I have heard to the contrary, that he considers me of so little value. I would be betraying all the hopes which you have allowed me to nourish if I now accepted any other possibility. To leave my homeland, to go to the court of Bonaparte, to leave far away all my friends, to marry someone who I have hardly met, to accept a new position of which I know nothing : all these difficulties, very real though they are, I might be able to overcome so as to please you and to make easier your relations with the emperor. But happily your situation is not so very bad that I must feel myself obliged to sacrifice what I have so long believed to represent my hopes of a happy future."

Dorothea, with real affection, tried to kiss her mother's hand but the duchess pettishly snatched it away, tears of frustration and self-pity in her eyes. At that moment, she had good cause to regret the selfishness and indifference which had led her to play so little part in her daughter's development, almost to ignore her very existence. Yet it is most unlikely that she reproached herself, rather reserving all the blame for her headstrong and ungrateful daughter. Now she began to try to argue Dorothea into acquiescence ; making much play with the dangers of incurring Talleyrand's rancour, the certainty that Napoleon would think the refusal dictated by hatred for France, the tribulations that would descend on all the family. She accused her daughter of obstinacy, coldness and hostility ; always, she said, she had considered Dorothea as her favourite child and now with what base ingratitude she was rewarded. Dorothea was far too upset by these reproaches to wonder for what she should have been grateful or, if the treatment she had received was really that of a favourite child, what the duchess could have done for her other daughters. Even through her tears, however, she would not give up the one vital point and admit that she was anything but engaged to

Prince Adam Czartoryski. At last a short period of armed neutrality was agreed to : Dorothea pledged herself to be reasonably polite to Edmond de Périgord and not to insist on any final answer being given for at least another two or three days ; " that way," said the duchess bitterly, " it will at least appear that you are giving the proposal some serious thought."

Though thoroughly displeased, the Duchess of Courland by no means despaired of eventually persuading her daughter into reason. The vulnerable point in Dorothea's position was her claim to be already committed to Prince Czartoryski ; this she had made the main justification for her resistance. Dorothea must therefore be persuaded that her prince did not consider himself engaged to her and had no intention even of proposing. To achieve this end, the duchess was prepared to tell any number of lies and to suborn everyone else into doing the same.

First Batowski was sent off to the death-bed of Piattoli at Altenburg. He must have, he said, a letter which would end Dorothea's dreams for once and for all. The poor, sick old man protested feebly that he had nothing to say which could discourage Dorothea further, all his arguments had been used already. Batowski waved these objections aside. All that was needed was an assurance that Prince Adam was to marry another ; for example young Mademoisclle Matuschewitz for whom it was known his mother had so long destined him. In the end Piattoli gave way. It is not pleasant to think how his last hours must have been tormented by the knowledge that he had lied to the pupil whom he loved so dearly and, in so doing, helped to bring her to a marriage to which she was bitterly opposed.

In triumph, Batowski brought back the letter and gave it to Dorothea. It was quite short ; only a few lines scrawled with a trembling hand, " All our hopes are destroyed . . ." he began. He had heard from a friend in Warsaw that Prince Adam was engaged and the old princess delighted. " This, then, is the explanation of his long silence. I am in such pain," he concluded, " that I can write no more."

Dorothea's immediate reaction was to order the horses and set out to visit Piattoli. She could not positively disbelieve his letter but no more could she believe it; only if she heard it from his own lips would she accept that all her hopes were baseless. She found him within a few days of death. At first he sent out a message that he must be alone and Dorothea had virtually to force her way into the sick-room. Before she could put any question he began to speak: " Be happy. Be good to your mother. Your passionate nature has given me cause to worry over you but you have plenty of intelligence as well; make full use of it in the difficult times which I see lie ahead of you. You have been the great preoccupation of my last years; forgive me for having tried to direct the course of your future and entrust yourself now to your mother." Dorothea tried to speak but with a feeble gesture he waved her away. Sorrowfully she returned to Löbikau, leaving the abbé to die alone in such peace as he could find.

Even now she was not entirely convinced. The old man might have been wrongly informed, pessimism induced by illness might have led him to see more in casual gossip than in fact was intended. But Batowski and the duchess had yet another card to play. Staying in the house was Countess Olinska, an old Polish lady and a friend of the duchess. Carefully she was groomed in her role and next day, when the family was assembled, she appeared holding a bundle of letters which had apparently just arrived from Warsaw. Everyone, she said, was talking about Prince Adam's forthcoming marriage. She went on to add a gloss of supporting detail but Dorothea was no longer listening. She found no more room for doubt. She was unhappy but, even more, she was bitterly, furiously indignant. If this were all that Prince Adam thought of her then she would show him just how little importance she attached to his defection. Rising, she asked her mother to come into the next room for a moment. There she told her that, in the circumstances, she was now ready to marry anyone that it might be thought desirable, even Monsieur de Périgord.

Not giving Dorothea an instant to change her mind her mother kissed her with an enthusiasm that for once was wholehearted, congratulated her on her proper show of pride and ran from the room to give the good news to Edmond de

Périgord. An interview with a satisfied suitor was altogether more than Dorothea could stand and she locked herself in her room and stayed there, weeping, for the rest of the day. She would have liked to spend the next day there as well but the duchess came herself to coax her into coming down; if Dorothea were going to go through with this thing, she reasonably pointed out, then she might just as well do so with good grace. Reluctantly her daughter trailed downstairs and was led into the drawing-room where Edmond was waiting. The two wooers stared at each other in consternation; Edmond, to be fair, having excellent reason for his dismay at the sight of the skinny child, huge eyes red with tears and pale face set in lines of hang-dog sulkiness. The duchess smiled on them like Cupid on a pair of rapturous love-birds. " Now I shall leave you alone together," she said archly. " You must have such a lot to say to each other." She left the room. There was a long, unhappy silence then Dorothea spoke. " I hope, sir, that you will be happy in this marriage which has been arranged for us. I must tell you, however, what you probably know already, that I am giving way to my mother's wishes, not with actual repugnance, it is true, but at least with the most complete indifference towards you. Perhaps I will be happy—I like to think so anyway—but I am sure you will understand my regrets at leaving my country and my friends and won't resent the sorrow which I will feel, at first at any rate."

It is doubtful whether Edmond could anyway have mustered much in the way of ardour ; these first words of his betrothed were certainly enough to dampen it.

" My God ! " he replied. " I find that perfectly natural. For that matter, I'm only marrying myself so as to please my uncle. At my age, you know, it's much more fun being a bachelor."

The young lovers then parted and Edmond de Périgord left next day without having sought for a second interview.

*   *   *   *   *

If this were only romantic fiction, the dénouement would not be hard to predict. Prince Adam would have heard of the deception and would have arrived in the nick of time to claim his rightful bride. The wicked Batowski would have been killed in the ensuing battle, the ugly duchess would have been left alone in her castle and Adam and Dorothea have ridden off together into the sunset. Reality was less well contrived. Just before Piattoli's death, Prince Czartoryski had written to him to say that he had at last overcome his mother's reluctance to the marriage and proposed to leave for Löbikau as soon as possible. The letter was delivered to the duchess and returned by her to the sender with a cold note informing him of Piattoli's death and of her daughter's engagement. Prince Charming missed his cue ; probably he knew nothing of the trick which had been played on Dorothea, certainly he took no steps to undo it. The marriage was fixed for the end of April, only six weeks ahead, partly to suit Dorothea's wishes but mainly so as to give him as little chance as possible of making mischief.

There remained a few hurdles to cross. The consent of Napoleon had to be obtained and Talleyrand at the moment was in disgrace. Alexander's support for the marriage was perhaps the decisive factor ; anyway, as it turned out, the emperor made no objection. Then there was the question of religion. Dorothea was completely indifferent as to the form of service ; Edmond was, of course, a Catholic ; around Löbikau anything but a Lutheran service was impossible. It was therefore decided that the marriage should be celebrated at Frankfurt according to the Catholic rites. Finally there was the opposition of friends and family. The Prussian royal family were outraged at the engagement, all Berlin society followed suit and urged the duchess to change her mind. Dorothea's three sisters were rabidly anti-French and Wilhelmina's marriage with the émigré Prince Rohan, total failure though it had already proved, did not dispose her to kindly feeling towards Napoleon. If the marriage went through the Duchess of Courland realised that she would be going a long way towards cutting off herself and her daughter from all her German friends. Such considerations could not make the duchess change her mind but they could cause her much regret. It grieved both her and Dorothea that German society largely boycotted the wedding and that not one of the three elder daughters was there to see their sister married.

In a desolate apathy, Dorothea drifted towards her wedding

day. Grief for the dead Piattoli, injured pride over the defection of Adam Czartoryski, regrets for a vanishing Germany, dread of an approaching France : all these blended to produce in her a numbed dismay which yielded only to flashes of sudden, unreasoning panic. Her future husband was among the least of her troubles ; from him she could expect, she wrote, at least indifference and a certain respect. In her present state she asked for no more. It was a chill conclusion to the childhood of a girl who, from the first moment that she had been able to feel, had longed above all to be loved and to be allowed to love in return.

4

This moment of her life, when she was pitchforked so uncivilly from childhood into the responsibilities and difficulties of married life, is a convenient time to consider how far she had developed from the shy, suspicious schoolgirl of a few years before and whether she was in any way equipped to meet what lay ahead. Her character was very far from formed in 1809 but all her strengths and weaknesses were already apparent. The Duchess of Dino of twenty years later was superficially so different as to seem another woman but in the girl of sixteen almost all the elements were assembled.

Dorothea's education had been spasmodic. Certain subjects had been neglected altogether, others pursued even to excess. She had had almost no religious instruction and was pitifully ignorant of all aspects of modern life which had not happened to engage her interest; she knew quite a lot about Voltaire and Rousseau and had a fair acquaintanceship with the intricacies of the French aristocracy but would have been at a loss if asked to identify the industries of France or even the leading members of the Government. But her ignorance did not stem from incapacity or even disinclination to learn; it simply had not occurred to her that these were subjects on which at least a minimal knowledge would be of use.

Once she set her mind to a problem, however, she approached it with application and considerable efficiency. Her powerful and analytical intelligence—of a kind which men at least are apt to describe as " masculine "—had been sharpened and disciplined by her childhood passion for mathematics and astronomy. Even at the age of sixteen, it provided her with an uncommonly effective weapon for the clear understanding of complicated issues and a quick decision as to the necessary consequences. The usual corollary to this kind of intelligence is a lack of imagination. Dorothea was no exception. Though idealistic and often romantic she had no room for fancy or, indeed, for anything which was not demonstrably regulated by the rules of logic. In her personal relationships this lack was redressed by an acute sensitivity ; though never good at predicting how other people would react she was quick to perceive their thoughts and to adjust her own conduct accordingly.

Whatever she did, she did thoroughly and with an undeviating determination. If she decided that a certain course was right then she would hold to it, regardless of the consequences and in defiance of opposition. Her marriage provides almost the only instance in which she acted consciously against her considered judgment and even then she only gave way in a moment of apathy. She noted down in her memory the unhappy consequences of her surrender and resolved that it should never be repeated.

The same quality of steadfast conviction was apparent in all her likes and dislikes. Once her loyalty was given to one whom she loved and trusted then the gift was absolute ; no sacrifice was too much and no risk too great to run in their defence. But the gift of such loyalty was rarely made and she demanded that, in return, as much be done for her. One fall from these exacting standards and friendship was lost for ever. In time she was to learn a degree of tolerance but for Dorothea at sixteen there could be no such thing as a second chance. Her dislikes were as implacable as her loves were firm. " If gratitude is one of the most prominent characteristics of the good part of my nature," she confessed in a letter, " I am afraid that I have a compensating amount of rancour. I have never forgotten a service or a friendly word but I have perhaps too often remembered an insult or an unkind remark." An enemy once made was to be hounded ; the word " forgiveness " existed in her vocabulary but it was to be used only sparingly and with reluctance.

Dorothea was never unconscious of the great position which was hers by birth. She was not, however, beset by the blind pride of caste which made rigid and intolerable so much of the aristocratic society of Europe. She was aware, indeed, that there was an aristocracy of talent as well as of birth, and that each had their own importance and their own privileges. She often found it difficult to establish the proper relationship between the two and at the best of times found it a delicate piece of social tight-rope walking. Yet she felt that she understood the principles well enough. For her to have married outside the higher reaches of the nobility, for instance, would have been an inconceivable betrayal of her position, yet when Schiller came to visit her in her salon at Berlin she recognised that the honour was being done to her and not to him.

Such openness of mind, creditable though it may have been for the age, did not extend far beyond the ranks of apparent genius. She admired greatness and sought after its possessors but for the second-rate she felt nothing but indifference or contempt. She judged the pretensions of mankind by harsh and unrelenting standards and made no concessions to those who failed to meet them. The suffering of fools gladly was not in her nature and even the sensible man would meet with little appreciation unless his qualities in one direction or another verged on the extraordinary.

To say that Dorothea worshipped success would suggest a vulgarity of mind which was not hers. If the necessary qualities were there then success would probably follow but this was relatively unimportant ; a symptom of greatness but never a guarantee of its presence. As to her own capacities, she had few illusions. Though her mind was as quick and her judgment considerably sounder than that of, for instance, Madame de Staël, she lacked the ebullient creative genius which enabled this latter to impress herself so indelibly upon the consciousness of an age. Such limitations she recognised and did not much regret. But she was still intensely ambitious and longed to use her abilities to the full in playing a part in the affairs of state —any state would do, provided that it were of adequate importance.

" If she had lived at the time of the Fronde she would have been one of the great women of history," said Talleyrand to Charles de Rémusat[1]. At the time of her marriage Dorothea probably did not know whether the Fronde was a hair-style or a kind of vegetable but she had realised that in the nineteenth century there was little room for her in public life save through the activities of the men she influenced. It was not till many years afterwards that Count Molé wrote of her : " The dream of her imagination and the ambition of all her life has been to govern a man of distinction, a man vested with great power. Nature has given her the talents to fill such a role, even to fill it brilliantly," but the judgment could as well have been passed in 1809. It was this perception of the sort of role she felt that she should play which made her feel regret when she learned how she had at one time been considered as a wife for the Duke of Berry. In part, at least, it was for the same reason that she had resented with such bitterness the apparent defection of Prince Adam. To have become Princess Adam Czartoryski might have been delightful but to have been the wife and Egeria of the liberator of Poland would have been sublime.

From her childhood Dorothea had learnt prudence and suspicion ; she had learnt to expect the worst of motives from others and not to look for any sympathy in her own troubles. She had learnt to cloak her natural warmth and longing to love and to be loved under an air of cold neutrality. But not all the unhappiness she had endured or the indifference she had encountered had sufficed to tarnish the essential virtues which still held strong within her : honesty, integrity, sincerity, a deep capacity for affection. In 1809 she was a formidable machine with all the parts ready mounted, needing only the touch of genius to put the finishing touches and set her moving. That touch of genius she was to find but one thing at least was certain, even on her marriage day ; it did not, could not lie in the hands of her husband.

*   *   *   *   *

Count Edmond de Périgord and Princess Dorothea of Courland were married at Frankfurt on the 22nd of April, 1809. Within forty-eight hours of the wedding Edmond had left his bride and was on his way to rejoin Berthier's headquarters in Austria. It must have afforded him the most exquisite relief to leave behind this shy, unhappy girl with all the unwanted complications in which she involved him and to find once more the life which suited him so well of drinking, gambling, wenching and making war.

Reluctantly the new Countess Edmond de Périgord, still escorted by Mlle Hoffmann, set out after her mother for Paris. She knew that she was leaving Germany behind her for a long time, for all she knew for ever. Batowski had given her glowing accounts of the life and society at Paris; of the great position she would occupy there as a Princess of the House of Courland and a niece of the Prince of Benevento. Most of this Dorothea had discounted as sugar intended to garnish an exceedingly bitter pill but enough had been absorbed to leave her wondering whether her new life might not, after all, have certain compensations. It was with much apprehension, but also with a certain curiosity and even hope that Dorothea set off on the journey to her new home.

Paris in 1809 existed in the shadow of Napoleon. When he was there, all life revolved around his court; when he was absent, his doings and his whereabouts were the first subject of conversation. In the previous September at Erfurt his power had reached its zenith. The kings and princes of all Europe had gathered together to do his bidding; it had seemed that nothing could be beyond his powers and that he could create a new continent carved to suit his whim and blindly subject to his will.

That Napoleon should have imposed his will on France and on all Europe was one thing, that he should have succeeded in imposing it also on Parisian society was another, in its way perhaps even more remarkable. Yet even in the heart of the old nobility, the *Faubourg St. Germain*, the pattern of the emperor's wishes was accepted. Many of the aristocratic refugees from the Terror were still in exile but quite enough remained behind, or had since returned, to make a respectable showing and give to the imperial court some of the glitter of the *ancien régime*. With remarkable docility the holders of the oldest titles of France accepted that the empire had come to stay and submitted to jostling at court with the new Napoleonic nobility; men who, ten years before, they would not have been ready to nod to in the street. Mental reservations there were, of course, and into certain of the drawing-rooms of the *Faubourg St. Germain* no parvenu, however resounding his title or splendid his fortune, could hope to penetrate. In general, however, the new order was accepted, and as a result, Parisian society of the time was more fluid, more international, and, by and large, more entertaining than it had ever been before or than it would be again for another fifty years. The elegance, the fastidiousness, the lightness of touch of the *ancien régime* had perhaps vanished but in their place was a turbulent energy, a spirit of discontent and adventurous inquiry which made of Napoleonic society something new and uniquely stimulating.

Arrived in Paris at the end of April, Dorothea and her mother stayed with Talleyrand at his huge house in the Rue de Varenne ; now the Hôtel Matignon, official home of the Prime Minister. She was perhaps more curious about her new and formidable uncle than anybody else whom she was likely to meet in France. She knew that he was fifty-five years old, had been born the eldest son of one of the most ancient families of France but had been permanently crippled by an accident and had therefore seen title and inheritance pass to his younger brother. She knew that he had entered the Church, had become Bishop of Autun, had played a leading part in the early days of the revolution and, in 1791, had resigned his see and, not long after, been excommunicated. As the Terror rose to its height he had fled the country, returned to France under the Directory, aided Napoleon in his rise to power and become Minister of Foreign Affairs under the consulate. She knew his reputation as a libertine and womaniser, the legends that were told of his cunning and wisdom, his immense wealth and power. She knew that he had been among Napoleon's few intimate advisers and that, abroad, he had long been considered as the most important Frenchman after the emperor. What she did not know but was gradually to find out was that this intimacy with the emperor was now over, that the two men lived together in uneasy co-existence and that Talleyrand devoted his principal energies to planning the downfall of the empire which he had done so much to create.

It would have been remarkable if, at first glance, Dorothea had found her uncle altogether prepossessing. " Monsieur de

Talleyrand is the most disgusting looking individual I ever saw," the Duke of Argyll had written robustly a few years earlier. "His complexion is that of a corpse considerably advanced in corruption. His feet are distorted in every possible direction . . ." Croker put it quite as emphatically, " He looks altogether like an old, fuddled, lame, villainous schoolmaster and his voice is deep and hoarse." Certainly Talleyrand's physical deficiencies seem to have been more apparent to men than to women ; the history of his life is sufficient evidence that he possessed a power of fascination which could easily overcome his conspicuous disadvantages. The charm of his conversation and the force of his intelligence were at all events quickly sufficient to dispel any hostile first impressions and it was not long before Dorothea's feelings towards her uncle were those of trust and dazzled admiration.

Talleyrand's early judgment of his niece, though temperate, was also one of satisfaction. He did not find her particularly attractive, but she was, after all, no more than a girl. For the same reason he looked tolerantly on her other weaknesses. "Exaggeration and affectation he always hated." wrote Dorothea many years later. " At the time of my marriage I was somewhat to blame in those directions." Talleyrand would not have denied it but he benevolently attributed this to her education and German background and trusted to a few years in Paris to put it right. His friend Choiseul told him that she had intelligence and would one day achieve distinction ; he replied that he would never have suspected it but, all the same, looked more carefully at Dorothea and noted the remark for future reference. " I am very well pleased with the young niece whom I owe to your good offices," he wrote to Caulaincourt a few days after the first meeting. " I am doing my best to help her endure her separation from her husband during this first period. The mother is charming. After a fortnight in Paris . . . they are going to Rosny."

Rosny is a large and grandiose house which was built originally for Sully, the finance minister of Henry IV. It lies about thirty miles from Paris near the town of Mantes-la-Jolie ; *jolie* perhaps in 1809 but now a stinking little industrial town. Rosny itself is an attractive building surrounded by a park and large formal garden of the kind always described in France as a *jardin anglais* and in England generally considered to be one of those gardens which one finds in France. However attractive the house or pretty the village, most girls would probably have resented this rather cavalier dismissal from the pleasures of Paris to a country exile. In the circumstances, however, Dorothea asked for nothing better than to be ignored. Thankfully she postponed the moment when she would find herself exposed to the full blast of French society and settled down to fortify herself with brooding, reading, thinking and her other country pleasures.

" The mother is charming." Talleyrand was in fact a great deal more interested in his new niece's mother than in the niece herself. The Duchess of Courland had all the qualities he found most desirable. Her birth was beyond reproach, her fortune splendid, her wit and *savoir-faire* the equal of that of any woman in Paris. Talleyrand saw in her a companion worthy of his intelligence, he saw an extra piece to be made use of in his perpetual chess game with Napoleon, above all he saw an extremely attractive woman whose mature beauty and distinction of feature appealed strongly to his exacting palate ; " still beautiful," wrote Coulmann, " she shone with a brilliance accentuated by her surpassing grace and dignity."[2] Their common interest in Dorothea and Edmond was rapidly found to extend to many other spheres ; their friendship became intimacy ; in a few months the duchess was the most constant element in the firmament that always flickered around the Prince of Benevento and became the recipient of his most passionate and eager letters.

The Duchess of Courland had come to Paris as a convinced admirer of Napoleon. Talleyrand was in semi-disgrace and among the most determined and the most effective of Napoleon's enemies. In the end the duchess was going to have to choose between the objects of her admiration but, to begin with, she saw no reason why she should not be on excellent terms with both. Talleyrand, indeed, encouraged her to enter the royal circle ; an extra ear at court would never come amiss. It would have been remarkable if the duchess had been unflattered by the reception that she found awaiting her. Emperor and empress vied to do her honour ; Josephine presented her with a ring as a souvenir of her stay in France and Napoleon accorded her the distinction, almost unique for a woman, of being received alone in private audience. She spent her first few months in Paris in the euphoric conviction that she alone was loved by all ; even, perhaps, that through her intercession with her dear friend the emperor, her dear friend the Vice Grand Elector might be received back into favour.

In October, 1809, peace was signed in Vienna and Edmond de Périgord came back to Paris. Her six months at Rosny had probably done a lot to reconcile Dorothea to the idea of his return. Life in the country was all very well but after the initial relief at being alone had worn off she would have been most unnatural if she had not begun to pine a little for the unknown pleasures of Paris. For Edmond, too, the return must have produced a pleasant surprise. Dorothea was at an age where, physically, she was developing fast. Already the skinny schoolgirl was vanishing and the lines of the face taking on the rich fullness which alone could provide a suitable frame for those great dark eyes. It was only in the bloom of young motherhood that Dorothea was to arrive at real beauty, but though she was still only sixteen the returning soldier had already the gratification of finding a handsome woman awaiting him.

For two years Count and Countess Edmond de Périgord lived together in Paris and were to be seen at every event in the social calendar. Dorothea made no attempt to outshine her mother in Parisian society, her youth and inexperience would have ensured the futility of any such an enterprise ; but she still managed to achieve a considerable reputation for wit, vivacity and beauty.

Even the new Empress Marie-Louise, fresh from the imperial splendours of Vienna, had found Paris a revelation of gaiety and sophistication and life at the Tuileries infinitely more exciting than at the Schönnbrun. For Dorothea, used only to the provincial society of Berlin and the stark barrack-room grandeur of the Prussian court, the transition was still more dazzling. She was delighted by French society and the rich variety of Parisian life ; a little intimidated at first but quickly gaining confidence as she went around and got to know more people. There were bound to be many prejudices against her ; the Prussians had but recently been at war with France and, though it is always easier to be gracious to the conquered than to the conqueror and though Dorothea might fairly be considered as more of a cosmopolitan than a German, she was at first treated with some suspicion. But the suspicion did not endure for long. Her youth, her charm, her readiness to be pleased all acted in her favour : " although still almost a child " wrote the Countess de Boigne, " she was exceedingly pretty, engaging and gracious ; already the distinction of her intelligence shone through brilliantly. She had every quality except that of being natural but in spite of the absence of this, which is the greatest charm of youth, I found her most agreeable."

Though generally well-liked and sought after, it does not seem that Dorothea made any particular friends. All her life she was to prefer male society to female ; quite apart from any physical relationship she found man's intellect more satisfying, his interests more absorbing and his company generally more stimulating and rewarding. For women on the whole she had little use except in so far as their capacities seemed to her to measure up to masculine standards. Her relationships with them tended to vary between prudent neutrality and out-and-out war. At the age of sixteen, newly arrived in Paris and saddled with a husband who still felt it his duty to be possessive, she had neither the liberty nor the experience to develop those friendships among men of talent and position which were later to play so large a part in her life. Yet she had no inclination to substitute for such relationships the sort of close alliance with someone of her own age and sex which is so easily entered into and which, for most girls, yields so much pleasure. She retained always a certain aloofness and, though superficially one of the crowd, was lonely among a host of glittering acquaintances.

In so far as anyone was charged or charged themselves with keeping an eye on Dorothea in her first years in society, it was Countess Kielmannsegge. This child of a princely Saxon house had been born in 1777 and was now in the full flush of beauty.

Her first husband had died abruptly in 1800, gossip having it that his wife had poisoned him. Two years later she married Count Kielmannsegge. From the start it seemed improbable that the marriage would ever be much of a success. The couple seemed antipathetic emotionally, physically and—most damaging of all—politically. Countess Kielmannsegge was a convinced admirer of Napoleon; Count Kielmannsegge devoted most of his energies to anti-Napoleonic plots including one full-blooded effort to assassinate Jerome Bonaparte, King of Westphalia. During the greater part of their married life the husband pursued his crusade against the emperor and left his wife to her own devices. The countess filled her time with lengthy visits to the Duchess of Courland during which the two ladies vied with one another in enthusiasm for the imperial cause.

After Dorothea's wedding the duchess suggested to her friend that she should come and join her in Paris. The countess arrived in the autumn of 1809 and, at the first opportunity, sought an interview with the emperor. It was granted and she took advantage of it to ask for the release of her husband who was now under arrest in Hanover as a result of the misfiring of one of his plots. Napoleon was well pleased by his beautiful Saxon admirer. He granted her request on two conditions : first, that the countess should settle in Paris ; second, that the count should not. Nothing could have been more to the taste of Countess Kielmannsegge who at once settled down with a clear conscience to enjoy the pleasures of Paris. Dorothea she was attracted to from the start and, though they were not to become close friends till a year or two later, she still saw much of the Countess Edmond de Périgord and of her dashing soldier-husband.

*   *   *   *   *

Through 1810 and 1811 Dorothea continued to live in comparative harmony with her husband. Both parties to the marriage were increasingly convinced that they had neither interests nor tastes in common but there were sufficient distractions to make the relationship perfectly tolerable in spite of this. There was only one major disturbance to her

social round ; when, in March of 1811, she gave birth to her
first child, a son. The event was celebrated with gratifying
pomp and both emperor and empress condescended to stand
god-parent. The boy was christened Napoleon-Louis. The
name, so appropriate at the time, was to prove something of
an embarrassment in the future and as happened so frequently
with children of the period, the " Napoleon " was to vanish,
rarely to be heard again, before the child was three years
old.

One minor incident in this period stuck very vividly in
Dorothea's mind so that she remembered and recorded it
some fifteen years later. At this time a certain Mlle Lenormand
from Alençon was enjoying great vogue as a fortune-teller.
She was said to have been constantly visited by Robespierre
and St. Just and it was counted to her credit that she had
prophesied Danton's fall and Bernadotte's rise to a throne.
Her career received no more than a temporary set-back when
Napoleon, in a fit of pique, sent her to prison for having had
the temerity to predict some imperial calamity. Captain
Gronow, an English officer in Paris, described her a few years
later as " a monstrous toad, bloated and venomous. She had
one wall eye but the other was a piercer. She wore a fur cap
upon her head, from beneath which she glared out upon her
horrified visitors. The walls of the room were covered with
huge bats, nailed by their wings to the ceiling, stuffed owls,
cabalistic signs, skeletons."[3]

Dorothea, in common with all her friends, went to visit her,
taking the precaution of giving a false name and address when
she made the appointment. After the usual rigmarole of
questions about dates of birth, favourite colours, etc., Mlle
Lenormand got on to the fortune proper: " She said that I was
married . . . that, after much pain and trouble I should be
separated from my husband, that my troubles would not cease
till nine years after this separation and that, during these nine
years I should experience all manner of trials and calamities.
She also said that I should become a widow when no longer
young but not too old to marry again, which I should do. She
saw me for many years closely allied with a person whose
position and influence would impose on me a kind of political

81   F

position and would make me powerful enough to save someone from imprisonment and death. She said also that I should live through very difficult and stormy times . . . I should still be alive, she said, at sixty-three . . ."

The news about her marriage did not come as a complete shock to Dorothea but she must have wondered who the " person of position and influence " could be before dismissing the whole matter from her mind.

In the summer of 1810 the Duchess of Courland left Paris for a visit to her estates in Germany. She was expected to stay away until the beginning of the following year. Her departure must have been something of a relief to Dorothea. It can never be altogether pleasant for a girl just entering society to be so patently overshadowed by her mother and the duchess had too few of the qualities of a parent to give her daughter much cause for regret at her going. Not long afterwards Countess Kielmannsegge left to visit her husband and see whether he might still not be converted to the true or Napoleonic faith. Dorothea, therefore, found herself left to her husband or to her own devices. The latter, she was more and more tending to conclude, were likely to provide a more satisfactory employment of her time.

Not long after her mother's departure Dorothea found herself given a new importance in Parisian life. After divorcing Josephine, Napoleon, on the 1st of April, 1810, had married the arch-duchess Marie-Louise of Austria. In September of the same year twelve ladies-in-waiting were named as members of the new empress's household. The majority of these were drawn from the nobility of foreign countries subject to the emperor's sway and Dorothea was among the few who, at least, bore a French name. Since she was also the only one of them who happened to speak German as her native tongue, she must have hoped to grow particularly close to the empress. But the part played by the ladies-in-waiting left little scope for the establishment of intimacy or even friendship ; they only appeared on formal occasions and never penetrated into the domestic life of the empress.

Talleyrand was delighted with this honour paid to his niece. Though open rupture with the emperor would have to come in the end, he wished to postpone it for as long as he could. Shortly before the announcement he had written to Caulaincourt. " There is a question of creating some ladies of the palace ; they say six. Probably Mme de Périgord will be one of them ; I hope so, because anything suits me if it provides a tie between me and the emperor." Dorothea had no idea at all of her uncle's calculations and never even suspected that she might be of use to him. She welcomed the distinction, was bored by the duties and decided that, compensations though it might have, the life of a court was not altogether to her liking.

One other step she also took towards her integration in French society. Sometime in the course of 1811 she sent for the priest at Rosny and informed him that she proposed to adopt the Roman Catholic faith. It does not seem that she asked for much in the way of preparation or that the priest was allowed the luxury of explaining to the young convert exactly what she was accepting. Dorothea had made up her own mind, was quite clear in what obligations it involved her and now wished her decision to be carried out with a minimum of fuss and bother. Any theological disputation would indeed have seemed to her an unnecessary irrelevance. So far as one can tell the conversion was actuated by nothing more profound than general sentiments of propriety and social convenience. " I have never busied myself with dogmas or mysteries," she wrote some twenty years later, " and if I prefer the Roman Catholic religion I do so because I think it most useful to society in general. Individual religion is a different matter and I think any religion based upon the Gospel is equally good and divine."

When she wrote that passage she probably had in mind by " usefulness to society " the part the church could play in imposing stability on a social system ; in 1811 it is unlikely that there was anything in her mind beyond a feeling that, on balance, a family is happier if all its members profess the same faith and also that, having married into French society, she had better conform to the outward and visible pattern of French morality.

*   *   *   *   *

When the Duchess of Courland and Countess Kielmannsegge returned to Paris the intimacy between them was at first resumed as warmly as if it had never been interrupted. But their relationship was not to be proof against political differences and affairs in France no longer left the duchess the possibility of being the friend of all the world. Countess Kielmannsegge remained loyal to Napoleon ; well before the end of the year the Duchess of Courland had thrown in her lot with the opposition.

The ever-increasing probability of a war between France and Russia had reminded the duchess that Russia was still the source of the greater part of her income. The wisest course would probably have been to retire from France altogether, but to do so would have meant giving up her close alliance with Talleyrand. This she could not endure for it had become uniquely satisfying to her. At one level the relationship was passionate, on another it was a highly intelligent and dis-passionate partnership. Under Talleyrand's influence the duchess came to dislike Napoleon's methods and mistrust his aims ; once the glamour of his achievements had worn off she saw him for what he was—a man of prodigious talents and supernatural force but whose policies and very existence were incompatible with peace and stability in Europe. Napoleon himself did nothing to check the progress of her disillusion. Always ready to accept her adulation, his gracious welcome chilled as soon as he thought he detected a trace of opposition. He showed his disapproval by treating her with indifference and even played with the idea of expelling her from France. This, in its turn, fostered the duchess's resentment and what, with tactful handling on either side, might have been no more than a temporary coldness, grew quickly into implacable hostility.

" The Duchess of Courland had altogether turned against Napoleon," wrote Countess Kielmannsegge after her return from Germany, " and if there was one thing which seemed to her to be an unforgivable weakness it was to admit to any sense of loyalty towards him." This might have been expected to lead to a complete rupture between the two women but the

countess did not see the matter that way. In the summer of
1811 the Duchess of Courland settled in a little house at St.
Germain, a few miles from Paris. It had two virtues essential
to Talleyrand, comfort and seclusion, and he set up there an
informal headquarters for the pursuit of intrigues against
Napoleon. Far from shunning so unsavoury a spot, Countess
Kielmannsegge in her turn installed herself at St. Germain. She
had grown to know well Savary, Duke of Rovigo, Napoleon's
Minister of Police. Savary, without using so indiscreet a word
as spying, suggested that it would be of value to all parties
concerned and particularly to the emperor, if she was to
exercise a discreet surveillance over the duchess. The countess
saw nothing unworthy in the proposal and from that time
submitted occasional reports to the minister on the current
activities of her friend and of Talleyrand.

Judging by her memoirs, life at St. Germain appears to
have been a constant whirl of conspiracy and intrigue. One
day she claims to have gone unexpectedly into a room where
she found Talleyrand, the Duchess of Courland and another
friend, the Viscountess de Laval. Talleyrand had just finished
expounding what must have been some particularly nefarious
plot for he finished with the words, " and that is how we shall
destroy him ! " " We shall destroy him ! We shall destroy
him ! " echoed his fellow conspirators, clapping their hands
together and clasping each other around the neck.

The most relevant point about this picturesque but somewhat unconvincing anecdote is that Dorothea was not featured
among the plotters nor does she seem to have been associated
in any way with her mother's activities at St. Germain. She
could certainly not have been ignorant of Talleyrand's breach
with Napoleon—it provided a constant source of gossip for
all Parisian society—and she must have been aware how closely
her mother was associated with all aspects of Talleyrand's life.
It may have been that, as a lady-in-waiting, she felt inhibited
from working against the régime. More probably, however,
she had not yet developed any very lively interest in politics,
and was perfectly content to enjoy herself in Parisian society
and leave conspiracy to her elders.

From time to time, however, not even the most perfect

observance of the principles of non-intervention could save her from being the victim of her uncle's unpopularity with the Emperor. One such occasion arose in August, 1811, when she was on duty with the court at St. Cloud. Napoleon had been grumbling for days at the insubordination of his Vice Grand Elector and, with his astonishing capacity for absorbing trivial gossip, had also picked up a story against Count Edmond de Périgord. In the course of the evening he suddenly rounded on Dorothea.

" Really, your husband is guilty of too many idiocies. How can he possibly have spent ten thousand francs on cameos ? "

" Sire," replied the startled Dorothea, " Your Majesty has been misinformed. My husband has never done anything so foolish."

Ignoring this, Napoleon turned to Berthier, " You ought not to tolerate this sort of thing on the part of one of your aides-de-camp." Berthier remained discreetly silent and the emperor turned back to Dorothea. " In fact it is a good deal easier to forgive this particular folly than many of the others which your husband is in the habit of committing. Anyway, as you know, for a long time I have ceased to take any interest in these poor Périgords."

Tears came to Dorothea's eyes but she had enough spirit to reply angrily : " Sire, my husband and my uncle have at all times served Your Majesty with zeal. It rests with you to make further use of them. And surely their earlier services have at least deserved that Your Majesty should not ridicule them."

The court stood aghast at this audacious reply to the emperor from a mere girl and waited apprehensively for some fresh outburst. The emperor, however, said no more and Dorothea, now crying openly, ran from the room.

Few men can have had less of the instincts of a gentleman than Napoleon but even he seems to have suspected that in this unprovoked attack on a young and innocent girl he had gone a little too far. Next day, when all the courtiers with Berthier at their head were ostentatiously cold-shouldering Countess Edmond, he called her to sit at his table and, when she sat in a respectful but reserved silence, plied her with the choicest pieces of fruit and made a point of being agreeable to her. The courtiers, Berthier still at their head, at once joined in and began to flatter and cajole her and Dorothea found herself the most sought after person at court. She knew well what value to attach to these protestations and, when Berthier was particularly fulsome, she remarked coldly how pleased she was to see that a few pieces of fruit from the hands of the emperor earned her so many graceful compliments.

Talleyrand's comment on the scene at court was as temperate as it was devastating: " It seems," he said, " a poor way of proving his power."

Countess Kielmannsegge was well aware that Dorothea did not take any part in her mother's political activities. She transferred to the young countess all the affection which her mother had forfeited by her contumacy. " My friendship for Countess Edmond de Périgord," she wrote in the summer of 1811, " firmly based as it was on mutual confidence, was born at this period." Towards the end of the year Dorothea was expecting a second child and was always glad of a chance to escape from the rigours of court life to spend a few days in the country at Rosny. There Countess Kielmannsegge would frequently follow her and play her favourite role of confidante ; convincing herself if not her hostess that, at the age of eighteen, Dorothea could still do with an older head to advise and help her. " Countess Dorothea needed me," she wrote to a friend, " and her husband, whose intelligence and serious nature may not shine beside hers but whose honesty and kindness are obvious on every occasion, has always been quite as insistent that I should come to stay."

It would be surprising if Dorothea felt any very urgent need for the presence of this interfering busy-body. However, she does appear to have had a genuine regard for Countess Kielmannsegge and there is no doubt that Edmond was always glad to have her at Rosny. This was in itself an excellent reason for Dorothea to welcome her company. After all, if somebody else was ready and anxious to entertain Edmond there was all the less need for her to do so.

In a cryptic, confused but still revealing metaphor, Countess Kielmannsegge compared Dorothea at this period to " a young girl . . . stranded on a ship-wreck in the midst of the waves, who impatiently lifts a corner of her veil in an effort to see the promised land which she feels is close ; like a sailor to whom appears by an odd trick of sight the shores of his native land before they have actually appeared on the horizon." Dorothea in 1811 was indeed looking for the promised land ; what it would look like and where it would lie she did not know but of one thing she was certain—that she had not found it yet and need not hope ever to find it in her marriage.

*   *   *   *   *

With 1812 came the looming certainty of war with Russia and every soldier in Napoleon's empire prepared himself for what everyone knew was going to be the greatest and hardest of all the emperor's campaigns. Edmond de Périgord had risen to the rank of colonel by the age of twenty-five and had no doubt that this promotion was owed entirely to his own merit rather than to any avuncular pressure. He looked forward to the coming battles as being certain to set him still further on the road to glory. Countess Kielmannsegge encouraged him, saying that he had always succeeded in the past and would certainly continue so to do in the future. An unkinder or more dispassionate acquaintance might have replied that he had already got further than he deserved. On 25th of January he set off to join his regiment at Brescia. After his departure he wrote several letters to the countess, entrusting his young wife to her care. Her simplicity and innocence, he said, were sure to lead to suffering ; he asked the countess to help her in these troubles.

The absence of her husband was bound to curtail Dorothea's social life but she found his companionship little loss. She was anyway at this time expecting her second child and had no objection at all to spending a few months waiting peacefully at Rosny. Unfortunately, her mother and Countess Kielmannsegge were also there for much of the time. The presence of these two warring women can hardly have helped to provide a reposeful background. Dorothea was soon on bad terms with her mother. Amicable enough when they saw each other rarely and could lead untrammelled their individual lives, it seemed that they were doomed always to clash as soon as they lived together in any intimacy. It did not take long before each felt strongly that the time had come for a change. Luckily it was not to be long delayed for the duchess was making plans for another visit to Löbikau and neither Dorothea's inclinations nor her health made it at all possible that she should accompany her.

It was an unfruitful stage in Dorothea's life; unfruitful, that is to say, in the metaphorical sense only since, in April, 1812, she gave birth to her second child, Dorothea-Charlotte-Emily. Looking back long afterwards at these empty months, Dorothea saw little to remember with pleasure. She was restless and dissatisfied. All her friendships seemed superficial, her marriage was a parody, in no one could she confide her unhappiness or her longings. Indeed, she would have been hard put to it to define with any precision what it was for which she longed. A nagging sense of incompleteness, of a life stunted before it had had any chance to blossom or mature, was with her always and prevented her from settling with resolution to any of the occupations which might have filled her time. Many of Dorothea's illnesses were undoubtedly psychosomatic and there is no reason to think that anything was seriously wrong with her; nevertheless her unhappiness was reflected in a physical malaise which in its turn accentuated her boredom and restlessness.

A passage in a letter which Countess Kielmannsegge wrote to a friend in March, 1812, throws an odd light on this period and suggests that Dorothea had troubles even beyond her loneliness and discontent.

" Everything which the Duchess of Courland says is based on falsehood and it pains me to have to admit that it is no longer possible for anyone to put their trust in her. The complaints which she is constantly voicing against her daughter seem generally to produce the opposite effect to what she expects. Talleyrand, who certainly does not sin in the direction of being too fond of Dorothea, as time goes by will hardly be able to prevent himself from esteeming her; though to-day, old roué that he is, he may be apt to ask himself whether virtue and a decided character can really be the property of a young girl of nineteen. He has, judging by appearances, already forgotten the many overtures which he has already made towards Madame de Périgord in this respect."

The most obvious innuendo to read into the last sentence is that Talleyrand had made several attempts to seduce his niece and had been always rebuffed ; no doubt due to the sterling moral support given to Dorothea by the virtuous Countess Kielmannsegge. It would be idle to pretend that such a tentative would have been completely contrary to Talleyrand's nature but there is not the slightest evidence to suggest that he made it. Indeed, everything that is known of Talleyrand's life at this period suggests the contrary. His interests were heavily engaged elsewhere and he hardly began to know his niece at all well or to consider her with any attention until after the departure for Germany of her mother in the summer. The future development of the relationship between the prince and Dorothea cannot be reconciled with the idea that, at one time, they had played the roles of vicious old libertine and indignant innocent. It is, of course, possible that the countess did not refer to sexual seduction in her letter but meant no more than that Talleyrand had tried to persuade his niece to play a part in his political plotting. More likely, however, she had allowed spite to overcome discretion and was busily embroidering on some scrap of gossip which she had garnered in the Paris drawing-rooms. Certainly she had always a weakness for the melodramatic ; in the same letter she wrote that :

" Dorothea is overwhelmed by a thousand agonies which she looks on as so many acts of penitence offered out of love for the God to whom she prays to help her accomplish her duty. She accomplishes this duty with the purity of an angel and with a self-abnegation which earns her all the favours of providence and must ensure that no impure breath can ever come to blacken her innocent intentions and her ever irreproachable conduct ". . . . " She has only one fault," concluded the countess more prosaically, " she talks too much."

Besides acting as genteel spy on the Duchess of Courland, Countess Kielmannsegge also undertook to perform the same duty by her daughter. Her friend Savary took her aside one day and, claiming to speak on the direct instructions of the emperor, asked her " to watch unceasingly over Madame de Périgord, to encourage her good qualities and to help her keep on the straight and narrow path of principle." " They counted on me," wrote the countess exultantly, " they entrusted her to me so that I might provide a shelter against the perversity of her uncle."

Evidently the countess submitted favourable reports for Dorothea's stock at court remained high. She was promoted in the hierarchy of ladies-in-waiting and Napoleon, after unleashing one of his onslaughts on the wife of Marshal Ney, went so far as to turn to the young Countess Edmond and tell her, " As for you, I know that you behave well." " Make sure that it goes on like that," he continued more prudently. Even more to the point, he took steps to ensure that certain properties which had been given to Talleyrand should be entailed on Count and Countess Edmond de Périgord and not be left free for the prince to dispose of as he thought fit. Countess Kielmannsegge, of course, claimed much of the credit for this. Napoleon, she said, had sent for her and Savary and asked whether they considered that the Périgords deserved this mark of favour. Both the countess and the minister had assured the emperor that they saw no reason to change their views as to the virtues of the young couple.

*   *   *   *   *

In June, 1812, the Duchess of Courland left for Löbikau. Dorothea would not have been sorry to have remained quietly at Rosny but court duties forced her to be most of the time in Paris. With the duchess out of France, Talleyrand naturally saw more of his young niece and took a keener interest in her doings. The last traces of the immature child had now vanished. At no point in her life would it have been reasonable to describe Dorothea as pretty ; her haughty, acquiline features and great, burning eyes, " gaslight eyes " as Lady Granville called them, made any such petty epithet quite inappropriate. Sometimes beautiful, always distinguished, Dorothea, even at the age of nineteen, had a presence and vivid personality which few women ever achieve. It was perfectly possible to dislike her—

most women did indeed—but she was hard to ignore and for men she provided a challenge, a shock of excitement which was far outside their normal experience.

Talleyrand was as delighted with her mind as with her appearance. He found in his young niece a keen intelligence, a knowledge of and readiness to be engrossed by the intricacies of the political scene and a maturity of judgment coupled with a refreshing absence of prejudices and preconceptions. Certainly Dorothea shared the instinctive class-consciousness of the European aristocrat ; of, indeed, the European of any social level, but apart from such inevitable preconditioning she was open to every new impression. Her armoury of basic principles was meagre and applied as well to the field of public as of private life. Loyalty, integrity, persistence, a regard for decorum, a distrust of drastic innovation, a profound consciousness of the duties of a member of society : these were the factors which conditioned her own life and which provided the framework for her view of the world at large. Within this framework her convictions were unformed and to Talleyrand fell the task of shaping them in accordance with his own conceptions.

From the start, Dorothea showed a deference for her uncle's person and an interest in his ideas which completely beguiled this cynical and hardened philanderer. There was no trace of hypocrisy in her attitude. Talleyrand's wisdom, wit and intimate knowledge of the political world ; his unique combination of tolerance, almost one could say indifference, with certain deeply-held and passionately defended convictions, seemed to offer Dorothea exactly what she was looking for and most needed. He opened for her a new world, a world in which she knew her future must lie if she were ever entirely to fulfil herself, a world far removed from her circle of smart friends in Parisian society and the oafish mundanity of her husband's pleasures. In those first months of companionship with her uncle she laid the foundations of her future life. She also, incidentally, killed for ever the possibility of achieving even a tolerable *modus vivendi* with Edmond de Périgord.

While Dorothea was growing away from him in Paris, Edmond was seeking the distinction which Countess Kielmannsegge had told him was sure to come his way. A few months carousing with his regiment in Germany did little to advance his chances but as Napoleon's army ploughed deeper into the heart of Russia the pleasures of the mess gave way to the more serious business of war. Talleyrand watched his progress with anxiety. For better or worse, his nephew carried with him the future of the House of Périgord and, however low the prince might rate his qualities, he was still anxious to push him forward considerably further than his natural abilities could take him.

Edmond was, in fact, by no means so pitiful a character as his uncle sometimes imagined. In battle, he was an excellent junior officer[4], cool, sensible and never hesitating to risk his life if he saw one of his men in danger. The more one considers Edmond the more it seems that he had the makings of a worthy and honourable, if dull and sluggish, member of society. The pity as much for him as for Dorothea was that such qualities as he had were those least likely to earn the notice of his wife. In part at least it was the sense of inadequacy and inarticulate resentment which she induced in him which led him to indulge his vices to the extinction of all his finer parts. A pretty little woman to admire and adore was all that Edmond needed ; how could he be expected to cope with a blue stocking beauty who treated him increasingly with arrogant indifference.

But the gallantry of ten thousand Edmonds would not have been enough to stem the French defeat. His winter was spent not, as Talleyrand had feared, at the gambling tables of Moscow but in the icy desolation of Napoleon's first retreat. Late in the night of 18th December, the emperor, having abandoned his shattered army, arrived unexpectedly at the Tuileries. Dorothea was on duty at the palace that night and was one of the first to have the news. As soon as she had a free moment she dashed off a note to her uncle telling him of Napoleon's return. She must have suspected that to Talleyrand the news would have a particular significance. With Napoleon in Paris prudence was reimposed on all those enemies of the régime who had begun to make their voices heard without concealment. In Duff Cooper's words ". . . for the last time treason hung its head, criticism sank to a whisper and conspiracy crept underground." With her midnight scrawl,

Dorothea was testifying that, in the future conflict, she would make common cause with her uncle.

In the wake of his emperor, Edmond de Périgord returned to France. He only stayed in Paris for a few days—long enough for Dorothea to conceive a child but not for her to resume any real life with her husband—and then went off to rejoin his regiment. Edmond and Dorothea had spent less than half their married life together; it would have been a shaky start to a union far more soundly based. After a few months' dissipation, he set off with the army against Austria. The Napoleonic adventure was entering its final phase. After four days of ferocious fighting, the French Army was defeated at Leipzig. Its demoralised fragments began to pour back across the Rhine. Edmond, fighting with his habitual blend of gallantry and imprudence, was cut off in a skirmish and taken prisoner.

His imprisonment caused him remarkably little inconvenience. At any rate among the aristocracy, the obligation to hate one's enemies had not yet been generally accepted and Count Edmond de Périgord found himself treated far more like an honoured guest than a prisoner. He settled down philosophically in captivity to comfort himself for this further separation from his wife by a vigorous bout of gay living and the inevitable gambling.

Talleyrand was by now fairly sure that any amount of damage done to Edmond's career by external circumstances would be trivial compared to the damage he daily did to it himself. In prison, indeed, his chances of promotion were probably quite as good as elsewhere. However, he diligently occupied himself with the string-pulling necessary to secure an exchange or, at any rate, a release on parole. He had little difficulty. In January, 1814, Edmond was authorised to return to France.

Dorothea meanwhile had other preoccupations besides the misfortunes of her husband. She had spent most of the summer and autumn at Rosny awaiting the birth of her third child. The birth of her last child, Dorothea, had been a hard one and this time she was extremely ill. When, on 15th December, she gave birth to a second son, she must have wondered whether the bearing of children by a husband she did not love was really a rational or profitable occupation for a life-time. But whatever the demerits of the father, she loved the children dearly and was determined that they should have a better chance of happiness than had been offered her. This son was christened Alexander - Edmond. Her eldest son, Napoleon-Louis, had been named in honour of the Emperor of France. It is a mark of how far the family's politics had evolved and of Talleyrand's assessment of the situation that her second son bore the name of the Emperor of Russia.

The Duchess of Courland was back in France in time for the birth of her grandchild. Helped by a long separation and the self-confidence which Dorothea had already gained from her friendship with her uncle, the duchess got on a good deal better with her daughter than she had used to. It might have been expected that she would have resented the importance which Dorothea had now assumed in the eyes of Talleyrand. Certainly there could be few women so broad-minded as not to feel a sense of injury at the growth of even a modest friendship between their lover and their daughter. But in fact there is no reason to believe that she felt any real jealousy. She still considered her daughter as something of a little girl and saw no more reason to object to Talleyrand's partiality towards her than any other mother would feel at the affection of an uncle for a favourite child. So simple an account, of course, would never for a moment have satisfied the Parisian gossips. They had it that the duchess was bitterly distressed at finding herself supplanted by Dorothea and gleefully commiserated with her on finding her daughter seduced and herself jilted in a single operation. If there is any evidence for this theory it has never been produced. All the letters of the period between Talleyrand and the duchess contradict it and suggest that, if it were true, a most complicated and pointless game of mutual deception must have been in progress.

One reason for the better relations between Dorothea and her mother was quite simply the absence of Countess Kielmannsegge. This venomous busybody had finally retreated from Paris and was now living in Germany turning over the possibilities of divorcing her husband. She wrote from time to time to Dorothea but was beginning to suspect that her protégée was in fact little better than her mother when it came to loyalty to the emperor.

*   *   *   *   *

Napoleon's world was crashing about him. Beaten back within his frontiers and fighting with a brilliant yet desperate ferocity he was forced step by step back towards Paris. On 20th March Edmond arrived in Paris to find that his wife and mother-in-law had been packed off to Rosny in case the city was besieged. Talleyrand, indeed, was doubtful whether Rosny was really far enough from Paris to be secure and considered sending the women to Valençay, his estate in Berry. On 12th March came a report that Cossack skirmishers had penetrated as far as Beauvais ; he hesitated for the last time, then sent a consoling letter telling the women to stay where they were. Soon all would be over.

The end was, indeed, growing very close and Talleyrand had made all his plans to benefit by it. The history of the previous few years had, to some extent, divorced him in people's minds from his imperial master. He was implicitly trusted by the Emperor Alexander of Russia. He was disliked by the Bourbons but had not made himself so repugnant to them as to be altogether unacceptable in their eyes. The key to the future of France was in his hands and he had no intention of allowing anyone but himself to turn it. Impassively, he awaited the moment when at last the long years of waiting would be over and treason to his emperor dignified as loyalty to his king.

Little news came through to Rosny and such as did was most of it inaccurate ; for a true picture of what was going on Dorothea and her mother depended on Talleyrand's occasional laconic notes. On 1st April, Dorothea was supposed to be on duty at the Tuileries. She felt she ought to attend and announced her intention of coming to Paris. Talleyrand knew better than she did how fast events were moving. He told her to stay where she was and began to manufacture an alibi for her absence by spreading rumours of her illness. In the event no alibi was needed. On 29th March the empress left Paris on the way back to her family at Vienna. Two days later the allies were in Paris. The Emperor Alexander made his way to Talleyrand's house and lodged there as his guest. The conquerors of France vied in paying their respects to the only man who held their confidence among the conquered. It was perhaps the most triumphant moment of the statesman's life. From Rosny Dorothea was summoned to come and share it.

5

On the 31st of March the first detachments of Cossack cavalry arrived in the outskirts of Paris. The Parisians watched their entry with a strange mixture of relief, suspicion and stupefaction. To some they came as conquerors, to others as liberators ; but few could watch their entry without mistrust and a certain bitterness that France, so long triumphant, should now herself see the invaders in her capital.

Arriving amidst the vanguard of the Cossacks, said the gossips, was the young Countess Edmond de Périgord. Someone claimed to have seen her galloping into Paris, perched astride a horse behind a Cossack soldier[1]. Somehow this wildly far-fetched tale gained credence and soon all Paris was talking of Dorothea's sensational arrival ; as politically ill-judged, it was said, as it was socially indecorous. This fantasy was, of course, so incredible as to be hardly worth denying. The canard however, was to haunt her for all her life ; forty years later she was protesting to the King of Prussia at its resurrection in a book by the German historian Gervinus. Dorothea, in fact, arrived in Paris two days later and prosaically by carriage. She did however actually enter the city with an escort of Cossack cavalry and in that perhaps lay the genesis of the legend.

Dorothea found her uncle in a position of greater power than that enjoyed by any other Frenchman ; almost, through the influence which he exercised on the Emperor of Russia, than that enjoyed by any other man in France. The crumbling of the Napoleonic edifice had left a gap which the Bourbons had not yet arrived to fill. Whether they ever would, depended upon the will of the allies and for advice the allies looked to Talleyrand. Talleyrand himself was without doubts. Little affection though he had for their persons or respect for their talents he had convinced himself that only the return of the legitimate ruling family could give France the stability that she needed and the position in Europe which he held to be her right. He knew that the Bourbons themselves were never likely to look on him with other than suspicion. That was a handicap he had to accept ; he was a great deal cleverer than they were and reckoned that he could probably handle them when it came to the point.

Though technically living with her husband at their house in the Rue de la Grange-Batelière, Dorothea in fact saw little of Edmond at this period. The latter spent much of his time with the army and Dorothea was anyway largely occupied in helping her mother and her uncle entertain the Emperor of Russia and his suite in Talleyrand's vast house in the Rue St. Florentin. It was essential for the successful carrying out of Talleyrand's plans that Alexander should continue to treat him as an intimate friend and should not subject himself to other, possibly hostile influences. The continued goodwill of the temperamental and volatile emperor was not easy to guarantee and the work of Dorothea in keeping him happy and making Talleyrand's house agreeable to him was a considerable element in the process. Certainly, her failure would have made her uncle's task more difficult. The emperor was by no means committed to the return of the Bourbons and was known to be playing with the idea either of handing over the throne to the family of Orleans or of a regency during the minority of Napoleon's son. Only Talleyrand's insistence on the need to call back Louis XVIII to his brother's throne and the implicit faith which Alexander had learnt to place in the judgment of his host made possible the Restoration ; if that faith had been shaken or the good relations between the two men disturbed, then Louis XVIII might have found his exile indefinitely extended.

Dorothea was seeing her uncle in an entirely new light. By the time she had arrived in France, Talleyrand had lost the trust of Napoleon and had begun his long course of sub-terranean opposition. She had known him only as the furtive plotter, never revealing his true thoughts except in seclusion with his intimates. The authority with which he was now acting and the dexterity with which he managed all about him impressed his niece as a startling revelation. Before she had admired his wit and intelligence, responded to his obvious affection for her. Now, suddenly, she realised that he was a great man. She saw him dominating all in the salons of the Rue St. Florentin : " at once the heart and the brain of Paris " as Lacour Gayet described it ; saw him effortlessly pulling the network of strings which governed the destiny of France, and felt that, for the first time, she appreciated him at his true worth.

*   *   *   *   *

The Bourbons duly returned and Talleyrand in turn was duly installed as their Minister for Foreign Affairs. As a mark of favour to his uncle, Louis XVIII did what Napoleon had for so long refused to do and promoted Edmond to the rank of brigadier-general. Talleyrand had also suggested to the king that the Countess Edmond de Périgord should be nominated lady-in-waiting but this Louis XVIII refused to do. It was bad enough for a Bourbon to see effective power resting with a man who had been associated with the revolution and had worked so closely with Napoleon. It would have been intolerable to be constantly reminded of the fact by the presence of ornaments of the late imperial court around his person.

Dorothea did not take the news too hardly. In spite of her childish memories of the exiled court at Mittau, what little she knew of the Bourbons did not dispose her to look forward to their society with much enthusiasm and her experience of the imperial court as well as of her life in Berlin had taught her that palaces were not the best places in which to seek entertainment or even congenial society. She found that life in Paris outside the Tuileries was quite complicated enough to fill her life sufficiently.

Unlike the majority of her friends, Dorothea had no doubts about the presence in Paris of Prussian, Russian and British troops. For her they were liberators emphatically on the right side and that was all there was to it. It was true that a few months ago her husband had been fighting against these same liberators and had actually been made their prisoner, but that unfortunate interlude was mercifully over and now life could revert to properly regulated lines. Her international birth and upbringing had given her a complete absence of patriotism, almost of any national sense at all. For a time she had become an enthusiastic Prussian but the phase had not long survived her marriage. People to her were primarily wise or foolish, noble or common, right-minded or wrong-minded—not French, Russian or Prussian.

However, the attitude of others was more ambivalent. Few French aristocrats regretted the downfall of Napoleon and the restoration of the Bourbons but between that and actually welcoming the presence in the heart of Paris of the foreign troops who had brought about these miracles a gulf of bitterness was fixed. To make matters worse, the Prussians, who were the element among the invaders with which Dorothea was most closely associated in the eyes of her Parisian friends, were also by far the worst-behaved. They had some grudges to repay from the times that the French had occupied their country and they repayed them with enthusiasm and a cheerful disregard of national susceptibilities. Gangs of Prussian roughs wandered freely around Paris doing any mischief which occurred to them : one night a group of more than a hundred of their soldiers poured into the Palais Royal, smashed windows, assaulted men, insulted women and were only prevented from setting the whole place on fire by the efforts of some English officers and men.

Such incidents did not make Dorothea any the more popular in French society and the first months of the Bourbon restoration brought her considerable chagrin, few new friendships and a final rupture of one of long standing. Countess Kielmannsegge passed forever from Dorothea's life. Shortly after the occupation of Paris the countess had received a letter from her former protégée which included a passage of glowing praise for Wellington. All her old imperial loyalties were shocked and she replied in terms which put a sharp end to the correspondence. " For a long time now," she wrote sadly to another friend, " the heart of this young woman has trampled underfoot all thoughts of dignity . . ." She herself was meddlesome, mischievous and, at times, malign. Still, in her own way, she was capable of loyalty. Her admiration for Napoleon was never to be shaken and yet she had got as close to loving Dorothea as her chilly heart would let her. It is much to her credit that when she was forced to choose between them she quarrelled with the friend on the winning side rather than allowing to pass unchallenged an affront to the loser.

These uneasy months brought another far more painful loss to Dorothea. At the end of April, Dorothea-Charlotte, her second child and only daughter, developed what appeared to be a not particularly dangerous attack of measles. The disease was taken a good deal more seriously in 1814 than it would be to-day but even so no one was inclined to worry and, by May 7 or 8, the child seemed to have passed the crisis and to be well on the way to recovery. Then, abruptly, things took a turn for the worse. A letter written by Talleyrand to the Duchess of Courland on the morning of 10th May shows his anxiety —though, admittedly he seems to have worried as much for the mother as for the child.

" Dear friend, I am very worried about our little Dorothea. After leaving you yesterday evening, I went by their house and was told that her illness was taking on a more dangerous character. . . . I beg you to keep Madame de Périgord at your house and not let her go home ; it is quite essential for her health which is not strong enough to bear the shock which the child's suffering would be for her. Besides, she wouldn't do any good there. I would be sorry to see her expose herself to such danger in any case, but if she could do something which no one else was able to do then I would not try to argue with her duty as a mother. But here there is no reason at all for her to go as the child is as well looked after as possible."

The authority of the Duchess of Courland was not put to the test ; Dorothea-Charlotte died in the afternoon of the same day.

Dorothea suffered intensely from the death of her daughter. It seemed to her peculiarly unjust that someone so young and innocent should be so ruthlessly destroyed. Formally, she accepted that it was the will of God but, in practice, her pity and regret were tinctured with an impotent resentment which could find no target at which to direct itself but remained poisoning the wounds which sorrow had inflicted. The pain was all the worse since pride and suspicion—the two great legacies of her childhood—had robbed her of the capacity to ask for sympathy or to confide what she was feeling in someone else. Her mother was, of course, out of the question; the Duchess of Courland would have been embarrassed and slightly offended if her daughter had tried to make her share her sorrows. Talleyrand was kind and understanding but Dorothea still did not know him well and anyway, distracted as he was by the affairs of Europe, would not have thought of laying on him any additional burden. Only the right husband could have entered into her sorrows and so won her trust as to help her bear them; intellectually and emotionally, weak, affable, stupid Edmond was quite incapable of establishing any sort of contact with her or even of noticing her pain. With his failure there faded also the last meagre hope that their marriage might be invested with any reality. It was only in suffering that Dorothea realised how much she was alone.

*   *   *   *   *

Throughout the summer of 1814, Talleyrand was preparing himself for what was to be the most formidable test of his career. It is not within the scope of this work to consider the purposes and consequences of the Congress of Vienna; it is sufficient to say that, for more than twenty years, Europe had known continuous war, almost every frontier had been violated, almost every dynasty overthrown. Now the moment had come to re-draw the map of Europe in a form that it was intended would be handed down from generation to generation. The shape of the nineteenth century was to be decided around the conference tables of Vienna. Meetings of heads of state may not always achieve considerable results but at Vienna something had got to be worked out or the ruins left by Napoleon would never be reconstructed; what cannons had destroyed only skilful and arduous negotiation could restore.

There was never the slightest doubt that Talleyrand would represent France at the Congress of Vienna; no other Frenchman could possibly match his wisdom, experience and prestige.

Besides, Louis XVIII saw a certain advantage in removing from his country this embarrassing relic of the revolution. What was much less certain was that even Talleyrand would be able to make himself listened to when questions vitally important to the future of France were being discussed. France, after all, was responsible for the catastrophic war from which Europe was now emerging and it was France which had been vanquished. True, the Bourbon government was not responsible for the misdeeds of Napoleon and had indeed been reinstated by the conquering allies. But the allies did not find this always easy to remember. The analogy is patently both superficial and inexact but it is not altogether misleading to compare the problem which faced Talleyrand in 1814 with that of de Gaulle in 1944. Both represented countries recently defeated, both feared that they were to be excluded from the formulation of decisions which they deemed vital to the interests of France and both resolved to make the application of any such decisions impossible until they had been given a say in their making. The tactics which each statesman was to pursue were as widely different as the circumstances which made them necessary but the broad lines of their strategies were not so very far apart.

Talleyrand selected with care his team for the negotiations. For the real work he chose La Besnardière, " the most out-standing man to have appeared at the Ministry of Foreign Affairs for many years." For his German connections and old time's sake, he chose the Duke of Dalberg " to broadcast those of my secrets which I wish everyone to know." As representative of the Pavillon Marsan, home of the Count of Artois and hence heart of the extreme right wing, he selected Count Alexis de Noailles ; " if one must be spied on at least it is better to choose the spy oneself." The Marquis de la Tour du Pin would ornament the delegation by his lineage and social graces ; also " he would do to sign passports." Quite as important as any of these was Carême ; greatest chef of the epoch and deemed by many to be as considerable an artist even as the great Vatel. There was still one serious omission however. If there was one thing of which Talleyrand could be certain it was that the social life of Vienna would be brilliant and onerous and that quite as many of the major decisions would be made in drawing-rooms and ballrooms as around the conference tables itself. If he was to do his job properly, his house in Vienna would have to become one of the centres of society and if the Viennese aristocracy and the *beau monde* of Europe were to be drawn in he would have to find a hostess whose beauty, breeding and wit would overcome the rancour which France's imperial adventures had inspired.

Propriety, no doubt, decreed that Talleyrand take his wife with him to Vienna, but propriety was here at variance with both political expediency and personal inclination. Princess Talleyrand—with the Restoration the imperial title of Benevento had been tactfully forgotten—would have made a pitiful ambassadress. Catherine-Noël Worlée had been the daughter of a minor government official. At the age of fifteen she married a Mr. Grand of the East India Company, was seduced by Sir Philip Francis, a member of the Supreme Council of Bengal, discarded by her husband and found her way to Paris where she set herself up in the only career for which she was abundantly qualified, that of *grande cocotte*. That she became Talleyrand's mistress is not surprising, that she became his wife is almost inexplicable. It seems that the principal credit must go to Napoleon who, feeling that his court was not sufficiently respectable, bullied or cajoled his Vice Grand Elector into regularising the liaison. Talleyrand himself, when asked to explain his marriage, could only say that in the conditions prevailing at the time it had not seemed to matter much one way or another.

Certainly, at the time of their marriage he had been deeply attached to Mme Grand. She had all the charm which comes with youth, exuberance and outstanding beauty and sufficient social cunning to gloss over her lack of intelligence and ignorance of the world. But by 1814 the youth and exuberance had gone and the charm with it. All that was left was a blowsy, vapid, over-dressed old tart, preening herself on the relics of her former beauty and quite incapable of filling the place in society which was open to the Princess Talleyrand.

The prince had no compunction in cutting her out of his life. She had proved as promiscuous in her second marriage as in her first. Marital constancy was not among the principles which Talleyrand prized highly but she acted with such blatant indiscretion that Napoleon was able to use her affairs as a convenient reason for abusing his minister. This Talleyrand found harder to forgive and when Napoleon insisted that she be exiled from Paris he acquiesced with satisfaction and relief. Since then they had met but rarely and any pretence at a united married life had long been abandoned.

It would have been disastrous if this pattern of vulgarity had been thrust into the midst of the most snobbish and arrogant society in Europe or this blandly stupid woman involved in the mesh of subtle and intricate political intrigue which was to underlie the social life of the Congress. " At Vienna France had to bear itself in a way quite different from that which one had grown to expect from her over the last twenty years," wrote Talleyrand in his memoirs. " It was essential that the dignity which she would show should be displayed with nobility, even with brilliance." The brilliance the Princess might once have managed but dignity and nobility had never been within her range. Talleyrand did not have far to look for a substitute. Without doubts or hesitation, he urged his niece to undertake the task.

*   *   *   *   *

Dorothea de Périgord was as well equipped for the work as Princess Talleyrand would have been incompetent. In intelligence she was not put to shame by any of the statesmen who were to surround her ; in beauty she could stand comparison with any other flower of the European aristocracy ; by birth she was entitled to a place of honour in even the most exclusive drawing-rooms of Vienna. All she lacked was the sophistication that comes from experience and an exhaustive training in high society and even this was to prove an advantage; after an evening of hard-boiled brilliance with Princess Bagration or Countess Zichy it was a relief to turn to the innocence and comparative simplicity of this girl of just twenty-one.

Her family connections were invaluable. Dorothea could claim relationship with a remarkable number of the assembled aristocrats. The royal house of Prussia were her childhood friends, the Emperor of Russia an old ally of her mother's. Her three sisters were all at Vienna and strategically placed for the provision of information: Wilhelmina, Duchess of Sagan, was jostling for the position of mistress to Prince Metternich; Pauline, Princess of Hohenzollern-Hechingen had a husband among the ruling princes and a lover among the leading negotiators and Jeanne, Duchess of Acerenza was formally mistress of a Dutchman but still found time for a spirited flirtation with Frederick Gentz, Secretary General to the Congress and an infallible source of well-informed gossip.

Dorothea accepted her uncle's suggestion without hesitation. Dissatisfaction with her married life, irritation with Parisian society, regrets for her daughter, all made her ready for a change. But even though her married life had been an idyll and Parisian society a paradise without thorns she would still have followed her uncle to Vienna. For Dorothea, the Congress was to be her entry on to the great stage of public life, her promotion to a world of power and high policy. To have elected to stay with her family in Paris when the future of Europe was being worked out in Vienna would have been to betray what she believed to be her real role in life. Not that she could have defined with any precision just what she imagined this role was going to be. In part at least her reaction to Talleyrand's invitation was that of the stage-struck schoolgirl who dreams irrepressibly of footlights and a star billing. She wanted to be where great and powerful men were gathered, to shine in the highest society of Europe and to feel herself at the centre of affairs. Few girls of her age would not have felt the same. But Dorothea did not wish only to be there, to be seen and to be noticed; she wished also to contribute. It was in this that she differed from most of the other women of her generation and it was this which lent a certain seriousness to her decision. She had formed the sober and genuine belief that there was tremendously important work to do and that it would be less well done if she were not there. She knew that she could be of use to her uncle and that, in serving him, she would be serving also the best interests of Europe. In Vienna she felt that she might at last make full use of her capacities and fulfil herself in a way which she had never been able to do in France.

It was, all the same, a drastic decision to make and one which many were to criticise. For one thing, it was the first time that she had ever left her children for more than a few days at a time. Traditionally, children do not bulk very large in the life of an aristocratic French family but Dorothea was a fonder mother than most and rarely allowed her social adventures to distract her from the nursery. There was no question of taking them with her to Vienna; to act as ambassadress to Talleyrand was to be a full-time job and it would have been impossible to reconcile the demands of the Congress with any but the merest parody of family life. Dorothea was never a hypocrite; she admitted to herself that she was cutting herself off from her children for a quite unspecified period of time, regretted that this must be so, but never doubted that the sacrifice had to be made.

The decision to part from her husband was easier for her to make but far more permanent in its implications. It would have been possible for Talleyrand to attach his nephew to the embassy in some decorative capacity; Edmond might even have been set to signing the passports in the place of the Marquis de la Tour du Pin. The fact that he was left behind certainly shows that Talleyrand was heartily tired of his folly and extravagance but it shows also that Dorothea had no wish for her husband's company. It is impossible to believe that Talleyrand would not have taken Edmond along with him if Dorothea had wished it or had made it a condition of her coming. It seems possible, in fact, that Edmond visited Vienna during the Congress but if so, he lived alone in hired apartments and there is no reason to believe that he visited the embassy or even saw his wife.

For Dorothea, the journey represented the break-up of her marriage. Count and Countess Edmond de Périgord were, for one further period, to live again in the same house; the legal separation was not to take place till 1818; but, the moment that she decided to go alone to Vienna, represented Dorothea's final decision that life with her husband on anything but the most formal terms had now become impossible.

For much of her world, this same decision was taken also to announce her final surrender to the importunities of her uncle. Talleyrand's reputation as a libertine and womaniser was notorious. Dorothy's beauty was patent to all the world, so also was her discontent with her marriage. To smart Parisian society the news that Talleyrand and Dorothea were going together to Vienna and that Edmond was being left behind could only mean one thing, and they did not hesitate to announce the fact at the top of their voices. Later there will be more to say of the relationship between Dorothea and her uncle ; for the moment it is sufficient that when Talleyrand invited her to come with him to Vienna there is not a trace of evidence that he considered her in any other light than as someone to whom he was attached and who he knew was admirably qualified to do the job he had in mind.

But no one so worldly wise as Talleyrand could have failed to realise that the gossips of Paris would not stop to ponder the truth of their accusations before linking him and his niece in unholy alliance. Even if Dorothea had not seen this for herself, her mother and friends must have pointed it out to her. It must be accepted that she left for Vienna with her eyes open, in complete awareness of the consequences and with a readiness to accept them in their entirety.

For the rest of society, the departure of Talleyrand and Dorothea was a target for pleasurable malice ; for one woman it was a source of tragedy. Princess Talleyrand still hoped, against all reason, that one day her peccadilloes would be forgiven and that she would be taken back into favour in the drawing-rooms which she felt she graced so well. Countess de Boigne was visiting the princess's house in Paris when someone came with the news that Talleyrand had decided to take his niece with him to Vienna and that the couple planned to meet discreetly in a country house near Paris and continue the journey together. Madame de Talleyrand did not try to hide from herself the importance of the news ; she realised that it meant the extinction of all her hopes, the closing to her for ever of her husband's door. She played with the idea of going to Vienna herself, arriving without warning at the prince's door as one who had come home. When Napoleon's return to France forced her to flee from Paris she almost brought herself to the point of action; then at the last moment lost her nerve and went instead to London.

" I shall always regret that I gave way to a false moment of pride. I knew what airs Mme Edmond was giving herself in Monsieur Talleyrand's house in Vienna and I had no wish to see it for myself. This susceptibility prevented me from going to rejoin him as I should have done . . . If I had been in Vienna instead of London, Monsieur de Talleyrand would have been forced to receive me. I know him well enough to say that he would have done it with perfect grace and that the more irritated he might have been the less he would have shown it . . . I knew this perfectly but I have a horror of that woman. I gave way to this dislike, wrongly I know . . ."

And so, a forlorn, pitiable figure, she abandoned the field to the young Countess Edmond de Périgord.

*   *   *   *   *

Talleyrand and Dorothea arrived in Vienna on the 23rd of September, 1814. It is probably true to say that no other town of Europe in any epoch has drawn to it such a galaxy of crowned heads, statesmen, soldiers and aristocrats not to mention celebrated actresses, chefs and courtesans. It was the last, flamboyant flourish of the old régime, the ruling élite of the ruling continent gathered together to recreate the pattern of life which Napoleon had failed to demolish but which was shortly to fade like an insubstantial pageant before the grey reality of an industrial age.

It was the last fling of the cosmopolitan aristocracy before it succumbed to the bourgeois prejudices of nationalism. When the host himself was an Austrian Emperor, Italian by birth and speaking French by preference, how could the guests be conscious of their races ? National aims were one thing but personal nationalities quite another ; the Russians set a good example by having in their delegation three Germans, one Pole, one Greek, one Frenchman . . . and one Russian.

Everyone who was anyone was there, from the eighty-nine year old Prince de Ligne, doyen of European chivalry, to thirteen-year-old Master David Whittier from Selby who thought that the horses and uniforms were pretty but that everything was a little slow after England. A hundred thousand foreigners were believed to be in the city for the occasion, of whom ninety-five thousand at least had no part at all to play in the negotiations but were there to provide a sumptuous back-cloth and savour the unparalleled galaxy of beauty, wit, elegance and plain vulgarity.

The extravagance and variety of the social life was dazzling. After twenty years of privation the European smart set were at it again and intent on proving that they had lost nothing by their abstinence. Every night there was at least one great ball interspersing an endless stream of banquets, concerts, hunts and every kind of reception. Fortunes were spent on clothes and jewellery or dissipated even more rapidly at the gambling tables. A perpetual cycle of scandals and romances kept the gossips busy and provided a touch of savour to even the most formal evenings. Amateur theatricals were vastly popular. The Empress of Austria loved to organise evenings of this sort: for opera, Prince Antoine Radziwill was in great demand, Countess Esterhazy starred in German tragedy, while Dorothea, who took to acting with an enthusiasm born of her childhood in Berlin, was sure of a major part whenever comedy was on the programme.

For intrigue, either amatory or political, one could not do better than frequent the salons of the great hostesses, where each one gathered around her a coterie of the faithful and tried to outshine the rest in the brilliance of the conversation and the nobility of the guests. The most distinguished families of Europe held open house: Liechtenstein, Esterhazy, Bagration; each had their speciality: for gaiety one patronised Mme de Fuchs, for serious conversation one did better with Princess Furstenberg; each had their regular evening: on Monday, all society flocked to Princess Metternich, Thursday was the turn of Princess Trauttmansdorff and on Saturday it was socially unthinkable not to be seen in the drawing-room of the lovely and brilliant Countess Zichy.

Through these salons glided gracefully all the most beautiful women of the European aristocracy. Most of them were depraved, many of them were no more than exquisite simpletons, but they knew how to talk, they knew how to dress and they knew how to dance. They provided a supremely ornamental setting for the real business of the Congress about which, for the most part they knew and cared nothing at all.

The most remarkable thing about the Congress of Vienna was that, in spite of the innumerable distractions, the work did get done and what is more that it got done with skill and profound deliberation by men who nevertheless contrived to play conspicuous roles in the feverish social turmoil which surrounded them. In an age where work and play are neatly segregated and the business lunch and diplomatic cocktail party, barren though they may be, are the only unions between the two, it is hard to understand the game of international politics as played in the eighteenth and early nineteenth century. The salon, the ballroom were not merely agreeable places of relaxation after the day's work was done ; they were an essential complement to the conference table.

". . . No such weighty and complicated issues have ever been discussed in the course of so many pleasures. A kingdom might wax or wane in the course of a ball, an indemnity be settled during a dinner, a constitution be drafted at a hunt ; sometimes an epigram or a happy remark might clinch a treaty which constant meetings and exchanges would otherwise have had to drag painfully to its conclusion." The witness was admittedly prejudiced in favour of this sort of negotiation ; the quotation is from Count de la Garde-Chambonas who existed throughout the Congress in a euphoric mood of exalted snobbery and devoted a volume of memoirs solely to its social side. He was essentially right however : treaties really were settled at dinner-parties, bargains really were struck at balls and ladies of fashion, if they had the intelligence and the desire, really could exercise a considerable influence on their admirers and lovers.

Thanks to the efficiency of the Austrian police service the pattern of social life and its inter-relationship with the real business of the Congress can be traced with remarkable precision. Baron Franz Hager von und zu Altensteig, President of the " Oberste Polizei und Censur Hofstelle," had been entrusted by the emperor with the task of watching over all the principal participants of the Congress and reporting on every aspect of their activities. With the aid of an elaborate network of spies he performed this task with exemplary efficiency and filled volume after volume with meticulously verified details on the comings and goings of his victims. Talleyrand, who had settled with Dorothea in the vast Italianate Kaunitz palace almost in the shadow of the cathedral, was rash enough to boast that he had turned it into a fortress immune from espionage. He would have been disconcerted if he had known that one of the doorkeepers, a chambermaid and a minor official in the Chancery were in Hager's pay and that every scrap of paper left lying around found its way to police headquarters. Talleyrand himself and Dorothea were both reasonably careful with their papers but Dalberg left enough love-letters lying around to provide food for a dozen major scandals. After every dinner party a list of the guests was submitted for Hager's information ; one time there was an intriguing flicker from the past when it was reported that, in the middle of dinner, Countess Edmond de Périgord had received a note from Prince Adam Czartoryski ; the agent had unfortunately not been able to see what it said.

A favourite target for police supervision was Dorothea's eldest sister, Wilhelmina, Duchess of Sagan. Fifteen years of luxurious debauchery and complete freedom from responsibility had ended the work which her unbalanced, empty childhood had begun. She was beautiful, witty, flamboyant, intensely ambitious, a creature of violent passions but no trace of sentiment, devoid of the smallest perception of right and wrong. Her wealth, birth and calculating mind gave her a position in Vienna second only to that of the crowned heads themselves. Almost the only woman who could match her was Princess Bagration, widow of a Russian general and great-niece of the Empress Catherine.

" These two tempestuous foreigners," reported one of Hager's society spies, " rivals alike in taste and in ambition, by a curious and fatal hazard are lodged in the same mansion which, to the shame of our nobility, is the only one available for our illustrious visitors. It seems to me very probable that in view of the preference which, for the moment at any rate,

Metternich shows for the Sagan, and the frequent visits which Talleyrand makes to her house that the pro-Austrian party will be established there and the pro-Russian party at Princess Bagration . . ." " It will not be the first time," concluded the reporter sententiously, " that the intrigues of women have had an influence on the policies of states and of the greatest states at that. Such are men."

Sharing a house was not such a hardship as might be imagined from the shame felt by Hager's spy. The Palm palace in which both ladies lodged could have housed half a dozen such households without much risk of their ever meeting. Nor did the rivalry between them take quite the shape that he had predicted ; rather it turned into a battle for the possession of the Emperor Alexander. Wilhelmina, strongly encouraged by Talleyrand who saw her as a useful instrument for reasserting his influence over the Russian monarch, used every wile she knew to lure Alexander from the salon of his devoted subject Princess Bagration. At first she had little success. As soon as the emperor had arrived in Vienna he hastened to pay his respects to the princess. Their friendship ripened along traditional lines. On the 3rd of October Princess Bagration retired to bed with a migraine and sent all her servants out of the house for the evening. If the emperor called the porter was to ring the bell four times. After dinner four rings disturbed the silent house. The princess, dressed only in a charming negligee, opened the door herself. She was overcome with confusion at discovering the identity of her guest but recovered sufficiently to usher him timidly upstairs. She *had* been ill, she explained, but now felt suddenly better. A jarring note was introduced when Alexander found a man's hat in her bedroom but the princess luckily remembered that it belonged to a decorator and both laughed heartily at the mistake.

The Duchess of Sagan was not discouraged. " Everything has been done to help her get off with me," complained Alexander to the princess. " They have even shut us up *tête-à-tête* in the same carriage. But they have had no luck. I appreciate the passions but I need some wit as well." Whether he discovered that the Duchess of Sagan had more wit than he had realised or whether he was worn down by her attentions, he underwent a sudden change of heart. On 23rd October, the Emperor Alexander arrived at the Palm palace. Princess Bagration assumed that it was to call on her but he took the other turning and ended lunching alone with the Duchess of Sagan. By 1st November he was so taken by his new favourite that he grew jealous and threatened to make difficulties over Wilhelmina's money—most of which was still in Russia—unless she broke with Metternich. The Duchess of Sagan was always receptive to new ideas, a little reflection showed her the reasonableness of this one and she politely explained to her former lover that, in the circumstances, there was nothing she could do but concur.

Metternich was furious ; still more so when he discovered that Wilhelmina was already mistress of the English chargé d'affaires and was just embarking on a violent affair with the new minister, Lord Charles Stewart. He never forgave her and four years later was still working off his spleen in letters to Princess Lieven. He claimed that she had continually pestered him to become her lover but was still incapable of fidelity : " I sacrificed myself without love in the hope that I would settle her, make her life moral and balanced."[2] His faith in the therapeutic powers of his love-making is impressive but the suggestion that, for a time at least, he was not desperately in love suggests either a faulty memory or an enviable capacity for self-deception.

*   *   *   *   *

Though she knew well all the protagonists, Dorothea did not appear often in her sister's house ; she found Wilhelmina a little intimidating and the way of life not altogether to her liking. Metternich, however, became a close friend of hers and Alexander did not associate her with the increasing distrust which he was beginning to feel for her uncle.

Dorothea's social life was brilliant and intense enough but rather more innocent and considerably less raffish. She threw herself into the fantastic diversities of Viennese life with a capacity for sheer enjoyment which neither she nor anyone else had suspected she possessed. She knew that she shone as a particularly bright star in the spectacular blaze of the European constellation and the knowledge delighted her. Belatedly she discovered the pleasures of youth and made the most of them with enthusiasm and unquenchable energy.

It is not necessary to labour at length the extravagance and the brilliance, the futility and the prodigality of the social life of Vienna during the Congress. One party perhaps epitomised all the rest ; the famous Carrousel. It is uncertain who originally conceived the brilliant idea of adorning the Congress with a medieval tournament but he deserved the gratitude of all Vienna. The superb baroque hall of Fischer von Erlach's Imperial Riding School was taken over for the occasion. Twenty-four of the most dashing young noblemen of Europe were selected to act as cavaliers and twenty-four *belles d'amour* picked out from the flower of the old world's aristocracy. Two tribunes were erected and smothered in the most sumptuous draperies— one for emperors, kings and the like, the other for the *belles d'amour* ; dukes, marshals, ambassadors and the rest were left to do the best they could for themselves in the gallery. For months beforehand the *belles d'amour* had been poring over books describing the court of Louis XIV ; they were determined that their costumes were going to outshine the past for elegance and luxury. " To tell the truth," wrote Dorothea, " I think we will be wearing all the pearls and diamonds of Hungary, Austria and Bohemia. Every relation or friend of these ladies has had her jewel box rifled and many a family jewel which has not seen the light of day for a hundred years will be adorning the dress or the forehead of one of us."

The great moment came and the twenty-four *belles d'amour*, swathed in white scarves, filed into the tribune and then, at the entry of their cavaliers, whipped off the cocoon and revealed themselves brilliantly to the expectant crowd. For an hour or so the cavaliers cantered around, putting lances through rings and slashing at dangling apples. The grand climax was the joust in which the cavaliers tried to unhorse each other. This caused much enthusiasm. " The *belles d'amour*," noted La Garde-Chambonas approvingly, " did not urge on their champions with shouts but confined themselves to expressive glances and gracious smiles. Nevertheless, this mute expression of a tender feeling seemed no less to tell their gallant knights,

' You are jousting for the sake of two fair eyes.' " Whether on account of the gracious smiles or from a healthy dislike of their opponents, the pace of the joust grew hectic. The stewards tried to maintain the peace but were not in time to save the young Prince of Liechtenstein from being violently unhorsed. He was carried insensible from the ring and his life was in danger for several days. This stroke of realism, however, seems to have done little to diminish the prevalent euphoria. Afterwards at dinner Dorothea sat at the table of honour next to her squire, Count Trautmannsdorff. " No less remarkable by the brilliance of her beauty than by the taste of her dress, she held the attention of all by the charm of her conversation, as lively as it was witty."

Count Trautmannsdorff, the Master of the Royal Horse and son of a distinguished old gentleman who had once been Minister of Foreign Affairs, was squire to Dorothea on many occasions during her first few months in Vienna. The arrangement was agreeable to both. For Dorothea, without her husband and not content always to adapt her pace to a sexagenarian uncle, it was useful to have a personable young man of impeccable birth ready to dance attendance and escort her where she wished to go. For Trautmannsdorff it was a pleasure to be accredited squire to someone as beautiful and distinguished as Dorothea who had moreover the inestimable advantage of being married. Existence was agreeable for a bachelor Master of the Royal Horse with a snug little mistress and not an honourable intention in his head. For anything except social trivia, Trautmannsdorff was not at all Dorothea's sort of man. She was eminently serious minded, intensely interested in the political side of the Congress, happiest in the company of men like her uncle, Metternich, Humboldt, men of affairs who thought and worked, who decided the fate of others. Her affable, empty-headed cavalry-officer was all very well at a ball or a dinner but for real life she looked elsewhere. The Viennese police busily reported to Hager that the two were seeing ever more of each other but not even the most imaginative of them suggested that the affair was brushing the frontiers of indiscretion.

In fact, during these first few months, Dorothea would have

had little time for a serious love-affair. To be a social success was delightful and, indeed, a large part of the reason for her presence in Vienna, but Talleyrand demanded more of her than that and she had no intention of failing him. Her first responsibility was to be a good hostess, to make the Kaunitz palace into the centre of the life of Vienna ; a centre agreeable to the friends of France and attractive even to her enemies. There was more to this than just the natural wish of an ambassador to feel that the life of the capital was revolving around him. France was still suspect in Europe ; the royal family tarnished by twenty-five years of exile. Their embassy in Vienna was required to be a vivid demonstration that this suspicion was ill-placed, that France was still as rich and powerful as ever and that her representative, Talleyrand, could speak with as much weight and authority as any other man at the Congress.

The art of running a great household, of presiding at dinners and receptions, of making a party a success, in short of being a hostess on the grand scale, is not one which many people enjoy. When they do it is usually the product of gruelling experience. Dorothea was born with it in her blood. She handled the vast diversity of guests who flowed through the embassy with an ease and confidence astonishing in one so young ; suffering their vanities, humouring their suscepti-bilities, more than holding up her own end in conversation yet never so that others felt themselves excluded or out-shone. " Countess Edmond de Périgord," wrote de la Garde-Cham-bonas, " did the honours of her drawing-room with an enchant-ing grace. Her brilliant yet playful wit would temper from time to time the ponderous political reflections which were bound to intrude into the conversation."

But though, when Talleyrand brought Dorothea to Vienna, he may have had little in mind save that she would make a competent and decorative hostess, it was not long before she was doing much more than that. It might fairly be imagined that Talleyrand would have found little use for the advice or the diplomatic talents of even the most intelligent girl of twenty-one. Certainly Dorothea was never thrust into any close contact with the day-to-day business of the Congress.

But there can be no doubt that Prince Talleyrand began increasingly to trust the judgment of his young niece and to consult her on questions far outside her official sphere. The French historian Villemain devoted a remarkable panegyric to the part she played in the embassy[3]. After listing the names of Talleyrand's colleagues he continues:

". . . less for the dazzling of frivolous society than for the wisdom of her advice and the hidden resources of her talent, he added another influence, intimately attached and devoted to him. Madame de Dino, brought up in all the elegance of the best French taste, nevertheless united a capacity for serious concentration which was entirely German with a cosmopolitan wit and gift of tongues. By her beauty, the imperious charm of her expression, the fire of the south blended with the haughty grace of the north, the inexpressible brilliance of her eyes, the perfection of her acquiline features, the dignity of her forehead framed as it was in such beautiful black hair, she was one of the people most naturally destined to do the honours of a palace or ornament a great occasion. But already this brilliant queen of society loved solitude and study and had had enough of mere worldly triumphs which gave her little pleasure . . .

Superior even to her beauty and, like her beauty, at once gracious and imperious, delicate and severe, her intellectual force appeared irresistibly powerful and one can well believe that, better than any professional diplomat, she could sense the political views of those whom she met and, at will, open them to conviction, insinuate advice, appease mistrust and bend their will to hers. On more than one occasion this reinforcement came aptly to the help of the consummate science of M. de Talleyrand : smoothed out the contradictions, removed the obstacles from his path, coaxed others into his way of thinking ; all before Talleyrand himself had had need to act or perhaps even decided what it was at which he was aiming.

Sometimes this fine yet sturdy intelligence, the more redoubtable because it was concealed beneath such graces, was of still more direct service to the great ambassador, fortifying his resolution or, with subtle art, making more palatable the form which he wished to give to it. On the minds of those who have endured much, who have seen much, hesitated often and failed sometimes, the ascendancy of a young and courageous spirit may be as healthy as it is powerful. This ascendancy showed itself in various forms. In notes written by Talleyrand, in his letters to King Louis XVIII and to other sovereigns, even in the most intimate of his letters, copied out by him for the sake of secrecy, are to be found the lively and delicate touches, the subtly persuasive shades of meaning which indicate the hand of Madame de Dino . . ."

Villemain was writing in 1855. He had met Dorothea quite often but only in later years. The picture of her life in Vienna, he built up from intelligent research conducted in the light of what he had seen. As a result, though it was not unreasonable or untrue, it showed her more as she would be in fifteen years than as she was at the date of the Congress. Dorothea at the age of twenty-one was not the detached and capable paragon whom he painted ; indeed she would have been quite insufferable if she had been. Worldly triumphs did not give her little pleasure ; on the contrary, though she was quite well aware of their real significance, she drew from them a vast amount of satisfaction. Her intellectual force did not appear " irresistibly powerful " ; though her husband and Count Trautmannsdorff may have felt her to be something of a blue stocking there is no reason to suppose that anyone else found her so unsociably intelligent. She was an enthusiastic and high-spirited girl of twenty-one, interested in everything, determined to enjoy herself and not in the least ashamed of herself for doing so. Any other description would do her less than justice.

Least of all was Villemain right when he described her as exercising on Talleyrand " the ascendancy of a young and courageous spirit." Certainly Dorothea in 1814 was growing to count for more and more in her uncle's life but at no time during their stay in Vienna did she cease to regard him with a slightly apprehensive awe. She enjoyed no ascendancy over Talleyrand and never deluded herself for a moment into imagining that she did. Nor, indeed, did she wish to. On reading Villemain's piece her immediate reaction was to feel irritation that something should have been written so unfairly disparaging to the memory of her uncle. When Talleyrand had made up his mind, she knew well that she had no power to shift him.

But this does not mean that she underrated her importance. " If I ever did more than just stick up the envelopes," she wrote, " I never had the bad taste to boast of it." She does not deny and probably meant to imply that in fact she did a great deal more. As their stay in Vienna wore on Talleyrand grew to attach ever more importance to the acumen, judgment and integrity of his young niece. It was a new sensation for him to trust anyone entirely and once he had got used to it he found it altogether agreeable and a most necessary relief. Here was someone in whose loyalty he could have implicit confidence, who sought no promotion or patronage, who respected him without seeing any need to resort to flattery, whose youthful convictions and energy complemented his discreet and sometimes over-subtle intelligence. It could not be long before she became indispensable. Dorothea came to Vienna as a young and attractive girl who would serve to lend attraction to an embassy ; she left it a mature, self-confident woman with a profound understanding of the personalities she had to deal with if not actually of the intricate business which engaged them. She came to Vienna as Talleyrand's favourite niece, to be pampered, amused and made use of. She left it as his most trusted friend and counsellor on whose judgment he was to depend for the rest of his life.

*   *   *   *   *

But though uncle and niece grew thus closer together and though Talleyrand, almost without knowing it, looked more and more to Dorothea for the pleasure of his life, there is no reason to believe that there passed between them anything even slightly unsuitable to their relationship. The light-hearted gossips would not for a moment have given up their fun by admitting anything so prosaic, but the police reports, which also had no incentive to ignore scandal if it were there, were entirely free of any reference to indecorous behaviour in the Kaunitz palace. The house was riddled with Hager's spies and any titbits concerning the habits of the French ambassador would have been especially welcome. But there was nothing ; nothing that is which could be read as in any way discreditable to Dorothea's morality. The infidelities of the Duchess of Sagan, the tentative forays of the Emperor Alexander, the nightly orgies of Lord Charles Stewart, all these were dutifully reported to Hager and the material meticulously checked and counter-checked. Talleyrand's movements were carefully followed, Dorothea's life subjected to the same study ; but still not a word implied that the old statesman, for all his reputation as a libertine, had even looked covetously at his beautiful young niece.

What is more, when, in March 1815, the Duchess of Courland made a belated appearance on the scene of the Congress, she chose to stay with Talleyrand and Dorothea in the Kaunitz palace. There was no need for her to do so. Even if she had found the splendours of Wilhelmina's home a little too ill-famed to be congenial she could easily have chosen to visit either of her other daughters. If her old lover had really been stolen from her by Dorothea, is it likely that she would have sanctioned the liaison by staying in the same house as them both ? In fact, however, she seems to have regarded their undoubted intimacy with perfect equanimity and the letters which she received from Talleyrand both before and after her visit to Vienna never varied in their tone of devotion and of assured affection.

The Duchess of Courland was a cold and selfish woman, well capable of turning a blind eye to anything which it did not suit her to see. The seduction of her daughter by Prince Talleyrand would not have disturbed her by its immorality ; the only fault she had to find in Wilhelmina was that she attracted too much unsavoury publicity. But though her feelings as a mother might not have been stirred, as the mistress of Talleyrand she would have been fiercely resentful. Her relationship with the prince was the most precious thing which remained to her in life. The pain which she would have suffered if she had found that her daughter had supplanted her in so short a time would have made the mere sight of her intolerable. The duchess was fifty-four years old. Age and illness were soon to blunt the edge of her passion and to soften her bitterness but in 1815 she had not yet arrived at such detachment. It is impossible to believe that she could have continued to stay in the Kaunitz palace if she had discovered that her daughter had become the mistress of Talleyrand; given the characters of the three protagonists it is quite as incredible that, if such had been the state of affairs, she would not have known of it within a few hours of her arrival.

If this were not enough there is another reason, still more conclusive, for dismissing any idea of a liaison between Talleyrand and his niece during their stay in Vienna. For the first time since her childhood infatuation with Prince Adam Czartoryski, Dorothea was in love. It must have been some time towards the end of 1814 that Talleyrand invited to dinner at the embassy young Count Clam-Martinitz, a major in the Austrian cavalry, then serving as aide-de-camp to Marshal Schwarzenberg. He could hardly have presented a sharper contrast to Dorothea's other admirer from the Austrian cavalry, Count Trautmannsdorff. Clam was only a year older than Dorothea but had risen quickly in the service and was generally acknowledged to be one of the most brilliant of the young officers. Of an ancient family, handsome, intensely ambitious, he was already well launched on a career which was to have brought him, a field-marshal, to the threshold of great power, when he died suddenly, at the age of only forty-eight, some twenty-five years later.

Count Clam brought to his courtship of Dorothea the same vigour and determination as were manifest in all his enterprises. Marriage was, of course, out of the question, but to have the beautiful and celebrated Dorothea de Périgord for a mistress would have added lustre to any career. Quite apart from such calculation, he seems anyway to have been head over heels in love with her. For Dorothea he represented something new and exciting. The vacuous flowers of the Viennese nobility were agreeable enough for an evening but not to be taken seriously. The men whom she respected and in whose company she was most nearly content, Metternich,

Humboldt, Talleyrand himself, were brilliant and fascinating enough, but she could not always forget that she was only twenty-one. Clam had the youth of the first and the talents of the second; he was handsome, witty, romantic; he was desperately in love with her. Given the emptiness and the longing of her own heart it would have been amazing if she had felt nothing for him.

By January, 1815, their liaison was an accepted feature of Viennese society. Talleyrand does not appear to have distressed himself unduly over his niece's misbehaviour; he knew that, in a few months, the Congress must end and probably calculated that the return to Paris would soon drive the affair from Dorothea's mind. For the moment the two lovers were seen together on every possible occasion and seemed every day to be more in love. Back in Paris, Count Edmond de Périgord heard of his wife's infidelity, sullenly wondered whether he ought to challenge his Austrian rival to a duel, then sought solace in his usual diversions of whoring and gambling.

*   *   *   *   *

During the morning of the 5th of March, 1815, Dorothea was sitting at the end of her uncle's bed chatting gaily of the events of the previous night and of a rehearsal which she had to go to that afternoon in the house of Princess Metternich. A messenger arrived with a letter from Metternich. Talleyrand left to his niece the trouble of opening and reading it.

" It's probably to tell me what time to-day's meeting of the Congress is to begin."

Dorothea glanced at the note. Her reaction would have quickly put at rest the fears of anyone who believed with Villemain that, at twenty-one, she had put aside childish things and lived only for grave conversation and high policy.

" Napoleon has escaped from Elba," she cried. " Oh, Uncle, what about my rehearsal ? "

Then she took in the full enormity of the disaster and anxiously asked what was going to happen next. Talleyrand knew quite as little as anyone else; blandly he assured his niece that, in any case, her rehearsal would certainly take place. Then, with his usual deliberation, he began the lengthy ritual of washing, powdering and dressing which had to be observed in full every time that he left his bed[4].

The rehearsal did take place but the news heralded the disintegration of the Congress. As Napoleon advanced towards Paris and his old soldiers rallied to him in every town he reached, Talleyrand watched bitterly while all that had been achieved in his months at Vienna was put in jeopardy. His own position was singularly awkward and he was in doubt as to what to do next. Of one thing at least, however, he was certain, that Europe would never know peace until Napoleon had once more been defeated and driven, this time for ever, from the continent which he had done so much to trouble. During the last months of the Congress, before the final act was signed on 9th June, Talleyrand devoted all his skill and energies to ensuring that it was against Napoleon that the wrath of the alliance was turned and that France, under the lawful government of Louis XVIII, was classed not as an aggressor but as the first of the victims.

Dorothea had her own reasons to be disturbed. On the 21st March, when Prince Antoine Radziwill called on her with the news that Napoleon had reached Lyons, he found Dorothea in tears and ill with worry. For several days she had had no news of her mother who had left Paris on her way to Vienna without giving any indication of the route she was planning to follow. Such intense anxiety for her mother, who, after all, was more than capable of looking after herself, might have seemed somewhat perplexing if it had not been that the duchess had apparently half-promised to bring Dorothea's children with her to Vienna. The thought of her family in the hands of Napoleon or involved in some local skirmish filled her with dismay ; mercifully she soon received news that her mother was out of France and her little sons safely left behind in the country.

Her husband was another worry. Dorothea believed Edmond capable of any folly and was afraid that he might have been seduced by old loyalties into rallying to the emperor. Here also she soon received comfort ; a letter which arrived on 10th April told her that Count Edmond de Périgord, whether on principle or out of prudence, had spurned the romantic

gesture and refused to accept any office under Napoleon. He
hoped soon to escape from Paris and join the king at Ghent.
There also, once the Congress was concluded, Talleyrand felt
that it was his duty to go. At the end of May he fixed his
departure for a date some ten days later. Dorothea could have
stayed in Vienna but Clam had already left to join Schwarzenberg at Heilbron and she felt no urge to linger among the ashes
of her love affair. To return to France was impossible, to
join the court at Ghent thoroughly inconvenient. Dorothea
decided the time was propitious for a visit to her estates in
Silesia. On 3rd June, 1815, she left Vienna ; a week later the
Congress was over and the curtain came down on the greatest
diplomatic festival of recorded history.

6

". . . Vienna. The whole of my destiny is contained in the name of this city. Here began my life of devotion to Monsieur de Talleyrand and here that strange and unusual association was formed to which only death was able to put an end . . . At Vienna I entered on that troublesome and yet so attractive life in the public eye which wearies more than it gives me satisfaction. I found much to amuse me here and many occasions for tears : my life became complicated and I was swept up in the storms which have so long raged about me . . ."

Dorothea's departure from Vienna marked the start of one of the most violent storms which was ever to disturb her existence. For the next fifteen months she was to wander uncertain of her path ; all her clarity of purpose temporarily distracted, torn by incompatible desires and uneasily conscious that, whichever way she might finally go, she would never be sure that she had chosen right. In June, 1815, the France to which she had pinned her future seemed to have disintegrated, for all she knew for ever. Her husband no longer played any real part in her plans, her uncle was in exile with the king at Ghent, her lover with the Austrian army ; if it had not been for her children she would have found herself with no obligations at all and nowhere which she could reasonably think of as a home. Even after Waterloo, when there was no obstacle in the way of her return to France, it would still have been easy for her to slip into the shiftless, drifting life of her sister Wilhelmina, to have become just one more amongst the band of noble, international libertines who ebbed around Europe seeking entertainment in the ante-rooms of power and picking and discarding lovers with the listless fervour of the very rich craving a new sensation. " I am ruining myself on husbands," remarked the Duchess of Sagan as she rid herself of her third with a handsome monetary endowment. Dorothea's newly acquired religion protected her from this embarrassment at least, but spiritually she could have ruined herself in the futile, distracting search for pleasure in which all her sister's world was engaged.

*   *   *   *   *

On 8th July, 1815, Louis XVIII returned ingloriously to Paris. With distaste, he yielded to expediency and appointed Talleyrand his President of the Council. It was natural for Dorothea now to return to Paris and rejoin her family. But she did not find it easy to resume her former habits and, above all, was not prepared to take up again the arid, wearisome routine of life with Count Edmond de Périgord. Total indifference had quickened into positive dislike and life in a common household became impossible. For a start she installed herself on the first floor of Talleyrand's immense palace in the Rue St. Florentin, leaving her husband alone in their old family house. Parisian society was large enough for them to see little or nothing of each other and Dorothea felt herself bound by few of the inhibitions of a married woman.

But even this large measure of liberty proved insufficient when, shortly after the second Restoration, Count Clam followed her to Paris. At once the whole city seemed too restrictive. The months of separation had done nothing to dull Clam's passion ; as for Dorothea, the return to Paris had merely underlined how far superior was her Austrian lover to her French husband. The liaison which, in Vienna, had been half lost among a wilderness of similar intrigues, in Paris became a public scandal and the unfortunate Edmond, who really cared very little what his wife might be doing, found himself compelled to take some notice. A report to Baron Hager, dated 14th August, from an Austrian spy in Paris, reported :

" An Austrian major has fought a duel with the Count de

Périgord, the same man as married the youngest of the Princesses of Courland . . . I do not know the reason for the duel but I know that Périgord was wounded by a sabre-slash across the face and that the Courlands, including his wife, are delighted. It is known that she is already trying to get a separation from him."

The failure to identify the Austrian major or the reason for his duel is certainly odd but Clam was in Paris at the time and it is stretching coincidence a little far to suppose that Edmond de Périgord would have had good reason to fight duels with two Austrian majors, both of them simultaneously in Paris[1].

By the autumn the constant embarrassment and anxieties of her life in Paris were becoming too much for Dorothea. The allies were back again and felt even less well-disposed towards the French than after the previous liberation ; they despised King Louis XVIII and all his ministers, distrusted the army whom they believed to be secret Bonapartists to a man and concentrated on demonstrating that they were in Paris as victors and had no intention of tolerating a second Hundred Days. Rumour had it, and every Parisian firmly believed, that the Duke of Wellington had been seen in the Louvre, himself unhooking and taking down the pictures which Napoleon had accumulated from every corner of Europe. The anecdote, though attractive, may not be altogether convincing but the fact that the Parisians accepted it shows how little love was lost between occupier and occupied ; an acrimony which extended even into the rarefied atmosphere of the cosmopolitan aristocracy in which Dorothea had her being.

Dorothea took little pains to spare the feelings of her countrymen by adoption. When Wellington first visited Talleyrand's house after Waterloo, reported Lady Shelley: " Madame Périgord ran up to the Duke and kissed him on both cheeks. She showed the most naïve joy and called him her saviour . . . She is a very pretty little woman and expressed, without the slightest hesitation and with a natural impulse, the adoration which I also feel for Wellington." The gesture may have endeared Dorothea to Lady Shelley but it is hardly surprising if to those French present it seemed, to say the least, in doubtful taste.

Her social life embittered and her friends estranged by political dissension, constantly embarrassed by the hostile presence of her husband, her loyalties torn between her Austrian lover and her children; every week in Paris was filled with pain for Dorothea. Talleyrand, whose experience and wisdom might have saved her from the worst of her suffering, was more than preoccupied with holding together his ramshackle government against the assaults of the right and the antipathy of the king; anxious though he was to help he simply could not find time to devote to his niece's affairs. By the end of October the situation had become intolerable. In the first days of November Dorothea and Count Clam left Paris together for Italy and thence Vienna.

*　　　*　　　*　　　*　　　*

There had perhaps been one more element in the complex of reasons which drove Dorothea from Paris. Since her return from Vienna she had been conscious that her relationship with her uncle had in some way changed. She had scarcely dared to analyse in what the difference lay, only she was aware of a vague discomfort, a feeling that the atmosphere of mutual trust and friendship which had existed so happily around them had been vitiated by new and unwelcome influences. In no way was Dorothea running away from her uncle, rather she was running away from a force which she feared might divide them for ever. She was afraid for their relationship and she was afraid even to ask herself what it was she feared.

Talleyrand himself was perhaps even less aware of what was happening. It took the flight of Dorothea to jolt him into an awareness of his feelings. Then all at once he realised how intensely he had learnt to love her and to value her society. The belated discovery filled him with consternation and dismay. The chancellor, Pasquier, for long an intimate of Talleyrand, described his plight:

" As for Monsieur de Talleyrand, if one had not seen it for oneself, one could hardly credit that, at this moment of all others, when he should have been occupied exclusively with business whose weight and responsibility would have terrified the most skilful and confident of statesmen and though already more than sixty years old, he should have chosen to indulge himself in a passion so intense as completely to absorb his mind . . .

Pasquier was as malicious as he was unreliable. But other witnesses, including Count Molé, a close friend both of Talleyrand and of Dorothea, testified that his niece's departure threw the prince into a state of utter despair and probably contributed to his lack of fight when Louis XVIII dismissed him from office. " Hardly had he been separated from her," wrote Molé in his Memoirs, " than he began to wither, to change, to languish. It was a strange thing to see him, sixty-year-old that he was, eaten away by the slow fever induced by the loss of his mistress and, in a word, dying of a broken heart." This helpless passion is hard to reconcile with the image of cold, impassive calm which Talleyrand was accustomed to present to the world ; that he should have felt Dorothea's defection so strongly is surprising enough, that he should have betrayed his state of mind to the rest of the world is proof that the calamity was so great as to overturn all his normal patterns of behaviour.

In spite of such evidence, it is impossible to be completely certain about the feelings of Talleyrand when he found himself separated from his niece, for all he knew for ever. Certainly he did everything he could to induce her to come back and to enlist others to the same end ; letters he wrote to the Duchess of Sagan and to Friedrich von Gentz betray his anxiety. Certainly he regretted intensely her absence and found that his life without her was achingly incomplete. But he was still not entirely single-minded in his misery. The letters which he wrote to the Duchess of Courland at the time were as ardent and enthusiastic as ever. Talleyrand felt no obligation to be sincere or honest in his correspondence ; least of all where a pretty woman was concerned. It would have been no new departure for him to be in love with one woman while writing passionate letters to another. But it is still impossible to read Talleyrand's letters to the duchess and to believe that he was interested solely in the latter's daughter. The constant reiteration of his affection, the eagerness with which he pressed her to come to visit him at Valençay, seem too simple to be hypocrisy and too straightforward to be insincere. Talleyrand loved Dorothea deeply, of that there can be no doubt ; but that he loved her to distraction and to the exclusion of anyone else is not entirely proven.

Her uncle's appeals to her to return, so startlingly in contrast to the restraint and strength which she had learnt always to expect from him, came as a shock to Dorothea. She arrived in Vienna some time towards the end of November, 1815 and, for the next three months, was almost constantly in the company of Clam. We can only guess at the progress of her thoughts over this period ; no letters or memoirs remain to document the struggle going on inside her. But no one of her sensibility and conscience can have failed to be deeply disturbed by the rival calls upon her love and upon her loyalty. Pleasure she certainly derived from these few months but it must have been pleasure marred and contaminated by an ever-present sense of unreality and dismayed perplexity. Dominating everything was her vain struggle to reconcile the various strands of her life and to win happiness without doing injury to those she loved.

She had managed her departure from Paris with sufficient discretion to make return quite possible ; some awkwardness there would be but nothing that would not be forgotten within a few weeks. But did she want to return ? On the one hand there was her lover, independence, a life of gaiety and irresponsibility, a distinguished role in that aristocratic clique of the demi-monde which is far more exclusive than the monde itself. On the other there was her family, her life with Talleyrand, all the promise that it offered for power and influence. The choice was clear-cut but the decision can have been none the easier to make because of that.

Yet, viewed in the knowledge of her life to come, it is hard to think that she was ever in real doubt. Though she may have told herself that it was open to her to plan her future as she willed, she must always have kept thrust to the back of her mind the certainty that, in the end, she would go back to

Paris and that the hectic gaiety of Vienna was time borrowed from reality, to be savoured and enjoyed but in no way considered as a substitute for real life.

Count Molé found no difficulty in explaining the workings of her mind. Dorothea's ambition was " to govern some famous and really powerful man. Nature had fitted her to play such a role and to play it not without brilliance." In Talleyrand she had her instrument to hand; a man whose intelligence and position could hardly be matched, whose name rang throughout Europe, yet over whom, through his age and his devotion to her, she saw her way to establishing her authority. So she sacrificed her dashing, young lover to the alluring promise of fame and power and returned to the side of her uncle.

The explanation had the merit of simplicity but contained only enough truth to be thoroughly misleading. Certainly she was ambitious, she did long to play her part in great affairs and to work through men of power. In part it was this longing which led her to turn her back on the seductions of life as led by her sister Sagan and follow the starker path of responsibility. But simple ambition was no more than a part of the reasons for her return. Dorothea never believed that she could " govern " Talleyrand. She felt for him respect and love without a glimmer of half-contempt for a fond, old man. She hoped to influence him but never to over-persuade. Her instinct was to serve and not to rule.

But beyond and underlying mere ambition there was a far more profound and far less definable force which drove her back to France, her uncle and her family. Under the luxurious texture of her daily life, Dorothea possessed a hard and constant core of principle which still survived even when she was most bored or dissatisfied. Save for rare moments of abandon she was incapable of irresponsibility. In her single-mindedness, in her strict and scrupulous observance of a certain code of rules, in her adoption of a given principle to the complete exclusion of any thought of self-gratification, in her determination, in her intellectual austerity, she had indeed many of the Puritan qualities. At times she regarded her seriousness of purpose almost with resentment and wished herself possessed by the same fundamental frivolity as so many of her friends. But the mood never lasted for long. " There's nothing young about her except her freedom from affectation," remarked Talleyrand on one occasion. Dorothea took it as a compliment and knew that it was not in her to hanker for long after childish things. Always she was sure that, in the end, she would not be able to resist her sense of purpose. On the whole, she was grateful for this certainty.

Clam had no part in this stern pattern. Much though she felt for him and hard though she must have tried to delude herself during the first weeks of the adventure, she was never convinced that he could become essential to her being or that their life together could offer her the fulfilment which she sought. The society and the love of Clam gave Dorothea keen pleasure, but, though she sought pleasure, she could not enjoy it for long if it seemed to her that duty called another way. Now the needs of her children, the happiness and political future of her uncle, her own chances to count for something in the history of Europe ; all seemed to summon her back to Paris. Against such a call, the plaintive appeal of a discarded lover could count for little.

We do not know at what moment Dorothea decided that life with Clam offered no acceptable prospects for the future. The arrival at Vienna of the Duchess of Sagan on 15th February may well have been the deciding factor. Wilhelmina had been recruited by Talleyrand to help persuade his niece to return and her additional arguments may have been of weight. More probably, however, her presence provided a vivid and disagreeable reminder to Dorothea of the sort of existence which awaited her if she chose the path of irresponsibility and luxurious dalliance. It seems anyway that Dorothea's mind was made up either just before or just after her sister's arrival ; within a week of it she was on her way to Paris.

The return from Vienna spelt the end of Dorothea's affair with Clam. At first the Austrian could not accept that this was final. At the end of March he was back in Vienna with his master Prince Schwarzenberg, confiding in his friends the depth of his disappointment and his plans for rising above it. In a series of letters he pleaded with Dorothea to change her

mind and to come back to him. She was obdurate and in the
end he was forced to abandon hope. On 4th June, Dorothea,
then living in the country, wrote to her uncle in Paris a letter
which announced that all was now finished[2] :

" A thousand thanks for your letter of the 2nd. ; I need to
know that every day will bring me some new proof of your
affection. The two fat letters which you forwarded to me
are from Monsieur de C—— ; one dated 16th May, six days
more recent than the one I told you about in my last letter,
the other containing nothing but a portrait which I had
written to ask for . . . He took advantage of sending it
to me to repeat many of the same disagreeable things which
he had said in his last letter. However, I am very glad to
have the portrait ; the more so as he assures me most
generously that he has forgotten me altogether and adds
that he is trying to wipe from his mind the memory of the
humiliations which he has endured and which every day are
renewed for him. He says that he has read my letters to
Gentz and to my sisters from which he sees that I am
delighted to be back. Now he is only angry that I did not
arrive more quickly at this result which has turned out to
be so agreeable to me and thus drawn him earlier from the
dream which every day made him the laughing-stock of the
whole world. He finishes by saying that he begs my pardon
if he wronged me in not at first believing the news that I had
sent him but that I would well understand that he could not
give up the dearest hope of his life just on the word of
someone as changeable as me. He adds no more on this
subject. His conclusion is an eternal farewell which I echo
with all my heart . . .
" The illness was too serious for the cure to have been easy
but the cure has been too complete for me not to feel shame
at having been so much subject of a whim . . .
" This latest proves to me that I must reply only by the
most profound silence. I hope soon to take everything which
comes to me from that quarter in the same way as you read
the stupid and impertinent articles which a few malicious
journalists print against you. But how many sad memories

for the rest of my life ! You have often reproached me with not resenting enough certain kinds of offensive behaviour ; if you knew how much the indelicacy of those people makes me detest them you would be fully satisfied . . ."

Neither Clam nor Dorothea come with credit from this letter. The piqued vanity and bitterness which Clam must have shown does not dispose one to be sympathetic ; his only thought seems to have been of his humiliation and his foolishness in the eyes of the world. But he was, after all, the injured party. It was he who had been abandoned, left nursing his injured heart and pride in Vienna, robbed of " the dearest hope of his life." Dorothea could have afforded to be generous. Even if no trace of affection was left for her former lover she still need not have indulged in the rancour which appears so clearly in this letter to her uncle. But gentleness was not conspicuous in Dorothea's character and forgiveness not a word which bulked prominently in her vocabulary. Now Clam had offended ; for reasons which can only half be known she had turned against him. He must be driven from her life and every trace of their love erased from her memory.

Dorothea's acrimony too may well have been exaggerated. In writing to Talleyrand, her principal purpose was to reassure him that the affair was over and that Clam would never reappear to disturb their lives. It could be that, though to Talleyrand she described her love for Clam as an illness, where she herself was concerned she reserved some more agreeable memories. But whatever her reasons or whatever memories she cherished, the sentence of exile was as complete as her words had promised. Clam may not have been forgotten but he was excised from her life. She was to meet him again but only as an acquaintance. The affair as such was over.

It may be that this is not the whole story. Family tradition has it that, before his last meeting with Dorothea, Clam was already deeply in love with Lady Selina Meade, daughter of Lord Clanwilliam, the beautiful Irish girl whom he was later to marry. According to this account it was he who, with some brutality, told Dorothea that the affair was over and it fell to Talleyrand to comfort her and rebuild her confidence.

The story is not impossible. Dorothea's pride might well have led her to conceal the real facts and her bitterness against Clam would be more natural if it were she who had been jilted. But there is no documentary evidence to support it and it seems improbable that she would have taken the trouble to maintain her own version even in her letters to Talleyrand. In default of any evidence to the contrary the generally accepted story seems the more plausible.

*   *   *   *   *

Once returned to France, Dorothea proceeded to lay down the lines along which her life was to progress for the next fourteen years. Though she had come back to her children she had no intention at all of resuming common life with her husband. Of that she had had quite enough. Her home was now with her uncle. But so long as Talleyrand had a wife in evidence Dorothea's position in the household remained ill-established. Large the house in the Rue St. Florentin may have been but Versailles itself would not have been large enough to shelter both Princess Talleyrand and her niece. Dorothea was never a good sharer; if she could not have something to herself she would rather not have it at all. She resolved that Princess Talleyrand must be driven finally from her uncle's life.

It is no light thing to set out cold-bloodedly to destroy a marriage and to usurp the place which is rightfully another's. For Dorothea, however, the problem did not present itself in these terms. The marriage, she considered with good reason, was already destroyed. Rightly or wrongly, Talleyrand had not the slightest intention of resuming any real relationship with his wife; the only question was whether she should be pensioned off into decent retreat or allowed to remain in Paris, sharing her husband's house, wasting his money, bringing constant shame on him by her folly and vulgarity and, incidentally, making her niece's position difficult if not impossible. For Dorothea this question allowed of only one answer and she set herself assiduously to make sure that her uncle arrived at the same conclusion.

With the return of Napoleon, Princess Talleyrand had fled to England. Her husband was delighted; he had no immediate intention of crossing the Channel himself and, within the realm of the practicable, there were few places where he would rather see his wife. After the Restoration he pointed out to her the advantages of keeping a stretch of sea between them. But the princess was soon homesick. After some painful negotiations, the most that she would agree to was to avoid Paris and to spend her winters in Brussels and her summers in Pont-de-Sains ; an estate of Talleyrand's in the Ardennes which he had given her.

To Dorothea this looked suspiciously like the thin end of the wedge.

" I have given a lot of thought to Madame de T's reply," she wrote[3] to her uncle in June, 1816, " and I become more and more afraid that, one of these fine days, she'll suddenly appear in your room. She will start off by saying that she only means to stay a few hours but that she wishes to have an explanation with you ; it will all end up in her getting more money out of you. The only proper thing for you both is that she should be made to stay in England, assuming that Europe must continue to possess this treasure. With an appearance like hers, she can hardly complain about the bad effect of the climate, which, anyway, she's already managed to put up with on several occasions already. It's obvious that what she wants is to be either in France or in the Low Countries . . .

" As money is the only motive behind all Madame de T's actions, in dealing with her it is always necessary to look at everything from this point of view. I am being so bold to give you some advice which will spare you a painful conversation of the kind you most dislike. Here it is. Send her at once, not some trimmer like Monsieur Roux but Monsieur Perrey armed with a letter of credit and with instructions to tell Madame de Talleyrand that she will not touch a penny of the income you give her until she arrives in England and that she will forfeit it all if she leaves England again. Let Monsieur Perrey accompany her as far as Paris or Ostend and not come back until he has seen her embark. I swear to you that my advice is sound and that you will be wrong not to follow it."

This letter reflects no credit on its writer. Its gibes at the wretched princess are cheap and unnecessary, its whole tone vindictive and cruel. In defence of Dorothea it can only be said that Madame de Talleyrand had already caused her husband much distress and that Dorothea was determined that no more damage should be done. But it illustrates well her implacable determination to carry through whatever course seemed to her desirable. In later years she would not have regretted the intent of the letter but only that it was not phrased with greater skill. It cannot have given Talleyrand much pleasure to read. Little though he liked his wife and accurate though he may have felt his niéce's judgment to be, he must still have felt uneasy at its harsh logic. Perhaps Dorothea's ruthlessness stirred some long dormant loyalty to the miserable woman who had enjoyed such beauty and vitality when he had first known her. Perhaps he tried the tactics recommended by his niece but met with no success. It is at least certain that the princess did not return to England. Indeed, within a few months she was to be seen in Paris again. But there the matter ended. Never again did she cross the threshold of her husband's house or in any way make her presence felt in his life. From the Restoration to the death of Talleyrand, Dorothea was undisputed mistress of her uncle's houses.

*   *   *   *   *

Of these, the palace in the Rue St. Florentin was by no means the largest. In 1803, with the help of a handsome subsidy from Napoleon who felt that his Minister of Foreign Affairs needed a country house to do his entertaining, Talleyrand had bought the chateau and estate of Valençay in Berry. This grandiose monument of the Renaissance had been built at about the same time as Chenonceaux and Chambord. Dorothea found it less original but more imposing than the first and less fanciful but more possible to live in than the second. Even so, and in spite of her familiarity with palaces and great houses, she confessed to finding it *unheimlich* and doubted whether she would ever be at ease there[4].

In the next few years she was to have every chance to get used to the surroundings. In the autumn of 1815, Talleyrand had offered the resignation of his Ministry to Louis XVIII and had heard his offer accepted with alacrity. The Duke of

Richelieu took his place. " I have spent thirty years of my life," Talleyrand wrote a little disingenuously to the Duchess of Courland, " without thinking of anything except whether I could be of use to my country. From to-day, I am going to look after my own interests which I have so totally neglected." In the spring of 1816 both the wish to be away from a Paris which had ceased to need him and his expressed intention of looking after his own interests drew him to Valençay. Certainly there was much that needed doing there ; the estate itself had been run down and allowed to become unprofitable and the house reduced to a shambles by the diversions of the two Spanish princes to whom Talleyrand had played the part of reluctant gaoler.

In April, 1816, Dorothea and her uncle left Paris for Valençay; a journey of some twenty hours by coach. They settled down to the serious business of putting the house in order. One of the first tasks was to refurbish the room which had been assigned to the Duchess of Courland who was on the point of leaving for a visit to Germany. " I am going to concern myself personally with your room," Talleyrand wrote to her, "have the carpet taken up, clean everything and make sure that you will be well installed in October. It gives me the greatest pain to see you setting out on so long a journey, but I hope that you will be able to arrange things so that it will not be necessary in the years to come and that, dear friend, we will pass our life in the same places, in the same occupations, in the same way of life. I know nothing comparable to the happiness of passing my life with you."

The relationship between the three must have been difficult for all of them. Time had softened the bitterness of her injuries, but Dorothea still did not trust her mother and had little reason to love her. She knew too well the habitual extravagance of Talleyrand's style of letter writing and, if she had seen them, would not have taken too seriously the protestations in this letter. But if she had really thought that Talleyrand was only happy in her mother's company and dreamed of building his life in common with her, then her position would have become at once intolerable. That Talleyrand should derive great pleasure from the society of the Duchess of

Courland she could accept, but that anyone but herself should play the leading role in the prince's life would have been altogether inadmissible.

Playing the country squire could not satisfy Talleyrand for long and the role of squire's niece was even less congenial to Dorothea. A short visit to Paris for the wedding of the Duke of Berry did no more than whet the old statesman's appetite and, after a visit to the waters at Bourbon l'Archambault with Dorothea had restored his vigour, he made up his mind to winter in Paris. October found them both installed once more in the Rue St. Florentin.

Paris with her uncle in opposition cannot at first have appeared so very different to Dorothea from what it had been when he was in power. The prince seemed to command the same esteem, the drawing-rooms of the Rue St. Florentin were still as full of all that was brightest, richest and most influential in the cosmopolitan society of Paris. But there was a change, a subtle variation in atmosphere that told of power slipped away, a new note in the deference that showed it was paid to age and reputation and not to a man who could make or break the visitor. Grandeur and distinction were all very well but it was to power that Dorothea had wished to ally herself. She was too young to go down with the setting sun and she knew that her uncle too would never be happy so long as he were kept from office. Resolutely she dedicated herself to preparing the way for his return. It was a task at which she did not, at first, show herself particularly adept.

In her previous stays in Paris one of her closest friends had been Count Molé ; a romantically handsome young aristocrat who had endeared himself to Napoleon " by his historical name and his capacity to listen " and served him conscientiously though without enthusiasm. Talleyrand had made him Minister of Transport in his short-lived government and had arranged for him to be created a peer of France. Dorothea felt no doubt that here at least she would find a sure ally. To her surprise and chagrin she found him equivocal in his attitude ; sympathetic certainly but showing no great eagerness for engaging in battle against the Government. She wrote on the subject to her friend Madame Aimée de Coigny, and

Decazes, Louis XVIII's favourite and Minister of Police, intercepted the reply and showed it to Molé. In his memoirs Molé professed the most virtuous indignation at this invasion of the privacy of correspondence but this did not stop him reading the letter with attention. He found it full of spiteful comment on himself. Dorothea's chances of enlisting him in the cause were not improved.

Then, in November, came a sharp set-back. Another former protégé of Talleyrand was Pasquier, a mediocrity who had accepted office as President of the Chamber under Richelieu. With an indiscretion extraordinary in a man of his experience, Talleyrand chose a reception at the British Embassy to insult first Decazes and then Pasquier himself in the latter's presence. An unpleasant scandal followed. The offence could not be overlooked and Talleyrand was banished from court until further notice. His actual exile lasted only three months but the real damage was not so quickly repaired.

A reconciliation with Pasquier, at least, seemed essential if Talleyrand was not to forfeit a large part of his potential support. Molé offered to act as go-between and left in his memoirs an account of his reception when he came back to report that Pasquier had no wish to renew his former intimacy.

" Madame Edmond de Périgord was at her uncle's when I returned. On learning that Pasquier was throwing over the patronage of Monsieur de Talleyrand, her rage was such as I do not remember having seen in a woman, even in the street. Her face was livid and she was trembling from head to foot. Instead of replying to her abuse I turned my back on her and, with an impassive face, continued to address Monsieur de Talleyrand as if we had been alone. This made her weep with rage and she looked ready to devour me. At the same time I read in her uncle's face and appearance that he could never forgive me any more than he could Pasquier."

Molé is not the most reliable of witnesses but there is no reason to believe that he was over-dramatising. Dorothea rarely lost control of herself but when she did the result was formidable. Nothing would have been better calculated to provoke her to fury than this example of what must have seemed to her the vilest treachery. It would never have occurred to her that her uncle had behaved intolerably and that Pasquier's sulkiness was not unreasonable. Pasquier's desertion could not be excused and she had neither the self-control nor the inclination to conceal her anger. That Molé should have drawn her fire was unfortunate for everyone though it seems. unlikely that he was in fact quite as unprovocative as he made out. The scene, however, gave him the necessary excuse in his turn to shrug off Talleyrand's patronage. In 1817, Molé joined the Government as Minister of the Marine. Though he remained formally on good terms with Talleyrand and Dorothea it was nearly twenty years before the latter could bring herself to consider him as a friend again.

Another of her allies proved more constant. Baron Vitrolles was a well-remembered figure of her childhood. Now in Paris he was playing an important political role as councillor and friend to the Count of Artois, later to become Charles X, whose home in the Pavillon Marsan was a fertile centre for every extremist right-wing enterprise. Vitrolles at this time was in the early forties, fanatically royalist, a dashing, honourable, slightly stupid figure whose devotion to his odious master was as creditable as it was inexplicable. For Dorothea he had a love half avuncular, half passionate, and a keen admiration for her intelligence and strength of character. Knowing that Talleyrand was thoroughly disgruntled with the present Government, Vitrolles dreamed that he might build a new and bizarre alliance in which the prince, at the head of the right-wing extremists and anyone else who might happen to feel that they were unfairly excluded from office, would upset the Government of Richelieu and take charge on behalf of the Pavillon Marsan.

Talleyrand was sceptical but not in a mood to reject outright any alliance which might be helpful to him. Dorothea was frankly delighted by the idea. Her uncle's liberal ideas never soaked very deeply into her naturally authoritarian mind and at no time of her life, if two ladders to power had presented themselves, would she not have chosen the more traditional and the more conservative. But what really mattered to her was not political ideas but personalities and the facts of power. Vitrolles she liked and trusted ; through him her uncle might be restored to office, through him the loathed Decazes might be brought down. She had no hesitation in engaging with him in a joint crusade.

Vitrolles's first idea was to persuade Talleyrand to give his name as author to a secret memorandum which he himself had written at the instruction of the Count of Artois. It was intended that this note, which was a commentary on the present state of France, should be presented to the Emperor Alexander at the Congress of Aix-la-Chapelle where a final term was then being put to the occupation of French territory by the allies. Vitrolles rightly felt that the memorandum would carry far more weight if Talleyrand would accept its parentage. Uncertain whether he alone could persuade the prince of the efficacy of this course, Vitrolles, who somewhat over-estimated Dorothea's influence in affairs of such a nature, began by enlisting her aid. " Her quick and subtle understanding " he wrote " lent itself to every subject, she helped Monsieur de Talleyrand to think and forced him to define and complete his ideas which, without her, would have remained vague and futile. Often she was a source of inspiration to him. Her intelligence moved with amazing speed and she could follow his thoughts with less need of words than anybody else . . ."

Dorothea was quite ready to do what she could but, source of inspiration or not, she had no pretensions to match Talleyrand's skill in conspiracy. She made it clear to Vitrolles that she would not try to over-persuade her uncle. It would have made little difference if she had. Talleyrand showed no enthusiasm for Vitrolles's oblique manœuvre. He pleaded that he had nobody whom he could trust sufficiently to act as go-between and, though he never directly refused to participate, saw to it that the idea was let drop. As always in such matters he showed good judgment ; the secret memorandum was published and Vitrolles identified as the author, several plotters from the Pavillon Marsan were arrested by order of Decazes and the Count of Artois looked sourly upon his favourite.

Wounded, Vitrolles retreated into an empyrean of ultra-royalist unreality and, with Chateaubriand and Mathieu de Montmorency began to edit an extremist newspaper, the *Conservateur*. He was forced to resign his office as Minister of

State and the *Moniteur* announced his disgrace. Dorothea wrote from the watering-place at Cauterets to console him: " You will easily be able to guess my reactions when I saw the *Moniteur* of the 26th. You always tell me that I am not easy-going enough so you will not find it hard to believe that one item in it drove me mad with indignation. I suppose that you will take it more calmly than any of your friends ; I can assure you that those of them in Cauterets are thinking of very little else."

* * * * *

One consolation came to solace her wounds. At the end of August, 1817, Talleyrand had been given the title of Duke by Louis XVIII. Satisfied with his princedom he arranged for it to be passed to his younger brother Archambaud, father of Edmond de Périgord. Archambaud thus became Duke of Talleyrand. Then, in December, 1817, Ferdinand the First, King of the Two Sicilies, in his turn offered a dukedom to Talleyrand. The honour together with a handsome income for life had in fact been bestowed as long ago as 1815, but only now was the territorial title added to it. Archambaud being already fitted out with a French dukedom, Talleyrand felt free to pass this honour on to his nephew Edmond and thus give himself the pleasure of transforming Dorothea into a duchess. " The King of Naples," he wrote to the Duchess of Courland in December, 1817, " has just granted to Edmond and Dorothea the title given to me to go with my Neapolitan duchy. They are going to be called the Duke and Duchess of Dino. It is the name of one of the royal estates in Calabria . . . From to-day Dorothea will enjoy all the advantages which the title of duchess carries with it at court . . ."

Talleyrand derived immense pleasure from his niece's promotion and, even if Dorothea had not found the honour agreeable in its own right, she would have been happy in his satisfaction. But in fact she was well pleased by her promotion. To a Princess of Courland a Neapolitan duchy may not have seemed very wonderful but a duchess is always a duchess and, apart from the prestigious ring of the title, the precedence which it gave at court was most acceptable. Countess Edmond de Périgord had been all very well as a name for a young and unformed girl but now that she was mature and well-established she felt the need of something which would reflect more accurately her real significance.

Whether the territorial title appealed to her is less certain. The Duchess of Dino is euphonious enough but Dino itself was nothing much. It was in fact a tiny islet in the Gulf of Policastro. Sparse and rugged, it has been almost entirely ignored by the history books. The only information that Lacour Gayet[5] could find about it was in a manual of 1775 : " A prodigious number of rabbits are to be found on the Isle of Dino. Near the coast it is possible to catch large quantities of anchovies . . ."

Anchovies and rabbits, even in prodigious numbers, hardly seem to be the stuff of duchies. The title too gave rise to many ribald comments among the lesser wits of Paris. Dino, if divided into two words, made *dis* " no " ; a word she was supposed to have rarely used. ". . . or if ' No ' in whatever language," commented Lord Glenbervie[6], " that it has amounted to *un doux nenni avec un doux sourire.*"

But on the whole the name was to serve Dorothea well. Though she was to change it twice more in her lifetime, it was as the Duchess of Dino that she was above all to be remembered and to figure in countless anecdotes and memoirs. It was as Duchess of Dino that she was to live out almost the whole of the twenty years which she was still to spend with Talleyrand, as Duchess of Dino that she was to reign in the embassy at London and play so large a role in the opening years of the July monarchy. It was as Duchess of Dino that she was to stir up as many enmities as any woman of Paris and win the devotion of a circle of constant and admiring friends.

7

For Edmond, the honour of his dukedom arrived almost simultaneously with the final collapse of the fortune which might have allowed him to enjoy it with pomp if not distinction. From his mother he had inherited three million francs and the magnificent house and estate of Rosny. By the end of 1817 he had gambled away the one and on 24th December of the same year he reluctantly sold the other to Monsieur Louis-Charles Mourault, a Parisian business-man. Thence it soon found its way into the hands of the Duchess of Berry who was to spend much time there after the murder of her husband and profoundly shock the locals by shooting rabbits and returning to the house with their bleeding ears strung as trophies around her neck.

But the price which Edmond got for Rosny was barely enough to cover his existing debts and nothing in his way of life suggested that his extravagance would become less outrageous in the future. Dorothea took alarm for her own fortune which, substantial as it was, had already suffered from her husband's depredations. Early in 1818 she applied to the court for a separation of goods between herself and Count Edmond de Périgord and on 24th March the order was granted. Her marriage moved one stage closer to complete extinction.

It was however to flicker once more into apparent life. Sometime towards the middle of 1820, probably in May or perhaps a little earlier, Edmond gave up his solitary life to come and live with his wife and uncle in the Rue St. Florentin. In the autumn of 1820 his debts were paid in full. The reconciliation, which did not seem to be accompanied by any conspicuous revival of marital affection, astonished Paris but the astonishment took on a different note when, on 29th December of the same year, Dorothea gave birth to a daughter. Six months later, Edmond moved out once more. The couple were never to live together again.

Parisian society did not hesitate to assume that Talleyrand was the father of the child and that Edmond, in exchange presumably for a fat bribe, had been called in to lend some vestige of respectability to the birth. Madame de Souza— herself, as Madame de Flahaut, a former mistress of Talleyrand —wrote to her son in August of 1820[1], " Madame Dorothea has become mystical. Poor Edmond is a pitiable spectator of this pregnancy conferred by the grace of God. He fears his uncle may force him to stay in bed when Dorothea is delivered. He sees their minds so inclined to believe in miracles that for all he knows he may be asked to suckle the infant." With a cynical shrug and witticisms such as these the smart society of France gratefully accepted this addition to the season's list of scandals. Any inclination there may have been to give Dorothea the benefit of the doubt was finally silenced when the Dinos split up once more a few months later.

Yet doubt there was and is ; many refused to accept the word of gossip and certainly they have never been proved wrong. It is not agreeable to conceive this young and beautiful girl, mother of two small children, acting as mistress to her sixty-six year old uncle, himself crippled and of unsavoury reputation. It would be comfortable to ignore the possibility altogether, or, since there can be no certainty, to leave it as a mystery with no more ado. But if one is to understand Dorothea or her relationship with Talleyrand with any pretence at completeness then one must at least try to form an opinion as to whether she was his mistress. For neither of them could it have been the most important, still less the most enduring part of their association, but the whole quality of that association, let alone its future development, must have been affected if Talleyrand slept with Dorothea and she bore his child.

In the *Souvenirs* which she was to write two or three years later, Dorothea referred to the discrepancy of age which makes the idea that she was Talleyrand's mistress so repugnant.

" If, in the course of my life, people have felt surprise that

a great difference in age seemed to me only a minor dis-
advantage in the various relationships which life has to offer,
they should refer back to the time when, on the threshold of
womanhood, I accustomed myself to the idea of marrying a
man twenty-five years older than me. Indeed, not only did
I accustom myself to the idea but I welcomed it through a
self-esteem which made me think that I was the better for
behaving so exceptionally."

If this is to be taken literally it must mean that Dorothea
did not find the idea of sleeping with her uncle as repellent
as would have been the case with many women of her age.
After all the marriage of a man of sixty-six with a woman some
forty years younger is by no means unheard of and, though
Talleyrand may have been crippled and in poor health, he was
still notoriously attractive and had a great reputation as a lover.
Certainly there is no reason to believe that he himself would
have looked forward to the consummation of their love with
anything except keen enthusiasm ; she was, after all, only his
niece by marriage and if his nephew could not hold his wife
then he must expect to run the same risks as any other husband.
Even though Talleyrand were eager and Dorothea willing
there still remains doubt. For one thing, it cannot be certain
that Talleyrand was in fact capable of giving Dorothea
a child. Many accounts of the time stress the growing feebleness which made him seem ten years older than he was. Such
evidence is not strong but it does at least point out the inherent
improbability of the liaison. For another, the Duchess of
Courland could hardly have been kept in the dark yet her
friendship with Talleyrand remained as close and constant as
ever. She may by now have become reconciled to her displace-
ment by her daughter but so conspicuous a proof of it must
surely have been resented. Even if she felt no indignation as
a mother, one would have expected some coolness at least
between the duchess and her former lover.
Talleyrand himself did nothing to prove the gossip false.
Pauline, as the child was christened, was always his favourite
among the children who surrounded him ; he treated her with
constant and deep affection so that even as hostile a critic as

Sainte-Beuve had to admit " if there is one good side to M. de Talleyrand . . . it lies in this corner of pure affection."[2] In his will he left her his estate at Pont-de-Sains and his gold watch and chain with a miniature of Dorothea set in the cover.

Trying to balance all these straws of evidence and taking into account the peculiar circumstances of the birth, it is reasonable to assume that gossip was right and that Talleyrand was indeed the father of Pauline. If still more speculation were called for, it would not be too extravagant to guess that the liaison began sometime after Dorothea's final break with Clam in 1816 and that this passage of their relationship closed for ever after the birth of Pauline. But it is no more than a guess. The truth will never be known and anyone who wants to believe that Dorothea's relationship with her uncle was unsullied by any taint of sex can muster a reasonable case to justify his point of view.

What is however certain and what is really as important is that every petty figure in French society took it for granted that she was a loose and wicked woman. The reputation was to dog her all her life and preceded her wherever she went. Creevey was making no assumption which was not generally shared when he confided to his journal some ten years later : " We were interrupted by the arrival of the Duchess of Dino . . . As for D, villain as she is, I never saw anyone more striking and imposing. Her eyes brilliant beyond all example, her face extremely handsome, her figure that of perfect youth . . . her manners the most natural for a Frenchwoman I ever saw and quite perfect and her dress the same. And yet to think of this devil living as mistress with old T, the uncle of her husband and having three or four children by him. Was there ever . . . ? "

Not everyone had as lascivious an imagination as Creevey but this sort of gossip was a commonplace in London and Parisian society. For two generations of jealous women and idle men it was enough that Dorothea was seen in the company of a friend for him to be posted as her latest lover, enough that she spoke kindly of anyone for vicious tongues to spread the word that the duchess was launched on another of her affairs.

Even when Talleyrand was into his eighties and nearing his deathbed, it was still assumed that their lives were conducted on lines of unparalleled debauchery. Only the small hard core of Dorothea's real friends knew her well enough to assess this gossip and discount nine-tenths of it as totally unfounded.

One of the most remarkable attacks on Talleyrand and, by innuendo, on Dorothea came in an article by Georges Sand which appeared in the *Revue des Deux Mondes* in 1835. It is worth quoting at some length since it epitomises the shocked relish with which the French upper middle classes peered through an impenetrable barrier of ignorance at what they fancied to be the home life of Prince Talleyrand and his beautiful young niece.

The article is written in the form of a dialogue between two trippers—the author and her friend Paul—walking in the neighbourhood of Valençay. The two friends are standing in front of the chateau reminding each other of the various iniquities of the owner:

" Gripped by an uncontrollable loathing and a secret horror . . . A window opens. It is the Prince's. Since when have corpses grown too hot ? . . . A white and slender figure crosses a corner of the green lawn and we saw it mount the outer staircase of the tower at the other end of the castle.

' Is this,' asked my friend, ' the shade of some just soul whom you have evoked to dance and frolic in the moonlight and be the despair of the ungodly ?—No, for this soul, if indeed it is one, dwells in a body of much beauty.' ' Ah, now I see,' he went on. ' It is the Duchess. They say that . . .' ' Do not repeat it,' I cried, interrupting him. ' Let my imagination be spared these ghastly images and horrible suspicions. I can believe that this old man should have conceived so blasphemous a thought ; but she is too beautiful. It is impossible ! If rampant debauchery or sordid avarice are to be found in beings of such charm and hide themselves under a disguise so pure, at least let me know nothing of it, let me deny it."

Nobly Madame Sand thrusts away such painful thoughts

while her friend describes how, that morning, he had seen Dorothea driving in a carriage through the park.

" You seemed to throw out rays of light into the warm, damp wind from the south. Dressed all in white like a young girl, like one of Diana's nymphs you were borne as on wings by a splendid steed in a light and graceful carriage. Your hair was blowing about your candid brow and a magic radiance sprang from your great, black eyes (the most beautiful eyes in France, so they say) . . . but since then I have been into your room and seen the portrait which hangs within the curtains of your bed.

' That alone,' I broke in, ' is enough to prevent me putting any bad interpretation on the artless affection which springs from an almost daughterly gratitude for kindnesses done and protection legitimately given. No, no ; one cannot be corrupt with an air so brilliant yet so gentle, with so marvellous and youthful a beauty, with so proud and open a bearing, with so harmonious a voice, such easy manners. The God of good people who you invoked just now ; I invoke him too so that he may save me from learning of what I do not wish to believe, that vice lurks under so affecting an exterior, that there is some foul insect in the heart of every scented flower."

So, diligently hoping for the best, the two friends made their way back to the village where Madame Sand hastened to record the delicacy of her sentiments for the benefit of her admiring readers.

Shortly after the article appeared Dorothea wrote to her friend Adolphe de Bacourt :

" Living as I have done in the house of Monsieur de Talleyrand and in his confidence, how could I escape the licence of the Press and its attacks in this most libellous age of journalism ? It was long before I got used to it. I used to be deeply wounded, very much upset and very unhappy and I shall never become completely indifferent . . . However, as it would be equally absurd to allow one's peace of mind to be at the mercy of people one despises,

I have made up my mind to read nothing of this kind, and the more directly concerned I am the less I want to know about it. I do not wish to know the evil which people think or say or write about me or about my friends."

But in 1821 Dorothea had not found even this measure of self-protection. It was in reaction to her injuries that she developed a veneer of indifference to what the world might say of her, a veneer which hardened into real disdain and confirmed all who did not know her well in their conviction of her deep-rooted and cynical immorality. Too proud to dispute the verdict or to change her ways, Dorothea resolved to defy the world, almost to welcome its misrepresentations as fresh proof of its unworthiness. She never forgave society its calumnies and society never forgave her the little attention which she paid them.

* * * * *

Eighteen twenty-one brought more troubles to Talleyrand and Dorothea than those to which their own lives gave rise. As nearly every year, the Duchess of Courland was spending the summer at Löbikau. At the beginning of June she fell ill. Conflicting reports arrived in Paris, then she seemed to be definitely on the mend. Suddenly, in August, all was over. A friend, Countess Trogoff, was sitting by her bed and laying out the cards to tell her fortune, when the duchess choked and lost consciousness. She remained insensible for three days and then died.

Dorothea had little reason to love her mother. Nevertheless, over the last few years they had drawn closer together than ever before. The Duchess of Courland had taken with equanimity the rise of her daughter in Talleyrand's esteem. Herself nearly sixty years old she had ceased to disquiet herself much over the nature of Talleyrand's affection and was content in the certainty that the place she occupied in his life could never be filled. Her certainty was justified. Deeply, passionately though he loved Dorothea, she could never wholly take the place of her mother. Their relationship was in many ways both more extensive and more profound but, if only because her mother had been almost the prince's contemporary and she so far his junior, they were never to enjoy quite the same intimacy and absolute understanding. Long afterwards, Dorothea showed the prince a portrait of her mother which he had never seen before. His eyes filled with tears as he said, " I do not think that there can ever have been on earth a woman more worthy of being adored." " My heart is broken," he wrote to the Duchess of Sagan, " I shall mourn for her until my last day which I see approaching now without regret."[3]

In the affection which they both felt for Talleyrand and which he lavished on them in return Dorothea and her mother had grown fond of each other. Once the irritants which had stemmed from the duchess's role as a would-be dominant mother or from their direct competition for worldly position had faded, they found after all that they had much in common. Her mother's death came as a real grief to Dorothea ; real, indeed, to a degree which almost took her by surprise. " I am deeply distressed," she wrote to Vitrolles, " I have lost immensely, both for the present and for the future. She was very dear to my heart and always ready to extend a helping hand to revive, succour or defend." She would have deemed it improper to say much less whatever her true thoughts had been ; even to a close friend one could not admit that a mother's death was other than a tragedy. But in fact her sorrow was sincere. All her early bitterness had not been forgotten but in this case at least she had been able to forgive. Now with her mother's death the last close link with her childhood was broken and she felt herself suddenly alone. Her grief was for herself as well as for her mother but it was none the less unfeigned for that.

From now on Talleyrand was to depend on Dorothea as never before, and to treat her and her daughter Pauline as the only objects of his love. If ever Dorothea had contemplated making a new life for herself away from the shadow of her uncle, she now knew that to do so would utterly shatter the fabric of his life and kill him as surely as any weapon but far more cruelly.

*   *   *   *   *

From now until the July revolution nearly ten years later, Dorothea's life settled into a pattern which was comfortable, entertaining and varied enough to make the years pass without too much regret. What was lacking was close association with power. The life of a constitutional monarch would never have appealed to Dorothea; still less could she be content when sharing the lot of even the most renowned of former ministers. Never during these years did she cease to dream of Talleyrand's return to power or accept that the pleasures of retirement could compensate for the tribulations of office.

Life was divided, principally, between Valençay and the Rue St. Florentin in Paris. In his life Talleyrand had many houses, moving from one to another with indifference and parting with them without regret. In Valençay he made a home and a home he destined not only for himself but for his family in the future. Already he had tried to have the estate invested with the honours of a duchy which could pass eventually to Edmond and Dorothea. Louis XVIII had refused, pointing out that it would be a doubtful compliment to the King of Spain to name a duchy after his former prison. Talleyrand accepted the verdict but not without a private resolve to get it reversed when time had dulled the susceptibilities of the Spanish court.

But home though it might be, there was nothing cosy about life at Valençay. Dorothea had found it *unheimlich* on her first visit and she never had cause to change her mind. Life followed the lines of a small royal court rather than a country house. Quite apart from the constant flow of visitors, there was a retinue of doctors, lawyers, tutors and agents of one kind or another and constant entertainments were given by musicians or travelling troupes of actors. The company was usually distinguished, the conversation often brilliant and the food invariably outstanding. Dorothea would ride or drive her carriage in the woods, look after the welfare of her uncle's guests, read greatly and write many letters, pass the time at needlework, sketch, occupy herself in good works in the surrounding villages, join with enthusiasm in charades or private theatricals and with less enthusiasm in the prince's

interminable games of whist. It was pleasant enough but for
Dorothea it lacked the savour of great events.

Dorothea and her uncle were never alone at Valençay.
With them, as chaperon, confidante and friend was always to
be found Princess Tyzkiewitz, niece of the last King of Poland.
From 1826 until her death eighteen years later this forlorn
relic of a vanished kingdom lived on in the great west tower
of Valençay, occupying herself exclusively with the affairs of
her friends " who she loved with the most rare and the most
generous fidelity."[4] She never played any very significant role
but her unfailing calm, placidity and wisdom lent some
stability to a life which otherwise might have been wrecked
by turbulent emotion.

The presence of the princess also provided some sort of
buffer to the wit and spite of the Parisian gossips. None of
these would have admitted for an instant that the old lady
was anything but a derisory imitation of a duenna but her
presence gave a certain gloss of respectability to the household.
Without her, in fact, it is unlikely that Dorothea would have
agreed to share her uncle's house and even Talleyrand, little
though he cared for society chatter, would have hesitated before
so exposing his niece.

After the summer in Valençay came the winter in Paris.
Here there was never a moment for relaxation. Talleyrand's
social reputation had hardly been damaged by his political
eclipse and the house in the Rue St. Florentin was constantly
filled. Dorothea and the prince occupied apartments on different
sides of the courtyard and maintained their own establishments
but to all intents and purposes the Duchess of Dino was hostess
in her uncle's home. The occupation was not so trivial as it
might sound ; always present in Dorothea's mind was the
determination to win so much support for her uncle that in
the end it would prove impossible to keep him from office.
All the expense, all the contrivance, all the tedious hours of
preparation, all the spontaneous charm and not always so
spontaneous wit, all the evenings passed in tolerating bores
or flattering fools—throughout it all she retained her constant purpose and harnessed every occasion to the needs of
policy.

Her mastery of social techniques was not so complete that she pleased all the world. Lord Glenbervie spent an evening at Talleyrand's and reported with tepid enthusiasm, " Madame de Périgord was particularly attentive to Lady Charlotte and meant and tried to be so to me but was embarrassed. The world thinks she does the honours well and in general she is still thought handsome. But she is not improved since I saw her depart from Spa in 1814."[5] Lord Glenbervie was something of a dirty old man whose overtures to Dorothea had met with scant success. For every such critic there was at least one Henry Fox to find the Duchess " wonderfully clever, and full of wit and talent."[6] But it was not only her rejected suitors who failed to be enchanted.

Court life was an additional burden in this long-drawn-out campaign though Dorothea found the ritual there less intolerably stuffy than it would have been in any other house. Madame de Boigne, indeed, considered that she positively relished the pomposity and artificiality, " When, having put on a lot of diamonds, she can sit for an hour or two on one of the principal sofas in a room brilliant with candles and in the company of several other highnesses of the same rank, then she considers her evening very well spent." This does Dorothea less than justice, insipid conversation and pointless protocol held no charm for her, but it is true that never for a moment did she forget that she was an aristocrat with royal blood in her veins. Still less would she ever have challenged the conventions which ruled the society in which it was her lot to move : that way, she would have felt, revolution lay.

Save for his brief disgrace Talleyrand was always an honoured guest at court. But he was never made to feel that he was liked or his presence desired and his niece felt acutely the cold courtesy with which he was received and the deaf ear turned to his counsels. But there was another royal household where she and her uncle were better appreciated. There they went for their pleasure and for the sake of congenial company and there were many to note that they were seen more often at the Palais Royal than with the senior branch of the family at the Tuileries.

The Palais Royal, home of the Orleans family, was at this

time the centre of the smartest and gayest society of Paris. The Duke of Orleans may have been son of a regicide but he was still a prince of the blood and the wealthiest man in France. With the royal family he remained on terms of affability tinged with suspicion; for the rest of Paris he kept open house. He had a finger in every pie; never plotted to the point of indiscretion but contrived to give the impression that he did not positively abhor sedition; by his lavish spending won the favours not only of the aristocracy but—more important—of the middle classes and the mob.

Certainly a reception or ball at the Palais Royal was a more agreeable affair than its counterpart at the Tuileries. Men and women were not segregated into discontented herds, the sterile ritual of presentation was cut to a decent minimum—even below it, some starchy supporters of the *ancien régime* would complain—the company was less monotonous than the rigorous protocol of the royal palace could permit. The atmosphere was relaxed and gay; it was possible actively to enjoy one's evening—a delectation rarely allowed to those who patronised the rival and senior establishment. And yet the Duke of Orleans never let it be forgotten who he was; head of a branch of the royal family which, though junior to the Bourbons, was no less noble or distinguished and quite as legitimately descended from Louis XIII.

Dorothea was charmed by the Duke of Orleans and he, for his part, took great pains to please her. Though they became sincere and constant friends it is certainly true that, for the duke, the chief attraction of Dorothea at this period must have been in the power and influence of her uncle. A few years previously a man named Didier had been executed for organising a futile revolt at Grenoble. Before he died he was reported to have said, " Let the king keep the Duke of Orleans and Monsieur de Talleyrand as far from the throne and from France as possible." The words had an ominous ring. No one who knew Talleyrand could doubt that he had looked ahead and noted that, if the follies and obstinacy of the Bourbons finally became intolerable, a ready-made and sympathetic substitute would be available. Every time that the duke looked covetously at the throne he must have reflected that only in Prince Talleyrand would he find the wisdom, experience and skill which he would need if his ambitions were ever to be realised.

Finally, when holding court neither at Valençay nor the Rue St. Florentin, Dorothea, the prince and the faithful Princess Tyzkiewitz would go off on holiday to the mountains or a watering-place. Each would travel in their separate convoy, jolting across the roads of France, accompanied by a retinue of maids, grooms, footmen and the occasional doctor or secretary. In 1816 the procession wound its way to Bourbon l'Archambault, an attractive little watering-place in the heart of France. For the following three years they visited the Pyrenees, then it was back to Bourbon l'Archambault again.

Dorothea did not find this kind of travelling very stimulating. But her sense of duty towards her uncle imposed it on her ; the summer journey, after all, was undertaken mainly for the sake of his health. Even if it did not hold much excitement for a beautiful and energetic woman of thirty she had at least the satisfaction of seeing the old prince happy in her company.

*   *   *   *   *

Beyond this everyday round of gaiety and political intrigue, these fallow years were important to Dorothea because during them she laid the foundation of friendships which were to thrive until one or other party ended it in death. Dorothea was the most faithful of friends. Once she had accepted someone into her circle there was nothing she would not do to advance their cause or to promote their happiness. Almost all her friends were men, all were intelligent, all ambitious, all serious in pursuit of their aims. All were highly respectable though not necessarily from the higher reaches of the aristocracy, one or two indeed being positively middle-class. Most of them were drawn from the ranks of Talleyrand's political allies ; they tended to be liberal minded, thoughtful and occasionally a little dull ; they wrote innumerable letters to Dorothea and to each other and preserved almost all that they received with a care for which no historian can be too grateful.

Pierre-Paul Royer Collard, professor, lawyer and constitutional royalist was one of those whom Talleyrand sought out as an ally and kept as a friend. He was the leading spirit of the little group of the " Doctrinaires," the defenders of the fruits of the Revolution whose probity, tenacity and intellectual powers made them as much loathed by the right as they were respected by the rest of France. He lived close to Valençay in an isolated house perched on the top of a rock and perpetually battered by the winds. There Talleyrand and Dorothea arrived one afternoon without warning. Royer Collard greeted them coolly but their combined charm was too much for him and within a short time he was numbered among their most precious friends. " He was at once original and witty, serious and vivacious, showed much affection for me and made himself very pleasant to Monsieur de Talleyrand," wrote Dorothea. Madame de Boigne, as usual, saw things in a rather different light. " Monsieur Royer Collard is possessed by one of those mysterious ambitions which seek to gain everything while pretending to desire nothing . . . He has made himself a great career with little talent but a great deal of grandiloquence. One can credit him with two or three outstanding speeches and an immense quantity of words—more hollow than profound— which nevertheless had a great vogue for a time."

Dorothea never had any doubts as to Royer Collard's wisdom and sincerity and, indeed, few men were more generally respected. He was thirty years older than Dorothea and she considered him in many ways as a complement to her uncle; lacking some of the charm, the guile and the grandeur, but with qualities of honesty and purity which she could never pretend the prince possessed. Deeply religious himself, he made a considerable impression on the young woman and kindled in her an interest in the faith which she had accepted till then as no more than a social convenience. Their letters to each other are serious and severe. Royer Collard's letters, in particular, might be tedious were it not for the sudden and unexpected flashes of wit which break the monotony and reveal a lively mind behind the severe and dry-as-dust exterior.

Making a comparison between Thiers and Guizot, Royer Collard acidly remarked, " There is this difference between the two men, that God has not given Thiers the capacity to distinguish between good and evil while Guizot, who has the capacity, ignores it." It is hard to see how Dorothea can have had any sympathy for François-Pierre Guizot, a cold, proud, fish incapable of any action which was not calculated or any reaction which was not mean, a man conspicuously devoid of nobility even in a generation of little men. This friendship too began in political alliance. Guizot was another of the Doctrinaires, perhaps the most brilliant of them, certainly the equal of any in intellectual capacity. To Dorothea he seemed a man destined for success and as such a man worth knowing ; he was a man opposed to the present régime and as such a man worth encouraging ; the only surprising thing is that as well as admiring his talents, Dorothea seemed to have been attracted by his personality. Until the very end of her life she would never have counted Guizot among the closest of her friends but she valued and esteemed him and they wrote to each other regularly and warmly.

A third member of the Doctrinaires was Prosper de Barante. Barante, a diplomat and successful historian, had more in him of Royer Collard than of Guizot, though he lacked the stature of either. But he had a genius for friendship and represented for Dorothea all that was stable and permanently valuable. " Pleasant, kind and affectionate as ever . . ." " . . . My belief in him is as complete as my pleasure is real. He is upright, trustworthy and kind to such an extent that he can be entirely relied on." The virtues are, perhaps, not the most stimulating, but the number of people who counted him as the dearest of their friends shows that his qualities were very real. Among his distinctions he counted that of having fallen in love with Madame de Staël when she was forty years old and he no more than twenty-four. How far he actually advanced in her favours cannot be sure but, on his side at least, the relationship was passionate enough. By the time Dorothea grew to know him well the slim, idealistic youth had mellowed into a relaxed and middle-aged minor public figure comfortably fixed up with a handsome creole wife. But some traces of the romantic still clung to him and, though he never found another Germaine de Staël, he also never quite stopped looking for her.

Even with this amorous background, no one seems ever to

have linked his name with Dorothea's with more than a flicker of malicious innuendo. Still less did anyone seriously suggest that Guizot or Royer Collard was her lover. But this did not mean that Dorothea was free of scandal ; all her life she was destined to be its target. The excitement over her sharing a house with her uncle was beginning to lose its savour ; Parisian society began to look for some new man whom they could credit with possession of her heart and favours.

They found him in Theobald Piscatory. Piscatory, who had been born Theobald Arcambal but had changed his name after adoption by a rich Greek, was some seven years younger than Dorothea. Under the Restoration he had won a reputation as a romantic by travelling to Greece to fight with the insurgents. In 1824 he returned in glory to buy arms with which to continue the fight[7]. Either Parisian life distracted him or he felt things had gone too far for him to be of use—at all events he does not seem ever to have gone back to Greece. By 1826 he was a frequent visitor at Valençay and popularly believed to be the lover of its hostess.

There may be no smoke without fire, but in this case the smoke seems exceptionally wispish. Certainly Dorothea was attracted by this genteel adventurer. She was not so consistent that a brief but gallant service with the Greek insurgents did not seem infinitely more praiseworthy than her husband's equally gallant and considerably more protracted service with the emperor. But it is hard to be sure that there was any more to it than that. There are certain cryptic references to *cette affaire P* in her letters to Vitrolles. " I was wanting to speak to you of this *affaire P* but then, like you, I forgot. That's not so bad, is it ? " " I have a very serious need to see you. I want your advice and your help. Both my thought and my heart tell me that I should turn to you." And, considerably later, " The consolations of friendship become more necessary to me every day ; I ask of them that they should play a great part, fill a gaping hole, above all prevent me being aware of an emptiness in my life which I do not wish to see once more filled up by the force which has so shaken and marred my life . . ."

It is easy to read everything or nothing into passages like this. Dorothea was always prone to dramatise her emotions and it could well be that the force which had so shaken and marred her life—on this occasion at least—was a week-end flirtation in the woods of Valençay. But for Parisian society there was no room for doubt. Writing a few years later Stendhal[8], whose relish for the retailing of ill-informed and out-of-date gossip must come as a perpetual and disagreeable surprise to his admirers, reported that " she is more in love than ever with Monsieur P." At the date Stendhal wrote there is not the slightest doubt that he was wrong but the " more than ever " is the revealing phrase—the affair had been a staple of drawing-room conversation since 1825. There were many wild stories abroad, according to one of which Piscatory was supposed to have fathered a child whom, it was alleged, Dorothea had cunningly contrived to bear without being detected and to dispose of with equal dexterity and mystery[9].

What is at least certain is that the recipient of these confidences, Baron Vitrolles, played a much larger part in her life than Piscatory ever did. Over this period, indeed, she was probably closer to Vitrolles than to anyone except her uncle. The death of her mother and separation from her sisters had largely cut her off from the past. She was loth to lose it altogether. In this honest and spirited friend she had someone who knew a little at least of her childhood. For this reason he was exceptionally precious to her.

Vitrolles was far from satisfied with this not very romantic rôle of childhood friend and brotherly confidant. A letter Dorothea wrote him shortly after the death of her mother bears all the marks of an amiable but firm rejection:

" My fickle health is tolerably good this morning : my feelings towards you are not fickle at all. I am most faithfully yours but not to such a degree that either one of us be given the least cause for regret. It is better that I should now treat you a little harshly than that in the future we should experience any of those shocks which have become so much too strong for me . . .

" Tell me what you are dreaming of. I will be delighted to see you to-morrow at two o'clock but not, it must be clear, to give you any explanations or to tell you any truths. I have nothing in my heart or mind which is not filled with friendship towards you. I depend equally on your friendship and if my manner says anything else then it is false. My dear, very dear friend, I beg you not to ruin yourself as a friend by taking on the sullen touchiness of a lover."

It cannot be said that Dorothea treated Vitrolles very well. That she valued his company and friendship is obvious; that she was determined to retain them, equally so. Yet one does not feel that she gave much in return. She could reasonably have defended herself against a charge of coquetry with the plea that she unequivocally refused to act as his mistress from the start. Yet the defence would not have been really valid however many quotations she could cite to prove her case. Little real affection is to be found in her letters—there is an entirely different tone in those written at the same period to Royer Collard or other friends—and one seems to detect a false note in her constant self-reproaches for the pain she caused him. Certainly her protestations did nothing to disguise the fact that she expected to continue to inflict it in the future and there are a few hints that she sometimes led on her unfortunate admirer rather further than might otherwise appear. " I am in the habit of controlling my impulses " she wrote on one occasion " or, at least, of not letting them appear on the surface. I don't know what can have moved me so strongly yesterday that I allowed my determination to be overcome." The reference may have been to something altogether innocent but a little well-contrived weakness on Dorothea's part would not be inconsistent with the rest of her behaviour. One may wonder whether she would not have been a better friend to Vitrolles if she had treated him with rather less friendliness; there was a carefully cultivated lack of conviction about her declarations of indifference which must have kept her unfortunate would-be lover in the throes of alternate anticipation and despair.

Yet in a way Vitrolles was as much to blame as Dorothea. After the first year or two of close friendship he cannot have had many illusions about his chances of winning through to anything more gratifying. The fact that he was still prepared to put up with his quasi-avuncular status suggests that he did not find it too unsatisfactory. There was an element of the spaniel about Vitrolles and all his virtues—loyalty, trustfulness, patience—equipped him ideally to be the victim of one woman or another. Long after their friendship had ended, Dorothea referred contemptuously to his " cloying and inferior manner." He was an admirable character in many ways but one can understand that after a time anyone of spirit might have found irresistible the impulse to trample him underfoot.

*   *   *   *   *

Life at Valençay, life in the Rue St. Florentin ; Talleyrand, a small circle of friends, a host of acquaintances : these were much but not enough to fill Dorothea's life to her satisfaction. In the spring of 1822 her discontent, as was common with her, became reflected in her health. Without anything discernible being wrong with her she confined herself to her rooms and announced herself an invalid and tired of life. A friend called, to find her in tears and refusing to be consoled.

" Have you seen a doctor ? " he asked.

" Yes."

" And what did he prescribe ? "

" He told me to amuse myself."

" Very well, you must go more into society."

" I've had enough of it already."

" Theatres, walks ? "

" They tire me."

" Go to the country."

" And cut myself off from everyone I like ? "

" Dabble in politics."

" To do that I'd have to take part in a conspiracy and where would I find the other conspirators in this country ? "

" Try flirting."

" I've exhausted it."

" Then piety ? "

" I'm past it."

" All right then, try writing."

" Write ? Write what ? "

" Your memoirs."

165

" What rubbish."

" No. You've travelled a lot, you've seen a lot of the world. Your life has been an unusual one. Your character is freakish enough—certainly nothing in you or concerning you is like anything else I've ever met . . . You find the present disagreeable and the future frightening : you must be distracted from both. Live only in your memories and you can achieve it."

Dorothea did not at first take the advice seriously and, even after she began to write, approached the task from a strictly therapeutic angle ; noting with approval the soothing effect of authorship on her nerves. Gradually, however, she became absorbed in the work, delighted by the sense that she was discovering herself in the process, that the rule of absolute honesty and frankness which she imposed on herself in her writing led to a revelation of her own personality. On the whole the picture which emerged pleased her quite well ; " To discover sincerity at the end of a pen is not necessarily to lose all liking for it " ; but she did not flatter herself that it was particularly profound or even that it told the whole truth. " Volatile to excess, susceptible from every side, eternally changing under the irresistible pressure of outside things, could I hope to re-establish the steps of the ladder up and down which I go unceasingly ? I do not think so."

The most surprising thing about the *Souvenirs* to all those who have had cause to read court reminiscences and study the interminable joys and tribulations of those who spend their youth in palaces is the fact that they are remarkably easy to read. She obviously enjoyed describing the things which amused or moved her and did so in a vivid and straightforward style which neither treated her family and upbringing as subjects for a satirical attack nor cloaked their absurdities in a stuffy reverence. She had no hesitation in challenging the cherished prejudices of her parents and teachers, yet did so without acrimony or resentment. The Dorothea of the *Souvenirs* has a lively intelligence, wit, much sensibility and warmth, ambition, some selfishness, an unconscious arrogance rooted in birth and upbringing and a remarkable fund of common sense. The picture, as she said, was not displeasing ; the rest of her life bears witness that, on the whole, it was a faithful likeness.

*   *   *   *   *

The writing of her memoirs kept her agreeably occupied through 1822 ; by the next year she was in search of fresh distraction. She found it in a visit to Germany ; partly to see how her estates were doing, partly to take the waters at Baden. It was her first long absence from Talleyrand since the final break with Clam seven years before and she was nervous as to how well he would get on without her. She knew how completely the old man had become dependent upon her and she dreaded the thought of causing him unhappiness. "Absence seems to me to be a death placed suddenly in the midst of life," she wrote sombrely to Barante ; rather uncharacteristically concluding a little later on that the reason for her gloom was probably no more than a liver-attack.

She left France with regret. After an initial feeling of hostility and then a period of frigid co-existence, Dorothea had at last adjusted herself to life there. Paris she still distrusted and was to do so all her life. "Home of the most infamous slanders, of the monstrosities that a spirit of hideous partisanship can produce," she wrote to Barante after a particularly venomous attack on Talleyrand had excited her indignation. The only society there in which she could feel herself naturally at home was that of the aristocracy of the *Faubourg St. Germain.* And yet the *Faubourg* never really accepted her ; her separation from her husband, her relationship with Talleyrand, one of the fathers of the Revolution, later her close association with the July Monarchy : all combined to make the more rigid elements of the French nobility suspicious of this dangerous and disturbing foreign plotter. But in the country it was different. Valençay had become one of the most cherished centres of her life. She had grown absorbed in the life of the little town ; worked unremittingly for the welfare of the poor, for the school, for the convent, and had her reward in the affection and esteem which the people bore her. She was far too ambitious and worldly a woman to play the parochial Lady Bountiful for long but while she did it she knew that she was doing good. For a month or two at least, she could convince herself that she asked for nothing more from life. Her brief visit to Germany gave her little pleasure and did nothing to disturb her new-found loyalty.

* * * * *

Her distrust of Paris was soon to be fortified. In the summer of 1824 Dorothea set in motion the legal processes which were to complete her separation from her husband; a separation not only of goods now but of body.

Parisian society was outraged. That Dorothea and Edmond should live in unremitting disharmony and cuckold each other to distraction would have been taken as perfectly understandable, even natural. That Dorothea should leave Edmond to live with his uncle was more unusual but quite excusable. That she should have taken steps to protect her fortune from her husband's depredations was felt to be rather bad luck on Edmond but not unreasonable in the circumstances. But enough was enough. To drag the affair into the courts for a second time and to insist on a formal recognition of something which—to all intents and purposes—was already a fact, was an offence against the code of behaviour of the *Faubourg St. Germain*.

It was all so unnecessary, they felt. No one was going to insist that Dorothea live with her husband in fact; why not be content with that and let the theory look after itself? Few if any doors were actually closed to Dorothea and she continued to be received regularly if unenthusiastically at the Tuileries but there was a chill in the air around her when she went into society. Friendships were broken, others cooled off; more and more Dorothea was led to seek her companions among the liberal politicians who sympathised with her anger against the *Faubourg* and the royal family.

The most inexplicable thing about the separation is why Dorothea ever decided to ask for it. Her critics were not being unreasonable when they said that things could have gone on quite well as they were without any suffering on either side. She must have known how unpopular her action would make her in Paris. She seems to have gained nothing; any idea of divorce and remarriage was, of course, out of the question and any extra feeling of independence she may have achieved can hardly have outweighed the compensating discredit. Least of all does it seem likely that Talleyrand encouraged her in an action so damaging to the good name of his family and to her own interests.

It is possible that there were circumstances unknown to us which made the separation seem necessary to Dorothea. More probably the explanation lies in her own character. She hated half measures, untidy loose ends and relationships which could neither grow into real intimacy nor wither away to formal acquaintanceship. Her loyalty was strong and lasting but so also was her power of hatred and she had grown to hate her husband as she would have hated anyone with whom she was formally bound to maintain an appearance of intimacy yet whom she could not love. " Fire and water mix better together than Monsieur and Madame de Dino," she was to write bitterly to Vitrolles a year or two later. And she could not bring herself to maintain the formal pretence that fire and water could mingle happily when she knew that her whole marriage was a silent lie.

This would still not explain why Dorothea suffered several years of *de facto* separation before she decided to vest it with legal forms. Perhaps she felt that a few years must be allowed to pass between the birth of Pauline and her final separation from her husband. Certainly so much scandal already surrounded the birth of her youngest child that Dorothea could well be forgiven for putting expediency before principle and accepting the unreality of her marriage for a little while longer. It is that the separation came at all which is most remarkable, not that it came so late.

*   *   *   *   *

Dorothea in 1824 again set off on her travels without Prince Talleyrand. In June she arrived at Schloss Johannisberg to visit Metternich and regale him with accounts of the decadence of Parisian society and, in particular, the iniquities of Villèle, champion of the extreme royalists and at the moment head of the Government :

" The Duchess of Dino came to visit me from the other side of the Rhine," wrote Metternich. " She stayed with me for a whole day. She knows Paris from top to bottom : which is why I was so pleased to see her . . . Dorothea tells me that it is quite impossible to conceive the depths of degradation to which men at Paris have sunk wherever money is concerned."

Metternich had no love for the French Government of the day and must have relished this chance to establish contact with the opposition under cover of a friendly visit. Though he was careful not to obtrude too far into the foreground, Talleyrand was actively at work to frustrate and if possible put an end to the rule of Villèle. Dorothea both encouraged and abetted him. She was in fact a most valuable ally ; both because she could express opinions and criticise the Government with a freedom which the old prince would have felt imprudent in himself and because of the influence which her charm, beauty and intelligence allowed her to exercise over many men of high position but uncertain will.

Indeed, while actually staying with Metternich, she received news of a notable victory. Talleyrand was particularly anxious to secure the defeat of a financial measure for which Villèle was pressing. Voting in the upper chamber was likely to be close. The bill could probably be defeated if only Hyacinth Louis, Count Quelen, Archbishop of Paris, could be induced to throw his weight against it. This self-satisfied priest, whose ability was bound by limits his ambition was never to recognise, was a devoted royalist but had little love for Villèle and his Government. It seemed not impossible that he might be subverted to the opposition. Dorothea addressed herself to the task. ". . . At a moment when her heart was not otherwise engaged ; " wrote the Countess de Boigne a few years later, " impelled by boredom, idleness and perhaps a touch of malice, Madame de Dino entertained herself by turning the head of the archbishop. He fell passionately in love with her." " Passionately in love " is probably an over-coloured version of Quelen's satisfied vanity at finding himself the object of Dorothea's attentions and certainly the latter's motives were more practical than Madame de Boigne believed. Quelen, anyhow, responded as hoped. At Johannisberg the news came that he had spoken against the measure and that the Government had been defeated. " According to her, it is impossible to say in advance what effect his defeat over this bill will have on Villèle," wrote Metternich. " She has exactly the same opinion of him as me, though she knows very much more about him."

From Johannisberg, Dorothea went on to Switzerland. There she found herself staying in the same village as the Duchess of Broglie ; witty, intelligent, beautiful and a true daughter of Madame de Staël. Albertine de Broglie had put this last attribute beyond doubt when, at the age of eleven, she was asked why she was crying : " Alas," she replied resonantly " they think I am happy and yet there are bottomless gulfs in my heart." With womanhood her penchant for the dramatic had been curbed by an ironic humour. She was one of the few women in France for whom Dorothea felt affection and a certain respect. On this occasion she greeted Dorothea with genuine pleasure but still reported delightedly to their mutual friend Prosper de Barante that she had met Dorothea wandering in the meadows at six in the morning in a long silk dress and all her pearls[7].

Dorothea does not seem to have enjoyed Switzerland much. She found it " flooded with English who go everywhere without looking at anything ; make too much noise and spend too little money ; haggle over everything, even the view, and are perfectly intolerable to meet." The men who were supposed to make up the party had failed to turn up and she found herself isolated in a long drawn-out *tête-à-tête* with the Duchess of Ragusa, the jolly, unintelligent wife of Marshal Marmont. Dorothea rarely derived much satisfaction from feminine company, the chatter of this particular companion soon exhausted her patience and made her unusually glad to be in Paris once more.

Back in the capital she found Villèle still in office but Louis XVIII on his deathbed. The King had always been personally affable but had never distinguished himself by any real kindness or—more damning by far—done anything to help her uncle back to power. Dorothea was no doubt disturbed by the appalling details of his death in putrefaction which were whispered around the salons of Paris but what must have been far more interesting to her was the probable policy of the new King Charles X.

There was not much in the record of the former Count of Artois to suggest that he would offer any particular favour to Prince Talleyrand. In the past, indeed, the two had had several brushes and found themselves in the sharpest opposition. But at first Charles X seemed intent on living down everything for which the Duke of Artois had stood ; the censorship of the Press was abandoned and liberal ideas were all the mode. It did not last. A little discouragement was quite enough to damp the new king's frail, reforming ardour and Talleyrand's hopes of office vanished before they had even been more than a distant mirage. Discontentedly, Dorothea settled down for another period of opposition and intrigue ; waiting, always waiting for a return to the realities of power which she had once tasted but which now seemed to recede ever further into an uncertain future.

*   *   *   *   *

For several years Dorothea had been thinking that it would be pleasant to have a country home of her own. She had grown fond of Valençay but it was still her uncle's house and life there persisted in a stiff and immutable ritual which she herself had not dictated. She wanted a home where she could create or destroy as she thought fit and where life would follow the pattern of her own desires. Some time in 1825 she completed arrangements for the purchase of the chateau of Rochecotte in the department of Indre-et-Loire, some say as a gift from Talleyrand but more probably out of her own fortune. For the next twenty years until she handed it on to her daughter Pauline it was to be her favourite home. She found constant and undiluted pleasure in its improvement and, even through her long absences, she never forgot her concern for its development and for the welfare of the dependants who lived around it.

Though much of its contents have been dispersed, Rochecotte

still stands to-day substantially as Dorothea de Dino last saw it. The same great trees shade its lawns and windows, the same terraces cascade precipitously down towards the Loire, the same atmosphere of calm, dignity and repose hangs around its heavily creepered walls. It lies on the right bank of the Loire, a few miles below the massive fortified castle at Langeais and almost opposite the huge and eccentric chateau of Ussé. In fact a large house by any standard—large enough anyway to shelter Talleyrand, Dorothea and a score of guests—it seems small and self-effacing compared with these grandiloquent neighbours. This lack of pretension is as evident inside as out ; the rooms are small and the emphasis is on comfort and intimacy rather than formal grandeur.

The construction of the château is as original as its air is modest. The original owner, the Marquis de Rochecotte, wished to dominate the river without being exposed to the winds at the top of the steep slope. The house therefore tumbles haphazardly from level to level ; the ground floor at one point re-emerges as a second storey at another ; terraces and roof gardens jut out unexpectedly and add the pleasures of a Rajput palace to the grace of an Italian palazzo. Dorothea no sooner acquired it than she set to work to enlarge and improve. With the help of the architect Vestier she put in train the building of a new wing and the hollowing out of a chain of rooms under the existing terrace. Impatiently she supervised the work herself ; never content with its progress or satisfied that the plans were being carried out according to her ideas, yet with it all entirely happy in her occupation.

" Yes, certainly, I have a true passion for Rochecotte," she wrote to Barante two or three years later. " First, because it is mine. Second, because it has the most beautiful view over the most beautiful countryside in the world. Lastly, because it has an air in which one can live without cares. And then, what is more, I am always arranging, adapting, beautifying and adding to my property. To chase the moles out of my vegetable garden and to stock my woods with rabbits : doesn't it seem to you that that is worth a lot of trouble ? I have taken whole-heartedly to country life."

So far as Talleyrand was concerned, their life was full enough already; what with Valençay, the Rue St. Florentin and their summer travels. But as soon as the house was well established he went there to visit Dorothea and was immediately pleased by what he found. Soon he was to feel as much at home at Rochecotte even as at Valençay. His own rooms were reserved for him, his wishes scrupulously deferred to ; he found there an informality and ease which his great palace in Berry could never match and profited by it to consort with people with whom he would have felt vaguely out of sympathy amidst the traditional splendours of Valençay. Besides, it was Dorothea's own home. It gave her pleasure to welcome him there and he, in turn, found pleasure in her satisfaction.

It would be profitless to spell out the course of these years in any detail. For Dorothea, despite the many diversions which she contrived to pass the time, they were essentially years of service. She had dedicated herself to the task of helping in her uncle's quest for power and consoling him so far as she was able when power remained obstinately out of reach, of ministering to his health and acting as a buffer between him and those who sought to hurt or damage him. It was no easy work. Talleyrand was a sadly disappointed man. He was now more than seventy years old and felt himself still at the height of his powers. But he did not delude himself that this could last much longer. A little more delay and his chance would be gone for ever. He was tired, fretful and impatient and as he dragged his ailing body from Paris to Grenoble, Grenoble to Marseilles, Marseilles to Hyères, Hyères to Nice, always in fruitless search of some magic formula to restore his failing strength, Dorothea must have wondered from time to time whether her service would never end.

She stayed with her uncle because she loved and esteemed him, not because she saw his patronage as a short cut to the thrones of power. And yet how much she longed for him to return to office. Everything seemed to have gone wrong with her life. Intensely ambitious, she saw the man to whom she had pinned her destiny repeatedly passed over and with no apparent prospects for the future. Capable of deep and passionate love she saw her marriage in ruins and such poor affairs as she could contrive occupying only a corner of her heart. If she had been able to return to Germany she might perhaps have built her life anew, but she had already ruled out any idea of deserting Talleyrand when he stood in such need of her and she was not one to change her mind on such an issue.

To cap it all, Dorothea was often ill over these years and never rose far above a trough of mediocre health. In part this was a cause of her discontent, in part, no doubt, a result, for with Dorothea physical well-being could rarely come except with happiness. In particular she was beginning to suffer from violent attacks of rheumatism. Talleyrand insisted that she accompany him to his estate at Pont-de-Sains in the north of France, saying that the calm and solitude would do her good. So they might have, but the house was set in thick forest and perched on the edge of a lake. Cold and damp more than redressed the balance and her rheumatism, not surprisingly, grew no better.

In June of 1826 she decided that something drastic must be done to end the torture. Sea-bathing was at this time the prescribed cure and Dorothea screwed up her courage to undergo the ordeal. " I am undertaking this trip to Dieppe with the keenest repugnance," she wrote to Vitrolles, " and I would never have decided to go if I did not think it essential. Certainly I won't know anyone there and I have heard that the countryside is the ugliest in the world." In fact, since the Duchess of Berry had started to go there two years before, Dieppe had become almost excessively fashionable and Dorothea was more likely to suffer from a surfeit of acquaintance than a lack of it. Talleyrand was greatly encouraged by his niece's resolution and considered the victory already half won. " Madame de Dino has decided to get well," he wrote, " and that is a lot already, for in her case the will can do great things." Faith, however, could do no good if the sea-water was not available to supplement it. For the first few days the weather made bathing impossible and poor Dorothea had no recourse but to look forlornly at the ugliest countryside in the world and brood over the martyrdom which was in store for her. Then, when the storm died down, the real suffering began. She wrote to Vitrolles describing the ordeal which she was undergoing.

" Have you ever seen a woman bathing in the sea ? I got
the strangest impression of it from watching others at it.
They seem to be delivered over helpless to large and ill-
disposed men who duck them, shake them, turn them upside
down and push them in every direction. At any moment
they may be left to sink to the bottom of the cold, grey
ocean—so much less tempting than our own Mediterranean.
My maid, while she undressed me, commended my soul to
heaven and all the saints. At last I was dressed in huge
pantaloons and a little blue woollen blouse and my hair done
up in a cap. One of the men seized me under the arms,
carried me bodily into the sea and then, holding on at the
most to the end of a finger, abandoned me to the waves.
When he had had enough (for I had no control at all over
the proceedings) he took me under the arms and bounced
me up and down as if I had been a baby. Finally, when he
had exhausted all his tricks, he carried me back to my little
tent and told me I was a brave child not to have cried ; for
nearly all women did the first time they bathed."

To have her first bathe behind her did nothing to reconcile
Dorothea to her surroundings. " The town is ugly, the
countryside sterile, the sea saddens all and ennobles nothing."
And to cap it all her rheumatism remained uncured. " Madame
de Dino *suspects* that she is a little better," wrote Talleyrand[11],
but the suspicion was never confirmed and Dorothea left
Dieppe convinced that the ordeal had been in vain.

*   *   *   *   *

Perversely she began to feel better as soon as she arrived at
Valençay. There Dorothea was never at a loss for something
to do and knew that what she was doing was of real value to
her neighbours. The life she led seemed real and substantial
after the artifices of the city : " Here there is no romanticism,
no mysticism, no ill-defined impressions or anything like them,
no shadow of politics. We had good-will, hospitality, practical
employment of our time ; a well-being which, while lofty in
origin, is still most simple. I believe that it is at Valençay that

Monsieur de Talleyrand and I appear at our best." And with all this the countryside was some of the most beautiful in France, the life healthy and energetic. One day she hunted stags for eight hours in the rain and returned to the house drenched, exhausted and astonished at her own contentment. Her capacity to derive pleasure from simple things always came as a slight surprise to Dorothea. At such moments she was apt to wonder whether she was not making her life unnecessarily complicated and it often called for a concentrated exercise of will before she could think herself back into the atmosphere of distinguished melancholy in which she usually felt herself at home.

There were many visitors to Valençay that summer; among them Royer Collard, Piscatory her rumoured lover and the Marquis of Montrond. Casimir Montrond had been among Talleyrand's closest friends and business associates since the days of the Directory. *Le beau Montrond* was handsome, witty, dashing and with a gratifying reputation for wickedness. Although unscrupulous and totally untrustworthy, he seems to have had nothing really discreditable against him, save perhaps that of fathering that brutish millionaire, Lord Henry Seymour. Dorothea disliked and disapproved of him from the start. Her occasionally rather prudish rectitude made it certain that his flamboyant lack of principle would offend, but even more she resented his influence over her uncle. This was not just a matter of petty jealousy and a wish to keep Talleyrand to herself; she welcomed, for instance, the attention which Talleyrand always paid to the opinions of Royer Collard and went out of her way to cement the friendship between the two men. But Montrond seemed to her to appeal to all that was basest in Talleyrand's character; he was a relic of a period of her uncle's life in which she did not share and with which she could not sympathise; from the first he was identified as an unhealthy influence which had to be contested. For the time being Montrond and Dorothea lived in a state of uneasy neutrality but long before Talleyrand's death it was to mature into open war.

Dorothea's sense of frustration and emptiness was mitigated to some extent by the attention she gave her children. It cannot

M

be said, however, that they took up a very considerable part of her time or energies. Not that she was a cold or unfeeling parent but, in the great French families of the nineteenth century, there was little room for children and only in the most exceptional cases did parents play any significant part in the education and upbringing of their family. " With the departure of my children," wrote Dorothea to Barante from Valençay, " our huge and silent home . . . has lost the gaiety and movement which their games and sense of freedom spread around us." The regret was genuine and when her children were actually in front of her she took a keen and loving interest in their development. But intercourse normally was through a blanket of governesses and tutors and, even if mother and children chanced to be in the same house together, they probably lived in separate wings and only met by appointment.

Napoleon-Louis—the Napoleon long discreetly forgotten— was now fifteen years old. A plain, rather uninteresting little boy, he was studying at the Lycée Henri IV in Paris and making up in application and assiduity for what he lacked in inspiration. He was friendly, timid, docile, anxious to please ; never likely to do anything very wrong yet still less likely to achieve the conspicuously right. Dorothea loved him but in rather a perfunctory manner : probably she would have cared much more if he had sometimes given her cause for worry.

Alexander, her second son and two years younger than Louis, was as erratic as Louis was stable, as hot-tempered as his brother was placid ; intelligent, sensitive, quick to love and to hate, capable of sharp malice and with a streak of stubborn perverseness inherited from his father. " A very strange yet perfect little fiend," Dorothea described him and with all his faults she found him far more interesting than the virtuous Louis. He had early made up his mind that he wanted to be a sailor and it was decided that he should go to the Naval College at Angoulème. As was usual with him when he had set his heart on something, Alexander passed his entrance examination with ease and even distinction. The contrast between the two brothers was never more clearly shown than in their respective reactions to leaving home. Where Louis had accepted separation with equanimity even though he had no particular love for his school, Alexander was feverishly anxious to be started on his new life, yet overwhelmed with grief at the prospect of losing his mother and his home. Dorothea too was dismayed at the parting, but proud of her son's talents and convinced that in him was a future admiral and perhaps ruler of France.

Pauline, her youngest child by seven years and for that reason especially dear, showed already the gentleness and sweetness coupled with implacable determination which were to be the features of her character. At the age of six, however, she was too childish to be really interesting to Dorothea. It was her great-uncle, Prince Talleyrand, who most obviously doted on her; an affection which, even at that age, she most energetically reciprocated.

*   *   *   *   *

Life rolled on along its unsatisfactory course. In November Talleyrand and Dorothea returned to Paris but Dorothea stayed only to be in town for the admission of Royer Collard to the Academy. Then she retreated to her rabbits and vegetable garden at Rochecotte where she was to remain secluded for the winter and indeed, except for four brief visits to the waters at Néris and to Valençay, for the whole of 1827 and 1828.

" Yes, I shall stay here for as long as my duties towards Monsieur de Talleyrand allow me," she wrote to Barante. " If it were not for the excellent reason of being with him I would never emerge at all from my retreat. Probably by my own fault, there is now so deep a gulf between the world and me that we have become for ever strangers : it tires me, bores me, troubles my spirits and damages my health . . . I don't ask for the approval of the world any more than I fear its blame ; all I ask of it is that I should be forgotten."

The gossips of the day saw in Dorothea's seclusion fresh reason to suspect some hidden scandal in her life. Piscatory had a house not very far away in the neighbourhood of Chinon and Countess de Boigne for one referred archly to " personal relationships " which made the stays in Touraine of the Duchess of Dino very agreeable for her. In fact, she seems to have remained at Rochecotte mainly because she found it peaceful and agreeable, with the usual complex of subsidiary motives including dislike of Paris, disappointment at Talleyrand's perpetual exile from office and continued ill-health. Though in fact as well as most people, she lived in the conviction of her extreme frailty, both mental and physical, and husbanded what she believed to be her meagre resources against some quite unspecified threat.

" I have imposed on myself a strict moral discipline so that my health may be restored : that is to permit no looking back, no theorising, no meditation ; to live only with the most positive interests and, so as not to let myself become a complete imbecile, to rely on the wisdom of others as it appears in their books and not to put my own intelligence to any strain . . . The system seems to work well enough . . . "

Dorothea was not to be allowed to linger indefinitely in her rustic sanctuary. In the summer of 1828 Louis had passed his final examinations with considerable distinction. It was decided to send him to Italy to complete his education. Baron Vitrolles, whose political career had never really recovered from its set-back of ten years before, had recently been sent to Florence as Minister. Dorothea saw in his presence in Italy a chance to ensure that her son—aged only seventeen and young for his years—would not misspend his time. She never hesitated to make use of her friends—to be fair to her there was nothing she would not do herself for those she was fond of—and she now wrote to Vitrolles charging him with Louis' physical and moral welfare.

Vitrolles awaited the visit of a schoolboy ; yet when Louis arrived in Florence it was to find a letter from his mother summoning him to return at once to Paris to get ready for his marriage to Mademoiselle Alix de Montmorency. To Vitrolles Dorothea admitted that she herself was dumbfounded by the message she was sending : " She is the great match of the season and Monsieur de Talleyrand did not wish to let it escape from Louis whom he intends to vest with a magnificent fortune. His generosity, the charms and other recommendations of the girl, the great age of Monsieur de Talleyrand and the gentleness, calm and self-possession of my son, all helped to overcome my natural reluctance to marry off my son at the age of eighteen. One must hope that everything will turn out for the best. At least no one can say that I have neglected the interests of my children . . ."

The interests of Louis, in financial and social terms, she certainly had not neglected but it is all the same difficult to excuse Dorothea entirely for her part in this marriage or rather for her failure to play any part except that of acquiescence in the wishes of her uncle. With the memory of her own forced and unhappy marriage behind her, it is surprising to say the least that she should have pushed her immature seventeen-year-old son into marriage with a girl whom there is no reason to believe he had ever met, let alone expressed any love or even liking for. It is still more surprising if one considers that, when Pauline married ten years later, Dorothea was insistent that the choice of husband should be entirely her daughter's and that she should only marry a man whom she knew she could love.

There are probably several reasons for this apparent inconsistency. For one thing, Louis was to be heir of a great name and a great fortune yet his social position was far from secure. Dorothea, who knew herself in part responsible for this, felt that the damage must be repaired if Louis were ever to enjoy his proper position in life. The chance to marry him to a member of the great family of Montmorency and a rich Montmorency at that, might never recur. In accepting the match she was in a sense expiating her own social mis-demeanours. And then, as she told Vitrolles, there was Talleyrand's great age. He might not live for long and it was his dearest wish to see Louis well married and the dynasty secure. And finally, there was perhaps some feeling in Dorothea that it did not much matter who a man might marry. For a girl, an unhappy marriage could ruin a life ; for a man, she may have thought, so little was demanded in the way of fidelity or even formal good behaviour that he could get along quite happily even though his wife proved totally unsuitable. Louis would probably be able to establish a satisfactory relationship with Alix de Montmorency—" one must hope that everything will turn out for the best "—and, if he failed, then it would not be too difficult for him to find consolation elsewhere.

Louis accepted his wife with the same placid acquiescence as he had accepted the visit to Italy and as he would have accepted any other proposal which others told him was necessary for his happiness or education. The inducements to fall in with his mother's plans were certainly considerable. At Talleyrand's request, Charles X created the young man Duke of Valençay. Subject to a usufruct reserved to himself for life, Talleyrand passed on to the new duke the chateau of Valençay and all the dependent estates. Certainly they were tied up in such a way as to prevent Louis dissipating the whole fortune but the gift was still a princely one. Finally, since Dorothea felt every young husband should have something in the way of a career, Louis was attached to the Ministry of Foreign Affairs in a capacity which gave him a daily task if he felt so inclined without taxing too severely his time or talents. " My son seems happy," reported Dorothea, and on the whole he had reason ; he had found financial independence long before he could have hoped for it and it had probably never occurred to him that he might be able to marry for love.

In January, 1825 a series of glittering parties were given in the Rue St. Florentin to celebrate the coming marriage. The ceremony itself took place on 26th February. Dorothea was hectically involved in all the preparations ; after the wedding she wrote to Barante that she had just completed " the two most stupid months that I have spent since the time I had to pay calls for my own marriage." The sentimental always bored or sickened Dorothea. She went through all the social rituals with perfect grace and decorum—to have done otherwise would have been to defeat the object of the whole exercise—but she was not going to tell her friends that she did not find it wearisome and a waste of time.

Alix de Montmorency was attractive and highly self-possessed. A few months older than Louis, she was many times as mature and worldly wise. Before her marriage she had had something of an affair with Count Rudolph Apponyi ; man about town and cousin of the Austrian Ambassador. Apponyi had hoped to catch Alix for himself and bore the Duchess of

Dino a grudge for her intervention. He describes how, at a party given shortly after the wedding, the young Duke of Valençay " who suspected nothing, told me that his wife had often spoken of me and that he was exceedingly anxious to be counted among my friends. Both the Dinos . . . kept at a respectful distance of each other. They both told me, with a somewhat distracted air, that they were pleased to have Alix for a daughter-in-law."

" I now see a lot of the little Duke of Valençay," he wrote a few months later. " He is an excellent young man and so values my friendship that it would be ungrateful to refuse it. He is only eighteen years old ; we laugh a lot together about his respectable title of husband . . . He tells me many amusing stories about his *début* in his new life and, when he speaks to me of his wife, often refers to her as Mademoiselle Alix."

Finally Apponyi indulges in a little spite towards the duchess who had robbed him of his prey. " What a woman Madame de Dino is ! Certainly she had the least heart of the daughters of the Duchess of Courland, even though she was the dearest to her mother. For myself, I infinitely prefer the Duchess of Sagan. I must mention something which the Dino said about her son at one of our dinners. As I had been sitting next to the Duke of Valençay at table it was natural that after dinner I should go over to his mother to say something agreeable about him. ' Yes,' she replied, ' He is a good boy. He knows when to keep quiet.' This answer chilled me, especially as little Valençay is always going out of his way to show his love for his mother." It did not occur to Count Apponyi that Dorothea's remark could possibly have been directed at other, not quite so young men who were too self-satisfied to imagine that their views on everything were not invariably welcome.

Talleyrand's prudence in so tying up his fortune that Louis de Valençay could not have free access to it was soon made evident. For Edmond was again in trouble. His appearance at his son's marriage almost constituted a good-bye to Paris. In 1828 he had been retired from the army and thus became free to concentrate entirely on the gambling tables. In spite of the handsome income which Dorothea allowed him he soon ran deeply into debt and by 1829 his position in Paris had become untenable. To evade his creditors he left for London.

In England he seems somehow to have negotiated a loan for three hundred thousand francs and promptly lost sixty thousand of it in a night's gambling. Soon he was hopelessly in debt again and this time jailed. The French Ambassador, the Duke of Laval, was naturally embarrassed to have so high-born a French nobleman imprisoned in his bailiwick. According to Princess Lieven, everyone including Lord Aberdeen, the Foreign Secretary of the day, urged him to declare that Edmond was a member of his Embassy and thus get him released on grounds of immunity. Typically, the Duke of Wellington alone stood out against the idea and said that, in such circumstances, he would rather pay himself. Laval agreed and, though far from rich, found the money to secure Edmond's release. Eventually the English debts seem to have been repaid out of Dorothea's pocket.

From London, Edmond continued his rake's progress to Brussels, promptly fell into debt again and was once more imprisoned. Louis de Valençay went to see him there and would certainly have paid his father's debts if he had had free access to his fortune. Apponyi in his memoirs enlarges on the shabbiness of Dorothea and Talleyrand in thus preventing a son from helping his father but it is hard to wonder that their generosity was exhausted. Finally a settlement was arrived at on the condition that Edmond settled at Florence. There it was felt that even he could not get very deeply into debt. He remained in exile for the rest of his life ; out of sight at least if not entirely out of mind and little missed by those who should have had most cause to regret his absence.

*   *   *   *   *

Dorothea's return to public life was made so as to marry off her son, she remained because at last there was life again in the political arena and work for her to do. Charles X, in Professor Brogan's phrase[10], was moving with the confidence of a sleep-walker and moving inexorably towards disaster. Villèle had been replaced by Martignac, who made some minor concessions to the liberals but ended by offending both the left and the extreme right and in losing the confidence of the king. He resigned, and in August of 1829 Charles X plucked from the embassy in London and placed in office his old friend Prince Jules de Polignac ; fanatical in all things and above all in defence of the divine right of his master. It was a declaration of war on the liberals or, at least, was interpreted as such by everyone less extremist than the ministers themselves.

For years Talleyrand had been biding his time. Now he scented that the moment had almost come and that the régime would shortly have to be swept away or drastically modified if the peace of France were to be preserved. He needed urgently to know all that was going on and to be fully in the counsels of those who were plotting revolution. He knew that his own wisdom and experience would be invaluable assets to the liberal cause and he was anxious that the liberals should avail themselves of it. Even more, he needed to prepare the way for his own return to office if the liberals were triumphant. And yet, with all this, he had too much at stake to risk provoking the Polignac Government into any action against him. In all the subtle manœuvring which these needs entailed, Dorothea de Dino was to play a leading part.

Of all the men of the July Revolution whom Dorothea knew and encouraged, it was a young journalist from Marseilles called Adolphe Thiers with whom she worked most closely. The friendship between these two is as improbable as it is creditable to them both, for Thiers would seem to have been everything which Dorothea most disliked.

A few years later Dorothea wrote from the embassy in London, " Three gentlemen from Arras have been dining with us. They belong to the French middle classes and are very proud of the fact. One of the three was a little man of seventeen who is . . . already as talkative and positive as could be wished. He gives every promise of one day bellowing most conspicuously in the chamber."

Adolphe Thiers was the prototype of all the little gentlemen from Arras for whom Dorothea felt so much disdain. By birth, indeed, he was barely even of the middle classes. The illegitimate son of a small business-man from Marseilles, he achieved first legitimacy, then bourgeois respectability, finally by the time Dorothea got to know him, even a touch of dandyhood. Of bursting energy, voluble, impetuous, ambitious, self-confident to the point of arrogance, he quickly made his name as a journalist in Paris. Talleyrand first met him in the drawing-room of the liberal banker Laffitte, was amused by his presumption and appreciative of his intelligence and forcefulness. " An urchin of genius," he described him, and mentally marked him down as a useful instrument to be made use of in a campaign against the Government and the Bourbons.

Dorothea took longer to warm to him and he was still little more than an acquaintance when the Polignac Government came to power. Even then she had not much love for his radical theories and bourgeois instincts and only the coincidence that both were in opposition made possible their unnatural alliance. Once allied, however, they quickly became genuinely fond of each other and there is a note of something near flirtation in their correspondence. Accustomed to the restrained, almost languid attitude of her circle, the explosive enthusiasm and vigour of Thiers came to Dorothea as a new and disconcerting experience. After some hesitation and once she had savoured the real talent which lay behind, she decided that she liked it.

" The life of Rochecotte," wrote the Countess de Boigne, " was not agreeable to Talleyrand. The new intimacies of the Duchess of Dino had peopled it with a mass of young literary figures who claimed already that importance which youth has attributed to itself since 1830. Towards Monsieur de Talleyrand they lacked that deference which would have seemed proper to anyone with more knowledge of how to behave.

" He began by suffering under this treatment. However, as his health came back so his energies returned and he decided to make use of these young talents which thought that they could dominate him. Ambition awoke again in him and he had no difficulty in picking out Thiers and settling to work to exploit him."

The concept of Dorothea thrusting a reluctant Talleyrand into contact with young, liberal society is, of course, absurd. She was highly suspicious of their methods and motives and would never have got to know Thiers at all except for her uncle's recommendation. But Dorothea had a mind of her own. She was far more likely to make it up on the basis of personal friendships than of abstract political principles but she was as capable as anyone of understanding the principles and rejecting those which seemed to her unacceptable. She gave all the help and encouragement she could to Thiers because it suited her uncle's plans—certainly—but also because he had by then become her friend and she had convinced herself that what he was trying to do was in the interests of France and of society in general.

Dorothea would never have made a revolutionary. Her ideas were too settled and moderate for that. The Duke of Broglie noted her anxiety lest Talleyrand compromise himself by dining in the same house as Lafayette. " She would like to make popular revolutions by means of crêpe dresses and silver turbans," he noted in his journal the following day, " to stir the masses by witty sayings and to upset society without interfering with her soirées."

The criticism was just. Politics was something of a game for Dorothea, a game in which she liked the players on one side and disliked them on the other. But she had taken the trouble to master the rules and she played it with enthusiasm and authority.

* * * * *

In December, 1829, Thiers arrived at Rochecotte. With him came his fellow Provençal, François Mignet and, perhaps the most brilliant of the three, Armand Carrel who was to die in a duel seven years later. General Donnadieu, the army commander at Tours who was under instructions to keep a watchful eye on the doings at Rochecotte, was not unnaturally alarmed at this gathering of the dissidents and reported it to Paris. No action was taken but the general had good reason to be disturbed. What was being discussed was the foundation of the *National*, a newspaper which was to contribute much to the atmosphere of discontent and unrest which made possible the downfall of the Bourbons.

" Messieurs Thiers, Mignet, Stapfer—the translator of Goethe—and Carrel have founded the *National*," wrote

Stendhal to an English friend early in 1830. " They have put all they have into it and Monsieur de Talleyrand has found the rest. The beautiful eyes of the Duchess of Dino inspire Monsieur Thiers . . . Old Talleyrand has said in public that he recalled the Bourbons so as to have peace, now it is necessary to drive them out again so as to have tranquillity."

Dorothea played a larger part in this than that of the society hostess whose beautiful eyes inspired the rebels, whose house sheltered them and whose rich uncle provided the necessary funds. Dorothea was a clever woman, she knew the personalities of the Government and royal family far better than Thiers and his friends could ever hope to do, her long association with her uncle had taught her political wisdom and an appreciation of the realities of power. Now she enthusiastically put her experience, her energy and her intelligence at the disposal of her guests.

In Paris, too, Dorothea continued to do all she could for the liberal cause. The Rue St. Florentin became the centre of the opposition ; not the apartments of the prince, which might have seemed too directly compromising, but in the part of the house reserved for Dorothea. There Talleyrand could make what friends and allies he chose while assuring himself that he was at least not talking treason in his own home.

For Dorothea her new activities had one sad consequence. Little though the Bourbons had done to make Vitrolles grateful to them, this loyal and simple man still gave them his complete allegiance. Knowing this, Dorothea had told him nothing of her liberal ideas and friendships. In her letters she had, indeed, been disingenuous to the point of deceit. " Politics do not interest me any more," she wrote to him in July of 1829. " I won't say anything about politics for I spend no time on them at all," in September.

But in October of the same year Vitrolles came home. One of his first visits was naturally to the Rue St. Florentin where he was astonished to find so many unknown faces. He asked Pasquier for the explanation. The names of the guests gave him his answer. Disillusioned, he left the house. He was too whole-hearted to be able to keep his friends if he disapproved of their activities and he knew that he could never accept the existence of treason against the Crown.

On 2nd December, Dorothea wrote to him from Rochecotte reproaching him with not having come more often to visit her. She can hardly have expected that the invitation would be accepted. Though she may have done her best to deceive herself, she knew that an intimacy which had lasted nearly all her life was ended. It must have distressed her to inflict yet another wound on this unfortunate man who sought only to help her. But her first loyalty was to her uncle and she had convinced herself that the future of Prince Talleyrand, not to mention that of France, depended on the overthrow of the régime. In the face of this, sentiment could count for nothing. If Vitrolles could not accept her politics, then he must be allowed to go his way.

8

When the July Revolution broke over a Paris long racked by anxiety, Dorothea was living quietly at Rochecotte. For three tormented days she waited for news ; her house " ringed around with violence and fire," as she dramatically described it in later years though in fact there seem to have been only the most trivial disturbances in that part of Touraine.

For all she knew, anything might have happened in Paris. The Bourbons might have quelled the rising, in which case her uncle's liberty, perhaps even his life would be in danger. Even worse, the extreme left might have got out of control and 29th July become a second 14th July. In that case nobody would be safe. At last a messenger arrived bringing with him news so good that it could scarcely be believed. Charles X, last King of France, had fled the country. Louis-Philippe, Duke of Orleans, first King of the French had been called to take his place. The July Revolution was over. The July Monarchy had begun. For Dorothea it was a moment of the most pure pleasure ; pleasure for herself, but even more pleasure in the triumph of her friends and of her uncle. " You know how I have always loved the Palais Royal and hated the Tuileries," she wrote to Barante. Now the Palais Royal had triumphed and the forces of evil—that is to say, the forces which had failed to return her uncle to office—had been vanquished.

On 1st September, Dorothea arrived in Paris to pay her respects to the new monarch. She found her uncle in a state of unusual hesitation. The fruits of victory were his but he could not decide which one he ought to pluck. The new king had no such doubts. Alone among the foreign ambassadors in Paris, Lord Stuart de Rothesay had shown himself a champion of the new régime. Alone among the foreign Governments

London had provided a somewhat grudging acceptance of the Orleanist dynasty. France still lived in the shadow of 1814 and the king was satisfied that the stability of his Government would depend on its acceptance by the rest of Europe. Equally, he believed, the acceptance of the rest of Europe would surely follow if first he could win the full support of England. And who was better qualified to do so than the wisest and most experienced of French statesmen, the old friend of the Duke of Wellington, the perennial champion of the English alliance, Charles-Maurice, Prince Talleyrand. It was made clear to the prince that the appointment was his if he would take it and that it was the urgent desire of the king that he should do so. But Talleyrand could not make up his mind. His memories of London were not entirely happy. He was seventy-six, old to be setting out on his travels again. He knew that he could have the pick of all the jobs available. Perhaps some post at home would be better. Secretly he may even have had hankerings to head another ministry in Paris.

Dorothea had made up her mind. She had had enough of life in France with all its social uneasiness and unsatisfying minor love-affairs. She longed to get back on to the stage of international politics. This was the world which she really understood and enjoyed and in which she knew she shone. Above all, she was convinced that this was the right job for her uncle ; that in no other capacity could he do work for which he was so well qualified and which would give him so much satisfaction. Certainly the appointment to London would suit her own requirements very well, but it was the belief that it would contribute most towards the happiness of Prince Talleyrand which led her to throw all her powers into persuading him to accept. The wishes of his king, the urging of his niece, and his own sense of duty were too much for Talleyrand. He accepted the appointment as Ambassador to the Court of St. James. On 24th September he disembarked at Dover. A week later Dorothea followed him.

* * * * *

The England of 1830 was conspicuously in transition. George IV had died in June, succeeded by his bluff, stupid, but essentially good-hearted brother. William IV was popularly credited with liberal ideas. Few people would now claim that he had a single idea in his head, liberal or reactionary, but at least he seemed unlikely to pose much of an obstacle to reform. And the clamour for reform was growing every day more urgent. Tory rule, which had lasted for virtually sixty years without a break, was dying on its feet. The general election which followed the death of George IV had cost the Government fifty seats. The Duke of Wellington might still have purchased a little time by conceding something to the champions of parliamentary reform but he was too proud to swim with a tide of which he deeply disapproved. " I am not only not prepared to bring forward any measure of this nature but, so far as I am concerned, so long as I hold any station in the Government of the country, I shall feel it my duty to resist such measures when proposed by others." When Dorothea landed in Dover it was already clear that this slogan was to be the epitaph of the old Tory party.

Yet, though the reign of the middle classes had already dawned, the England which Dorothea was to see was still strikingly reminiscent of the England of the eighteenth century. It was above all a country which, so far as she could judge, was still effectively controlled by the hereditary aristocracy, an oligarchy whose vast estates and princely fortunes would have stood comparison with those of any age or any empire. It was a country in which the Duke of Devonshire's annual income was conservatively estimated at £440,000 and where Mr. Lambton jogged along on a mere £40,000 a year. It was an England where the reformers seemed as well-born and as rich as the reactionaries, so that Lord Grey could boast that his own Cabinet surpassed all previous records in the acreage owned by its members. It was an England in which the foreigner could be forgiven for imagining that all the legislation in the world could make no difference to the immutable hierarchy of wealth and power. Only the closest examination and understanding could reveal that not only was the hierarchy itself in the process of being dismantled but that even within its framework there was a constant renovation and amendment which made our seemingly rigid aristocracy the most flexible in Europe.

Certainly Dorothea saw little evidence of flexibility and quickly formed the conclusion that only an earthquake could upset the social order ; an earthquake which would utterly destroy the whole existing pattern of English life. In spite of her own great wealth and pride of ancestry she was startled by what seemed to her the improperly great disparity between rich and poor and the apparently unbridgeable social gulfs between the various classes. " When I see to what heights of power and glory London has risen, I ask myself if it can ever change ; it is only when I am revolted by excesses of misery which exist alongside the excesses of luxury, that I answer ' Yes '." It may be that the July Revolution had inspired Dorothea with the illusion that something had been done to better the lot of the poor in France but, even so, such a remark made about the English and coming from the niece of the French Ambassador may fairly be considered a little cool.

Dorothea landed at Dover on the 30th of September after a crossing which took nineteen hours and made her atrociously sea-sick. Even through her misery, however, she found time to appreciate the attentions she was paid. At first she was taken for a lady of the *Faubourg St. Germain* fleeing the revolution but as soon as it was discovered who she was, no pain was spared to welcome her. A French flag was hoisted, brandy and sherry pressed on her as sovereign cures for sea-sickness, the passengers crowded around her asking questions about the revolution and there were resounding cheers as she arrived in port.

This was a good start and she was well-disposed to England before she set foot on its soil. But even so, London came as something of a shock. She found it, she told Thiers, " far from offering the same gaiety and life as one finds at Paris. Coal and steam, which here usurp the place of all human sources of power, plunge this immense city into a thick atmosphere, evil-smelling and dismal, which makes gloomy all it surrounds. But I forget that I have only been here twelve hours ! "

Second impressions were more favourable, though some part of the depression lingered. " If I tried to describe London I would only bore you and not even give you any real impression. To understand this extraordinary marvel, made up of the magnificent and the fantastical, of vast establishments and of childish little nonsenses in bad taste, you would have to come, to look, to admire, to wonder ; but always to find something to please. As for society, it is as much under the rule of fashion as the country is under that of steam. Happily fashion is very favourable towards us at the moment ; when I say us, I mean as much towards France as to ourselves."

Dorothea knew well how tough her uncle's task was going to be. The enthusiasm of her first reception had done something to reassure her ; at least it had shown that the English people were not basically ill-disposed towards the new régime in France. But the opinion of those who counted had been much disturbed by the July Revolution. Charles X had not been highly thought of and Polignac's foreign policy had been sufficiently alarming to leave little regret at his disappearance. Still, there were many people left to remember the first revolution. The English asked themselves nervously whether the Terror was with them again and the French launched on another disastrous cycle which would drag all Europe into war. The Government of Louis-Philippe had been recognised but only with hesitation and reluctance. The English did not propose to trust it very far until they knew that it was going to last and conduct itself in an orderly fashion. As for King William IV, he considered Louis-Philippe to be an infamous scoundrel and said so frequently in public until the Duke of Wellington hinted that slightly greater reticence would be more in keeping with his position.

And then Talleyrand himself was not universally loved or admired. The Duke of Wellington was pleased to see him but even he, according to Princess Lieven, would have preferred the French to send a marshal as Ambassador. William IV would probably have preferred an admiral ; anyhow he declared himself very much displeased with Talleyrand's appointment. Most of the English were ready to be friendly but still suspicious of this figure from the past, grey, sinister and immensely old. " He crawled past me like a lizard along a wall," wrote Lady Granville, and a vague unease before this reptilian figure was the most common reaction of London society. Dorothea's reputation, too, had preceded her; or rather a dramatised and distorted version of it. " The Queen . . . would have had no time for any private meeting with the Dino," wrote Creevey in his diary, and the gloating venom of this " mischievous toad " as Lady Holland well described him was typical of too many of his fellows.

Talleyrand and Dorothea had another most embarrassing handicap in the presence in England of their former king and most of his family. Charles X was at this time at Holyrood Palace. The Government were anxious to move him from there, feeling that his presence so near to the coast was an invitation to malcontents from France to gather round him. They offered him one of Lord Arundel's houses about fifty miles inland but secretly hoped that he would leave them altogether and settle on the Continent. In the meantime life was a continual jostle between Charles X and his emissaries on the one hand trying on every occasion to underline that he was the only true ruler of France and Talleyrand on the other seeking to disparage the claim without weakening his moral case by too openly attacking his former master. The English court found themselves caught between the two; aware that, whatever they might do, somebody was sure to be offended. At Ascot, Queen Adelaide apologised to Dorothea for having accepted some trinkets from Holyrood for a charity bazaar which she was organising. The Queen of France, she felt sure, would understand the reasons of state which made it necessary. No doubt she said very much the same sort of thing to Charles X when apologising to him for receiving his successor's ambassador.

Sometimes the presence of these discomfortable exiles could be turned to the advantage of the Orleanist court. In October, Princess Esterhazy, the wife of the Austrian Ambassador and niece of the Emperor of Austria, told Dorothea that she felt bound to call on the Duchess of Berry. Dorothea said nothing to discourage her but urged that, as a *quid pro quo*, the princess should at least make a point of passing through Paris on a journey she was shortly to make to Vienna. A similar call at the Palais Royal would redress the diplomatic balance. In the circumstances, Princess Esterhazy could hardly refuse. Typically, the Duchess of Berry, who no doubt knew that the princess was a friend of Dorothea's, treated her visitor coldly, only gave her an audience of a few minutes and showed no gratitude for the visit. When Princess Esterhazy duly arrived at the Palais Royal, Dorothea had made sure that she found a very different sort of reception. She continued her journey well disposed towards the Orleans dynasty. The hostility of the Austrians was proving an embarrassment to the new French Government and the good-will of the Esterhazys did much to sweeten the atmosphere.

*   *   *   *   *

For Talleyrand, the chief problem was the Belgian question. In August, 1830 the Belgians had revolted against the union with the Dutch which had been imposed on them at the Congress of Vienna and broken away to independence. The French could naturally be expected to sympathise with their neighbours to whom they were bound by ties of religion and language and for whose revolution they felt in part responsible. The English as naturally took the part of their traditional allies, the Protestant Dutch. If exacerbated, the difference could have grown into a European war. Talleyrand was determined that it should not. Over the next four years the principal aim of his diplomacy was to achieve the independence of Belgium without forfeiting the friendship of England. To have even a chance of doing this he had to win the trust and friendship of the men with whom he would have to deal. It was there that Dorothea came in. Policy in England was controlled by a small group of men in each of the two parties, nearly all of them rich and aristocratic. The prejudices of these men against a usurping monarch had to be overcome, their confidence won and their sympathy engaged. Talleyrand could win their respect by his intelligence and experience but he needed help if he were to bring them to the point at which they could consider what he said objectively and in a spirit of good-will. The rôle of Dorothea, in part at least, was that of a glorified public relations officer. It was a rôle which called for the highest possible degree of charm, patience, wit, pertinacity, perception and sheer, grinding hard work.

The first task was to make the embassy a place to which men of taste and intelligence would wish to go. Their first address was 50 Portland Place, a not very satisfactory building which Dorothea resolved to change as soon as they were well enough established to be able to spare the time. Within its limitations, however, she found little difficulty in organising a household dazzling enough to satisfy even the most exacting Englishman. It was not long before Talleyrand was famed for keeping the best table in London and Dorothea had nothing to learn in the arts of making a salon agreeable, stimulating and, above all, smart. The only trouble was the expense. " As soon as the Belgian affair is finished, whatever the result, we are going to leave England," wrote Dorothea to Thiers, " Monsieur de Talleyrand . . . does not want either to wear himself out or to ruin himself. The latter he could hardly fail to do. You could never imagine how much we are spending here or the stinginess shown by the Ministry of Foreign Affairs." This perennial wail of the ambassador's lady abroad was to be repeated continually over the next few years. No doubt it was well justified but it must still be admitted that when Talleyrand and Dorothea finally left London some four years later the style in which they lived had never noticeably been reduced and yet their respective fortunes seemed substantially intact.

Grandeur and elegance came naturally to Dorothea and they were necessary if Talleyrand's Embassy were to do all that was asked of it. The July Monarchy was not a very glamorous affair and the English aristocracy were ready to sneer at the citizen king with his bourgeois air, his pawky manners and his undistinguished court. Yet they could hardly sneer at a king who chose to live modestly himself but could still be so brilliantly represented abroad. Dorothea's old admirer, Prince Adam Czartoryski, visited them in London and paid tribute to her success. " Dorothea . . . had great influence over Talleyrand and used to preside at the magnificent receptions in the French Embassy . . . The rooms . . . were fitted up with all the splendour of the great French aristocratic salons of the eighteenth century ; the cuisine was perfection ; and the inexhaustible wit of the host and the amiability of the hostess

made these receptions the most brilliant and the most sought
after in London."

Visitors from France were equally impressed and dazzled
by the style in which their country's reputation was upheld
by their ambassador. As Count Alexis de Saint Priest remarked,
" the July Revolution can sometimes be a little bourgeois,
but thanks to Monsieur de Talleyrand, it is carried off in very
grand style in London. Madame de Dino contributes finely
to the total effect." The Duke of Broglie also visited London
specifically to see what was going on in the embassy. His
admiration however was tinged with sympathy, " I do not
think that it is possible for any official position to combine
more magnificence with more tedium."

As much magnificence combined with as little tedium as
possible was an admirable recipe for entertaining but closer
alliances than those which could be made in balls or receptions
were necessary if Talleyrand's mission was to succeed. Perhaps
the greatest handicap under which an ambassador can labour
is the hostility or mistrust of his fellow diplomats. Talleyrand
and Dorothea found they had a singularly tricky collection to
get along with. Nearly all the stars of the diplomatic
firmament were now concentrated in London. Most of them
were already known to Dorothea. Baron Bülow, the Prussian
Minister, later to become Minister for Foreign Affairs, was
an old ally from her life in Berlin. Prince Esterhazy, the
Austrian Ambassador, she had known and been friends with
during the Congress of Vienna.

But the most influential couple in the diplomatic circle were
always agreed to be Prince and Princess Lieven ; not that they
operated much as a couple since the prince, though in title
Russian Ambassador, played no more than a depressed and
ineffective second-fiddle to his wife. " Madame de Lieven,"
wrote Dorothea some years later when Prince Lieven's recall
to Russia made a generous obituary in order " is of all women
the most feared, respected, sought after and courted. Her
political importance, which was due to her wit and knowledge
of the world, went side by side with an authority which no one
dreamed of questioning . . . Her house was the most select

in London and the one to which the *entrée* was the most valued."

Inevitably the two women found themselves in strong and constant rivalry. Both found the competition stimulating and there was surprisingly little antipathy on either side. Madame de Lieven had in her favour eighteen years' residence and an intimate knowledge of English society, keener political acumen than Dorothea would ever enjoy, a remarkable capacity for engaging the affections of outstanding men and driving, insatiable ambition. Dorothea on her side had the prestige of Talleyrand instead of the burden of a make-weight husband, youth, good looks and unassailable charm—" her eyes brilliant beyond all example, her face extremely handsome, her figure that of perfect youth . . ." In wit and intelligence the two women were well matched.

The rivalry between these two was notorious and a regular feature of London entertainment. " The female Lieven and the Dino were the people for sport," wrote Creevey. " They are both professional talkers—artists, quite, in that department. We had them both quite at their ease, and perpetually at work with each other ; but the Lieven for my money ! She has more dignity and the Dino more grimace." But the competition was more serious than just for social prestige. Princess Lieven was close to many English statesmen, closest of all to Lord Grey who was soon to become Prime Minister. She enjoyed great influence and used it diligently for her master the Emperor of Russia. Dorothea was her only effective rival and something at least of the success of Talleyrand's policies depended on how far she could win the ear of the Lieven's victims. The princess did not underestimate the opposition. She admired as well as liked Dorothea, " whom I hold as a most excellent and kindly person, whatever they may say to the contrary, and this in addition to her many brilliant social qualities." Both women prepared for a long and protracted struggle.

*　　*　　*　　*　　*

And then there were the English themselves, with whom, after all, it was their principal job to get along. " But what must one do ? " asked Dorothea, with little hope of an answer. " What must one be in order to please them ? It's impossible to say, for I see a miscellany of types succeed and yet the most perfect people fail completely. Pompous Monsieur de Chateaubriand is to-day the object of their mockery. The simple Monsieur de Latour Maubourg and the amiable Duke de la Châtre have kept a fond corner in their memory. Monsieur de Polignac made the great mistake of marrying an English girl who came from the second rank of society and was spendthrift instead of mean. As they are very frank and never make polite phrases we must suppose that we suit them well ; there are five or six houses to which I can take along my needlework and invite myself to dinner when I wish. That is something so rare that one must count it as a great success. They will never forgive any affectation, any pretentiousness, any extravagance, any pedantry. They think the better of you if you quickly pick up their customs which are filled with the most childish rules. It's greatly to your credit if you speak their language . . . There is no envy here, no meanness, no malice ; reserve and coldness, yes, but a true superiority in common sense and simplicity and good manners which make them excellent to live with. All my life I shall guard deep gratitude and affection for certain people in England. If this country had a climate and some brightness and it were possible to live here in style but without ruining oneself, one would never wish to leave."

The English, in fact, with their reserve, dignity and common sense appealed strongly to Dorothea who had not really been equipped by her German upbringing to appreciate fully the brilliance and vivacity of the French. Certainly she prized these qualities and regretted that they had been dimmed in the smoke and steam on this side of the Channel. But in England she found a new self-confidence ; she felt that she knew where she was, that she was not being flattered to her face and ridiculed or reviled behind her back, that she was judged for what she was and not what gossip believed her to be. Gratefully she contrasted the attitude of the English with what she had known from the French and had no doubt which race had the most claim to her affection. The English, after all, had made it clear that they liked her and nothing could have been more certain to make her like them in return.

Dorothea did, in fact, make herself very popular in England. The unsavoury notoriety which had preceded her was never wholly dispelled but, in face of her dignity and total propriety, it soon dwindled to a little cloud of ill-informed gossip. The faint whisper of wickedness which hung around her past, in time, indeed, became something of a social asset adding glamour to an otherwise almost too correct exterior. Lady Granville, who disliked her heartily, came back from dinner at Stafford House reporting crossly, " Lady Stafford has a sort of *engouement* for Dino. She can talk of nothing else and her manner to her is affectionate homage. She can say nothing but ' Is she not beautiful ? Is she not interesting ? ' " It would not be too much to say that, for a time at least, almost the whole of London society shared Lady Stafford's infatuation and Dorothea found herself the most courted figure in town.

* * * * *

One of the first of Talleyrand's duties was to present his letters of credence to King William IV. The ambassador had no illusions about the antipathy with which both he and his master were liable to be met at the Court of St. James. He could not afford to have the King of England permanently against him, and this first interview might well set the pattern of the future. Talleyrand's apparently nonchalant approach to the problem was typical of the man and his methods. He was already dressed and his valet was actually pinning on his decorations when Talleyrand turned to his niece and remarked that perhaps it would be a good idea for him to make a little speech.

" Let's see ; Madame de Dino, would you mind jotting down a few sentences in your largest hand-writing ? "

A little disconcerted but always ready to oblige, Dorothea sat down and prepared a few sentences. Talleyrand read them, changed a word or two and proceeded tranquilly to his interview. The speech was well received, despite a rather risky reference to the king's descent from the House of Brunswick; a bland reminder that the Hanoverians were quite as much usurpers of another's throne as the family of Orleans.

This was no isolated instance of Talleyrand's methods of

drafting, though usually he would give his niece a little longer warning. "All the letters of this period written by Monsieur de Talleyrand to the king, Madame Adélaïde and the Duke of Wellington were first thrown on paper by me and then rehandled by him," wrote Dorothea. There is no reason to believe that she exaggerated. Talleyrand had always disliked drafting his own papers, and now, burdened with the frailty of a man of nearly eighty, he was not likely to change his ways. His niece had his complete confidence and, though she could not follow him through the maze of negotiations over the Belgian question, on all the broader problems of policy and in the constant battles of personalities, she seconded him with competence and aplomb. The problem, indeed, is to say where the mind of the uncle left off and where the hand of the niece took over. The relationship between them was so close that probably both of them would have found it hard to say. What is undoubted is that, as their stay in England wore on and Talleyrand grew weaker and more uncertain, so Dorothea's influence grew till, by the time of retirement, her authority seemed predominant in almost every field of business. This was no case of usurpal of power; her respect and love for her uncle were far too great for that. Rather it was a gradual adoption of burdens which the old man was too tired or too bored to bear himself. Certainly Dorothea did not regret the extra authority; she throve on power and delighted in the intricate web of diplomatic manœuvre. But the indignation with which she rejected any suggestion that it was she and not her uncle who was in control shows clearly that, in her own mind at any rate, she was only the instrument of the prince's will.

Talleyrand having made his *début* at court, it was now for Dorothea to do the same. Her status was uncertain and potentially embarrassing. Technically, she had no right to the rank of ambassadress and William IV was not inclined to make an exception in her case. The Duke of Wellington came to the rescue, pleading that at Vienna she did the honours of Talleyrand's house and was received on that footing by the emperor and empress. "Oh, very well," said the king grudgingly, "I will tell the Queen, and you had better tell her too."

The society to which this decision gave an appropriate *entrée* was neither gay, cosy nor intellectually stimulating. It had not yet acquired the paralysing formality and tedium of the Victorian court—its unpleasantness one feels was caused more by the sheer incompetence of the royal hosts than by deliberate intent—yet in its way it was equally unattractive. Dorothea describes one particularly gruesome royal drawing-room " more crowded than ever, and consequently so long and fatiguing that Mexico, Spain and Naples were successively placed *hors de combat*." As a result of these ladies fainting one after the other what was left of the diplomatic corps had to exert themselves even more than usual. Madame de Lieven, with a determination as admirable as it was characteristic, plumped herself down on the steps of the throne to have a rest, then passed on into the king's room to look for some lunch. " She came back and told us that she was neither tired nor hungry. She all but added that our legs should be rested because hers were, and our stomachs satisfied because hers had been stayed."

Still, Dorothea was never entirely miserable. She had enough humour to appreciate the comic in even the most austere of London entertainments and enough curiosity to find something of interest in everyone she met. Occasionally she longed for the peace of Rochecotte but on the whole the life suited her well. Certainly never for a moment did she think that she had been wrong to come ; it is doubtful indeed whether it can ever have occurred to her that an alternative existed.

*   *   *   *   *

Dorothea's old friend Count Molé had been appointed as Louis-Philippe's first Minister of Foreign Affairs. Though his relations with Talleyrand had been formal rather than affectionate over the last fourteen years, they should still have been able to work tolerably well together. Unfortunately they had radically different ideas as to the proper relationship between ambassador and minister, particularly when it came to the negotiations over Belgium. Talleyrand considered that he should be left free to handle them as he thought best, keeping

Monsieur de Molé informed so far as it was convenient for him to do so. The minister's rôle was to keep his ambassador posted on what was going on in France and on French relations with other countries. Molé, on the other hand, would have liked to transfer the conduct of the whole affair to Paris. Failing that—and the attitude of the Duke of Wellington made it quite clear that he had no chance of succeeding—he felt Talleyrand should report fully on every stage of the negotiations and await instructions before going any further. Molé was, of course, entirely in the right by all the normal standards of diplomatic procedure. Talleyrand however was no ordinary envoy. He was the most distinguished Frenchman of the age and he had no intention of admitting any superior in his own profession. He would accept instructions from the king but no minister so far his junior as Molé was likely to impress him.

In the early stages, Dorothea made some efforts to pour oil on the waters. On 15th October, 1830, she wrote to Molé, " The Duke of Wellington's courtesy has been most marked. I often speak to him of you and you know the way I speak about those of whom I am fond. I wish that you could be as powerful in your office as he is in his ; he runs it like a general his head-quarters . . ." But the time was already past when such palliatives could do any good and, even as she wrote, she knew that either Molé or her uncle would have to go.

Dorothea busied herself with enlisting Thiers and Madame Adélaïde on the side of Talleyrand. To Thiers she complained about the tone of Molé's dispatches and his failure to let the prince have the news from Paris ; she was particularly indignant that he had even had the artfulness to write directly to the Duke of Wellington himself. Since she feared Molé would not wish to give any publicity to Talleyrand's doings, she sent Thiers a copy of the speech he had made at the presentation of his credentials to the king and asked her friend to ensure that it was published in the French papers. To Madame Adélaïde, sister of the king and with much power to influence him, her approach was more oblique. Dorothea had written to Bertin de Veaux, the French representative at the Hague, suggesting that Talleyrand and he should enter into direct correspondence. Bertin de Veaux very properly submitted the idea for approval to his minister[1] and Molé rejected it out of hand. Ingenuously, Dorothea repeated this to the king's sister, remarking how curious it was that Count Molé should wish to prevent an arrangement so beneficial to everybody. Madame Adélaïde was also left in no doubt as to the success the prince was enjoying, " It would be impossible to be treated more graciously by the court than we have been," wrote Dorothea " All the drawing-rooms, Whig or Tory, are equally attentive to the French Ambassador and nothing is lacking in John Bull's goodwill towards us."

A situation in which the Ambassador to the Court of St. James corresponded with his king behind the back of his minister and the minister corresponded with the Prime Minister of England behind the back of his ambassador was not a happy one, nor could it long continue. Inevitably it was Molé who had to yield or go altogether. He chose the latter. The first time he offered his resignation to Louis Philippe it was refused and a temporary reconciliation patched up between him and Talleyrand. The second time it was accepted and the more docile General Sébastiani took his place. Talleyrand settled down to continue his negotiations in his own way.

In November, 1830, the Duke of Wellington resigned and the long Tory reign was over. To Dorothea, whose constant misjudgment of English politics can usually be traced to her readiness to find parallels with the France of 1789, this seemed like the beginning of the end. Even she, however, could not find anything very sinister about the new Prime Minister, Lord Grey, a conscientious and incorruptible aristocrat whose abhorrence of revolution was quite as obvious as his adherence to reform. Much though she personally regretted the parting of the Duke of Wellington whose almost avuncular kindness had done so much to make her life in London agreeable, she felt sure that in time her relationship with Grey would grow as close.

Lord Palmerston, successor to Lord Aberdeen at the Foreign Office, looked like being another matter. Shortly after the new Government took office Dorothea commented that both Grey and Palmerston seemed personally well disposed towards France. It was almost the last amiable remark she was ever to make about the latter. "This flamboyant Harrovian with his dyed whiskers and striped pantaloons "—in Duff Cooper's admirable phrase—was exactly of the quality to displease Dorothea most deeply. No amount of political disagreement or of resentment for his off-hand treatment of her uncle can alone explain the sustained rancour which she bore him or the delight with which she greeted news of his set-backs many years after she had left England for ever. "It is seldom," she wrote to Barante, "that a man has a face so expressive of his character. The eyes are hard and pale, the nose turned up and impertinent. His smile is bitter, his laugh forced. There is no dignity, or frankness or correctness either in his features or his build. His conversation is dry, but I confess not wanting in wit. He has on him a stamp of obstinacy, arrogance and treachery which I believe to be an exact reflection of his real character."

Luckily not much harm was done to relations between France and England. Talleyrand fully shared his niece's feelings but was far too good a diplomat to allow it to disturb him. He continued to work with Palmerston with equanimity, patience and, at least over the Belgian question, a high degree of success.

*   *   *   *   *

It is sometimes hard to imagine how Dorothea, who was never physically strong, managed to get as much done as she did each day in London. It is no light task to run one of the largest and most luxurious houses in town and this constant preoccupation, coupled with the crushing social round which even in those leisurely days was the lot of a senior ambassadress, would have been enough for most people. In addition to this, Dorothea worked assiduously with her uncle as a sort of private secretary-cum-counsellor and undertook a great deal of semi-official correspondence on his behalf. Yet somehow she found time to read voluminously, mainly among works of the seventeeth and eighteenth century, and to conduct an enormous private correspondence. Every day page upon page went out from the embassy in her thin, uneasy hand; to her relations, to her children, to her friends, Barante, Royer Collard, Guizot, Thiers to mention only a few of those that have survived. " I don't think she writes to all her former lovers but she does to a great many . . ." wrote one spiteful commentator[2] and certainly her output was remarkable even in an age where massive letter-writing was a commonplace.

In February, 1831, she had intended to spend a few weeks resting in France but at the last moment hesitated to leave Monsieur de Talleyrand when he was so preoccupied by his work. In the end, though she got over to Paris for a fleeting business visit in May, for her holiday she had to satisfy herself with a cottage at Richmond. " I must stay close to Monsieur de Talleyrand," she wrote from there to Barante. " He so often needs someone to whom he can confide the plans, doubts and hopes which unceasingly occupy his mind."

There was perhaps another slightly less unselfish reason for Dorothea's reluctance to leave England. At the end of 1830, a young, provincial nobleman named Adolphe de Bacourt had been added to the staff of the embassy. Bacourt was only twenty-nine, eight years younger than Dorothea. A slender, graceful young man with spaniel eyes and an ingratiating manner, he was only removed from the truly romantic by premature baldness and a slightly too evident sense of self-interest. Women longed to protect him ; men, sometimes at least, to kick him. But this too facile description does not do justice to his modesty, honesty and considerable good sense. Talleyrand, who was never sparing towards his subordinates, thought highly of him. He wrote appreciatively of his " energy and sagacity." He was hard-working, intelligent and anxious to please ; an admirable follower though not of the calibre ever to achieve leadership.

Bacourt entered diplomacy on the advice of the Baron de Vincent, an old acquaintance of Talleyrand. He had been at The Hague for the previous seven years and, though tagged with a legitimist label, had not been considered of sufficient significance to be purged with the more important Carlist sympathisers after the July Revolution. Talleyrand had heard well of his work and asked Molé for his services when looking round for a capable staff for the embassy. He may have thought benevolently that he would be company for Dorothea ; if so, he succeeded beyond his expectations.

A letter written to Bacourt[3] somewhat later by his friend Charles Bresson, then first secretary in the French Embassy at Brussels, gives some indication of the way things were going.

". . . And how about you, my fine Alcindor . . . they tell me that you have been set on fire by those same bright eyes which touched me too in their time. I advise you not to limit yourself to a love as respectful as mine : to act has its advantages and life is short."

Whether or when Bacourt took his friend's advice can never be proved, though there seems little doubt that for a period at least he was Dorothea's lover. At all events during their years in London there was nurtured a friendship which was to last until Dorothea's death. For thirty years it was to Bacourt that she wrote most constantly, Bacourt whose advice she sought, Bacourt with whom, after a long separation, almost estrangement, she found it such sweet relief to meet again. And this affection Bacourt repaid tenfold with complete devotion ; never in his life was anyone to challenge Dorothea's paramount position. Loyalty was Bacourt's most conspicuous virtue ; if he had had less of it he would perhaps have been a happier man but could never have retained Dorothea's affection and absolute trust.

*   *   *   *   *

After about eighteen months in London Dorothea at last got her way and left the embassy in Portland Place behind her. The new house was in Hanover Square and altogether better suited to their needs. It belonged to the Duke of Devonshire and had formerly been lived in by Lord Grey. The latter waited until Talleyrand and his niece were well installed and then obligingly told them that it was haunted by a man with a pale, sad face and piercing black eyes. Lord Grey had discovered him lurking behind a pillar and the ghost had blown on the face of his daughter Georgina while she slept. Dorothea was temperately disquieted but does not seem to have lost much sleep over it. The servants took the news more hardly and for months afterwards refused to move around at night except in couples.

Somehow into this crowded life she managed to fit visits around England to admire the beauties of the country and of man's contrivance. Though she found ghosts in her own house a little too macabre to be enjoyable she had all the fashionable affection for the depressing. Eridge Castle in particular pleased her well. It belonged to the Earl of Abergavenny, " a rich and misanthropic octogenarian." His own apartments, she noted with approval, were excessively dismal. The view too came in for applause. " I have never seen a prospect so romantically wooded and at the same time so profoundly melancholy. It is not English, still less is it French ; it is the Black Forest, it is Bohemia. I have never seen ivy like that which covers the towers, the balconies and indeed the whole building. In short, I rave about it." Knole proved even better, " venerable and lugubrious . . . which for melancholy has no rival." Dorothea, one feels, could have paid an enjoyable visit to Northanger Abbey.

She was also introduced to the English week-end house party : " twenty or thirty persons who know each other but not familiarly are invited to be together for two or three days." Unfortunately, as the hosts only went to their house to receive their guests and left as soon as they were gone, they themselves had the air of being on a visit which gave the whole party rather an unsettled effect. At Woburn though they played cards on Sunday she found that the splendour and size of the house dulled into cold formality everyone except the duchess, who was anyhow notoriously foul-mouthed. At Warwick Castle the great drawing-room was lit only by about twenty candles, like " will-o'-the-wisps which deceived the eye rather than illuminated the room. I have never seen anything more chilling and depressing . . . I kept thinking that the portrait of Charles I and the bust of the Black Prince would come and join us at coffee . . ." Instead, there arrived Lord Eastnor, a mighty hunter and his brother, a parson, who had not shaved since Christmas and never opened his mouth except to eat. But not even rigours such as this could dim her affection for the English countryside which she found richer and more varied than that of France and more sympathetic than that of Germany.

Every Eden must have a serpent and Dorothea, who was not really content without something to dislike, would probably have introduced them if they had not been there. Among the English there was Lord Palmerston; among the French her special enemies were Montrond and the Count and Countess Flahaut. Montrond was Talleyrand's jackal. He existed on the scraps which the prince would throw him from time to time, some mysterious lien which he seemed to enjoy on the secret service funds and a considerable allowance of charm and wit. In November, 1830, he arrived in London, announcing to the world that the ambassador had sent for him as he had found his services indispensable. Indignantly Dorothea wrote to Madame Adélaïde to deny the imputation : " Monsieur de Talleyrand finds himself here in such a position that he has no need of anyone. Besides, the sort of help he would get from a person of whom no one here has any good to say except that he is very amusing, would not be of much use either in the service of the king or even for our social position."

It is possible that the jealousy and distrust which Dorothea felt for Monsieur de Montrond would never have flamed into open war if it had not been for one of those complicated and obscure scandals which from time to time rejoice the hearts of the French. The only detailed authority for the story is Prosper Mérimée[4], that avid scandal-monger whose correspondence with Stendhal provides a mine of malicious libel for any student of the period. According to him, Montrond (thinly disguised in the story as Monsieur de Colline Ronde) entertained himself by persuading a son of Lord Palmerston that the Duchess of Dino (10 no) was ripe for seduction and a worthy target for any young man of dash and virility. He then warned Dorothea that he feared the young man meant mischief. In the event, it is said that young Mr. Temple got much the worst of the encounter and retreated with a badly scratched nose and the loss of half his hair.

Even if this inherently improbable skirmish ever took place, no more might have been heard of it. Montrond, however, now made sure that it got back to Paris and, in particular, that it was published in *Figaro* by the journalist, Latouche. Then Piscatory came into the picture. Relishing the idea of a little favourable publicity he proceeded to name himself Dorothea's champion and challenge Monsieur Latouche to a duel. Piscatory missed, Latouche fired his shot in the air, the two men fell into each other's arms. All was forgiven but, by Mérimée and the Parisian public at least, nothing forgotten.

This squalid and trivial affair was probably dramatised in the telling but there is no doubt that Montrond made the maximum use of whatever material was at his disposal. It was not the sort of liberty Dorothea could forgive. It took several years before she finally persuaded her uncle to break with him but in the meanwhile she devoted her energies to denigrating and abusing him. From this time on there was a new note of venom in her voice as she spoke of the *âme damnée* of Talleyrand.

Her other pet hates, the Count and Countess of Flahaut, were less vulnerable. Count Flahaut was—as near certainly as makes no difference—Talleyrand's son by the pretty wife of an old and complaisant husband. He was affable, gallant and tolerably distinguished, outstandingly attractive to women, a devoted follower of Napoleon who had come back into favour with the July Revolution. Left to himself he would probably have got on quite well with his father but once he had married Margaret Elphinstone he had little chance of being left to himself on any subject at all.

Meg Elphinstone was the daughter of a tough old admiral, Lord Keith, whose title, fortune, temper and determination she was to inherit. At one time seriously tipped as a future Lady Byron, she had later failed to catch the Duke of Devonshire, fell passionately in love with Flahaut on the rebound and married him strongly against the will of her family and even somewhat against the will of Flahaut himself. Intelligent, ingenious and ferociously ambitious, she had resolved that her husband should be French Ambassador in London. Talleyrand having got there first, she decided that, the reversion at least must be Flahaut's. In the meantime she settled down to push her husband into intimacy with the Prince Royal, eldest son of King Louis-Philippe. If plotting and calumny could achieve anything, she was resolved that the embassy in London should be empty in the near future.

At the end of November, 1830, Flahaut arrived in London

armed with a plan which he had worked out with the new Minister, Sébastiani, for the solution of the Belgian problem. Talleyrand treated the plan with scant respect and the bearer with less. What was worse, when the time came for him to recommend a chargé d'affaires to look after the embassy during his absence on leave he asked, not for Flahaut, but for Durand de Mareuil. Flahaut had to content himself with Berlin, a post of much lesser importance though still beyond the capacities of the new incumbent.

Meg Flahaut put the blame for her husband's discomfiture on Dorothea; probably without justification, since Talleyrand was perfectly well able to decide for himself that he did not want the co-operation of a man whose only proved ability was that of making a nuisance of himself in as ostentatious a manner as possible. The two women, however, had loathed each other at sight and Count Flahaut quickly adopted his wife's prejudices. A " horrid little serpent," he called Dorothea, and " a lying little devil," but the wife's intrigues were more dangerous than the husband's invective. Meg Flahaut was a close friend of the Greys and had many liberal connections. She made it her business to warn them all that the French Ambassador and his niece were closely allied with the Tories and that Talleyrand was plotting with the Duke of Wellington. The accusation was a damaging one; especially in the case of Dorothea whose right-wing sympathies were well known. The Countess de Boigne indeed went so far as to allege that the reason she got on badly with Lord Palmerston was her notorious liaison with the ultra-Tories.

The animosity between Dorothea and her cousins by bar-sinister became one of the set pieces of the London and Parisian seasons. " The Flahauts are both gone to England," wrote Lady Granville. " I think there will be a great row-de-rowing amongst them all." There always was and there was always going to be. Several years later the same informant reported, " Madame de Dino in great beauty. She and Meg meet and dine each other, but it is like the meetings in cock-and-bull fights. The night before last Dino ran into Lieven's salon, saw Meg and shrieked : ' *Oui, ma chère, c'était un cri épouvantable.*' She did not apologise or say for why. Explanations have been asked. Dino says it was a *cri de surprise*, Meg says it was a *cri de horreur*." That cry, in one form or another, had been heard many times in Paris and London over the previous years.

*   *   *   *   *

In June, 1832, Lord Grey's third Reform Act was made law. Modest though its measures may seem to-day, to the right wing of the time it was held to open the flood-gates of revolution. It is hardly necessary to say that Dorothea was among the gloomiest of the prophets. She recognised the crying need for social change and the appalling disparity between the rich and poor but, as soon as it came to opening the way to reform by extending power outside the small aristocratic élite, then she heard in her ears the rumbling of the tumbrils and saw already the guillotine reared on the Horse Guards Parade. Comparing life in London after the Reform Act with life in Paris during the early stages of the revolution she found "the analogy is striking, the copy a trifle too servile . . . Aristocracy, minority of nobility, *tiers état* have each their counterpart in the Tories, Whigs and Radicals." Dorothea's dread of innovation and reform became more marked with the years ; as she grew older she retreated further and further into an ultra-conservatism which could only be overcome if she found herself, through some question of personalities, emotionally engaged on the side of the reformers. It is an odd fact that almost all her French friends were liberal by tendency and yet, left to herself, she would have drifted inevitably towards the arcane and medieval mysteries of the transcendental right.

In France, too, things were restless. The Prime Minister, Casimir Périer, had died in the cholera epidemic that was then ravaging France. The future of the régime seemed to depend on finding a successor of sufficient stature. His friends thought that only in Talleyrand could the necessary wisdom and experience be found. Charles de Rémusat, son of an old friend of Talleyrand and a leader of the younger Doctrinaires, was selected as the emissary. Before approaching Talleyrand himself he decided to sound out the duchess. He left a circumstantial and malicious account of his interview :

" Dorothea of Courland was then thirty-nine years old. She was still almost at the peak of her beauty which had, anyhow, never been that of youth. She was of medium height but elegant and carried herself with such grace and dignity that she seemed taller than in fact she was. She had a great air of distinction. She was thin, and her dark and slightly sickly complexion always stood in need of a little rouge. Her features were handsome though not perfectly regular. Most striking was her nose, like that of a bird of prey but delicate and finely sculpted. Her teeth were fine and white ; from her mouth, with its thick, expressive lips, came slightly hesitant speech, which minor mistakes of pronunciation in no way made disagreeable. Her small and rather pointed face under a broad forehead ringed with jet black hair was lit by incomparable eyes of deep blue-grey . . . whose burning and caressing look could cover the whole range of expressions. Being short-sighted, she would half-close them and in so doing add to their softness. Yet she was so much alive that when she was no longer in sight one could swear that her great eyes were black as coal. Her mouth and eyes were extremely seductive ; the only fault in fact was that there was too much seduction about them.

" And so I was going to lunch with her. It was served in her drawing-room. ' I hate having people around,' she said, and sent away the footmen. So there we were for our chat, with very much the air of those who act out their politics in a thoroughly worldly atmosphere. I felt that I was playing a part in a society game. For a moment I wondered whether I should not fulfil all the characteristics of the rôle by mixing gallantry with business . . . I had heard often that formerly in good society every *tête-à-tête* automatically had to become a love scene. The duchess seemed to have preserved the principles of the *ancien régime* so perfectly in this respect that it occurred to me that I should tell her how beautiful she was. Happily neither the temptation nor my self-esteem so far blinded me ; I saved myself from ridicule and contented myself by eating my eggs and cutlets and trying to keep my wits about me as well as I could. We discussed many subjects but the object of the conversation was to tell me the following :

" ' You want to make Monsieur de Talleyrand into a head of Government ? Save yourself the trouble of trying ; it would not suit him at all. He would not wish to do it and, even if he did, I would not permit it.'

" At these last words, or something like them, ' That's enough, Madame,' I said, ' I know when I'm beaten.'

" Her own personal reluctance showed clearly how she would have dreaded the responsibility of exercising her own real or supposed influence in the midst of a Government open to view and to all the noise of publicity. From this moment, I did no more than bring to bear on Monsieur de Talleyrand the minimum of pressure needed to show that I had not given up too easily . . .''

Dorothea found her visitor outstandingly disagreeable ; supercilious, captious and rigidly set in his own ideas. He began their conversation by promising to tell Dorothea what was going on in France. " It takes a long time to learn," wrote Dorothea wistfully after his visit, " he has been teaching me for more than two hours ! " She referred briefly to Rémusat's mission ; " Monsieur de Talleyrand is too much determined not to take part in any administration to give way on this point."

That was the truth of it ; Talleyrand was perfectly content where he was and Dorothea knew it. It is highly unlikely that she boasted of her influence in the way Charles de Rémusat described. Her respect for Talleyrand was far too great to let her speak so arrogantly even to a close friend, let alone a mere acquaintance whom she distrusted and disliked. At the most she may have said that she personally disliked the idea and would advise the prince against it. Rémusat's imagination would have done the rest ; in his mind at least there would have been little difference between such a statement and the direct boast that she would not permit it.

It is interesting, though largely profitless, to speculate whether Dorothea could in fact have persuaded Talleyrand to return to France and lead the Government. Probably she could not ; greatly though Talleyrand respected her judgment and much though he would have done to please her, he knew where he was of most service to France. It would have needed a great deal of pressure before he would have left England for work which he knew to be thankless, exhausting and totally unsuited to his present powers. As it was, Dorothea felt this even more strongly than he ; for her own personal reasons she would have been most reluctant to return to Paris but for the sake of her uncle's happiness she would have resisted any such move to the death.

9

In June, 1832, Dorothea left London for France where Talleyrand and she were to spend a few months' leave. The prince followed her a day or two later. Then, after the shortest possible visit to Paris she moved on to Switzerland where her doctor had prescribed her baths of whey. By the end of August she was at Rochecotte where she stayed until it was time for her to rejoin her uncle in London towards the end of October.

Inevitably she drew comparisons between the French and English and on the whole she was still inclined to favour the latter. Her views of the English were conventional and close to those which would be voiced by most sympathetic foreigners to-day. They show at least that she had taken pains to try to understand and to like them. Of English women she wrote :

" The brilliancy of these splendid, English complexions, the beautiful, blonde hair falling in long ringlets on the rosiest cheeks and the whitest necks in the world, almost prevent one from lamenting the absence of expression and movement which characterises these beauties. It is the fashion to criticise English women for their want of style. They walk badly, it is true, but in repose their nonchalance is not ungraceful. They are usually well made and less pinched in their *toilettes* than French women. Their proportions are finer and more developed. They sometimes dress without much taste but at least each pleases herself and there is a diversity in their dress which brings out each one very well."

But English women interested her no more than those of any other race. When she turned to the subject of Englishmen her views may not have been any more original but, at least, they were not limited to reflections on dress and complexion.

" Their conversation," she wrote, " is cold, reserved and unimaginative to a degree which, for a long time, strikes one as very tedious. But this feeling gives way to one of real pleasure if one takes the trouble to look for the good sense, the kindness, the learning and the cleverness which are concealed beneath the shyness of their exterior. One has hardly ever reason to regret having encouraged their timidity, for they never become either familiar or indiscreet . . . Detestable caricatures when they are copying others, the English are admirable when they are themselves ; they are well-fitted to their own territory and they should be judged only on their own ground. An Englishman on the continent is so much out of his element that he runs the risk of being taken either for an idiot or a coxcomb."

Yet even more than the hidden values of the Englishman it was the virtues of our politics and constitution which pleased her most. The appalling gap between the rich and poor still seemed to her deplorable, yet she thought that she had discovered compensating features in the English system. In their personal liberty and their equality before the law, she decided, the English workmen found consolation for their lack of means. Arguing from her own character, she concluded that since to her independence was immeasurably more important than comfort, it must follow that the poor in England, though often working long hours in bad conditions for a derisory reward, must nevertheless be happy since they could speak their minds in public without much fear of arrest. This concept of the noble and disinterested workman who put liberty so far before the problems of malnutrition and keeping a roof over his family's head may seem a trifle naïve. In fact Dorothea had not the least idea whether the poor were contented or not. But her praise for the liberty which all in England enjoyed had a certain validity and argued, at least, readiness to see the better side of our national life.

Less questionable was her praise of the English for not extending their parliamentary rancours to their private lives.

The diplomatic corps, she noted with astonishment, went with equal freedom to the houses of the Opposition and the Government and no one appeared to find it discreditable. Most foreign observers tended to attribute this to deep-rooted English frivolity ; Dorothea saw in it the triumph of reason over factionalism and benevolence over bitterness. She compared it with favour to the profound jealousies and hatreds which were racking the body politic of France.

*   *   *   *   *

All in all, it was a relief to Dorothea to get back to London. But though she found that life was as agreeable as ever she could not help noticing that the power and importance of her uncle was diminishing. For one thing, the Duke of Broglie had taken the place of Sébastiani in Paris, and the Duke of Broglie was quite another Foreign Secretary ; a man who knew his own mind and was determined that his ambassadors, however lofty, should know it too. For another, Palmerston seemed now resolved to make things as difficult as possible for Talleyrand and in every way to assert his indifference to the French Ambassador's views and wishes. A cartoon in a London paper entitled " The lame leading the blind " had shown Palmerston groping his way under the guidance of Talleyrand. There was enough truth in the cartoon for it to rankle. It became Palmerston's preoccupation to ensure that whatever else might happen he should never again be accused of following the lead of this crafty old intriguer.

Dorothea, however, lived in constant hope that she would see the enemy vanquished and the Tories returned to power. With the Duke of Wellington back in office then, let Broglie do what he would, the old partnership would be restored and the French Embassy in London become once again the real seat of power in the formation of French foreign policy. It would, indeed, be hard to say whether Dorothea was more anxious to see the Whigs defeated for the chagrin it would cause Lord Palmerston, for the assistance it would give her uncle or for the ruin from which it would rescue England. That England was on the road to ruin seemed to her evident and when the elections of December, 1832—the first since the electorate had been enlarged—passed off without serious disturbance, her reactions were of amazed relief coupled with the natural irritation of a Cassandra who has cried woe at the beginning of the wrong scene. When the results of the election were announced and it was seen that less than one in five constituencies had returned a Tory she felt that her gloom had after all been justified but the new House settled down peacefully to discuss education and the only man who appeared to be conspicuously more powerful than before the election was the conservative Robert Peel. Such unreasonable behaviour was troubling to Dorothea's Germanic nature but at least it left her free simultaneously to fear a revolution and to hope for a Tory revival without either contingency seeming ridiculously remote.

By the end of 1832 the Belgian question had been effectively closed. Talleyrand was tired. He was seventy-eight years old and beginning to wonder whether it was not time that he left public life to the younger men. At least, he thought, it was time that he had another holiday. He would probably have left early in the spring of the following year if he had not felt bound to stay in London to receive the Duke of Orleans, eldest son of King Louis-Philippe. All royal visits must present much tribulation and hard work to those who organise them ; this one set exceptionally testing problems because of the uncertain standing of the French royal family and the presence in England of so many friends and supporters of their Bourbon predecessors. A good reception for the young duke in England could do much to fortify the Orleanist régime in France. The prince was determined that the visit should succeed.

Dorothea was mainly responsible for seeing that it did. Her uncle was too old and too frail to undertake the innumerable *démarches* which were necessary if London society was to be cajoled or bullied into greeting the duke with the requisite enthusiasm. No one else in the embassy had the necessary social contacts or could hope to shift the English aristocracy from the attitude of cautious dislike which they would probably have adopted if left to themselves. Even for Dorothea it demanded infinite patience, finesse and skill in negotiation. Lord Sefton, for instance, a close friend, was easily persuaded to give a dinner for the royal visitor. But in his dining-room hung a portrait of Charles X. Obviously the Duke of Orleans could not be asked to sit opposite it; yet equally Lord Sefton could not be expected to suppress the portrait altogether. Eventually a compromise was reached; the portrait continued to hang but in another room and the Duke of Orleans was able to take his dinner without being disturbed by this tactless reminder of his father's uncertain seat upon the throne.

In the end all went brilliantly well. Government and opposition vied in honouring the heir to the throne of France and even the court were more gracious than Dorothea would have dared prophesy. Almost as important, the Duke of Orleans was entirely satisfied by his reception and gave most flattering accounts of the embassy to his father on his return. Handsome, open, intelligent, of a sensibility and distinction rarely found among the ruling families of Europe, he made a great impression on Dorothea and in his turn was captivated by her grace and wit. Though eighteen years older than the young duke, her beauty was scarcely if at all diminished and her power of fascination unimpaired. In this brief visit were laid the foundations of what was to become a close and lasting friendship.

*   *   *   *   *

It was September before Talleyrand returned to France. Though it was announced that he was only going on leave there was much doubt as to whether he would come back. "His arrangements would seem to indicate that he has in view either death or the Presidency," wrote Madame de Lieven. She gave a dinner in his honour and afterwards wrote to Lord Grey: "from the tragic manner in which he and Madame de Dino both take their going away, I greatly fear that they are not coming back . . . I shall not feel at all amiable to any successor." A few days later Grey replied, "I had letters from Talleyrand and Madame de Dino both expressing an anxious wish and intention to return but both also in a tone of low spirits denoting a presentiment to the contrary. They will both be a great loss to society . . . Where could he lead a life more suited to his health than here, with just occuption enough to interest him and a society which is more in accordance with his aristocratic habits than that of *la nouvelle France* ? "

There is no doubt that the path of return was open to Talleyrand ; certainly he had enemies in the French Government but none bold enough to try to dispossess him if he decided that the embassy should be his for another spell. Dorothea was unusually irresolute. " There are so many real inconveniences in entering on active political life. On the other hand, there are so many real inconveniences in staying in France that, even if I wished to advise, I do not know what advice it would be best to give him." If she had wished to suit only her own wishes there is no doubt at all that she would have decided to stay in London. Everything about the life suited her : the grandeur of her position, the friends she had made, the fascination of her work. Conversely, there was nothing in Paris to attract her ; quite apart from the social complications in which the new régime was certain to involve her, it was plain that her uncle's retirement could, at his age, only mean his final retreat from the political scene. Though Dorothea was a considerable personality in her own right, she knew that her role was bound to be diminished once she had ceased to profit by her close association with her uncle.

It was this strong predilection for a return to London which made Dorothea reluctant to press her uncle one way or another. She could not feel sure that, if she tried to make up her mind as to what was the best course for Prince Talleyrand, she would not unwittingly be swayed by her own self-interest. She therefore decided not to make up her mind at all. Her first inclination, indeed, had been to fly in the face of her own desires and urge her uncle to retire. She had been persuaded from this, however, by Royer Collard, who felt strongly that both the prince's happiness and the well-being of France demanded that he remain in office. With a certain relief Dorothea retreated into discreet neutrality. With his niece offering no discouragement, the old man speedily let himself be persuaded by King Louis-Philippe into the course which, secretly, he knew he wished to follow. Before the end of 1833 it was settled that Talleyrand and Dorothea were to return to London.

*   *   *   *   *

For Dorothea, the short stay in France marked a certain shift in the close-knit circle of her friends. For one thing, she began to wonder whether Adolphe Thiers was indeed as admirable as she had previously thought. A desirable political ally he certainly remained, but was he really suitable as a close friend ?

Thiers had committed the offence of marrying. This in itself was pardonable, his wife Elise Dosne was a member of an immensely rich family of industrialists and the match was therefore perfectly justifiable on the grounds of interest. But Thiers also professed himself to be in love and this Dorothea found much harder to excuse. " I sincerely hope that his philosophy will not be tried too severely," she wrote with resolute, if unconvincing benevolence, " but, as the proverb has it, ' the sin brings its own punishment'."

In December, she and her uncle went to dinner with Adolphe Thiers. To her satisfaction if not surprise, she found the new Madame Thiers perfectly intolerable. She had pretty eyes and a good figure, Dorothea grudgingly admitted, but a disagreeable mouth, an unpleasing smile and a too prominent forehead. " She says nothing herself, hardly answers when she is spoken to and she seems thoroughly bored with us all. She has no presence and no idea of how to behave in society . . ." The idea that the poor child—who was only sixteen—was probably terrified at meeting the redoubtable Duchess of Dino evidently never entered Dorothea's head. It can never be easy for a young bride to get on with the women friends of a middle-aged husband ; when the friend has a European reputation for sophistication, wit, beauty and— incidentally—immorality, the experience must become almost intolerable. Given the circumstances, it is remarkable that Madame Thiers managed to open her mouth at all.

The dinner, graced as it was by the presence of Madame Dosne, mother of the bride, whose dress was " pink and girlish, and affectedly simple to a degree which quite astonished me," confirmed Dorothea in all her aristocratic prejudices. Thiers as an individual, a man of charm and extreme talent divorced from his *milieu*, she could accept as a friend. Thiers, the bourgeois, encumbered by his provincial wife and his frumpish mother-in-law, was quite another matter. The alliance of interests continued and in the future Dorothea was to make herself intensely active on Thiers's behalf, but the charm of the association had faded for ever.

Her affection for Thiers had absorbed a considerable part of Dorothea's thoughts and energies. Disillusionment left her free to concentrate on her other Adolphe, Adolphe de Bacourt. So well had this egregious young man succeeded in convincing Talleyrand of his qualities that he found himself appointed chargé d'affaires when the ambassador went on leave in September. Talleyrand wrote to the Duke of Broglie praising Bacourt's virtues and assuring the minister that the Embassy would be safe in the hands of his subordinate. The compliment, if he ever heard of it, must have gone far towards consoling Bacourt for his separation from Dorothea but he showed little appreciation of it in his behaviour.

The two wrote to each other diligently during Dorothea's stay in France. Literally hundreds of Dorothea's letters to Bacourt survive and they provide, indeed, the bulk of the so-called memoirs edited by her granddaughter Princess Radziwill. Unfortunately, in their editing, discretion and family loyalty triumphed over a sense of history. The letters have been harshly truncated and almost everything of a personal nature cut out. The originals returned to Germany and seem to have been lost there during the last war. As a result the letters, in the form available to us to-day, portray only a shadow of the true relationship between the two. One letter[1] from Bacourt, dated 10th November, 1833, has survived without emasculation. It is for this reason worth quoting at length.

In the letter, Bacourt first congratulated himself on feeling much better and attributed this to the fact that in his ambassador's absence there was no one to plague him :

" I assure you that it is this thought which makes me so reluctant to submit myself once more to the yoke of Monsieur

The Duchess of Courland

The Duchess of Dino aged seven

The Duchess of Dino
aged seventeen

ount Edmond de Talleyrand-Périgord,
ter Duke of Dino

Count Clam-Martinitz   Prince Talleyrand

The Duchess of D

Chateau of Rochecotte: water-colour painted at the time it was
bought by the Duchess of Dino

Chateau of Rochecotte today as altered by the Duchess of Dino

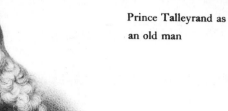

Prince Talleyrand as
an old man

The Duchess of Dino, from
an engraving

The Duchess of Dino

The Duchess of Dino aged fifty-n[...]

Sagan, from a contemporary engraving

de Talleyrand's ill humour. You were right to picture it as being the existence of a sheep. Between us there is a gulf which can never be filled. I can forgive him the injuries he has done me, attributing them to his age, his health, his preoccupations, but all the same I have resolved in future to live here only in independence and never to become again what I have been for him. Once we no longer have to work together and can meet on neutral ground, then things will be changed and we will be able to get on perfectly well together. I do not want you to accuse me of trying to set up an insuperable barrier to our meeting. No, in my heart I will never be wanting towards you, nor in my deeds when the deeds depend on my own will.

" In your letter, my angel, you wrote a very fine passage on those false women who steal the lovers of others or stir up the poison of jealousy by their indiscretions. I share all your ideas on this and that is why I am convinced that the less people who know about an intimate friendship, the better it will be. Still more do I agree with you that those who love each other must flee the world and find themselves some well-secluded corner . . .

" No, *ma belle dame*, I never find your letters tedious because for me nothing which concerns you can ever have in it anything of tedium. So chatter on, my little magpie ; you will never chatter as lengthily and as foolishly as I have done in this long letter . . ."

This querulous petulance of an underling who does not feel himself sufficiently appreciated can hardly have been very pleasing to Dorothea, and his strictures on her uncle must have offended all her loyalty. Yet in a way it was Bacourt's weaknesses and pettiness which Dorothea found endearing. Herself strong, self-confident and in an unchallengeable position of grandeur and importance, the feeble blustering of Bacourt, based as it was on a wish to impress and a badly-concealed sense of inadequacy, was filled with a plaintive charm. From someone less talented, less attractive, above all less devoted to her it might have jarred but Bacourt had real qualities and the weakness she would have condemned in another, in him she found beguiling. Dorothea could never have loved Bacourt as an equal ; he could not match her in status, in intelligence or in will ; but she loved him as a protégé, as someone she could mother, flatter, defend from the affronts of a hostile world. Most of Dorothea's friends were much older than her ; almost all, Thiers, Guizot, Molé, Vitrolles, Royer Collard, were men of determination and force who stood by themselves, confident of their abilities and unable to conceive that the rest of the world should not appreciate them also. Bacourt was something new for her and his deep diffidence, masked by a façade of social graces, awoke unexpected sensations in Dorothea's heart. She loved him with a warmth and tenderness which no one had induced in her before and only one other man was to rekindle.

As she must have suspected when she received the letter, Bacourt's brave protestations of his future independence came to little or nothing. When Talleyrand returned, his chargé d'affaires was there to greet him and life went on very much as it had before. With increasing age the prince, perhaps, became easier to work for. Dorothea too may have done something to smooth the relationship between the two men. But it would have been astonishing if Bacourt had shown the courage to defy his master ; he relapsed swiftly into the role of faithful follower and continued to play it so long as the relationship existed.

*　　　*　　　*　　　*　　　*

It was not long after their return to London that Dorothea realised that her first instinct had been right and that they would have done better to remain in France. The insufferable Palmerston was still firmly in office and, though the Government of Lord Grey seemed to be tottering towards collapse, his Minister of Foreign Affairs betrayed no awareness that his own tenure of office would not be sempiternal. He seemed, or so it appeared to Dorothea at least, to take a vicious delight in transacting all business of any significance through the British Embassy in Paris and to miss no chance of belittling the wisdom and status of Prince Talleyrand. The Tories made it plain that Monsieur de Talleyrand was the French Ambassador of their choice but, for all the feebleness of the present Government, the Tories were still in opposition and likely to remain so if the king could have his way.

Everything that year seemed designed to cause irritation or humiliation. From France came a stream of unwanted and embarrassing guests. The Prince of Moscow, son of the martyred Ney, arrived and insisted on being presented at court ; in view of William IV's ferocious dislike of all things Napoleonic his reception can hardly have been very gratifying. Lucien Bonaparte, " cringing in his manners and false in his look," expressed an even less appropriate wish to meet the Duke of Wellington. " I saw him cross the room," recorded Dorothea, " and come up bowing and scraping to be presented to the victor of Waterloo, whose reception was as cold as such baseness deserved." But at least Lucien was less of an irritation than Jerome Bonaparte who insisted on playing the king and startled Londoners by keeping two gentlemen-in-waiting standing behind his chair whenever he appeared in public.

No less unwelcome to Dorothea was Monsieur de Montrond. " For the last eighteen months he has had the management of a thousand louis of the foreign affairs secret service money," wrote Dorothea sourly. " I doubt if he ever gives them back the change." In May he announced that he was about to pay them a visit. Dorothea would have liked to have persuaded her uncle to forbid it but she knew the time was not yet ripe. Instead, she received him as coldly as possible. The long-standing friendship which bound Montrond and Talleyrand together was as galling to her as ever. This time, she noted with satisfaction that his charm seemed to be wearing off, leaving behind only a sense of fatigue and oppression.

"Monsieur de Montrond talks of returning to Louêche to put his poor body in a bath. It would be a good thing if it were possible to put his soul in also," she noted venomously in her journal. " His visit here was an even worse failure than that of last year. When you have survived yourself, your fortune, your health, your wit and your manners and when there does not remain even the faintest reflection of your past glories to give you a little consideration in the world, the spectacle which you present is deplorable. I said one day to Monsieur de Talleyrand that in my opinion nothing was left to Monsieur de Montrond but to blow out his brains . . ."

Diplomatic society in London seemed to be crumbling. At the beginning of the year the Esterhazys had been recalled to Vienna, now it was the turn of the Lievens. Palmerston insisted upon sending as Ambassador to St. Petersburg Sir Stratford Canning, probably the only Englishman alive whom the tsar would have found it completely impossible to accept. As a result, Lieven had been recalled ; to be consoled with some honorific office in the imperial household. Madame de Lieven was distraught ; her whole life was centred around the intrigues and confabulations of international politics and seclusion in St. Petersburg seemed to her a crueller sentence than any judge could have imposed. Dorothea felt for her not only as a friend in distress but, as a fellow victim of Palmerston's malevolence.

As the time drew near for Madame de Lieven's departure her gloom became ever deeper and cast a sombre shadow over the whole season. At Palmerston's farewell dinner the nadir of dejection was perhaps achieved. Dorothea went reluctantly and solely for the princess's sake. " Lady Cowper was making visible efforts to appear at ease. Monsieur de Bülow was pale and embarrassed and looked like a pickpocket caught in the act. Poor Dedel (the Danish Ambassador) resembled an orphan at the funeral of both his parents." So painful was Madame de Lieven's distress that Dorothea felt it kinder not to increase her agitation still further by going to see her off.

One of Madame de Lieven's bitterest complaints against Palmerston had been that the minister had poisoned her relationship with the royal family. Now Dorothea was beginning to wonder whether Talleyrand and herself were not being treated in the same way. Her relationship with the queen had always been close, and William IV had gone out of his way to be gracious to her uncle. Now the atmosphere seemed cooler. When they had gone on leave in 1832 she noticed that the king had said, " I have charged my Ambassador in Paris to tell your Government that I insist on keeping you here." In 1833 he had said, " When are you coming back ? " In 1834 he asked, " When are you leaving ? " The old king was as stupid as he was coarse and seemed to be well down the royal road to madness, but even so, his lack of friendliness was disquieting. Dorothea was not invited to Windsor. The omission was politely regretted and it was explained that the absence of the queen made it impossible for her to be received. The excuse was accepted as gracefully as it was given but that did not stop Dorothea from noticing that the queen's absence had not prevented Lord Grey's wife and daughter from going to Windsor. Fairly or unfairly, another score was notched up against Palmerston.

The Prime Minister did what he could to keep the peace between the Foreign Office and the French Embassy. Dorothea chanced to be visiting Lord Grey the day after Palmerston had offended Talleyrand with a typical piece of ill-manners and lack of consideration. Lord Grey ran down the staircase after her to assure her that Lord Palmerston had had no ill intention and to ask her to make excuses for him to Talleyrand. Dorothea replied that the road to hell was paved with good intentions. " I promise you to tell Monsieur de Talleyrand that Lord Palmerston is as innocent as an unborn child," she added dryly, " but I don't believe a word of it."

Surely it was high time for the prince to go. There still seemed a chance, however, that Palmerston might be thrown from office and someone more friendly replace him. By July, the Grey administration was obviously on the point of falling. Despite her liking for Lord Grey, Dorothea's sympathies were all with the opposition and, even if they had not been, her hatred of Lord Palmerston must have led her to pray for the rapid decease of the ministry. She found it unconscionably long a-dying. First the Prime Minister and the Chancellor of the Exchequer resigned. This might have seemed to close the matter, but the Lord Chancellor firmly stated that he was still in office and had no intention of giving up the Great Seal until formally ordered to do so. Lord Holland, for his part, declared that he had not resigned but that he considered himself to be out of office. Baffled, Dorothea appealed to Lord Grey. Surely a Prime Minister's resignation involved all the other members of the Cabinet? " In theory, yes," replied Lord Grey, anxious, as ever, to be helpful, " but in fact, no."

Theory and fact were eventually reconciled and the ministry was officially held to be out. The Tories were avid for office and felt that it was theirs by right. Little by little, however, it became clear that the king had no intention of offering it to them ; on the contrary, a laborious operation was going on designed to patch the rubble of the last administration into an alternative Liberal Government. Sitting next to the Duke of Wellington at dinner, Dorothea found that she agreed with the Tory leader in every particular ; Lord Grey's Government represented the last stage between innovation and revolution and the king was now on the point of pitching himself into " an abyss destined to engulf the monarchy and the country."

The king went his own way and eventually appointed Lord Melbourne as Liberal Prime Minister. The bulk of Lord Grey's ministers were retained with the addition of Sir John Cam Hobhouse. On hearing of the appointment of this last worthy, Dorothea characteristically remarked that he was " celebrated for his friendship with Lord Byron, his eastern travels and his very liberal opinions . . . This shows that the Cabinet has taken on a more decidedly revolutionary character." Her chagrin was complete when it became clear that Lord Palmerston was to remain at the Foreign Office. " It seemed as if everything in the greatness of England was dwindled, shrunken and soiled," she commented in obituary vein. Now indeed, she knew that it was time for Talleyrand to go. " Lord Grey's example," she wrote on 17th July, " is another proof that the great figures of history should themselves choose the circumstances of their retirement and should not wait till it is imposed upon them by the mistakes or the perfidy of others." There can be little doubt what moral she drew from the reflection.

*   *   *   *   *

Talleyrand was due to return to France in August, 1834. As a year before, he was uncertain whether or not he should come back to England. He knew that he was old and tired, in frail health, incapable of working at full pitch for any length of time ; but he knew also that his clarity of mind and intelligence were unimpaired, that his prudence, experience and wisdom were as valuable as ever. He knew that he could never work effectively so long as Palmerston was allowed to remain in office but he knew too that the Liberal administration could hardly last more than a few months. He appreciated the pleasures of freedom from office and the chance to live in peace at Valençay but had little doubt that within a few months he would be thirsting once more for a place in public life.

Dorothea had the same calculations to make. For herself alone there cannot be the faintest doubt that she would still have liked to stay in London. Her inviolable social position, her wide and unqualified popularity, the pleasures of her relationship with Bacourt, above all her ability to influence policy and the men who made it : all these were assets she was loath to exchange for the uncertain attractions of a Paris she had learnt to distrust and fear. Still more so than a year before, life in France with Talleyrand, enfeebled as he would be and living for the most part in retirement, could only mean something close to a withdrawal from public life. It is infinitely to her credit that, at this moment, she never stopped to consider her own desires but thought only of the needs and wants of her uncle.

Whenever she wished to express her thoughts with particular emphasis and precision, Dorothea liked to put them in writing. Especially under the cynical eye of her uncle she found her eloquence dry up, her train of thought grow muddled, her best points remain unmade. Now she had something to say to Talleyrand which she felt to be of quite peculiar importance. She sat down and wrote a letter and put it into his hands the day before he left for France. It is a good letter and no one can doubt its sincerity or the unselfish love which inspired it.

" I have a serious duty towards you which I never feel more acutely than when your glory is at stake. I irritate you a

231

little sometimes by talking, and then I stop before I have said all I think. So let me write to you and please forgive anything I may say which annoys you because it is my love for you which drives me to say it.

" I do not claim to be very clever but I feel that I cannot be wrong when I am thinking of you, whom I know so well and whose troubles and difficulties I am so well placed to understand. It is only after much reflection that I urge you now to leave public life and to retire from the scene on which a society in disarray is playing such a dismal part. Do not remain any longer at a post in which you are bound to find yourself asked to destroy all which you have worked so hard to achieve. You know what fears I felt last year when you returned to England. I foresaw all the pain in store for you, given the task you had to perform and the means at your disposal. You must admit that the greater part of my fears have proved real. This year there are a thousand new reasons why the position is worse . . ."

Dorothea enumerated the woes of England: a society divided by party spirit, a frivolous, presumptuous, arrogant minister, a Government swept away on the current of revolution, a new diplomatic corps " as impudent as it is vulgar," and as for the support of his own Government: " pettiness, indiscretion, vanity and intrigue dominate everything in Paris."

" You did not come here four years ago to make your fortune, your career or your reputation: all these were secure long ago. You did not come out of love for those who are ruling our country; you like them as little as you respect them. You came with no other object than to render a great service to your country at a moment when its very foundations were shaken. At your age it was a perilous adventure: to reappear after fifteen years of retirement when the storm was at its height and still it with a gesture. You did what you set out to do: let that be enough. In the future you can do nothing but whittle away the significance of what you have already done. " Remember the truth of Lord Grey's words, ' When one has kept one's health and one's faculties one may still at an advanced age usefully occupy oneself with public affairs. But, in critical times like the present, a degree of attention, activity and energy is required which belongs only to the prime of life and not to its decline. When one is young any moment is a good one for entering the lists ; in old age the only thing that remains is to choose the best moment for leaving them . . . ' The noble and touching farewell words of Lord Grey threw a last fleeting ray of light on his career. His retirement became a triumph yet, a day longer, and he would have been effaced. The last two champions of the old Europe should leave public life at the same time. May they carry with them into their retirement the knowledge that they have tried and done well and may history one day show that the coincidence of their departures does honour to them both.

" This and only this seems to me to be the fitting close to your public life. All considerations which might lead you to think otherwise are unworthy of you. You cannot be influenced by the possibility of a little more amusement, a few more social diversions. Are you to count the trifling excitements of despatches, couriers and news ? The interest of such things is often no more than that gained by a child from its toy. Are we even to consider the tranquillity which we enjoy ? Is the age of disturbance and revolution ended in France ? I do not know. Is it more or less distant in England ? I cannot tell. Shall we seek distraction in travel ? How are we to arrange our private lives ? What does it matter ? I am younger than you and therefore you may think that I would give more thought than you to the future, but I should think myself unworthy of your confidence and of the truth which I am now venturing to tell you if I let myself be swayed by the slightest consideration of my own comfort.

" If, like you, one belongs to history, one should think of no other future save that which history prepares. You know that history judges the end of a man's life more harshly than the beginning. If, as I am proud to believe, you think that my judgment is worth something as well as my affection, you will be as frank with yourself as I am with you now. You will have done with self-deceptions, specious arguments and the snares of vanity and you will put an end to a situation which would soon debase you in the eyes of others as of mine. Do not bargain with the world. Dictate its judgment, do not submit to it. Declare yourself old, lest people should say that you are ageing. Say nobly and simply to all the world ' The time has come'."

10

" Farewell to England," wrote Dorothea grandiloquently a few days after she had left for ever, " but not to the memory of the four happy years which I have spent there . . . Farewell once more to this hospitable country which I leave with regrets and gratitude."

When Dorothea wrote it was still not decided that her farewell was in fact destined to be as final as her words suggested. Talleyrand had been swayed by his niece's arguments, he had gone so far as to say that he would probably not be coming back but still he would not finally commit himself. To surrender office seemed to him to be loosening his last, tenuous grip on life itself; though logically he might be convinced that it was the right course for him to take, he would still postpone for as long as possible the inexorable application of the logic. When Dorothea rejoined him in Paris she found him depressed and bored, he said that he knew no one in France, that everyone was aged and worn out. She must have wondered for a while whether her advice was really right and whether Talleyrand would not have been happier letting his powers flicker out while he was still in harness. But her confidence was never shaken; her uncle's real happiness and, still more, his good name, could not be compatible with a course which inevitably must lower him in the eyes of the world.

She did not try to conceal her own personal regrets. In early October she wrote to Lady Holland saying wistfully how much better the fogs of London suited her than the brilliant suns of Touraine and Valençay. She was thinking of visiting all her old friends but was unable to leave Valençay before the Duke of Orleans paid them the visit which he had promised for later that month. An omen came to reassure her that no other decision had been possible when the Houses of Parliament were totally destroyed by fire. Dorothea promptly interpreted this as proof that the political edifice was " crumbling along with the material one and that the old walls refused to be dishonoured by the profane doctrines of to-day." Who could doubt that Talleyrand had done well to leave England before it had plunged altogether into the abyss of revolution ?

By the time that the Duke of Orleans came to visit them, Talleyrand had still not finally made up his mind. The visit in itself gave quite enough for both of them to think about. A visit by the heir to the throne of France is a great affair, however uncertain the title of the incumbent, and Talleyrand and his niece had prepared an elaborate programme of festivities and sight-seeing. The whole affair might in fact have been formal and rather depressing. However, with the social grace which consists so largely of doing the wrong thing at the right time, Dorothea after dinner firmly took up her needlework and proceeded to carry on as if her guest was an intimate of the house. Monsieur de Talleyrand found the example an excellent one and stumped off for his evening drive ; within a few minutes the rest of the party were cheerfully playing whist.

Dorothea had had a long conversation with the Duke of Orleans in Paris before she retreated to the country ; it seems probable that she then touched on the question of her uncle's future. Certainly the duke was quick to take up the subject with her when sitting next to her at dinner. His father, he said, was anxious that Talleyrand should return to London but he himself thought it was impossible, at any rate for as long as Lord Palmerston remained in office. Dorothea was cautious but agreed that it would be difficult for her uncle to go back. The Duke of Orleans spoke at length to Talleyrand ; both his own feelings and his knowledge of Dorothea's must have led him to discourage his host from seeking to return to London. Still no final decision was taken but Talleyrand at least went so far as to say that it seemed there was no more for him to do in London. One more grudging step had been taken down the tortuous path which led him to his resignation.

Royer Collard joined Dorothea in her efforts to persuade the old man to close the question for ever. In 1833 he had urged Talleyrand to return to London ; now he wrote to Dorothea in handsome apology : " Last year was the time he should have gone . . . From this very arm-chair from which I am writing to you to-day, I was blind enough to combat you, knowing nothing about it. You alone were in a position to know and to judge . . . I was wrong ; this is yet another piece of homage which I am anxious to pay you."

At last, Talleyrand, with the air of a man forced back on his ultimate defences, pleaded that the letter would be very hard to write. Within half an hour Dorothea had submitted a draft. Talleyrand changed a couple of words then, at Dorothea's suggestion, sent it to Royer Collard for him too to make one or two minor amendments. On 13th November, Talleyrand's letter of resignation was on its way.

Even now the battle was not over. Madame Adélaïde wrote to Talleyrand beseeching him to reconsider his decision and to Dorothea urging her to do what she could in that sense. The king wrote to reinforce his sister's pleas. On 19th November, the news arrived from London that the Liberal Government was out and the Duke of Wellington once more in office. The temptation to Talleyrand to go back on his decision must have been considerable but Dorothea never for a moment doubted that the essential facts remained unchanged. She made it her most constant pre-occupation to ensure that her uncle did not change his mind.

There was yet one more hazard. If the prince would not return to London, why should he not go somewhere else where the work would be less exacting ? Madame Adélaïde suggested Vienna. " Vienna would please me for many reasons," replied Talleyrand. " It would also suit Madame de Dino who, for all her devotion to me, finds it hard to console herself for leaving London where she was such a success. But at my age one should no longer venture too far from one's own home . . ." The offer was refused with thanks. Dorothea knew that her uncle was no more capable of undertaking the embassy there than he was in London. Resolutely she crushed down her own regrets. She wrote to give Prince Esterhazy the news and Metternich, hearing of it from him, speculated whether Talleyrand had not refused Vienna because he still dreamed of a return to London.

Dorothea could have disillusioned him ; whatever the future might hold for her and her uncle, she knew that his travels were over for ever. Now it remained to see that the last years of his failing life were filled with dignity and contentment.

*   *   *   *   *

The Paris to which Dorothea returned was vastly different to that which she had known before the July Revolution. The Government was slightly more to her taste but, as for the rest, she found it little if at all more agreeable. The supplanting of the Bourbons by the Orleans family had split Parisian society into hostile fragments. The aristocracy for the most part remained solidly loyal to Charles X and the Bourbons. Always exclusive, the nobles now became unapproachable. Retreating into their gloomy fastnesses in the Faubourg St. Germain, they tried to console themselves for their economic difficulties and political impotence by despising anyone who was not of their blood and hating anyone who was not of their opinion. Completely irreconcilable to the régime they yet, for the most part, lacked the energy or enthusiasm openly to combat it. It was an opposition of muted sneers and sulky isolationism which cut them off from the body politic and destroyed them for ever as an effective force in the life of France.

To the new royal family rallied the bankers, the lawyers, the rich merchants, and all those political figures whose fates were bound up with that of the régime. It was the world of Monsieur Leuwen, *père*, but the majority of the actors unhappily lacked his qualities of wit and tolerance. It was a vigorous society, forceful, varied, relatively free of prejudices and dogmas, but it was also raffish, vulgar, interested mainly in the acquisition of money or in the more sordid aspects of the struggle for power. It seemed somehow as if there had been just enough life in Paris to make one decent society. Now all the dignity and loyalty had gone one way, the energy, enterprise and open-mindedness another. All the arrogance, inertia and intolerance had been absorbed by the *Faubourg St. Germain* ; the *juste milieu* for its share had got the greed, the baseness and the gracelessness.

Lady Granville, wife of the British Ambassador, had

identified three main parties in Parisian society apart from those few loyal souls who felt themselves too out of sympathy with the régime to remain in Paris at all. There were the *Dames du Mouvement*, the supporters of the régime, among whose few aristocratic members were that insatiable gossip the Countess de Boigne and Dorothea's daughter-in-law, the Duchess of Valençay. Then there were the *Dames de la Résistance*, almost all the *Faubourg St. Germain*. "They wear mourning but it won't last—it is only for a very distant relation," remarked Lady Granville unkindly and, as it turned out, unjustly. Finally there were the *Dames de l'Attente*. "They are said only to be watching the weather." By those of zeal on either side they were held to be cowardly and unprincipled, by their own account they were reasonable souls trying to mitigate a situation which threatened continually to become altogether intolerable.

Dorothea, if she could have chosen freely, would have been with the neutrals. She could not afford to break altogether with the *Faubourg St. Germain*. For herself alone she might have become reconciled to a life in Paris shared only with a splinter-group of the aristocracy. But for her children it was unthinkable. All her prejudices told her that they must not marry below their social station. Louis was already safe, no one could cavil at a Montmorency, but Alexander was a problem and as for Pauline—Dorothea would rather have seen her immured for life in a convent than lowering herself by marrying out of the high aristocracy.

But equally she could not purchase the favour of the *Faubourg* by breaking with the Orleans family. After all, her uncle owed to them his return to office and the reinstatement of the Bourbons could only mean his final extinction. Almost all Dorothea's friends were active servants of the régime: Royer Collard, Thiers, Molé, Guizot, had all first banded together in opposition. To turn her back on them now would have seemed to Dorothea unthinkably disloyal as well as politically short-sighted.

The only course was therefore not to commit herself finally to any party ; to remain a supporter of the régime without appearing conspicuously as an enemy of the Carlists. But it was a difficult line to follow, filled with pitfalls and conundrums of protocol and comportment. Charles X died, for instance. Was one to wear mourning or not ? Whatever one did would be charged with political significance. Dorothea was at Rochecotte when the problem was finally posed. " Everyone wears mourning according to his own fancy," she wrote with wry humour to Bacourt, " from colours to deep black with infinite gradations and with fresh bitterness about every yard of crêpe that seems to be wanting . . . I am much puzzled to know what shade of white, grey or black I shall adopt when I reach Paris. Generally speaking the ladies of the neutral party who are also of society wear black in company and white at court."

The proud *Faubourg* was not impressed by this ambivalence. Those who were not with them were against them and there could be no doubt in which camp the Duchess of Dino with her foreign blood, revolutionary record and subversive friends was to be placed. So long as Talleyrand lived, at least, there would be little place for his niece in the temple of the godly. Her tentative overtures were rebuffed. There was not much open rudeness or hostility but she was never treated with warmth in a legitimist salon. Certainly she was given no reason to think that her search for eligible matches for her children was going to be an easy one.

But the greatest strain on Dorothea's policy of non-commitment came from the friendship of the royal family. Louis-Philippe was in that least enviable of positions ; a monarch boycotted by his own aristocracy. Considering that his family was of the blood royal and quite as ancient and far richer than the Bourbons, the contempt with which the majority of his subjects regarded him was perpetually astonishing. The king and all his relations were possessed by a haunting sense of inferiority and social uncertainty which would have been pathetic in a commoner and in a member of the royal family was either humiliating or profoundly touching according to the political opinions of the observer. Count Apponyi, for instance, tells that the Duke of Orleans found himself at a large ball where a few families of the *Faubourg* were also represented. He was struck by the charms of Mlle de Béthune, a young lady of impeccably aristocratic birth, but did not dare approach her for fear of a rebuff. He turned to the Duke of Valençay and asked him whether he thought it would be considered rude by Mlle de Béthune if he were to ask her for a dance. Valençay accused him of mock-modesty. " No, I assure you, I really am afraid of being snubbed." Eventually Apponyi went off to see if a dance could be arranged and found the girl taken aback but willing. " After all," she observed patronisingly, " he *is* a Prince of the Blood." The dance took place and Apponyi noted with surprised admiration that Mlle de Béthune was positively affable towards her royal partner.

It was inevitable that Dorothea should feel a little condescending towards a royal family treated with such disdain. Her duty and her sense of gratitude made it essential that she should put in an appearance at the large receptions at the Tuileries but there was no doubt in her mind as to who was doing a favour to whom. She found these evenings totally undistinguished, the dresses and uniforms dowdy, the protocol ill-managed, above all the company too mixed to be tolerable even in a palace. " A little man in uniform precedes their Majesties and asks each lady her name, a proceeding which in the case of three-quarters of them seems absolutely necessary." On their side, the king and queen did nothing to contest her view that it was the Duchess of Dino who was conferring the honour and they who were receiving it. Their pleasure at seeing her was touching and, on one occasion at least, special arrangements were made so that she could come and go by a private entrance and not be forced to wait amidst the riff-raff for her horses.

Dorothea liked the king and admired his taste and intelligence. She thought the queen worthy and respectable, though not a figure of much distinction. But the member of the royal family for whom she cared the most and over whom she was to exercise the greatest influence was the young Duke of Orleans. She found the frank admiration and respect shown to her by the heir to the throne of France both flattering and endearing. The relationship was never one of more than affectionate good-will but it was none the less valuable to both of them. Dorothea, indeed, would have been sorry to see any more profound feeling obtrude into their friendship. Her life was so full with the ailing Talleyrand that any fresh emotional complication would have been an intolerable burden.

Within forty-eight hours of her return to France, the Duke of Orleans had called at the house and spent an hour alone with her discussing his need of a wife and—perennial topic of heirs to thrones—the insignificance of the part which his father had allowed him to play in public life. Dorothea was sympathetic and helpful ; anyhow sufficiently so to induce the duke to invite himself to come and stay with her and Prince Talleyrand at Valençay a few weeks later. She found that the young duke possessed every virtue except that of judgment and flattered herself that this at least she was well qualified to supply. The future of the Orleans dynasty, of France itself perhaps, was tightly bound up with the development of this immature but potentially formidable young man. It was not going to be Dorothea's fault if every influence which could urge this development into the right paths was not forthcoming.

*　　*　　*　　*　　*

The urgent attentions of the royal family, the political obligations of her uncle, the suspicious hostility of the *Faubourg* : all these made it impossible for Dorothea to steer the middle course in Parisian society which she felt desirable. The result was that she was forced to live in a state of cold war with the great majority of those Parisians with whom, instinctively, she felt it right for her to consort. It was not surprising that she began to find Paris even more disagreeable than it had used to be and longed to escape from it to Valençay or, better still, to her own particular retreat at Rochecotte.

After her return from England, Rochecotte took on for Dorothea an almost mystical significance as a place to which to retire ; secure from the bitterness of the world and the calumnies of society ; tranquil in the affection and trust of a small community. She had only to be in Paris for a few days to be, " longing for the calm and sweetness of Rochecotte, with its wide horizon and its pure sky, for my clean house, my kind and simple neighbours, my work-people, my flowers, my big dog, my little cow and goat, the good abbé, the modest Vestier, the little wood where we used to gather fir cones."

The " good abbé " thus unceremoniously listed below the goat, was Jean Baptiste Girolet, a Benedictine priest now some seventy years old whose most noticeable characteristics were gentleness, innocence and a remoteness from human affairs as sublime in theory as it could be aggravating in practice. Vestier, the architect, fitted equally well into the pattern of life at Rochecotte. He was as sentimental as he was modest and devoted to his mistress. When Dorothea suggested to him that he might design her a tomb he burst into tears and was quite unable to undertake the work.

Calm, sweetness, simplicity : these were what Dorothea looked for in Rochecotte. She knew that in occupying herself with local affairs she was doing harm to no one and good to many. When she considered the pattern of her life in Paris it sometimes seemed to her that she did harm to many and good to none. She concluded that it was her life at Rochecotte which represented reality and in which she could hope to fulfil herself. Life in Paris was a meretricious sham, to be abandoned or, at any rate, indulged in as little as possible. Dorothea strove to adapt herself completely to the pattern of life at Rochecotte and to find there the security and peace which seemed to be lacking everywhere else:

> " *Well then ; I now do plainly see*
> *This busy world and I will ne'er agree*
> *The very honey of all earthly joy*
> *Does of all meats the soonest cloy,*
> *And they (methinks) deserve my pity,*
> *Who for it can endure the stings,*
> *The crowd, and buzz and murmurings,*
> *Of this great hive, the city.*"[1]

" If my friends will only love me," wrote Lady Grey more prosaically, " and I can possess a garden in summer and an arm-chair in winter, I am perfectly content in leading the life of an oyster." Dorothea quoted the sentiment and echoed it with all her heart.

Would Dorothea in fact have been gratified if oysterdom had been bestowed on her under such conditions or were her constantly reiterated dreams of retreat and the simple life no more than the sentimental vapourings of a spoiled society lady ? A rustic vocation does not come easily to the unpractised and Dorothea found that a little of it would go a long way. But this does not mean that she was hypocritical. She had a profound respect for the virtues and values of the contemplative life and the simple duties of the countryside. Her respect was enhanced rather than impaired by the occasional discovery that she herself was not yet fitted for such a life. And yet she was far more suited to it than she had been only a few years before. She had evolved considerably during her four years of intense social and political activity. She had learned, above all, which things in life she deemed vitally important and which could be allowed to fade with the insubstantial pageant. She had become a formed and coherent personality and, though the reality might differ widely from her ideal, there was sufficient resemblance that she might hope that the two could finally be reconciled altogether.

She was still overweeningly the aristocrat. Here there could be no compromise. She did not aspire to any further advancement, if such had indeed been possible in her eyes, or feel any jealousy of those few who were still more highly placed. Nor did she despise others for not being what she was ; her indignation and contempt was only aroused if they tried to ignore the gap or to deny its significance. Even then she despised them not so much for their impertinence as for the futility of their efforts. They were what they were and that was an end to it.

The complete rigidity of Dorothea's social outlook and her ineffable confidence in a divinely ordered universe of rich men in castles and poor men at gates was remarkable even in the 1830s. With such a viewpoint, it was not astonishing that she found the trim and ordered life of a country village more satisfactory than the crowd and buzz and murmuring of Orleanist Paris. The stage might be unduly cramped but at least the dramatis personæ knew their places. But it was not only pride of position which drew her away from the city to a life of partial retreat ; the decision was forced on her for more cogent and far more admirable reasons which involved the sacrifice of much that she deemed precious in life.

Dorothea was still intensely ambitious, as anxious as ever to be associated with and to influence those who controlled the progress of great affairs. But her ambition was no longer unqualified ; when she persuaded Talleyrand that the time had come for him to retire she was deliberately shutting herself off from the world of international politics in the interests of her uncle's happiness and good name. It was a selfless decision and one which proved what many might have doubted ; that she could weigh the joys of power against the well-being of those she loved and conclude that the latter was the more important. " When we are able to perform a complete renunciation of self," she wrote to Bacourt, " we find our burden lightened and the low and heavy flight of selfishness is replaced by the rapid sweep of outstretched wings, which is a pleasure in itself." Certainly she gloried in her self-sacrifice but it was no less painful to her for that.

Self-abnegation did not need to be carried to the point of complete isolation from the world she so much relished ; on the contrary she was to make herself very busy on the fringes of French politics over the next few years. Always, however, she knew that this was only a diversion, time and energy spared from the preoccupations with her uncle and her children which were her first responsibility. And forming itself as yet hesitantly in the background of her mind was the suspicion that even in the benevolent activities of a country lady and her duty to her family there was not a complete answer to the problems of her life.

Dorothea at the time of her return from London was far from having any strong religious convictions. What she felt was not so much a positive belief or desire as a profound dis- satisfaction with what she was and did. Something was lacking, but she did not know what ; she had to go somewhere, but she did not know where. All that she was sure of was that she was " immersed in the sorrow and grief which are the lot of worldly people and are the destruction of peace of mind, charity and purity." She was trying to escape from this morass, but " my efforts are usually impotent and my struggles vain and futile." ". . . When we have spent years amid the struggles of life and desire to change our path, we find ourselves a burden to ourselves ; we can neither go forward with our load nor throw it off straight away ; we stumble and retrace our steps ; we prove ourselves but feeble travellers and our goal recedes as our desire to reach it increases. Such is my case."

A lot of this was a more or less conscious effort in self-deception. Dorothea may have abhorred the struggle of life but another part of her relished it and would have been totally unhappy if deprived of its challenge, temptations and frustrations. She could never have been the contemplative oyster of Lady Grey's imagining or, if the role had been forced upon her, her restless disquietude would soon have made her an uncomfortable companion for others in the bed. But she did still long sincerely to be capable of adopting a life of contemplation and retreat. However inadequate her limbs and uncertain her sense of direction, Dorothea felt that she was groping her way towards perception of a hidden truth ; that she was within reach of the discovery of a way of life and thought which would somehow free her from all the wearisome bonds of her day-to-day existence. She had become—not a mystic—but a searcher after mystery. The fruits of her search were far from satisfying but they left her with the suspicion that all her life was dross and all her worldly interests of the most trivial importance. From now on her public life was played against a background of muted discontent and of uncertainty in the value of all she did.

*   *   *   *   *

Her duties towards Talleyrand and her children may have made it impossible for her to devote herself fully to the political world of Paris but equally they could not be reconciled with perpetual seclusion at Rochecotte.

The prince was a constant cause of worry and irritation. When he had agreed to return to London for the last time he had promised the Duke of Broglie that " once it is over, I shall at once return to my den to resume the torpor which is alone appropriate to my present condition." Now it was over ; but Talleyrand did not find his den at all congenial or torpor a condition which necessarily followed from the fact that it was appropriate. No sooner back in Paris than Dorothea found him depressed and bored, complaining that everybody else seemed to be aged and worn out. It was an ominous start to his retirement.

As time wore on, Talleyrand became better adjusted to his new condition; he began to accept that there might be recompense in increased leisure and freedom of action. He had the satisfaction of knowing that he was much missed in London and—always keen consolation for an ex-ambassador—that his successor, General Sébastiani, was far from filling his place. The latter complained that London society gave him indigestion and that the only person who was kind to him was Lord Palmerston—news that caused Dorothea some wry amusement. But, though Talleyrand grew less miserable, he was no less restless and compensated for his lack of activity by journeying endlessly from place to place. No sooner arrived at Paris than he would wish to be on the way to Valençay; from Valençay it would be Rochecotte which became the goal, from Rochecotte, Pont-de-Sains or Bourbon l'Archambault.

Much though she disliked them, Dorothea did nothing to check these futile peregrinations. If they brought some relief to her uncle then they were cheaply purchased at the price of a certain amount of inconvenience. Besides, she knew Prince Talleyrand might grow resentful if she seemed to interfere too often or too openly. There were limits to her influence and she wished to reserve it strictly for those occasions which were really of first importance. So long as there was any risk that her uncle might be tempted to engage once more in public life then she preferred to keep her forces in reserve. In little things it was to neither of their interests that she should oppose him.

Her children were less of a problem though even they presented trouble enough. Louis was dutiful as ever, his sins always of omission rather than commission. After the July Revolution he had respectfully followed his great-uncle's example and rallied to the new régime. True, he had not played any very noticeable part in its early days but he found that being the Duke of Valençay was in itself sufficiently exhausting an occupation. He conscientiously attended royal functions and became known as a friend of the Duke of Orleans. This done, he felt his duties to court and society to have been well acquitted. What was more he brought his wife with him into the Orleanist camp. As a Montmorency, all Alix's sympathies should have been with the Bourbons. But she was shrewd enough to see that, if Louis were to have a future, he must retain the favour of her uncle and of the present royal family. Privately she may have deplored the revolution but in her nature there was little place for sentimentality and she sacrificed her loyalty to the old régime to the interests of her future and solidarity with her husband.

Dorothea disliked Alix de Valençay and considered her a bad influence in Louis's life ; encouraging him in idleness and dissipation. She would have been a difficult mother-in-law for anyone and Alix was calculated to bring out the worst in her. The Duchess of Valençay had just enough obstinacy to provoke Dorothea's impatience, impertinence to sting her pride and intelligence to know how to irritate her most effectively without any of the integrity, purposefulness or distinction of mind which might have attracted Dorothea or, at least, won her respect. For a short time the two women were drawn together after the death at the age of two of Louis and Alix's first child, Yolande de Valençay. During the child's illness, when Alix too was much of the time confined to her bed, Dorothea took command of the household, organised everything and saw that all possible was done to save Yolande's life. When all efforts had failed she alone kept calm amidst the turbulent chorus of woe, comforted anyone who was susceptible to comfort and succeeded in making reason heard. But in Alix's gratitude can be seen the underlying antipathy between the two women. " At this moment," she wrote to Count Apponyi, " when everyone here had lost their head ; myself, my poor father, my mother, my sister, my brothers-in-law . . . we needed someone who felt less strongly than we did . . ." Only in Dorothea, she implied, was such superhuman—or, perhaps, inhuman—detachment to be hoped for.

The indifference which Alix displayed towards her husband and the loyalty which Louis continued to feel for his mother made the marriage a certain failure from the start. Louis was too young, too simple, too unassertive to have any chance of controlling his selfish and capricious wife. Both parties contributed to the disaster but Dorothea had no doubt that it was her daughter-in-law who was mainly responsible. She made her views plain to all who were concerned.

Alexander, the second son, presented another sort of problem. He had become a naval officer and was serving with his ship off the coasts of Latin America when the July Revolution put to the test the loyalties of everyone in royal service. Whether by genuine conviction or by reaction against his mother and Talleyrand, Alexander declared himself a legitimist. According to the diarist Raikes, he insulted his captain on his own deck for remaining in the service of a traitor, then resigned from the navy, challenged his former captain to a duel and ran the unfortunate man through the body. This is certainly the sort of thing which Alexander might have done but the facts, if true, seem to have been telescoped in time. Alexander remained with the navy until 1833 and did not finally resign until the end of 1835. Standards may have been different for a nephew of Prince Talleyrand but it is still hard to believe that any service could have tolerated from one of its junior officers behaviour of the sort which Raikes describes.

Alexander was never one for concealing his opinions and when he met his mother and the prince in Paris in the summer of 1833 there must have been some unpleasant scenes between them. Once more according to Raikes, there was a bitter quarrel and Alexander asked his great-uncle whether he imagined that " your eighty years of corruption can excuse the infamous part you have played ? " If indeed he did speak like this, Talleyrand must either have been exceptionally forgiving or Alexander subsequently most apologetic because no change was made to the will by which the prince left all Dorothea's children considerable fortunes.

His naval career over, Alexander now devised a new way of annoying his family. After a short stay in Paris he conceived a strong desire for his father's company and went off to Florence to visit him. There he stayed for nearly two years ; rejoicing, perhaps, in the remoteness of his creditors but also certainly in the vexation which he must be causing his mother and his great-uncle. Only in September, 1835 did he return to France.

Finally there was Pauline ; now some fifteen years old and

already dreaming of her entry into Parisian society. She presented little problem in her own character ; sweet-natured and obliging she had a streak of obstinate determination, but on all important questions tended to see things in the same light as her mother. So far as Pauline was concerned, the problem lay in the very fact of her existence ; the daughter of an Orleanist household who must nevertheless hope to find her social life and her husband among the supporters of the Bourbons.

If no reconciliation with the *Faubourg St. Germain* could be achieved then Dorothea would have had to look outside France to marry her daughter. She was not going to do this except as a last resort and felt reasonably hopeful that the need could be avoided. The first reaction of the *Faubourg* after her return from England had certainly been discouraging but it would be another eighteen months at least before Pauline would need to come out into society. Surely by then, even in France, some of the bitterness would have faded from public life ? And even if the Orleanist régime was as unpopular as ever, then surely assiduous courtship on her part coupled with an ostentatious caution in her relationship with the royal family would gradually soften the *Faubourg's* hostility ? For the moment Dorothea concentrated on fitting her daughter for the life of society. In December, 1834, Pauline was allowed down to dinner for the first time. She was young for such a privilege but Dorothea felt that it was no bad thing that she should learn how to listen to serious conversation without being bored. Whether or not she found the conversation to her taste it was not in Pauline's nature to show anything but appreciative attention. She seems to have survived the ordeal with credit.

Talleyrand's affection for Pauline was touching. Unlike her two brothers, she had gone to England with Dorothea and Talleyrand. It was one of the sights of London to see her waiting every evening in a carriage outside the embassy or the Foreign Office for the prince to finish his work and accompany her on their habitual drive. The old statesman spent almost as much time with the solemn, affectionate child as he did with her mother : when they were separated he wrote to her every day ; when Dorothea went for the cure to Baden,

Talleyrand and Pauline went off together to Bourbon l'Archambault. She went to Switzerland with her mother in the summer of 1835 and Talleyrand hardly knew which he missed the most ; with both gone he knew at any rate that there would be nothing left for him to live for.

*　　*　　*　　*　　*

The whole of the autumn of 1834 while Talleyrand was screwing his resolution to the point of resignation, was spent at Valençay. The great event of the season had been the visit of the Duke of Orleans but before that another guest had been and gone leaving, or so at least it seemed to Dorothea, a strong smell of sulphur behind him. Casimir Montrond came to stay at Valençay in early October. Dorothea had for long worked relentlessly to persuade her uncle to end the relationship. Montrond himself did much to help her ; the old dandy had become badly frayed at the edges and grew ever more curmudgeonly and hard to please. The wit and charm of his conversation had faded, leaving only coarseness and malice to testify to its former distinction ; his brilliant adventurousness had atrophied into a senile irresponsibility which made him impossible as a partner in any enterprise. Apponyi believed that he had been charged by Louis-Philippe to spy on Talleyrand and report his sayings. It seems most unlikely that the king would have had so much faith in the discretion of such a servant but Montrond had been known to spy on his friends and patrons in the past and it is quite possible that someone in Paris had promised him money in exchange for any interesting titbits of gossip.

The time had come to apply the *coup de grâce* and Dorothea did it without pity. There are several versions of what actually happened. According to the most detailed[2], Montrond made some injudiciously coarse remarks at table. Dorothea rose, scolded him like a schoolboy and rang the bell for a servant to bring round Monsieur de Montrond's horses as soon as possible. Dorothea's story that it was Talleyrand himself who took the final initiative sounds more like the truth. But whatever the details, the expulsion of Montrond was the culmination of a long and patient campaign which Dorothea had waged for many years. One could paint an unattractive picture of a scheming woman taking advantage of her uncle's age to destroy his oldest and dearest friendships. Jealousy of Montrond's influence over the prince was certainly an element in Dorothea's hostility. But it was concern for her uncle's welfare which inspired her actions. The bad manners, the incontinence, the disloyalty of Monsieur de Montrond had become intolerable. Talleyrand had ceased to derive much pleasure from his company and their friendship had become little more than a matter of habit. In so far as Montrond still had influence, it was unhealthy and malign.

Dorothea was justified in pursuing Montrond with such implacable dislike. In doing so, it was her love for her uncle which impelled her. But to be right is not necessarily to be sympathetic and implacability is not endearing as a characteristic. While admitting the justice of her cause it is difficult not to be a little repelled by the righteous executioner and to feel some pity for her seedy, shabby ruffian of a victim.

Hardly had Montrond left them than Lady Clanricarde arrived, accompanied by some other English friends. Lady Clanricarde was the only daughter of George Canning and an old friend from London. She paid Valençay the highest compliment at her disposal when she found it " spacious, comfortable and like an English country house." Apart from the house-party she noticed present " a drawing-master ; several persons more or less engaged in Mlle Pauline's education and a black gentleman " whose occupation she had not yet been able to define.

Montrond before leaving had promised faithfully to spread no word of the quarrel but Lady Clanricarde had barely arrived before the rumblings of his troubled pride began to filter in from the outer world. Lord Sidney wrote to one of the guests, Henry Greville, to say that Montrond was telling everyone that Valençay had become uninhabitable and that only Lady Clanricarde could put up with it. The letter was read aloud at table as was also a letter from Montrond to another of the guests asking for news as to what was going on and a third letter from the same author to Dorothea thanking her in the coldest possible phrases for her hospitality. Talleyrand, as

Dorothea had intended, was suitably annoyed and the possibility of any reconciliation much diminished.

A new vendetta arose to add spice to Dorothea's daily life. Lady Granville was wife of the British Ambassador and sister of the Duke of Devonshire ; gay, witty, inconsequential, mischievous, and in every way delightful. It was not surprising that Dorothea, predisposed as she was to see little good in other women, would find her flippant and artificial. The latter equally had little use for Dorothea's serious, almost intense nature, her *allemanderie*, as Talleyrand called it, her pre-occupation with her own soul. Dorothea was very capable of criticising herself destructively and acutely but it was rare that she found herself a proper subject for laughter. Lady Granville on the other hand was far less capable of serious self-examination, but found herself, as well as most other things, irresistibly amusing. The two women disliked each other from their first meeting.

Their antipathy soon became an ornament to the Parisian season. The two were constantly meeting : " Whenever anybody who hates me dines anywhere I am always fetched for them, poor souls," wrote Lady Granville plaintively. Their relations remained formally good : " Madame de Dino and I are as smooth as glass," but they took little trouble to hide their real feelings. Dorothea for some reason took umbrage at Lady Granville's habit of always leaving receptions at the Tuileries before dinner had been served. She arranged that the ambassadress should be invited to sit at the royal table and thus made it impossible for her to leave ; then, somehow contrived the seating at table so that Lady Granville found herself placed below the widow of a marshal. Only another ambassadress could hope really to appreciate the splendour of the insult. Lady Granville cared less than most for protocol, but even she cannot have forgiven the incident.

A few days later Dorothea was invited to dine at the British Embassy. Possibly Lady Granville had contrived a somewhat similar revenge, possibly Dorothea merely wished to express dissatisfaction with the food. Anyhow, she was ill at ease and showed it clearly. Apponyi described her " seated like a Sybil with her great black eyes at this table where wit was reigning.

She turned her gaze from one guest to another, plunging with her eyes to the very bottom of their hearts, as if she wished to discover their most secret and hidden thoughts. Then she would turn away with an expression of sadness or displeasure as if she had found nothing which did credit to the object of her study."

If forced into honesty, both of these women would have had to admit that they enjoyed the rivalry of the other. Their mutual dislike was genuine but not nearly so profound as each affected. As it was, they relished their antipathy and felt an extra satisfaction in the knowledge that it was the source of endless diversion to their friends.

But Dorothea's life was not solely inhabited by enemies. With Count Molé for example, she re-established a friendship as close as it had ever been in her early years in France. It was an anxious moment when Molé called to see her not long after her return to Paris but the event all passed off well. Molé was determined to please and, evidently, to be pleased : at any rate he told Dorothea that he found her much more likeable than she had been four years before. She in her turn found that he had lost none of the charm and brilliance which had delighted her long before. " He is in very good taste in an age when good taste is unknown " ; and few qualities were more likely to recommend themselves to Dorothea. The next stage was to bring him together with Talleyrand. Both men were nervous at the prospect and only agreed on condition that Dorothea was present. Her presence was presumably beneficial ; anyway, all passed off well. The reconciliation was soon complete and Molé welcomed back as a trusted friend.

Dorothea had always got a particular pleasure out of her correspondence with Count Molé. More of a man of the world than Bacourt, more of her own age than Royer Collard, more stimulating than Barante, he could always be relied on to understand her problems and sympathise with her point of view. During the spring and summer of 1835, as Talleyrand wandered disconsolately from place to place, content at nothing and tormenting the nerves of his companions, Dorothea found some consolation in pouring out her woes to Molé, and, incidentally, claiming a certain amount of credit for her patience and forbearance. " I'm finding it very hard to get back my health . . ." she wrote from Rochecotte in March, 1835. " But what does it matter ? It is worth a great deal to have a task which needs performing and whether it is easy or hard is not the question. What matters is to have an aim in life and to seek to achieve it worthily . . . When my spirit revolts then I silence it by saying that it is better to suffer than to expire, that there is no merit unless there is also effort, no triumph unless there is struggle, no progress unless there is sacrifice."

*   *   *   *   *

The querulous old age of Talleyrand was a cross which Dorothea was proud to bear but she added to it several supplementary burdens which at times seemed to her unfairly onerous. One of these was Princess Lieven. Dorothea met her at Baden in the summer of 1835. Since her exile from London the poor princess had found life in Russia quite intolerably parochial and now wandered pathetically around Europe trying to find her way back to the world of great affairs. " She finds nothing but a cruel void in the distraction which she demands of everyone," wrote Dorothea to Bacourt. " She finds no pleasure in occupation ; she lives in the street, in public places, talks inconsequentially and never listens, laughs, cries and acts at a venture, asks questions without interest in the answers . . . I have seen people, one after another, cease to pity her and care for her ; she saw it too and was humiliated."

Dorothea had always liked Madame de Lieven and was now saddened and shocked by her collapse. Perhaps she saw in it some parallel to what had happened to her uncle or even a hint of what she might one day suffer herself. She urged her old rival to settle in France and occupy her talents and energies in judicious meddling with the course of French politics. Madame de Lieven accepted the advice and Dorothea did much to help her, introducing her into the world in which she was herself so much at home. " Mme Dino is more than merely a kind woman," Madame de Lieven told Lady Cowper. " She has a great deal of subtlety and intelligence. . . ." The two ladies together made up a formidable partnership and for some time flung themselves wholeheartedly into the game of Government-making and breaking. Madame de Lieven indeed took up the game with such enthusiasm that she was never to stop until Louis Napoleon broke all the rules and made it, for a time at any rate, an unsuitable sport for amateurs. Dorothea was less wholehearted. She enjoyed promoting the interests of a friend but was not really prepared to practise politics for the sake of politics alone. If there was no friend to push, her interest would quickly flag.

Madame de Lieven in Paris was soon self-sufficient; Madame de Lieven in the country was a very different matter. Lord Grey had urged her to visit Valençay and she duly invited herself for June, 1836. Dorothea was apprehensive, especially as there would be no other guests at the time, but did not like to refuse so old a friend. The visit was a disaster. Madame de Lieven " yawned to desperation." Deprived of her newspapers and political gossip, with no possibilities for intrigue or for the high-minded flirtations in which she specialised, she had no idea how to entertain herself and grew nervous and distracted. This made her a singularly troublesome guest. Her first room, she complained, smelt of paint. It had last been painted fourteen years before but Dorothea obligingly moved her on to another equally grand bedroom. Here, Madame de Lieven found that the walls were too thick and gave her spleen. She was moved on once more, this time to the room usually occupied by the Duchess of Valençay, but warned that it was the last of the rooms in the castle fit to be occupied by so distinguished a guest. Unabashed, Madame de Lieven decided that she had really been happier in her first room after all and moved back there again. Even the gentle Pauline was moved to say that the princess seemed " rather whimsical."

Eventually Madame de Lieven taxed her hostess with unkindness in inviting her when there were no other guests. With considerable restraint Dorothea reminded her that this had been made quite clear before she came and that anyway she had invited herself. The princess seemed to see the justice of this. Anyway, she behaved very much better than Monsieur de Montrond and wrote a letter to Lord Grey describing her stay as most agreeable and the time as " flying by with wondrous rapidity." It is perfectly possible, in fact, that Dorothea, herself tired and restless, read more into Madame de Lieven's petulance than in fact was there. She was in a frame of mind to manufacture troubles where there were none and may well have read discontent and resentment into mild fits of boredom and a supercilious manner.

The future of Monsieur de Bacourt was still more troublesome. Separation had not made Dorothea any less alive to his wistful charms and now that he was deprived of the patronage of Monsieur de Talleyrand appeals for her help were more urgent and more pressing even than before. Competent and hard-working though he undoubtedly was, Bacourt was too soft a character to stand easily by himself in a world of harsh competition and jealousies. " He is not a man of action," she wrote to Thiers soon after her return to France. " He does not know how to make himself valued ; no one could be less of an exhibitionist than he—and yet a little exhibitionism is always needed, in this country above all."

The important passage of this letter was a plea to Thiers to render her " the most personal of services " by standing up for Bacourt's interests in Government circles. " That is what I must ask you because to me it is like my own affairs and there is hardly anything else in the world in which I feel more concerned . . ." In December, 1834, on a plea of ill-health, Bacourt returned to Paris and settled down to angle for a legation in which he could be his own master. He had hopes of Milan but was ready to settle for Karlsruhe if he could do no better. Himself a self-made man, Thiers had a thorough contempt for all who could not help themselves. He showed no inclination to exert himself in the matter and the powerful patronage of Dorothea and her uncle, supported as it was by a direct application to the king, could secure Bacourt no more than the second post. Even this took the best part of a year to bring about and it was September, 1835, before the Duke of Broglie reluctantly agreed that Bacourt should be posted as Minister to Karlsruhe.

Dorothea saw him go with regret. She was conscious of all his faults and had no illusions about his talents, but loved him no less well. When Bacourt tired of Karlsruhe and began to think that his talents should be rewarded with some larger post, she was once more indefatigable in his interests. This time it was to Molé, now Minister of Foreign Affairs, that she addressed her plea. " There are few things which interest me especially, few things by which I can be touched or wounded, but at last here is one . . . It is not often that one has a chance to oblige someone as independent in position, mind and heart as me . . ." No one really independent in position, mind and heart can enjoy asking favours from others, even from an old friend, and Dorothea's pride would have prevented her from begging for herself. But when it was Bacourt whose future was in question, pride went by the board and she did not hesitate to suggest to Molé that the legation at The Hague might suit Monsieur de Bacourt's abilities. Molé, a fundamentally selfish man, had as little intention as Thiers of putting himself out to suit the needs of the lovers of the Duchess of Dino. He played for time and was out of office by the time the appointment was made. Bacourt missed The Hague and when he was finally transferred it was to Washington ; a post which some people held to be of growing importance but which to Dorothea—as to most Europeans—seemed only unreasonably far away.

* * * * *

Though, for Dorothea, politics was primarily a question of individuals rather than of principles she was still intensely conservative by nature. All her adventures into liberalism were undertaken under the influence of friends or lovers with advanced ideas and were usually regretted afterwards. In spite of these lapses she seized every occasion to preach right-wing principles to anyone who seemed in need of hearing them. One of her most favoured pupils, who was, in fact, ready to pay considerable attention to her ideas, was the Duke of Orleans. Dorothea never hesitated to tell him where she conceived his duties to lie and to try to rescue him from the dangerous radical ideas which she feared he had been taught. At the time of the English elections they had two long arguments in which she tried to convince him of the need for a strong

Tory Government. At last the duke said that she might in the end convert him. " I should indeed be proud, Monseigneur," replied Dorothea, " to convert you to your own side."

But in general political ideas did not appeal strongly to her. In that, at least, she was well suited to her times. There can rarely have been a period in French politics where there was a greater dearth of outstanding ideas or idealists. Much of the effective power was retained in the hands of the king whose total contempt for his advisers did little to bolster the stability of an allegedly parliamentary régime. The residue of power was shared between a group of talented and ingenious politicians who replaced each other busily in the great offices of state with no perceptible effect on the state of France or of Europe. Thiers, Guizot, Molé, Broglie : all were men of intelligence, eloquence, and of reasonably high principle but there did not seem to be a great issue among them and they boxed-and-coxed in office without anyone being a penny the better except for the small band of potential political appointees who picked up the crumbs from their respective tables.

The field was open to the amateur who felt like taking a part without actually contesting any elections or appearing in the Chamber of Deputies. The first and perhaps most difficult thing to do was to decide upon a suitable candidate who had not yet been adopted by any other sponsor. Having done this all that remained was to denigrate all his rivals and to intrigue and lobby until eventually he arrived in power. After this consummation of all one's hopes one could either stick with him in the confidence that he would soon be out of office and then require rehabilitation or transfer one's allegiance and start the process with somebody else.

Dorothea had little hesitation in selecting Thiers as her candidate. The choice was not an ideal one. " Since his marriage," she had written a few months before, " he has been living in a kind of solidarity with the smallest sort of people, pretentious and of ill-repute . . . It is impossible, in spite of the floods of wit with which he deluges the mud which surrounds him, that he should not be bespattered if not smothered." Nevertheless, when it came to the point, he was a man of obviously greater talent than his rivals. She cared for him no more than she cared for Molé but the latter owed her nothing while Thiers was, in a sense, the creation of her uncle and herself. Madame Thiers was to be regretted but Dorothea was prepared to forgive her protégé's marital indiscretions and to throw herself into the battle on his behalf.

In 1835 Thiers had gone into a Government with Guizot and the Duke of Broglie. " He has made the wrong decision," Dorothea wrote to Molé, " to ally himself with people whose views he does not share." Guizot she could stomach but not Broglie. Someone had asked Talleyrand what he thought was the latter's true vocation. " To be not Minister of Foreign Affairs," the prince replied coldly. Dorothea shared her uncle's view and thought it almost treachery on the part of Thiers to serve in a Government with a man who had tried to erode her uncle's power in his last years in London and was now compounding his crimes by showing insufficient attention to the needs of Monsieur de Bacourt.

However, this could be remedied by bringing down the Government and Dorothea addressed herself to the task with the enthusiastic support of Madame de Lieven and a considerable amount of assistance and advice from Madame Adélaïde in the Tuileries. It is quite impossible to evaluate the effectiveness of her efforts, or indeed of the efforts of any of the amateur intriguers of the period. Thiers would have headed his own Government in the end, even though Dorothea's work on his behalf had not been forthcoming. A case could be made out for arguing that her efforts did not advance the forming of his ministry even by a day. But it would be wrong to underrate what could be achieved by a rich, intelligent and well-born woman intent on enlisting support for any given objective. Thiers owed the benevolent interest of the royal family almost entirely to Dorothea's friendship; her salon offered him opportunities possibly unrivalled in Paris for proselytising and making contacts; the support of Talleyrand—which everyone assumed to be in the gift of his niece—was a priceless benefit for any politician. It would not be too extravagant to hazard that, outside his own talents and personality, the support of Dorothea was the most valuable asset of which Thiers disposed.

By February, 1836, the time seemed ripe for an assault on the ministry. Urged on by his patroness, Thiers announced that he would resign even if the Government did not. This was enough to provoke the collapse of the others. A long and typically French crisis ensued. Molé refused to serve without Thiers, who refused to serve without Guizot, who refused to serve without Broglie. As Broglie was the most unpopular man in France the prospects did not look good. The king ruled that, whatever else might happen, he could not accept any Government which would disturb Europe. The Marquis of Sémonville thereupon produced from his pocket a list which he claimed would meet the case exactly. It turned out to include Madame Adélaïde as President of the Council, Countess Flahaut as Minister of War and the Duchess of Dino as Minister of Foreign Affairs.

Eventually things turned out as Dorothea had calculated. On 19th February, Thiers wrote to tell her that he had been asked to form a Government. Three days later he had succeeded. Neither Guizot, Molé or Broglie found a place. Not even in her most optimistic moments could Dorothea have hoped that Thiers's ministry would last very long. As it turned out, Thiers in office proved truculent, uncompromising and, to Dorothea's mind at least, insufficiently grateful to his benefactors. " Madame de Dino and de Lieven," wrote Molé to Barante after some three months of the new Government, " are still the most firm supporters of the result which their efforts have achieved and form for Thiers a court which one could hardly have predicted for him." But the support was in fact by no means so firm as Molé imagined. At the end of August, 1836, Dorothea heard from Madame Adélaïde that the king had finally fallen out with his minister over policy towards Spain and that Thiers had resigned. " Pity me, for I am heartbroken ! " ended the king's sister. More temperately, Dorothea decided that she was very sorry and saw in it an illustration of the need for conservative principles in public life. " I have a real interest in Thiers and I regret that his revolutionary instincts should have overcome his devotion, his gratitude and the recognition which he owed to the great wisdom, the prudence and the long experience of the king."

Any inclination which Dorothea might have felt to plunge back into the fray in support of Thiers was checked, not only by his revolutionary instincts but also by some foolish and bad-tempered remarks about Talleyrand and his niece which the defeated minister made shortly after his fall. Dorothea's comment to Bacourt was dignified, detached and distinctly smug. " Ill-temper and despondency usually find unmeasured expression in the case of persons whose early education has been deficient . . . I have no ill-feeling against him ; it was bound to be so. Moreover, there are very few people of whom I am sufficiently fond to hate them profoundly." What seemed to her to be the ingratitude and irresponsibility of Thiers left her with a discouraged distaste for French political life. Though she continued to take an intense interest in what was going on she never again descended completely into the arena.

*   *   *   *   *

Even if Dorothea had felt inclined to plunge again into politics, her business preoccupations would have made it difficult. In September, 1836, her German agent Herr Hennenberg died in Berlin. For more than twenty years Hennenberg had been left in almost sole charge of Dorothea's enormous German estates and had brought them from the ruin left by the Napoleonic wars to a state of conspicuous prosperity. Thanks to his efforts, his employer had become one of the richest women in Europe. A visit to Germany to settle her affairs seemed indispensable, yet she felt that she could not possibly leave Talleyrand while he was in his present precarious state of health. For the moment she decided to do what she could by correspondence and to run the risk that financial loss might follow. The decision hurt her, because the good order of her own affairs was something almost as precious to her as the good order of society in general. But her uncle's health and happiness had to be put first.

Her thoughts had been brought back to Germany by another event earlier the same year. The Duke of Orleans was anxious to visit Austria, Prussia and some of the German states. As in the case of the English visit, the first object was to secure support for the régime but the Duke of Orleans also felt that it was time to take a wife and that Germany was probably the best place for him to seek one. Dorothea had been in favour of the project from the start—too much in favour, grumbled Metternich, who accused her of gossiping to the Duchess of Sagan and endangering the whole enterprise. Eventually the visit was arranged for the summer of 1836. The Duke of Valençay, by his close friendship with the Duke of Orleans, his position in France and his great connections in Germany, was eminently qualified to form part of the royal party. " It was proposed to give him a title and an official position," wrote Dorothea with hauteur, " but I objected, as my son is sure to be well received anywhere."

Dorothea's pride was not misplaced. The Duke of Valençay was flatteringly well received wherever he went and in particular in Berlin. The Prince Royal told Louis that he had always considered his mother as a sister and that he proposed to treat her son as a nephew. Princess Louise and the Duchess of Cumberland were equally kind. The reception of the whole party in Prussia could hardly have been warmer. Dorothea congratulated herself that a part at least of this was due to her.

One last preoccupation of this summer must be mentioned. In May, 1836, Pauline made her début in Parisian society. The success of her coming-out ball was a tribute to Dorothea's efforts to reopen the door into the charmed circle where matches of sufficient wealth, birth and position were to be found.

Dorothea had contrived to win back a position in the *Faubourg* without severing the links which bound her to the Orleanists and their Governments. It had been a delicate operation and was as yet by no means successfully completed. Pauline's coming-out ball was not exactly exclusive ; too many loyal supporters of the régime and allies of Talleyrand would have been offended if it had been. But it was widely remarked that neither the Duke of Orleans nor the Prime Minister were present and that the *Faubourg St. Germain* were there in preponderant numbers.

But there was still a long way to go. In the course of this summer Dorothea proposed tentatively that Pauline would make an excellent wife for Antonin de Noailles, a junior member of a great family without much money but with the reputation of being the best-looking man in Paris. The offer met with no success; Monsieur de Noailles claiming that Pauline was too ugly. The accusation was unfair. Pauline was no beauty, "kind and charming, but pretty, no!" wrote Madame de Lieven about this time, but ugly was certainly too harsh a word. But, whatever the cause, Lady Holland reports that Dorothea found the set-back mortifying. However she continued her efforts undaunted and, except for a few irreducible pockets of hostility, met with much success. Partly this was due to the charm, dignity and quiet goodwill of Pauline herself. The hostesses of the *Faubourg* might disapprove of the mother but it seemed unnecessarily hard to go on from that to persecute the daughter; especially when the daughter was as well connected and likely to be as rich as was Pauline. " It is certainly better not to live in hostility with society and, if one has been wrong-headed or unfortunate, it is pleasant to make one's daughter a means of reconciliation," wrote Dorothea. Her first reason for wishing to reingratiate herself with the aristocracy was the welfare of her daughter; it seemed only justice that her daughter should have been one of the chief instruments in her campaign.

But more important than any of this for Dorothea's reputation in the eyes of the *Faubourg* was the work which she was known to be doing to secure Talleyrand's return to the Church before he died. It was this which, more than anything else, served to make her respectable. What was more, it was work which could be expected to earn the warm approval of the *Faubourg* without forfeiting the regards of the Orleanist party. On such grounds alone it would have been small wonder if the conversion of Talleyrand had become the principal preoccupation of his niece's life.

II

Talleyrand had returned from London to die. At the beginning of 1835 he was nearly eighty-one years old and the only question was how many months or possibly years his enfeebled form could bear the burden of living. Every minor accident or ailment seemed likely to prove the final straw, every exertion required of him taxed to the uttermost his dregs of strength. Yet in his weak and crippled body the old intelligence and acumen lay barely impaired by time; though he could not concentrate on anything for long, for short flashes he could be as brilliant a talker and profound a thinker as at any time of his life.

He knew that he could not last much longer but the reflection did not cause him much concern. His life had been a full one; he had enjoyed it thoroughly and his sins, though many, had been for the most part of an amiable nature and, with luck, venal. His relations with God did not cause him very much reflection; after all, whatever God there might be would presumably rather judge him on what he had made of his life than on what professions of faith he adopted in his closing years. If it had not been for the importunities of his niece and certain of his friends he would probably have given little thought to his relationship with the Catholic Church. Only the knowledge that he was causing distress to people whom he loved led him to consider what if anything needed to be done.

There was much to be done and to be done quickly. Talleyrand had begun his life as a priest and in the days before the Revolution had actually risen to be Bishop of Autun. His activities at the beginning of the Revolution had led to his formal excommunication : a fate he accepted with equanimity. Under the consulate he had been secularised but the Vatican found it beyond their powers to agree to the marriage of a former bishop, even as bad a bishop as Talleyrand had been. His marriage with Madame Grand had therefore ruled out the possibility of any complete reconciliation with the Church. He would regularly attend mass but never went to confession and was not admitted to communion. It was difficult to see how this situation could be bettered so long as his wife remained alive. Even if she were to die, however, much would need to be done and Talleyrand's friends asked themselves whether some preparatory steps could not be taken straight away.

Dorothea was quite determined that, if anything could be done at once, it should be. It would be unfair to suggest that it was primarily or even largely her own position which made her so anxious to see her uncle safely back into the bosom of the Church. It was her uncle's interests which concerned her but, at the beginning at any rate, she saw it as a social rather than a religious problem. The idea that her uncle should die without all the appropriate rites of the Catholic Church profoundly shocked her idea of decorum and good order. Anything disreputable about his death, any suggestion that he was being deprived of attentions paid to all good Catholics, must leave a taste of the hugger-mugger and unseemly. Already there were many prepared to accuse Talleyrand of every vice and commend him to Satan's particular care ; their voices would be vastly strengthened if it became known that the Church had turned its back on him even in his final hours. When Dorothea first began to ponder on the problem of her uncle's conversion her decisions were dictated almost entirely by a sense of what was owing to society and respect for her uncle's worldly reputation. It was only as the long struggle wore on that religious considerations began to play a larger and larger part in her thoughts.

*　　　*　　　*　　　*　　　*

It seems that Dorothea first took up the question of Prince Talleyrand's conversion in June, 1835, when Pauline was confirmed. She was then much in contact with Hyacinth Louis,

Count Quelen, the Archbishop of Paris. Quelen was a solemn, well-meaning man ; strongly addicted to the Bourbon cause and carrying his convictions to the point of refusing King Louis-Philippe entry to Notre-Dame. As a result he was very much a favourite of the *Faubourg St. Germain* ; an additional reason for Dorothea to wish to stand well with him. His bust is still at Rochecotte ; a fat, rather complacent face marked with courage and determination but very little in the way of humour, tact or sensibility. Dorothea appraised him with cool exactness and found him far from the ideal instrument for her purposes :

> " The trouble with the Archbishop is that he has not quite the intellectual grip which is needed if he is to play the difficult part which circumstances have imposed on him. Neither has he the intense energy which redeems, and sometimes more than redeems intellectual short-comings . . . He is kind, charitable, affectionate, grateful, sincerely attached to his duties and always ready to face martyrdom but he is too ready to receive impressions of every kind . . . He is afraid of criticism and is always provoking it by a hesitancy and a want of balance which arise from a vacillating intelligence and the scruples of a conscience which is never certain whether what was good yesterday is good to-day . . . However, as he has many noble and good qualities and he has the deepest interest in all who bear the name of Talleyrand, I wish with all my heart that his troubles may come to an end."

But though she could not see Quelen's ponderous reasonings having much effect on Talleyrand's subtle and disdainful mind, his co-operation was still essential if her uncle were to be restored to the favour of the Church. Quelen proved himself a willing ally. Indeed, sometime earlier, he had approached the Vatican and had received discretion to absolve Talleyrand and to receive him back into the Church. All that was needed was to dispose in some way of Madame de Talleyrand and to persuade the prince to make his peace by an admission of guilt and a humble request for readmission. Dorothea knew better than the archbishop how difficult it would be to persuade her uncle thus to sink his pride, especially when he was convinced than his actions throughout had been justifiable by any reasonable moral code. She refused to be rushed into a precipitate approach and explained that any direct overture to Talleyrand would probably produce the opposite result to what was intended. Her role would have to be passive and cautious ; her uncle might be gradually induced into the path to conversion but could never be driven and would revolt at once if he suspected that he were being led.

Sometime in November of the same year, Dorothea was reminded of her duties in a context far removed from arguments of social propriety. A cousin, Louise de Chabannes, had become a Carmelite sister and passed out of Dorothea's life. One day a letter came asking Dorothea to visit her in the convent of the Rue d'Enfer. Remembering her cousin as a sickly and unhappy girl she imagined that the harsh and austere life of the Carmelites had proved too much and that she was being called to a death-bed. Instead she was struck by the serenity and good-health which Mlle de Chabannes now enjoyed. As she was preparing to leave, her cousin handed her a little medal of the Virgin and begged her to make Monsieur de Talleyrand wear it, even without his knowledge. " This medal," she said, " brings back to the Faith even those who have wandered farthest from it." Dorothea was moved and impressed by a faith so sincere and so vivid. She promised to find some means of making sure that her uncle wore the medal. As she left the convent she reflected on her own grandeur and importance in the eyes of the world and the relative obscurity of her cousin. Uneasily she asked herself whether Mlle de Chabannes might not have found that very element in life which she was so conscious was missing from her own.

From the convent Dorothea went directly to the archbishop's house to discuss a marriage which had been mooted but was never to take place between her son Alexander and a rich heiress, Mlle de Fougères. They talked further of Talleyrand's conversion and Quelen undertook to call on the prince from time to time and see what he could do to advance the cause.

*   *   *   *   *

On 9th December, 1835, Dorothea received the news that Princess Talleyrand was dead. A few days earlier the prince had been told that his wife was dying; he received the news with equanimity tinged with cheerfulness and paid no attention to a tentative suggestion that he should put in an appearance at the bedside of the moribund. Dorothea still hesitated to tell him that all was over but she need not have worried, the prince was too tired to mourn except for those he loved and too old to pretend to regret which he did not feel. "That simplifies my position," was all he said and continued in a conspicuously good humour for the rest of the day.

Quelen thought that the death of the princess provided an excellent opportunity for taking up his idea of visiting Prince Talleyrand. The prince professed himself delighted and flattered, but unfortunately the date proposed proved impossible. So did another and another and it was soon clear that Talleyrand did not yet feel himself ready to be preached at, or at any rate not by such a man as the archbishop. He found it hard to consider the state of his soul a subject for rational discussion and, though preparing himself to make certain sacrifices to social propriety, felt it unfair that he should submit to being bored as well.

Dorothea, however, who had started in much the same mood of spiritual impassivity, now found that the thought she was giving to her uncle's case made it essential for her to examine certain fundamental principles in her own life. For the first time she gave serious thought to her relationship with God and began to seek consciously after the faith which had so far eluded her. Writing to Bacourt she reminded him of a conversation they had had at Rochecotte in which he had shown himself a deeper believer than she had ever claimed to be: "My experiences since that date have brought me more rapidly along the road . . . since I have seen all supports falling away around me, I have felt my own weakness and the necessity of some support and guide. I have sought and found; I have knocked and it has been opened to me; I have asked and it has been given to me; and yet all very incompletely hitherto, for when one thus walks alone and ill-prepared it is

impossible to keep clear of wrong paths or to avoid slipping
in the ruts . . ."

Meanwhile she missed no opportunity of bringing home to
her uncle what she considered to be the precariousness of his
position and his equivocal status in the eyes of the world.
Once, for instance, after they had attended mass together,
Dorothea said to him :

" It must have a curious effect on you to hear a mass."

" No, why ? "

" I thought that possibly you would not feel quite the same
as other people ? "

" I ? But exactly the same ; and why not ? I go in the
same way as you or as anyone else. You always forget that
I have been secularised ; that makes my position perfectly
simple."

" But after all, you have made priests."

" Not many."

Another time there was a violent thunderstorm which
threatened the castle. After a particularly loud clap Talleyrand
asked his niece what she had been thinking at that moment.
She at once replied : " If a priest had been in the room I should
have confessed myself, for I am afraid of sudden death. To
die unprepared and to carry with me my heavy burden of sin
is a terrifying prospect and however careful one may be to live
well we cannot do without reconciliation and pardon." Talleyrand made no reply and they went on playing piquet.

" I take every opportunity of making obvious my own belief
and thus attempting to arouse his, but never until I have an
opening. In such a matter a light touch is indispensable,"
observed Dorothea a little ingenuously. In fact, it seems sure
that the old prince knew perfectly well what his rather solemn
niece was up to and took a mischievous delight in evading her
snares. But he loved Dorothea too well and respected her
judgment too highly not to consider seriously anything she
might say. Unpromising though her uncle's reactions might
seem she was little by little preparing the frame of mind in
which he would be ready to negotiate terms, if not with the
Almighty, at least with his appointed representative on earth.
In October, 1836, at Valençay, he put the finishing touches to

a manifesto setting out the main lines of his career with a justification for his actions. It began with a declaration that he died a member of the Roman Catholic faith.

*   *   *   *   *

As 1837 wore on Dorothea congratulated herself that at last her patient work was beginning to bear fruit. In May they went together to the marriage of the Duke of Orleans at Fontainebleau. Scarcely were the festivities over than Talleyrand hurried off, in advance even of his niece. His reason was that the Archbishop of Bourges was visiting Valençay and that he wished to be there to receive him.

Dorothea noted with approval this new-found deference to the Church; she noted too the increasing effect which the deep religious convictions of Pauline were making on the old man. When Pauline had gone to her first communion she had asked the prince for his blessing. Talleyrand gave it to her, remarking with a tenderness which only this child could have evoked: "How touching is the piety of a young girl and how unnatural is unbelief " . . ." especially in women," he added prudently. However, his inclination was always towards moderation and in time he became alarmed by the passionate force of Pauline's convictions. Was it not more than likely that her teachers would try to set her against her great-uncle, held as he was in such formal abhorrence by the Church. Nervously he asked what Pauline's confessor used to say about him. The child replied that his name was never mentioned except with an injunction to pray earnestly to God on his behalf. Reassured on this count Talleyrand saw no cause to resent Pauline's deep religious life and seemed to feel even that he derived a certain vicarious grace from her faith and innocence. He observed that the confessor, a certain Abbé Dupanloup, appeared to be an intelligent and deserving man. Dorothea noted his approval and privately reflected that the abbé might well prove to be a more effective instrument for the salvation of her uncle than the well-meaning but heavy-handed arch-bishop.

In December, 1837, Dorothea fell seriously ill at Rochecotte with a violent fever and a sharp pain on the right side of her body. According to letters which Lady Granville received at the time, she was suffering from some sort of paralytic stroke. To the Duke of Noailles, Dorothea seems to have admitted that it was serious and even critical, but to others she was inclined to belittle her trouble. The seizure, though violent, must have been short-lived but, for two days or so her life was in some danger. Meeting her in January, Madame de Lieven found her greatly changed. The illness left its mark on the prince as well as the victim herself. For Dorothea, the realisation that she was close to death, brought to a head all the vague preoccupations with her spiritual life which had begun to occupy her over the last few years. She had already argued herself into a frame of mind where she could accept the dogmas of Christianity, but some sharp experience was needed if this intellectual appreciation were to be translated into a live and active faith. Her illness provided the shock that was required. " It seemed to me during the two days that I was ill," she wrote to Bacourt " that I saw something of the things of the next world and that it was not so difficult as might be thought to rise towards one's Creator . . . Providence can soften all the trials which He sends us by giving us the strength to bear them. One can never feel too thankful for all the Divine favours." Dorothea had arrived at Rochecotte a believer in the conventional sense of the word but with a life organised on lines that were rationalist and humanitarian and with no profound faith or capacity for spiritual experience. She left it a deeply religious woman who was never again to be able to escape from a sense of the Will of God and of the tiny part allotted to her in the divine scheme.

Talleyrand observed his niece's illness with consternation and the reinforcement of her faith with surprise and a slightly grudging approval. " So you have reached that point, have you ? " he asked. " And how did you get there ? " Dorothea explained her spiritual progress in so far as she herself understood it and Talleyrand listened intently. In conclusion Dorothea added that, among the many other serious considerations which had affected her, was her social position and the obligations which she felt it imposed on her. " In truth," he interrupted quickly, " there is nothing less aristocratic than unbelief." This formulation of her idea can hardly have appealed to Dorothea, rejoicing as she was in her new-found faith, but she was too prudent to argue with any line of thought which might help her uncle forward.

*   *   *   *   *

The beginning of 1838 found them back in Paris. Every day Talleyrand's strength seemed to ebb away and Dorothea did not dare to assume that he would live even another six months. On 27th January he stumbled and fell heavily while dining at the British Embassy. He was only kept to his bed for a few days but the accident had shaken what little was left of his frail forces. It was obvious to everyone that his death must be perilously near. Dorothea decided that the time for discretion and the oblique approach was now past. She invoked the help of Pauline's confessor, the Abbé Dupanloup.

Felix Dupanloup was an eloquent and impressive preacher who possessed all the qualities usually associated with the priest fashionable among the rich and ruling classes. It would be unfair to suggest that he was no more than this ; as director of the junior seminary of the archdiocese of Paris he acquired influence in the world of education fairly comparable with that of his contemporary in England, Thomas Arnold ; as Bishop of Orleans he was to be one of the major figures of the ecclesiastical life of France. But he was a worldly man ; not with the meaning that he was in any way a libertine but in his mastery of political techniques and his keen interest in the machinery of power.

Dorothea liked, admired, but never altogether trusted him. " It is possible that Monsieur Dupanloup is ambitious," she wrote to Bacourt. " I do not know him well enough to be positive. He is gentle, discreet, moderate, with a knowledge of the world, a fine command of language and conversational tact and, in short, possesses every quality which the spiritual director of a society parish should have. But this does not exclude ambition." However his talents seemed well suited to the purpose which Dorothea had in mind for him ; a lack of the finer spiritual qualities was hardly likely to jar on Monsieur de Talleyrand.

Pauline had spoken so much and so enthusiastically of the virtues of her confessor that it did not need much prompting from Dorothea for Talleyrand to invite this paragon to the house. Her plans were upset however when Dupanloup refused ; he knew that if he were to visit the prince the fact would be discussed all over Paris and he had no wish to risk his reputation. " He has less intelligence than I thought," remarked Talleyrand coldly, " for he ought to be anxious to come here for my sake and his own."

Dorothea did not let the matter drop. The archbishop assured her that he had not instructed Dupanloup to refuse the invitation and, what was more, that he would make it his business to see that Dupanloup accepted if Talleyrand could be induced to ask him to the house a second time. The prince was unexpectedly accommodating. Once more the abbé was asked to dine and this time accepted. Dorothea was delighted ; not only that the meeting was arranged but still more at Talleyrand's obvious eagerness to meet the abbé.

> " I cannot help ascribing his excellent frame of mind to my own feelings in my last illness and to the words which I was then able to speak to him. I bless God for the sign that He has been pleased to send me by His hidden yet always wonderful ways of working. If, to complete this great task, I should be called on to make a still greater sacrifice, then I would readily do so."

The dinner passed off well and Talleyrand was on his best behaviour. Dupanloup was delighted and amazed by the wisdom and good taste of his host. Talleyrand, too, was pleased. " I like your abbé," he told Dorothea and Pauline, " he understands what it is to live."

At the beginning of March, Talleyrand made what was to be his last important public appearance. He had been asked to deliver the funeral oration of Count Reinhard, a former Minister of Foreign Affairs, at the Academy of Moral and Political Sciences. He decided to use the occasion to deliver an apologia for his own career and an analysis of the whole science of diplomacy. The speech was an oustanding success and not least did it satisfy the Abbé Dupanloup, in whose honour

Talleyrand had inserted a passage on what he called the religion of duty. The abbé asked permission to call on the prince again. Talleyrand agreed with pleasure and the two men had a long conversation together, though without broaching the subject uppermost in the minds of both. As he was leaving Talleyrand asked him how he had found the Duchess of Dino.

" Not at all well," replied the abbé, " but much more worried about you than about herself."

" Yes, that is true."

" I found Madame de Dino and her daughter very deeply and seriously concerned about you."

On his way out, the abbé looked in on Dorothea. He seemed to feel there was some hope. This was no news to Dorothea, who understood her uncle far better than the abbé, but she knew also how little time was left.

" What a task it is and how terrified I should be of it if I did not tell myself that the most unworthy instrument which God is pleased to choose can become more powerful than the greatest saint if God's providence is pleased to make use of him."

One practical step at least was within her capacities ; in a series of conversations with the archbishop she established exactly how much the Church would demand of her uncle in the way of recantation. She prepared and secured Quelen's approval of the draft of a letter to the Pope which, if only Talleyrand could be induced to sign it, would secure his reinstatement as a full member of the Church.

The Abbé Dupanloup was quick to exploit the advantage which he believed he had secured. A few days after his visit he sent Talleyrand a copy of a book which he had written on Fénelon together with a long and carefully studied letter which ended by evoking the memory of the prince's dearly loved uncle, the Archbishop of Rheims, and with a tactful reference to Pauline. Talleyrand sent for Dorothea and gave her the letter.

" Do you know what's in it ? " he asked suspiciously.

" No, Monsieur."

" Very well, then read it ; read it aloud."

Dorothea read the letter but when she came to the final sentences, broke down and cried.

" Finish reading it," said Talleyrand sharply. " This is nothing to cry about ; it's a serious matter."

When she had finished there was a silence, then he said, " If I fell seriously ill I would send for a priest. Do you think that the Abbé Dupanloup would be glad to come ? "

" I am sure he would ; but, if he were to be of any use to you, you would need first to be readmitted to the Church which you have so unhappily left."

" Yes, yes. There is something I must do with regard to Rome, I know. I have been thinking about it for a long time.'

" Since when," asked Dorothea in surprise.

" Since the last visit to Valençay of the Archbishop of Bourges . . . I wondered then why the archbishop, who is supposed to be responsible for my soul, did not raise the matter."

" Alas, Monsieur, he would not have dared."

" But I would have taken it very well."

Dorothea took her uncle's hands in hers and, with tears in her eyes, asked :

" But why wait to have the matter raised. Why not yourself, freely, spontaneously and generously, take the step forward which is the most honourable for you and the most gratifying for the Church and for all people of good-will. You will find Rome well disposed, I know. The Archbishop of Paris is very fond of you. Why not try ? "

" I do not refuse to. I know that there is something which I must do. But do you know what they want of me ? Why can't they tell me that ? "

" Would you like me to tell you. I will do so if you would ? "

" I would be very happy for you to do so."

Without waiting for more, Dorothea wrote out and gave to her uncle the conditions on which she knew the Church would be prepared to welcome him back. Talleyrand raised an objection or two but nothing of importance. " Yesterday I had a most important conversation with Monsieur de Talleyrand," she wrote to Bacourt on 28th March, " and found him in a state of open-mindedness which seemed miraculous. I now hope to be able to push steadily forward. Though the goal is still far away I trust that no precipice will open in front of me to impede my progress."

★   ★   ★   ★   ★

There were to be no precipices but Dorothea was still to suffer much disquiet. Talleyrand was determined to take his time and time was the one thing which was lacking. A month after the conversation referred to above he had still taken no new initiative and Dorothea's carefully drafted list of conditions rested apparently unconsidered in his room. On 28th April, Talleyrand's brother Archambaud, father-in-law of Dorothea, died suddenly without regaining consciousness after a long paralytic attack. By his death, Edmond and Dorothea graduated from the dukedom of Dino to become Duke and Duchess of Talleyrand; the title of Dino descending to their second son, Alexander. But Dorothea had little time to concern herself with such trivialities. Archambaud's death had been a harsh reminder of what might happen at any moment to her uncle. She could not suppress the fear that he too might be suddenly struck down without a chance to complete his leisurely negotiations with the Church.

Talleyrand drew the same moral from his brother's death. On 1st May, as Dorothea was about to leave the house to visit the archbishop, the prince casually pulled a sheet of paper from the drawer. " Here," he said, " is something which should secure you a good reception where you are going. You must tell me what the archbishop thinks of it." It was the draft of his own retraction which he had quietly prepared without a word to his niece, " a kind of pleasant surprise which he wished to keep for me." She hurried with it to Monsieur de Quelen, who promised to recast it in more canonical form and let her have it back within a few days.

Talleyrand's sense of timing had not deserted him but the margin of safety was very small. On 12th May he fell seriously ill, on the 14th he was operated on for anthrax. Everyone around him realised that the end was near. In a hurried note Dorothea summoned the Abbé Dupanloup. She knew that this was to be the last chance.

The morning of the fifteenth the abbé arrived with the text of

Talleyrand's retraction as amended by Monsieur de Quelen, together with the draft of a letter to the Pope. Both these would need to be signed before the prince could receive the last sacraments. There was a period of tension almost unendurable for Dorothea as her uncle read through the papers. To her deep relief he declared them satisfactory. But he was not to be saved as easily as that. " Would you be good enough to leave the papers with me," he asked. " I wish to read them again."

The next day Talleyrand still had not signed the papers and it seemed that he could not live more than a few hours. First Dorothea and then Pauline pleaded with him. It was as at the time of his resignation ; though convinced of what he had to do he wished to postpone to the last moment possible the decision which would finally commit him. At that time he had put an end to his career, now it must have seemed to him that he was being asked to put an end to his very life. The Abbé Dupanloup spent most of the day in the Rue St. Florentin and added his prayers to those of the women. Talleyrand repeated that he was willing, that he would sign in time, that he wished to go through the text once more with Madame de Dino. His ultimate concession was a promise that he would sign between five and six next morning.

Would he still be alive by then ? By eight o'clock that evening he was obviously failing and the chances seemed high that he would not last the night. Haggard and sleepless, Dorothea and Pauline spent the hours by his bed, helplessly watching the life ebbing from the frail form. At half past two the doctor said that the prince could not remain in command of his faculties for much longer. Dorothea once more approached the bed and Pauline stood beside her with the papers and a pen in her hand. But obstinately Talleyrand refused to be hurried out of the schedule which he had fixed. " It is not yet six o'clock. I told you that I would sign to-morrow between five and six in the morning and I still promise to do so."

At half past four Dupanloup was back at his vigil. Behind him came the Duke de Poix, Sainte Aulaire, Barante, Molé and Royer Collard ; all old friends of the prince come to watch him through his last hours and—so Dorothea prayed—to bear witness to his return to the Church. Still Talleyrand played for time, extracting every last minute as once he had squeezed every last concession out of foreign negotiators. Once more he asked Dorothea to read through the papers and once more she enunciated the terms of her uncle's retraction.

" I found the strength to read the papers slowly and with deliberation," she wrote to Dupanloup long after all was over, " because I neither wished nor had any right to reduce the merit of my uncle's action. It was essential that he should understand exactly what he was about to do. God be praised, his faculties were still too much in his own possession and his attention too acute to let him be satisfied by any disturbed or gabbled reading. I had to justify his touching confidence which had made him wish that it should be I who gave this crucial reading. I could only do it by the firmness and clearness of my speech. In that way I could leave him complete freedom of choice up to the final minute and a perfect understanding of what was in question."

Painfully and carefully, with eyes shut and one hand holding the pen aloft, Talleyrand followed his niece's voice. Close as he was to death he must have detected the pain and fatigue behind her firm and unemotional tone. Physically exhausted as she was by three days and nights of watching by his bedside, tormented by anxiety lest at the end all her efforts should fail and her uncle's soul go unredeemed : the effort of self-control called for by this last test must have driven even her strong spirit almost to breaking point. But there was to be no more prevarication. The time that he had fixed had come and with a last effort of will he dipped his pen in the ink and put his name to the two papers. Charles-Maurice, Prince Talleyrand, had made his peace with God.

For Dorothea it should have been a moment of triumph and yet how sad a triumph it was which carried with it the death of the real victor. Still a few more hours of her ordeal were left. During the morning King Louis-Philippe came in person to pay his last respects to the old statesman to whom he so largely owed his throne. There was one more grinding effort of civility, one last struggle with herself before she could plunge into the pit of exhaustion and misery. Then the king left ; the end was very near. At twenty-five minutes to four in the afternoon of 17th May, Talleyrand's head dropped to his chest in final token of death. Dorothea looked for the last time on the dead man and then quietly turned and left the room. As the door closed behind her there closed with it the relationship which had dominated her life for more than a quarter of a century.

12

In May, 1838, Dorothea was nearly forty-five years old. She was still beautiful ; some said as beautiful as she had ever been. Though her constitution was not strong there seemed no reason why she should not live in reasonably good health for at least another quarter of a century. Ever since she had grown from girlhood her life had centred around one man. The relationship, once passionate, had been always absorbing. It had demanded from her almost everything, emotional and intellectual, which she had to give. Occasional conflicts of loyalties had arisen but all had quickly been resolved. There had been no real challenge to the cause to which she had chosen to dedicate her life. Only death had been strong enough to free her from her self-imposed enthralment.

To free her ; but to free her to do what ? " Everything has grown sadly empty, both in me and around me," she wrote to Molé some months later. " I care hardly at all what goes on in the outside world and very little more what happens inside myself. The emptiness, the lack, the remoteness which surrounds me becomes every day more evident and to-day, now that all my different tasks are completed, I feel only the pain of my own uselessness and search in vain for some outlet for my energies . . . People look after me and are gracious and kind ; but it all means nothing to me. What I need is not to be the object of other people's good offices but myself to care for others, to be devoted and useful to them . . . I have lost Monsieur de Talleyrand either fifteen years too late or fifteen years too soon ; at the age when it is most difficult to begin life on a new footing."

At the moment of Talleyrand's death, Pauline and Alexander were still unmarried, the prince's estate called for much arrangement and Dorothea's own affairs were in considerable disorder. But she could not tell herself that these were occupations for a lifetime ; beyond them the future stretched bare and uncharted. If Talleyrand had died fifteen years before she would have been only thirty years old. She could have cut loose entirely from the past and devoted herself exclusively to the future. If he had died fifteen years later the course of her life would have been almost run. She could have relapsed into a life of retirement and occupied herself contentedly with her memories and her grandchildren. But at forty-five she felt herself too old for the one course and too young for the other ; too deeply involved with her own world to contemplate a fresh start elsewhere, yet too tired and discouraged to build for herself a new place in society. In the gloom that followed her uncle's death she felt herself all at once too old to live and too young to die. It was well for her that the preoccupation of existence quickly drove back her thoughts into more fruitful channels.

The most pressing question of all was where, in future, she was to make her life. It was a question she was to do her best to evade answering for many years. After nearly thirty years of Paris she still felt herself a foreigner. Among a handful of friends she felt secure but with all the rest she knew herself to be no more than tolerated for her wealth and position. She had learnt to distrust Paris and to dislike the Parisians. She could not think of deserting it until she had done her duty by her unmarried children and the pleasure of her friends' company was strong enough to ensure that she would never cut herself off from it altogether. But as a place to live for the rest of her life Paris seemed to Dorothea impossible.

She could, of course, have spent the rest of her life at Rochecotte amidst the little community which she loved so well. But she knew that the Duchess of Talleyrand was not yet of the stuff of a recluse and that within a few months she would be pining for the life of a great lady. Besides, though it was only to Paris that she actively objected, she felt for France as a whole the mingled affection and distrust which it so often earns from those foreigners who have settled within her borders. There were many things there which pleased her well, yet when she considered the future of her country of adoption she was filled with the blackest pessimism. She foresaw a time when it would be impossible for anyone to stay who preserved even a shred of regard for the advantages of civilised society, for respect, justice and a proper sense of order.

Yet she did not know that Germany would prove any better. Since she had left at the time of her marriage she had paid only the briefest of visits to the other side of the Rhine. To Berlin, her birthplace, she had never returned at all. If she felt herself a foreigner in France, might she not be even more of one in Germany? And would the Prussians welcome back this wanderer with her Frenchified ways and alien interests? And how would she herself support the transplantation? Would not the life of Berlin prove intolerably provincial after Paris and London?

Financially the future held little terror for her. In spite of the handsome pension she was still paying her husband, she remained one of the richest women in Europe. With Talleyrand's death her children too had all inherited substantial fortunes. Louis, Duke of Valençay, had already been made a gift of the great property from which he drew his title; with the death of his uncle he entered into possession of the estate. Alexander, Duke of Dino, received a legacy of two hundred thousand francs and some fine woods in the Eure valued at as much again. The bequest came just in time to rescue him from the mountain of debts which he had accumulated. To Pauline went the property of Pont-de-Sains, valued in 1838 at more than one and a half million francs. For Edmond, still lingering in his Italian exile, there was only the harsh instruction: " I do not wish Monsieur le duc de Dino (as he still was at the time the will was prepared) to have either the use or the administration of the property left to those of his children who are still under age. I much regret that the disorder to which he has reduced his own affairs compels me to take this precaution."

As for Dorothea herself: " I beg Madame de Dino," read the will, " to accept my most tender gratitude for all the happiness which she has brought me and which I know that I have owed to her over the last twenty-five years. I bid her a most loving farewell." After many other bequests to servants and dependents, Dorothea was named the residual legatee and the house in the Rue St. Florentin was specifically bequeathed to her. It was generally assumed that she thus inherited a massive fortune but, in fact, after all claims on the estate had been met it does not seem that much was left. At any rate she found it convenient to sell the house with almost indecorous haste. The purchaser was a Rothschild ; the price was unsatisfactory but at least, as she wrote to Barante, it was certain to be paid and in ready money. Within a few weeks Madame de Lieven had rented for herself the apartments in which Talleyrand had held court for so long : " She seems very anxious to cut me out of her life," wrote Dorothea bitterly, " for she has chosen the only rooms in Paris to which it will be quite impossible for me to go."

It may have been a need for ready money which led Dorothea to sell with such speed this house which was so inextricably linked with her former life but it must also have been, in part at least, a wish to have done with it all. The Rue St. Florentin stood for a life that was past, a life that had depended entirely on the presence and authority of Prince Talleyrand. Without him it became hollow and meaningless and she did not intend to cling on to such a simulacrum of the past. The quick disposal of the house was a personal gesture which symbolised her conviction that the past was past and that new foundations for her life must now be laid.

But the thought of laying them was a weary one. She was tired and life had lost its flavour. " My long intercourse with Monsieur de Talleyrand has made it difficult for ordinary people to get on with me. I meet minds which seem slow, diffuse and ill-developed. They are always putting on the brake like people going downhill while I have spent my life with my shoulder to the wheel in uphill work . . . To-day, I feel that I am being overcome, in a moral sense, by what the English call creeping paralysis." Dorothea looked bleakly into a world of ordinary people. As she walked from the death-bed of her uncle, there seemed to stretch in front of her a narrow and interminable avenue of mediocrity, leading nowhere save to the grave, lit only by the dusk of dull minds and inconsiderable spirits. That she must walk it, she knew, but for how long, she asked herself, for how long ?

* * * * *

Her first desire was to escape from Paris; from the sympathy, the curiosity, the pressure of public life and the demands upon her for decisions upon a hundred major or minor points of administration. The organisation of her move from the Rue St. Florentin inevitably took some weeks but before the end of June, Dorothea and Pauline were on their way to Germany.

It was at Baden that Dorothea had decided to seek the repose she needed before she could face the great decisions of her life. The choice of one of the smartest and most popular watering-places in Europe as a suitable spot to lead the life of a recluse may seem perverse, but she was always nervous of new experiments and in Baden at least she knew that the people she was avoiding would be drawn from the highest ranks of society. " Here I live only for my health and for that of Pauline," she told Barante. " Amidst the beauties of nature and under the tranquil routine which we have established we are slowly regaining our balance; our souls are more at rest, our spirits renew themselves and the weight which bears so heavily on our souls seems to be lifting. It is something of a *tour de force* to live in so rustic a style in a town where all Europe is to be found and where one is constantly rubbing shoulders with princes and princesses."

After two months at Baden, the return to France could no longer be avoided. Too much remained to do; the fortunes and futures of too many people depended on the decisions of the Duchess of Talleyrand. On the way she visited Rochecotte where she remained a few days in complete solitude. Once more she told herself that this was her true home and that it was here that she would pass the rest of her life. She resolved to build a chapel and a library—as for Paris, a *pied-à-terre* where she could pass the worst months of the winter would be quite sufficient.

There was a pilgrimage to make before she could immerse herself once more in the turmoil of Paris. Unless she had been once more to Valençay she felt that she would not properly have said good-bye to the prince who now lay buried there. Dorothea, Pauline and Pauline's governess, Mlle Henriette Larcher, arrived by moonlight at " this beautiful spot, so rich in memories and so deprived of life and movement." Talleyrand's old dog Carlos was waiting for them, strangely excited by their arrival. He pulled Mlle Henriette by the dress as if, Dorothea observed, he were trying to say, " Come and help me to look for the missing one."

The party stayed only long enough to say a mass for the dead and then moved on to Paris. For Dorothea, Valençay had much in common with the Rue St. Florentin. It stood for a way of life that was past. It was her son's home and she was often to visit it, but Valençay was henceforward a part of somebody else's life and not of hers. She put it behind her with regret but without a backward look. What the future might hold for her she did not know, but at least it would not be that.

Back in Paris, Dorothea found herself faced by the same conflict of loyalty as had perplexed her so often before ; the unremitting battle between her instinctive sympathy for the old-school aristocracy and her feelings of duty and gratitude towards the court. With the death of her uncle, however, some of the links which had bound her to the Tuileries had inevitably been loosened. Her temporary home was in the Rue de Grenelle in the very heart of the Faubourg St. Germain. Some people saw in this a symbol of her new way of life and Count Apponyi claimed that Dorothea, having partially ingratiated herself with the *Faubourg* by securing the conversion of her uncle, now proposed to complete the process by quarrelling with the court. This, he said, she was achieving by refusing to do as the king asked and hand over to him Talleyrand's letter to the Pope. Since the letter had long ago been given to the archbishop and from there sent on to Rome there seems no reason to believe the story true, but Apponyi was only voicing the sort of gossip which was a commonplace in Parisian society.

Princess Lieven went even further. Dorothea, she wrote to Lady Cowper " has assured herself a good position with the

Faubourg St. Germain. The Court is very bitter against her, so they say," In her eyes at least there was no doubt that Dorothea, in fact if not in title, had already changed her camp. " She has cooked her goose with the whole Liberal party," wrote the Princess, appearing to derive some satisfaction from her friend's new unpopularity.

Only Dorothea demurred. Shortly after her return, Montrond called on her and showed himself exceptionally kind and soothing. He could not resist an occasional thrust however and inquired " Do you propose to become a lady of the *Faubourg St. Germain* ? " Coldly Dorothea replied that she did not intend to become a lady of anything except of rank and independent means. It was out of the question for her not to remain on good terms with the Tuileries but equally she had no wish to quarrel with anyone because of her or their political opinions.

Indeed, Dorothea showed great anxiety to be on the best of terms with everybody. Her previous efforts to win the approval or, at least, the tolerance of both camps had met with only limited success. Undismayed, she went on trying— some said even at the cost of honour and dignity.

With all the goodwill in the world however she found it quite impossible to remain on good terms with Adolphe Thiers. Shortly before Talleyrand's death Thiers had been going through one of his periodical bouts of bad relations with the court. In his irritation he had criticised the prince loudly and repeatedly. His relations with Dorothea were therefore already strained when he called at the house in the Rue St. Florentin to ask after the dying statesman. As he waited with a crowd of similar visitors in the ante-chamber the news came that Talleyrand had signed the papers which reconciled him to the Church. " He has undone his whole life by this piece of mummery," cried Thiers irascibly. The words were overheard by Madame de Castellane and dutifully repeated to Dorothea. She never forgot or forgave them. Whether to show his disapproval of the prince's behaviour or out of mere casual bad manners, Thiers never called after Talleyrand's death and never wrote to express his sympathy. True, he wrote kindly of the prince in an article for the

Constitutionnel but this was not enough to reconcile Dorothea to his discourtesy. The two did not meet again for many years and she bore him rancour for the rest of her life.

Thiers may have been temporarily on bad relations with the Orleanist Court but he was, quintessentially, the man of the July Monarchy. His radical ideas, his bourgeois origins, the great part he had played in the eviction of the Bourbons, all made him totally unacceptable to the *Faubourg St. Germain*. His continued friendship with Dorothea would have been a grave handicap in her efforts to make herself acceptable to the right ; the fact that she had quarrelled with him was a corresponding mark in her favour. Almost against her will she was being drawn away from one camp and towards the other. Never did she quarrel with the Tuileries or give up her friendship for all the members of the family, in particular for the Duke of Orleans, but from the moment of her uncle's death, the bonds between them slackened.

*   *   *   *   *

Pauline was now eighteen years old. Rich, intelligent and of great family, the parents of the *Faubourg St. Germain* would have hesitated to turn up their noses at her whatever the defects of her mother. As it was, Dorothea's overtures were received with as much enthusiasm as they were offered. The question was not whom Pauline could find to marry but whom she would select from the multitude of suitors. Of one thing Dorothea was certain ; that Pauline should choose for herself. For Louis de Valençay it might be all right to select a wife and force the marriage through without much ado, but for Pauline, whose sensitivity and intelligence were so much superior, there must be more solicitude. Her daughter's life, Dorothea knew, could be wrecked by a mistake as surely as her own had been, but this time she could not believe that there would be another Prince Talleyrand to piece together the fragments.

Mother and daughter between them seemed to find fault with every suitor offered them. Jules de Clermont-Tonnerre, despite his resounding name, had the misfortune to look vulgar. The Duke of Saulx-Tavannes could certainly not be accused of this ; his distinction lay rather in looking like an elephant. There was also madness on both sides of the family. The Duke of Guiche was only nineteen and had a foolish mother. The Marquis of Biron was extremely stupid and a red-hot Carlist. Elie de Gontaut was a fop. It almost seemed as if against every noble name some disqualifying blemish must be recorded.

One young man, however, seemed if not impeccable, at least a good deal better than the rest. Henri de Castellane was the son of one of Dorothea's oldest friends. Dorothea found him clever, well-educated, hard working and ambitious. He was very correct and polite, lived a retired life and went only into the best society. He got on well with his mother though he did not seem so devoted to her as to cause difficulties in his relations with his mother-in-law. From the time of his marriage he was guaranteed an income of fifty thousand francs a year and, better still, had an eccentric and elderly uncle with no heir and forty-two million francs to dispose of. At his marriage his grandmother had promised to make over to him her property of Aubijou in the Auvergne. The archbishop and the Abbé Dupanloup both pronounced him an admirable young man. Madame Adélaïde considered the match an excellent one because the Castellanes, though of the *Faubourg*, had never broken completely with the Orleanists.

The match therefore seemed admirable if not outstanding in every worldly sense. There remained the feelings of Pauline. From the first she had liked Henri de Castellane but—with exemplary prudence—declared that she wished to make sure of his principles and beliefs before committing herself. Further study was evidently satisfactory ; at any rate, by the end of the year it was generally accepted that the marriage would take place. By April, 1839, the way was clear ; the marriage contract was signed on the eighth, the civil and religious ceremonies took place on the succeeding days. By the time of the ceremony there was no more talk of principles and beliefs ; Pauline was in love.

Alexander was now the only one of Dorothea's children to remain unmarried. She had always regretted that he had abandoned his naval career. She knew his talents and virtues but she knew also that the same vices of idleness and irresponsibility as had ruined his father were his in full measure too and that his lack of a profession could only draw him ever deeper into debt and dissipation. He might well have made a passable job as eldest son and heir to Valençay but he could never reconcile himself to the comparative poverty and insignificance which was the lot of a second child. " His position embitters his character and destroys the equability of his temper," wrote Dorothea with regret. She still preferred his turbulent rancour to the anodyne respectability of her elder son but Pauline was more important to her than either of them and Alexander added to the irritation which he felt over having an elder brother preferred to him financially and socially the still keener chagrin of seeing his younger sister supplant him in his mother's attentions.

Since his return from Italy in 1835, Alexander had been hanging around Paris accumulating debts and enemies. Talleyrand's legacy had temporarily rescued him from the first of these but he was by no means outstandingly eligible as a husband. He could still, however, have hoped to find himself a rather better match than Valentine de St. Aldegonde, the shop-soiled child of a family of decidedly secondary distinction. Mlle de St. Aldegonde was described by Apponyi as appearing at a ball " like a sunbeam striking through an azure cloud," though he qualified this lyrical description by observing that this perfection must have taken at least eight hours hard work to achieve. She seems to have been pretty, vain and rather silly ; totally incompetent to cope with the moods of her unpredictable husband. The marriage seemed destined to drift from rock to rock. The most to be hoped was that it would never arrive at total shipwreck. Dorothea shrugged her shoulders and congratulated herself that it was no worse. The wedding took place in October, 1839. At least, Dorothea must have reflected, she would now be able to enjoy a certain respite before she would have to occupy herself with the marriages of any more of her descendants.

*   *   *   *   *

The marriages of Pauline and Alexander had at last given

Dorothea the necessary liberty to undertake her long-awaited journey to her estates in Prussia. In spite of her largely successful assault on the *Faubourg* she saw little reason to linger in Paris. " Mme de Talleyand without her uncle is of no importance whatsoever " wrote Princess Lieven exultantly. " She feels this every moment of her day. . . . She has no friends. Her salon has no grandeur or dignity and no one goes there. She is bored, she quarrels with everyone in turn merely to pass the time. . . ." Madame de Lieven exaggerated but there was truth in her malice ; Dorothea's consequence had indeed diminished and she found the fact hard to stomach. It was an extra incentive to be gone.

Dorothea had long been nervous about the sort of reception she could expect in Germany but her fears had recently been set at rest by a letter from her old childhood friend, Frederick William, the Prince Royal, " I give you my word, madam," wrote the prince, " that the thing which delighted me the most in your letter was the prospect which it offered of our seeing you and your family here . . . For pity's sake, do not disappoint us again. That at least you owe us as reparation for all the vain hopes which we have cherished over the long years . . ."

Such effusive friendliness was flattering when it came from the heir to the throne of Prussia. In retrospect, Dorothea's childhood at Berlin seemed to her to have been a haven of calm and order. The indifference of her mother, the pains of her love for Czartoryski, the heavy solemnity of the court : all these were thrust into the background of her mind to give place to a pattern of bright innocence where everyone was benevolent and affectionate and all occasions ordered decorously and according to the soundest principles of social precedence.

The thought of a journey to Germany excited her with all its promise of a refound home and family. Yet also it frightened her ; it was so long since she had left there and so few of her old friends would still be alive to welcome her back. At one moment Germany seemed to her the promised land, at another a desolate unknown which would differ from France only in the nature of its unpleasantness. " Paris is bad and tiring for me," she wrote to Bacourt. " It is too difficult to find peace there and yet that is what I need above all. I still intend to go to Germany in the spring but what I shall find there is tombs and business problems and what I need is sun and rest."

Prominent among both the tombs and the business problems were those of her sister Wilhelmina, Duchess of Sagan. Wilhelmina had died in November, 1839, at her home in Vienna. Two years earlier she had come to stay at Rochecotte. Dorothea had been apprehensive before her arrival. " I am never entirely at my ease with her. I was accustomed to be afraid of her in my youth and am still somewhat overawed." But the flamboyant, brilliant creature who had amused and scandalised the society of Europe twenty years before had degenerated into a stout, old woman, raucous and garrulous ; too dignified to be a figure of fun yet certainly unlikely to inspire fear in anyone. " Fidgety, jumpy, fat, wrinkled, very partial to tobacco and wearing rosebuds on her head," was Princess Lieven's unflattering description and the artist's licence does not seem to have been stretched unduly. The sisters had co-existed amicably enough for a few days. It was the first time they had met for many years and they parted with protestations that they must not let so long a separation occur again. But the visit had not established any real sympathy between them ; they had few common friends and no common interests and neither sister showed any particular eagerness to put their pledges into practice.

The news of Wilhelmina's death provided an extra and cogent reason for her journey to Germany. Wilhelmina's huge estates—a principality as it really was—around the town of Sagan had been left to her second sister, the Princess of Hohenzollern. But the Hohenzollerns had no children, and it seemed impossible that they should now have any. The title and estates would pass at their death to Louis de Valençay. Both Dorothea and Louis therefore felt a particular interest in visiting Sagan and in ensuring themselves that everything was being administered with due skill and attention.

Not that Louis, despite the fact that one day he would be Prince of Sagan, was expected by his mother to play any very important part in their travels. He seems to have been considered by her as something rather similar to a professional companion ; useful for opening doors, remembering appointments and providing an audience when there was no one more interesting to talk to. " Docile," " obliging," " reliable," were the words which Dorothea used most frequently about him. She was certainly fond of him but fond as one might be of an amiable and not over-intelligent dog. He was her child and therefore her responsibility ; she would take his side in any conflict and even feel maternal pride at any of his inconsiderable achievements. But she did not find him interesting or stimulating and when he was not there to remind her of his existence was as likely as not to forget about him altogether.

Whether Dorothea was conscious of it or not, her future depended on the success or failure of her journey. If she was ever to settle again in Germany she had to do so soon ; already her German habits were forgotten, her friendships broken ; even the language came with difficulty to her tongue. And yet she knew that life in France without Talleyrand could never satisfy her. What was she to do ? She did not know, but must have hoped at the bottom of her mind that her journey would provide her with a ready-made solution.

*　　　*　　　*　　　*　　　*

Even before she left France, Dorothea was disappointed by her travels. To get to Liège she took her first journey in a train and was ill-pleased by it ; she found disconcerting its reluctance to stop at several attractively walled towns which she wished to examine and the uncompromising way in which it thrust its way across the open country rather than visit the villages that lay beside the route. From the frontier onwards the journey was a saga of disillusionments. At Cologne she was forced to choose between going without a fire or being suffocated by a cast-iron stove. The beds were uncomfortable ; " as regards bedrooms Germany is undoubtedly in a state of savagery." The weather was dreadful ; hail, rain, blasts and storms. The suburbs of Cassel were especially poor. There was frost at Nordhausen on 23rd May. The countryside around was ugly, but not so ugly as the town of Halle where matters were made worse by a crowd of wretched students who loafed round the carriages with pipes in their mouths and seemed quite ready to cause a disturbance. Except in Berlin, the food was invariably deplorable. " I am undoubtedly a very ungrateful daughter of Germany," she wrote to Bacourt, " as I am always being exasperated by material discomforts which, in past years, I never realised existed . . . To some extent I had forgotten my motherland and was surprised to find it so hideous."

Only when she got to Berlin did more proper sentiments prevail. The king was gravely ill so court life was cut down to a minimum and there was little in the way of entertaining. But this did not discourage all the personalities of the city from hastening to greet her with gratifying alacrity. The welcome of the royal children was somewhat muted but they were unfeignedly happy to receive and welcome her. Dorothea was particularly concerned to make a good impression on—and, incidentally, to form a good impression of—the Prince Royal who was so shortly to ascend the throne. It was a shock to find that her childhood friend—three years her junior indeed —had grown very stout and old. But he could hardly have been more affable, gossiped with enthusiastic interest of their common youth and continually pressed her to settle in Berlin. By his wife, a Bavarian princess, she was less enraptured ; the Princess Royal was polite enough certainly but a timid manner, a cold heart and a dull mind made an unfortunate impression beside the easy friendliness of her husband.

The Prince Royal had been married for seventeen years but had had no children. The king's second son, Prince William of Prussia, therefore enjoyed a prominence and influence even beyond that which his considerable ambition and talents would anyway have secured him. With his wife, Princess Augusta of the house of Saxe-Weimar-Eisenach, Dorothea quickly struck up a friendship which more than made up for the chill of the Princess Royal. More than twenty years younger than Dorothea and very ready to be impressed by her wit, her sophistication and her distinction, Princess Augusta was almost embarrassingly effusive in her welcome. She asked Dorothea to call the day after her arrival in Berlin, gave a dinner for her the following night and from then on over-whelmed her new friend with kind attentions. Neither by intelligence nor character was Augusta the companion Dorothea would have chosen if no other consideration had played a part. But the love and admiration of the Princess of Prussia could not fail to be flattering and Dorothea quickly learnt to prize the influence which she possessed over her. The Duchess of Talleyrand had shared her uncle's life too long for her to live in any country without wishing to have some finger at least in the management of its affairs. The wife of the heir to the throne would certainly be a useful ally in her endeavours.

On 8th June the King of Prussia died. The Prince Royal succeeded to the throne as Frederick William IV and Prince William was given the title of Prince of Prussia. The funeral of the late king might have been contrived as a demonstration of Dorothea's importance. The chief marshal was instructed to find her a good place, the new king sent word to her to go to her seat by way of the royal apartments and the newly created Princess of Prussia sent her liveried servants to make sure that Dorothea found the way. She could not be left in any doubt that she had been accepted as an old and valued friend.

But even with all this Dorothea could not feel that she had come home or that Germany was any more her country than France or even England. " I am a complete stranger both to things and people, entirely unconnected with the place, speaking the language with some hesitation ; in short, I am not at home. I feel ill at ease and ashamed at being so."

By birth, by upbringing and by inclination, Dorothea was a European. It was a heritage she was proud of. But it carried with it its own penalties. There were times when Dorothea felt that it must after all be pleasant to belong, to be inextricably involved with some society, however restricted and parochial. The sight of her cousins and childhood acquaintances in Berlin still leading the same life, still intent on the same interests, filled her at once with a sense of superiority and of envy. Superiority, because her life had been so much more varied and eventful than theirs ; envy, because they were at home and knew it while for her there seemed to be no home anywhere on earth.

*　　*　　*　　*　　*

Prussia had so far failed to strike any real chord of patriotism. Dorothea now wondered whether a visit to her own lands and her own house might be more successful in arousing her sluggish sentimentality. A few days after the death of the king, she left Berlin to visit her estates in Silesia. Her first destination was Günthersdorf; a large house at the centre of her properties. She found it strange to arrive at a home of her own at so vast a distance from the spot where her life was usually passed.

Günthersdorf was an oasis of gardens and fine trees among the desolate pine forests and sandy wastes of Silesia. The house was massively inelegant but comfortable and pleasant to live in. It had stood empty for many years and there was only a minimum of furniture, glass and plate. The peasants' cows had been allowed to graze up close to the house and the noise of haymaking filled the long summer days. Life seemed to have become a perpetual picnic and Dorothea rejoiced in the calm ; assuring herself, as she had done so often at Rochecotte, that pastoral pleasures were the best.

Soon after her arrival the senior officers of her estates came to pay their respects to her. At their head were an architect, a doctor, two bailiffs, two rent collectors, an agent, a treasurer, a head keeper, four Catholic priests, three Protestant pastors and the mayor of the town. The imposing march past of these deferential and well-spoken gentlemen delighted the seignorial instincts of Dorothea. For the first time she began really to savour the attractions of feudal life in Germany and to conceive that, in the splendour, solidity and autocratic powers of her present position, there might be something that could outweigh the wider and more cosmopolitan attractions of Paris and London.

In Prussia a great landlord still enjoyed powers little short of royal and the royal power itself had more than a touch of the divine. Everything seemed settled and well-ordered and everyone—in Günthersdorf at least—well satisfied with their position. After the turbulent unrest of France and the disturbing irresponsibility of the English aristocracy, this docile acquiescence in a properly constituted social system possessed peculiar charm for Dorothea. She gave herself up with satisfaction to all the duties and pleasures of her rank; visited the churches and schools, presented prizes, rode around her estates, patronised the tenants and visited the more distinguished of her neighbours.

Amidst the new pleasures she found sudden evocations of a past not always so agreeable. She chanced to open an old writing-desk and found inside a bundle of letters which she had received long ago from the Abbé Piattoli; letters which recalled irresistibly her lonely and distracted youth, the sweetness of her few childish loves, the sorrowful saga of her dreams of Adam Czartoryski and the reality of Count Edmond de Périgord. " There is something remarkably solemn in this past thus suddenly revived with such intense reality," she wrote to Bacourt. " Solemn " showed generosity on her part towards those who had done so much to mar it for her; she could with justice have used a harsher word.

But Dorothea was not left long in peace to recapture her past and savour the pleasures of a country lady. On 19th June, she got a letter from her new agent Herr von Wolff warning her that her sister, the Princess of Hohenzollern, was behaving deplorably over the estates at Sagan. Knowing that she had no son to whom the title could pass and totally unconcerned about the interests of her nephew, Louis de Valençay, the princess seemed intent on despoiling the property. The land was happily protected by the entail but she was ransacking the house, selling everything which offered a hope of profit and allowing what remained to go to rack and ruin. Herr von Wolff strongly urged Dorothea to go at once to Sagan to protect her interests.

Sagan was only six hours journey from Günthersdorf and Dorothea quickly made up her mind that she must take her agent's advice. With her came Louis, the principal victim of her sister's depredations, to examine for himself the estate whose name he was one day to bear.

Except for the great woods around the castle, the countryside near Sagan was anything but picturesque. The town too had little to be said for it. Stendhal had been intendant there for the Napoleonic armies in the summer of 1813. He had found little to interest him and had commented sadly that the only inhabitant who had ever written anything was the Roman Catholic priest and that the only work of this divine had been a monograph on a flood caused by the River Bober. Since then Sagan had grown in size but not in beauty or cultural attainment. It was a typical, dull north-German township, prosperous and undistinguished, remarkable only for the great castle of its dukes.

Feeling that, in the circumstances, she could hardly demand her sister's hospitality, Dorothea had put up at the inn. At the first opportunity, however, she hastened to visit the castle ; grandiose, richly decorated, dominating the town and surrounded by a finely landscaped park. All was as she expected except where certain gaps marked the ravages of the Princess of Hohenzollern. The family portraits at least were still on the walls and in the outbuildings she found the old gilt carriage lined with red velvet in which her father had left Courland for the last time. To her dismay she found that her sister proposed to include even this sentimental relic in a future sale ; that at least she could prevent and she snapped it up with a bid of thirty-five crowns.

Herr von Wolff urged Dorothea to buy the estate outright. Her sister Hohenzollern already owed her some money and the affair could be put through with little inconvenience or financial strain. Dorothea was tempted but hesitant. It would be a fine thing to crown her German estates with the principality of Sagan and the idea of restoring her father's seat to its former glories appealed to all her ideas of propriety. But it would also be a heavy responsibility and one that would tie her to Germany more firmly than she was yet ready for. If she were to buy Sagan she would be proclaiming to all the world that she had chosen to settle in Germany. As yet she was not prepared even to admit that any such choice needed to be made. She was, indeed, scarcely prepared to admit it even when the decision had long been taken. Seven years later she was to write to Barante:

" I am not giving up France at all ; that would not be right whether according to my heart or to the rules of society. I want to share my life between my two countries. My

property and my peace of mind are both tied up with
Germany and yet I will always be drawn back to France,
by my memories, my long past, my daughter, Rochecotte
and the crypt at Valençay."

Yet it was not going to be possible for the Duchess of Sagan,
mistress of the lives of more than fifty thousand people, to
share her life between France and Germany unless she neglected
altogether her feudal duties. Dorothea could never have
brought herself to do this ; if she bought Sagan it would be
to make her life there and accept the obligations of the ruler
of a principality. Her reluctance to commit herself to the
purchase of Sagan sprang from her wish to postpone a decision
which she feared must one day be made. For the moment she
did no more than promise to come back to Prussia in the
following spring.

* * * * *

The journey back to France was made in leisurely stages.
In Berlin the Prussian royal family were once more effusively
gracious to her. She went to Potsdam to stay with the king at
Frederick the Great's palace of Sans Souci and was treated so
much like one of the family that she almost wondered whether
the last thirty years had not been a hallucination and in fact
she had never left. Once more Augusta, Princess of Prussia,
outdid all the others in her acts of kindness and protestations
of friendship. The spell which Dorothea seemed to exercise
over this vain, ambitious, fretful woman is a remarkable
testimony to her powers. From everyone else Augusta
demanded flattery, with Dorothea she seemed content only
to bestow it. She had never loved or understood her husband,
was not particularly interested in her children, was felt
generally to be cold and self-centred. Yet for Dorothea she
seemed to reserve a warmth and admiration which was as
extravagant as it was sincere. Her invitations rained upon her
new friend, her carriage was put permanently at her disposal.
Dorothea left Berlin in the conviction that her status there
would be higher and her influence greater even than in France
as the niece of Prince Talleyrand.

There were two more duties which she felt bound to fulfil before she left Germany. First she went to Carlsbad where her two surviving sisters, Jeanne, Duchess of Acerenza and Pauline, Princess of Hohenzollern had foregathered for the summer. It was sixteen years since she had met either of them and even as children they had never known each other well. She found her sisters sitting opposite each other playing patience. Jeanne greeted her naturally, Pauline with some embarrassment. They indulged in small talk over tea, then Dorothea retreated to her own rooms across the street.

This start was hardly propitious but the initial discomfort wore off and family relations were soon re-established on a satisfactory level of intimacy undisturbed by strong feelings of any kind. The three sisters went for drives together around the countryside, visited friends and saw such sights as there were in the vicinity. Some pleasant hours were spent dividing up the papers which the Duchess of Courland had accumulated during her life. Dorothea's share included letters from Goethe, Fénelon, Louis XIV and a series of letters from Napoleon to Joséphine.

A fortnight of Carlsbad was enough to convince Dorothea that, though she was glad to have met her sisters again and would not be sorry to do so more frequently, she could not hope to find in their society any of the companionship which she had been lacking since the death of Talleyrand. For Pauline in particular she felt little sympathy; for Jeanne, nearer to her in age and perhaps also in temperament, she had more affection.

There was one last duty to tender to the past. At the end of July she set off with Jeanne to revisit the house where she had passed so much of her childhood. Jeanne had now been a widow for two years and spent much of her time at Löbikau. The house itself was little changed and Dorothea was plagued by a host of turbulent memories reminding her of what might have been. She had been happy there but she had also been driven to acute misery and depression. Every corner recalled to her her former sorrows and pleasures ; everywhere she felt the presence of a solemn, skinny child with great black eyes whose gaiety and tears had filled the house with life and whose longing to be loved still seemed to hang like a prayer about the silent rooms.

Dorothea refound the boys and girls whom she had known in her youth and admired their children and even grand-children. She revisited the summer house in the woods where she had taken refuge from her suitors and thought sadly for a moment of one who had never come. Finally, with her sister she went to visit her mother's unassuming grave at the end of the park. The Duchess of Courland had made her peace with her daughter long before her death. All bitterness had now faded. But as she looked at the mound of earth beneath which her mother lay ; as she remembered the cold indifference with which her childish love had been rebuffed and the callous betrayal with which she had been tricked into marriage, she must have found it hard not to resent the injuries that had been done her and not to mourn for the mother whom she had never had. At least, she must have asked herself, might not just a little kindness and sympathy have directed her life into other, happier paths ?

13

Back in France, Dorothea took stock of her position. There seemed no reason why her life could not be steered into a pleasant and unexacting pattern. Winters and springs could be spent renewing old friendships and seeing something of her family in France ; most of the time would be passed at Rochecotte but there would need to be occasional visits to Valençay and, for the worst of the winter, she had bought a little house in the Rue de Lille. Summers and autumns would be spent in Germany, visiting her estates and consolidating her alliance with the Prussian royal family. Thus she could lead her dual life without ever needing to choose between one country and the other.

So at least Dorothea assured herself as she spent a few happy days among her children at Valençay. Louis seemed genuinely delighted to welcome her and, far more important, Pauline and her husband came down from their arid stronghold in the Auvergne to spend some time with her. Both had grown thin and looked tired but their daughter Marie, who had been born earlier the same year and in whom Dorothea was to take an ever-increasing interest, was all that a baby should be : "fair, fat and fresh, always in a good temper, laughing and restless, a little angel . . ."

She seemed really to have found that united and happy family life which had so consistently evaded her in the past. She took the keenest possible interest in all the doings of her grandchildren and seemed bent on making up to them for the neglect which she had visited on their parents. "At one time I was able to do without children quite easily," she wrote to Bacourt, "but now I am entirely changed and feel that something is really wanting when one or more of these little people is not about me. I can give them my time with real seriousness and feel greatly drawn to these weak little beings for whom Providence may have such great and remarkable destinies in store. It is strange how age changes one's character . . ."

At Rochecotte, Alexander of Dino and his wife came to complete the family circle ; complete, that is to say, except for the unfortunate Edmond who was still expiating his follies in rancorous old age at Florence. Alexander was on his best behaviour and harmony was complete. Yet the political rumblings from Paris reminded her constantly of the stability, the good order and the common sense which seemed to reign in Germany. In December, 1840, the ashes of Napoleon were brought back to Paris amidst the hysterical fervour of the mob. Yet barely two months before, Louis Napoleon, nephew of the emperor, had been tried in Paris and was still in prison for seeking to overthrow the State. Truly the Orleans family and their ever-squabbling supporters seemed determined to miss no opportunity of ridiculing and undermining their own régime. Dorothea must have contrasted the ceremony unfavourably with a similar ceremony she had recently attended in Berlin when a statue to Frederick II had been unveiled. There, most of the spectators had burst into tears and the enthusiasm for the royal family had been intense. " Nothing of the sort could be looked for in a republican atmosphere or in our revolutionary regions." Never backward in predicting revolution and disaster, Dorothea this time seemed to have good reason when she gloomily predicted that France would soon once more be pitchforked back into civil war.

*   *   *   *   *

Over the next years Dorothea divided her life between Prussia and France on more or less the pattern which she had sketched out to herself on her return from Germany in the autumn of 1840. She herself can scarcely have been conscious that little by little her life was altering its course. In her letters the references to German politics gradually became more frequent and her interest in the minutiae of the public life of France correspondingly diminished. Her responsibilities in Germany became more absorbing as those in France began to disappear ; her friendships in Germany grew closer as her French friends died or grew away from her. The years between 1840 and January, 1845, when she finally dropped the title of Talleyrand in favour of that of Sagan, mark a steady drift away from France which was none the less real for being gradual and accomplished largely without the awareness of the principal actor.

Her visit to Germany in 1841 was followed by her first return to Vienna since the Congress. She went ostensibly to visit her sisters who had invited her there the previous year. As she grew older the ties of blood seemed to grow more important and she was anxious now to preserve an association which formerly she had considered as of little worth. But even more she was anxious to see once more the city in which she had found so much pleasure and distress and among whose plots and dissipations her life had become irrevocably linked to her uncle's. " Of all those who turned my head, misled me, thrilled me, no one remains ; young, old, men, women : all have disappeared . . ." " I doubt if I will sleep well to-night," she wrote her first evening in Vienna " I am beset by all the ghosts which this place has called back to me and all of whom speak to me in the same language ; the language of the utter vanity of worldly things."

The only survivor of those who had been close to her during the Congress was Prince Metternich, now more than ever in control of the affairs of Austria. Recently he had married for the third time ; to Mélanie de Zichy, a pretty girl more than thirty years his junior. The new Princess Metternich awaited the visit of the Duchess of Talleyrand with suspicion, apprehension and a certain amount of jealousy. Dorothea for her part was inclined to scoff at Metternich's sexagenarian passion and expected to be received with hostility by the new bride. As it turned out neither had any need to be concerned. Mélanie wrote in her diary next day, " I was very frightened of her before I met her but I found her quite different to what I had been led to expect. She has a fine profile but her beautiful eyes have a certain air of severity. She was most friendly and the deep affection which she has for Clement (Prince Metternich) at once makes her gracious and kindly to my eyes. We

remained alone for a time and took advantage of it to get to
know each other better . . . Later the duchess spoke a lot
of her uncle whom she admired greatly. One can see that she
has pledged him all the gratitude of which she is capable . . .
She talks very agreeably and speaks perfect German."

Dorothea saw a lot of the Metternichs during her stay in
Vienna. The prince she found as intelligent and charming as
ever and gratifyingly ready to agree with her about the
lamentable state of Europe and the dangers of bloody revolution. As for his wife, she seemed attractive and kindly though
noticeably lacking in polish. Among other subjects, they must
have spoken of Dorothea's former *bête noire*, Count Flahaut,
who was being generally tipped as the next French Ambassador
to Vienna. There were difficulties and Meg Flahaut had
chosen to smooth her husband's path with a letter to Lord
Beauvale, the English Ambassador, in which she said that
no one need be concerned at the proposed appointment since
it would be a long time before *she* would be able to follow her
husband to Vienna. Dorothea was delighted by this singular
recommendation. She does not seem to have profited by her
position to try to spoil the Flahauts' prospects and in the end
the appointment was confirmed. She would however have been
less than human if she had not drawn some satisfaction from
the sight of Meg Flahaut's unaccustomed self-abnegation.

*   *   *   *   *

Back in France, Dorothea failed to recover the sense of a
happy and united family which had so pleased her on her
previous visit. It had, indeed, been largely an illusion even
then. Neither Louis nor Alexander were happily married and
the respectable façade which they managed to preserve for
the world could not survive any very searching examination.
But so long as all was well with Pauline and her family,
Dorothea could support the miseries of her other children with
resignation if not with equanimity. On this household all her
dearest hopes for the future were fixed. " . . . I can feel at
ease and secure with them without ever being bored, I can
relax in the atmosphere of their home."

She planned her winter on the assumption that Henri and

Pauline would spend it with her. In the meantime she had plenty to occupy her. She had brought back from Germany copies of certain portraits of her ancestors, these she now proceeded to install at Rochecotte. With the arrangement of her library, the reorganisation of her garden and the resumption of all her duties in the neighbourhood, she promised herself a busy and tranquil season. But in September she got a letter from her daughter which upset all her plans. For some months she had known that Pauline was not well, now she heard that the illness was serious and that it was essential for her to winter in the south. Her doctors had recommended Nice and she now hoped that her mother would come to visit her there. Dorothea disliked the South of France but in the face of such an appeal she had no hesitation. She decided at once to go to Nice with Pauline in December.

For one who had hoped to devote her winter to the placid reconstitution of her forces, Nice in the 1840s could hardly have been more unsuitable. Outside Paris it was undoubtedly the gayest town in France and its social life, being narrower, was correspondingly more intense. She might have hoped that Pauline's illness would provide her with an alibi against all invitations but her daughter began to feel better as soon as she arrived and would have soon been discontented with the life of a recluse. Willy-nilly Dorothea found herself forced to mingle with society. The Grand Duchess Stephanie even prevailed on her to give a party for a hundred and fifty people and, what is more, to organise it on a new and daring pattern which Dorothea understood to be known as a *thé dansant*.

In spite of her often expressed conviction that the life was not at all congenial to her nor appropriate to her state of health, Dorothea managed to get quite a lot of pleasure from her winter at Nice. But it called for a constant effort on her part and it was an effort which she could ill afford to make. She returned to Rochecotte exhausted, though with the comforting reflection that duty had been well done.

Her rest was not to be allowed to last for long. On 10th May, 1842, she wrote to Bacourt describing an affectionate letter she had just received from Henri de Castellane and praising his loyalty, uprightness, sincerity, high moral dignity and perfect nobility of heart. " Louis, my son," she went on, " is also agreeable and is thoroughly reliable. Alexander has qualities too, but his position has embittered him and made him difficult to live with." Nothing could have shown more clearly that only the Castellanes among her children really counted for Dorothea and that her son-in-law meant far more to her than her own two sons.

She was therefore upset and alarmed when a few weeks later she got a letter from Pauline at their home in the Auvergne, telling of the serious injuries which Henri had incurred as a result of falling from his horse. Any danger to his life seemed now to have passed but for a time he had been in great pain, had run a high fever and had suffered from severe shock. With no doctor living within miles the responsibility on Pauline was a heavy one. Dorothea wondered whether help was needed but reassured by the news that the worst was over, decided to wait for a further letter. It arrived a few days later and was anything but encouraging. Henri was no better and Pauline sounded depressed and tired. At once Dorothea decided that she must go to Aubijou. The architect Vestier was enlisted as an escort and the same night they were on the road. For forty-eight hours without any stop they trundled along the lamentable roads that led to Auvergne. Dorothea had no reason to think the trials of the journey unnecessary. She found Henri a little better but suffering from shock and in a state of depressed irritation which wore on the nerves of Pauline and made her devoted nursing an almost intolerable burden. He was obviously still in pain but resisted obstinately any suggestion that he would do well to leave the torrid heat and savage countryside of Aubijou for some spot where he could be better cared for.

After Dorothea had been there forty-eight hours Henri's condition was, if anything, worse. The two women were beginning to despair when, to their immense relief, he suddenly changed his mind ; from a determination not to be moved he was all anxiety to be gone within the hour. All was packed up and the procession was on its way early the following morning. Henri was stretched on a mattress in the Castellane carriage at the head of the file while, either on horseback or in the escorting carriages, rode Pauline and Dorothea, the architect Vestier, two coachmen, a doctor, a ladies' maid, two grooms, a cook, a lawyer, an armed guard and a negro called Zephyr who played the French horn. Painfully the ponderous cortège ground its way over the tracks between Aubijou and Neris. The country-side, though stark, was not without its beauties but Dorothea, already worn by anxiety and her constant travelling, was so overcome by terror at the sight of the precipices cascading beneath the wheels of the carriages, that she broke down and cried.

Dorothea remained with the Castellanes as far as Clermont. There she was assured by a doctor that while the convalescence would be long and painful, Henri was no longer in any danger. Satisfied, she lingered only to make sure that they would be well housed and looked after and then set off for Rochecotte. Now, at last, she was going to have her long hoped for months of country retreat.

In spite of the fair words of the doctor, Henri was never to recover from his injuries. He was soon able to walk again and superficially seemed well enough, but the bones had failed to heal. Constantly the victim of sharp pain and always handicapped in his movements, he became gloomy and embittered. " My father, unfortunately, was harsh by nature, which cut him off from most people,"[1] wrote his daughter Marie, who was not old enough to remember him before his accident. Certainly, after June 1842, he was never again the brilliant and friendly figure whom Dorothea had so much admired and Pauline loved. The marriage endured in tolerable harmony but all the gaiety and youth had withered away, leaving behind only the dry bones of duty and decorum.

Henri's accident and his subsequent ill-health was obviously responsible for much if not all of the unhappiness which overtook the marriage. But it does not entirely explain the sudden withdrawal of interest, almost of revulsion, which now seemed to overtake Dorothea. She still cared as much as ever for the welfare of her daughter and her granddaughter but the Castellanes as a married couple seemed to have lost importance in her eyes. Her reference to them in her letters, their involvement in her future plans dwindled almost to nothing and her occasional mentions of Henri were neutral or even cold in tone. He had grown crotchety and ill-tempered and one can understand that he might easily have quarrelled with Dorothea but the speed and completeness of the break are still perplexing.

Dorothea's alienation from her son-in-law can perhaps be explained by a story told by Prosper Mérimée in a letter written to Madame de Montijo[2] after Henri de Castellane's death at the end of 1847.

" Have I ever told you the story of that son of Monsieur de Castellane who married a daughter of Madame de Talleyrand (who, incidentally, was in all probability also the daughter of her great-uncle, Monsieur de Talleyrand ?). As you know, he is dead leaving enormous debts. His widow was inconsolable ; not at all about the loss of her fortune but simply for her husband. At the height of her grief, while looking through some of the deceased's letters so as to be able to sort out his money problems, she came across a packet of love-letters. It was obvious that he had been unfaithful but the really strange thing about it was that all the adjectives which referred to her rival were in the masculine. Just imagine her surprise ! Monsieur de C. had discovered a very good-looking footman in service with Princess Lieven. He had persuaded him to enter his service, had made him doff his livery and turned him into his steward. This steward and the unsuspected rival were one and the same ! Can you, who have studied the human heart, tell me which is the more grievous ; to lose someone whom one loves and admires or to discover that the person one regrets deserves nothing but one's scorn ? One day Madame de Talleyrand came to Monsieur de C's house. She saw the steward in question dressed up as a gentleman and ready to sit down at table with her. ' It seems to me that I have already seen this " gentleman " somewhere,' she said. ' Yes, it was behind Madame de Lieven's carriage. Please see that he is served in his room.' "

The most that can be said for this story is that it would conveniently explain an otherwise mysterious passage in Dorothea's life. Though Prosper Mérimée was a notorious gossip and capable of embroidering all he heard he would still hardly have invented the story altogether. It does therefore seem that rumour had it that Henri de Castellane was a homosexual and—what would have been almost more shocking to Dorothea—that he so far demeaned himself as to conduct his sodomy with a servant. If word of this had got back to Dorothea—let alone if she had made the dramatic discovery with which Mérimée credits her—her first thoughts would have been to keep it from Pauline. But even though she had no proof of the allegation, even though she believed it false, the very existence of the rumour would have done much to poison her relations with her son-in-law.

However this may have been, she never found again the ease and intimacy which she had previously so much enjoyed when with the Castellanes. Pauline and Marie remained to her, but in the ruin of their family life one of the greatest sources of happiness in Dorothea's life was unkindly extinguished.

* * * * *

The summer of 1842 brought fresh unhappiness to Dorothea. The Duke of Orleans had always been her favourite among the royal family and he, for his part, had always treated her with particular deference and affection. In his hands she had felt that there was a future for the Orleanists and in that future it seemed that she might expect to play a distinguished and important part. Then, suddenly, came the news that the duke had been killed in an accident, that he had fallen or jumped from a carriage drawn by runaway horses and had been picked up dead. Sombrely Dorothea noted in her journal that the republicans of Tours had given a banquet to celebrate the happy demise: " With the loss of this link from the royal chain we have all lost some of our security. Our goods and our heads are worth less than they used to be."

A few days later she was in Paris and called on her old friend, Madame Adélaïde. The chateau of Neuilly was like a vast tomb and the old lady ill with grief at the death of the nephew she had loved so well. She greeted Dorothea as the friend who, outside the closest family, would regret most deeply the loss of the young duke. Dorothea was taken to view the coffin and to sprinkle holy water in the little chapel. She had been mentioned with particular affection in the duke's will and left as a souvenir a magnificent Algerian carpet which she installed in a place of honour at Rochecotte.

Not even the return of Bacourt from the United States and the renewal of their old friendship could restore Dorothea's spirits after this year of disaster. He spent the winter with her at Rochecotte sorting through the great bundles of papers which Talleyrand had left in London and which had now finally found their way back to France. The task, with all the memories that it evoked, depressed her still further, and she passed some gloomy months in her secluded home. The gloom, however, proved temporary ; by January, 1843, she was counting her blessings in a letter to Barante : " my health is good enough, my life restful, the weather temperate, and my soul at peace." Peace, she had made it plain in earlier letters, was the very most that she could hope for.

Henri de Castellane's illness and her own subsequent exhaustion had prevented Dorothea from making her usual journey to Germany in the summer of 1842. Now business made it essential that she should return. In March, 1842, she had heard that her sister, having finally failed to come to any reasonable agreement with her nephew, the Prince of Hohenzollern, was offering to sell the whole property of Sagan. Dorothea was in no doubt at all that the offer had to be accepted but the financial and legal complications were appalling and it was impossible to conduct them satisfactorily at long range.

By June, 1843, after a journey which seemed to involve visits to half the principalities of Germany, Dorothea arrived at Sagan. A pretty house opposite the castle which had formerly been lived in by her father's chief steward was taken over until the castle should be fit to live in and there she settled until such time as she could once more enter her property and live in it with dignity and comfort.

The Prince of Hohenzollern, fortunately for Dorothea, had little interest in the estate but much in ready money. He proved content to sell the usufruct over the parts of the property which were his for life. All that remained was to pay the money and reunite ducal title, possession and ownership in the same hands. By 16th October, the formalities were completed and the deed was signed.

There was no question of her returning to France that winter; the business was far too important and too exacting. Already the call of her German principality was beginning to supplant all other interests and responsibilities. The enthusiasm with which she was greeted in Sagan touched and delighted her. For four years the property had been sadly neglected since the Princess of Hohenzollern had given it no attention at all. Wilhelmina too had preferred life in Vienna to provincial preoccupations such as taking an interest in the welfare of her tenants, her subjects as indeed they were in most senses of the word. Now the promise of a duchess who would live on her estates and take seriously the affairs of the principality gave new hope to the inhabitants. Dorothea, on her side, responded to their welcome with a determination to see them well cared for and well governed.

In the summer of 1844 she left reluctantly for a short visit to France. Pauline was on the point of having her second child and, whatever Dorothea may have thought of the husband, she did not mean to leave her favourite child alone at such a moment.

But the visit did little to slow down the work of improvement and of installation and she was back before the winter had begun. Gone were the days when six months in Germany had to be balanced against six months in France; all Dorothea's thoughts were now with Sagan. She had anyway to return in time for an event which seemed to her of great significance and which symbolised all the changes which had come over her life. Each possessor of Sagan, within a year and thirty days of his taking possession, was bound to renew the feudal contract with the King of Prussia under which he enjoyed his princely rights. On 6th January, Dorothea was invested by the king with the powers and rights of a ruler of Sagan. The Duchess of Talleyrand underwent the last metamorphosis of her life and from now on styled herself Duchess of Sagan.

To all who knew her in France this abandonment even of the name of Talleyrand seemed to represent the renunciation of her friendships and the betrayal of her memories. To the Prussian court it confirmed her conversion into a German lady and her integration into their society. Dorothea alone did not accept that she had cut herself off from France. To Barante she wrote, protesting that she had no intention of choosing between the two and that it **was** impossible for her to give up either one or the other. But the day that she first heard herself addressed as Duchess of Sagan she must have known that, whether she liked it or not, she could never again be received in France except as a visitor and could never hope to convince her old friends that she had not deserted them for ever.

14

Generalisations about love are usually either superficial or positively misleading. To say that Dorothea " had a passionate nature " would be trite and facile ; a phrase conveying little and in some ways concealing more than it exposed. And yet it is hard to find words more precise or revealing. Dorothea perhaps had a great capacity for love—for love of an individual, that is to say, not for any generalised love of mankind. She was single-minded, loyal, had little sense of the ridiculous and invested all she did with peculiar significance. Though proud, she was capable of sacrifice and complete self-abnegation ; though suspicious, she was longing always for someone in whom she could have blind reliance and to whom she could surrender her destiny ; though aloof, she was far from disinterested in the cruder pleasures of the flesh.

Her childhood, denied as she was any response from the mother whom she was so anxious to love, taught her to hide her feelings but did nothing to quench her ardour. If she had married a man whom she could have respected then, even though she had not loved him at first, love might well have followed. To such a husband she would have been a pattern of devotion and have spent all her efforts in furthering his wishes and seeking for his happiness. But she married Edmond de Périgord, a man whom she could neither respect, nor like, nor even tolerate. All her affection, all her yearnings to adore or to serve, were left within her so that they had either to moulder into bitterness or find their way out by devious routes and in strange forms.

It is probably true to say that Dorothea had never been wholly in love in all her life. Of all those connected with her Prince Talleyrand alone had fully engaged her attentions.

314

Deeply though she had loved and admired him, faithfully
though she had served him, completely though she had
dedicated her life to him : even in this relationship there was
always something held back. If she gave herself physically
to him during the troubled years after the return from Vienna
it was in gratitude, in fascination, in respect. Never was there
that perfect realisation of a passion which she believed to be
within her powers and for which she was half unconsciously
searching all her life.

Now she was more than fifty years old. She must have
begun to feel that the opportunity had passed, that age was
robbing her of a promise still unfulfilled. Yet she was still
beautiful, almost uncannily so for a woman of her years. It was
in 1845 that Charles Bocher, a libertine of distinction, described
how he met her often in the drawing-room of the Countess
de la Redorte :[1] " Her tall figure was the same as ever. Her
beauty still enhanced the brilliant qualities which had won the
hearts of those on whom the destiny of France used to depend.
In my ignorance of her age I, who was thirty years her junior,
became really captivated by her charms. I confided in Madame
de la Redorte who told me, ' You should declare your passion.
Nothing would be more flattering to our dear duchess ; it
would please her immensely ! ' "

Still beautiful, witty, sophisticated, vastly rich, an intimate
friend of the royal family of Prussia, bearing about her the
glamour of half a dozen notorious scandals : it was small
wonder that she could turn the heads of men much younger
than herself. What was more remarkable was that she should
have allowed her head to be turned in its turn. And yet, in
the spring of 1843, when she first met the young Prince Felix
Lichnowsky, she was on the threshold of her final love affair
which was to set the winds of spring blowing through the
autumn of her life.

*   *   *   *   *

Dorothea's relationship with Felix Lichnowsky is as elusive
as it was undoubtedly intense. Painfully little evidence is
left beyond a handful of letters and references in contemporary
memoirs and journals. How much she cared for Lichnowsky,

how far she deluded herself that it was a relationship which could last beyond a few years, how far she saw herself as a mother helping and inspiring a much-loved son and how far as a woman urging on her lover ; all this must be guesswork and guesswork based on the flimsiest grounds. That he was physically her lover is common tradition and there is no reason to believe that tradition lied. But it is the truth behind the facts which must remain uncertain ; the deeds may be more or less established but their significance remains obstinately elusive.

About Lichnowsky, " thrice-blessed Felix " in Prince Pückler's phrase, quite a lot is known. The memoir he wrote of his service in Spain in the Carlist wars gives a fair indication of his character. He was born in 1814 of a Hungarian mother and a Prussian father. All his youth was spent in Vienna where he learnt to spend money which he did not have and to believe in ideas which he did not understand. At the age of twenty-three he became bored of the life of a German cavalry officer and went off to seek adventure in Spain. There he covered himself with glory ; he was quick, strong, enterprising and brave to the point of recklessness, all virtues which commended themselves to his commander. Two or three years of war, however, satisfied his appetite for that sort of excitement. By 1840 he was back in Prussia again, trying his hand at politics. His views were radical ; not from any particular conviction but because these seemed best calculated to annoy the Prussian bourgeoisie. His instability became notorious and all who studied his career with care predicted that though it might possibly be brilliant, it would certainly be brief.

From the moment she met him some time in 1842 until his death in 1848, Lichnowsky was the most constant interest of Dorothea's life. He would pay her long visits at Sagan or at Günthersdorf, he saw her constantly when she was in Berlin and gossip linked their names invariably together. Dorothea can have had little liking for his political opinions but she was too wise and too experienced to take them very seriously. Lichnowsky was not the sort of man to push his radicalism to the point of revolution. Though he was certainly far more decisive and forceful a character than Bacourt, Dorothea had for him some of the same affectionate tolerance and protective urge; he was so young, so vociferous, so enthusiastic, in many ways so foolish. And then, though such a child, he was good-looking, virile and gratifyingly ardent. The relationship was a rich one and for Dorothea one of its charms was its constant variety. She found herself called upon to play the role now of a mother, now an Egeria, now a mistress—sometimes all three at once. The experience was exhausting and occasionally alarming but on the whole she found it very much to her taste.

But though her affair with Lichnowsky was certainly absorbing, she never allowed it to become all-engrossing. In 1845 the death of Royer Collard came as a sharp reminder of her friends in France. He was eighty-two years old, far closer in age to her uncle than to Dorothea, and her affection for him had been that for a parent or a far elder brother. Always she had had great faith in his judgment and had prized immeasurably his cool reason and utter integrity. He had never hesitated to tell her if he thought she had acted foolishly or improperly and Dorothea at times had found his frankness hard to swallow. But equally he had never left her in doubt that his chidings were inspired only by his profound concern for her welfare and her peace of mind. In that certainty Dorothea accepted meekly rebukes which she would have resented from any other man except her uncle.

" Only a few days before his death," she told Barante, " he wrote to tell me that he was near his end, to bid me good-bye in the most moving terms . . . Soon there will be no one whom I know and love except you. Live, live for a long time, far longer than I ; I do not wish to have to mourn you too. You know how loyal my heart is and what I feel towards my friends. So you know that what I say is true, without the least exaggeration."

She still kept alive the fiction that she was dividing her life between Prussia and France. Three months later, when on the point of leaving for a holiday in Italy, she wrote of her surprise at finding that it was already eighteen months since she had last been across the Rhine and of her determination to come back soon to the land " where so many memories still find personification for me in a group of three or four dear friends and where there is a tomb at which I wish to pray once more before I rejoin in heaven he who has dominated all my life." The words sounded fine and no doubt she was sincere as she wrote them but it is still true that the ten weeks she was to pass in Italy were devoted entirely to sight-seeing and other diversions. If her anxiety to revisit France had been as keen as she professed it, then some part at least of her holiday could have been sacrificed. In Italy she refound some of the gaiety of youth, found perháps a gaiety which she had never enjoyed before. Rome in particular delighted her. The Pope received this distinguished convert and contrived to give the impression that it was he and not she who was honoured ; several cardinals were kind to her ; under the wings of the Princesses Borghese, Doria and Lamolatto she was introduced into everything that was most distinguished in Roman society. After the stolidity of Berlin and the meretricious brilliance of Paris, she felt that she had found at last richness and nobility coupled with moral worth, pleasure in life without frivolity, religious ardour without austerity or undignified fanaticism. " It is not the charm of the climate, the artistic splendours, the magnificence of the churches and palaces . . . no, it is the exquisite flavour of orthodoxy which permeates everything, raises it up and is to be found nowhere but in Rome."

From thence she went on to Naples and to Venice. Both pleased her but she remained faithful to her first love ; neither the glitter of the one nor the " nonchalant gondolas " of the other could shadow her delight in Rome. Perhaps in part it was only the relief of finding a great city in which she had no relations, no property, no responsibilities and no political axe to grind ; perhaps the visit was an escape from a love affair which was making demands on her exhausting and oppressive for a woman of fifty-four to meet. By all the conventions of romantic liaison it should have been the ageing duchess who found intolerable the separation from her lover while the young and dashing prince made merry in her absence. In fact, Dorothea derived unfeigned pleasure from her holiday, and it was Lichnowsky who did the pining. Throughout their relationship—or rather that small part of it which is visible to us—the evidence indicates that it was Lichnowsky who was the ardent pursuer and Dorothea who asked herself from time to time if it were really worth the trouble. Certainly she suppressed these doubts without much struggle, but an obstinate mental reservation always remained.

When at last she returned to Prussia in the spring of 1846 the relationship was resumed and all Berlin gossiped of the doings of the wicked Duchess of Sagan. But Dorothea had demonstrated to her own satisfaction that, fond though she was of Lichnowsky, she could manage quite well without him. The knowledge must have helped greatly towards her peace of mind and it is not inconceivable that her journey to Italy was a deliberate exercise in self-discipline designed to help her to arrive at it. Self-illusion was largely foreign to her and it would have been strange if she had not accepted that, in the end, Lichnowsky would make his life elsewhere. Now she could reassure herself with the belief, that when this happened, she would not find it too difficult to carry on.

* * * * *

The euphoria induced by her journeys in Italy was not allowed to persist for long. Henri de Castellane was plunging his family into debt with a zeal that recalled to Dorothea the worst excesses of her husband. Since 1845 he had sat as a deputy and become an enthusiastic supporter of Monsieur Guizot. His career was turbulent and gave little pleasure to his mother-in-law, who considered that any political life except that of a leader was undesirable and viewed with distaste the sight of her son-in-law as a mere back-bencher and a violent and ill-conducted one at that. Then in July, 1847, his old injury, which had never ceased to trouble him, became suddenly much worse. " If the only effect of my son-in-law's illness was to paralyse his political energies I would be tempted to rejoice in his sufferings," Dorothea wrote dryly to Barante, " but they are so harsh and so prolonged as to make my daughter unhappy."

There is little trace in this remark of the old affection which had once made Dorothea rate her son-in-law so far above her own son. Pauline's happiness however came before everything and though her marriage certainly caused her much misery and strain, Pauline still seemed sincerely to love her husband. For her sake, Dorothea dutifully hoped that Henri would soon recover. However the news from France grew worse. Soon he was unable to walk at all and it became obvious that his life was in danger. Dorothea hastened across Europe to her daughter's side but she arrived at Rochecotte only just in time to be present at Henri's death-bed. On 16th October he died, leaving his wife inconsolable and his mother-in-law distressed on her daughter's account but still inclined to think that every cloud had a silver lining.

Two or three months before, Dorothea had presented Rochecotte to Pauline as a home more healthy and close to Paris than the Castellanes' grim fastness in the Auvergne. The gift was a generous one and made without thought to her own needs, but with the surrender of her home she took one more step away from her life in France.

Before she left France, Dorothea spent a few weeks in Paris. Madame de Lieven has left an account of a dinner which she gave in honour of the distinguished visitor. She invited the Duke and Duchess of Noailles, Monsieur Guizot, Count Salvandy and others from the world of statesmen and diplomats. With such a party she promised herself an evening of intelligent conversation about Prussia at which all would perform, but Dorothea naturally take the starring role. The guest of honour however had other ideas. Madame de Lieven had been rash enough to make some tart remarks about the reality of Dorothea's mourning for her son-in-law and word of it had got back to the target of her wit. Dorothea was never one to repay unkindness with charity.

At dinner she was placed between Guizot and Salvandy. For a long time she said nothing at all. In dismay over this pool of silence at what should have been an animated table, Madame de Lieven began a general conversation and tried to draw Dorothea in by direct questions. The replies were monosyllables. " Very well," said Madame de Lieven to herself, " if she intends to sulk we will ignore her and go on

as if she was not there." She began to talk to Monsieur de
Salvandy. Hardly had she begun than Dorothea whispered
something in her neighbour's ear ; just enough to break up
his conversation with his hostess. This achieved she let him
drop and, turning to Monsieur Guizot, in turn whispered some
remark in his ear. The conversation on that side also
effectively disrupted, she relapsed into a moody silence from
which she only emerged at intervals to continue her sabotage
of dinner-party discussion.

For Madame de Lieven, who prided herself as an artist
among hostesses, the experience was almost intolerable. But
it was to get still worse. After dinner, instead of settling down
in a comfortable manner, Dorothea formed a circle around her
in the way common to German princesses and then went from
one to another of her courtiers talking to them in a low voice
so that any general conversation was impossible. " I was
astounded," wrote Madame de Lieven. " Who did she think
she was ? The Queen of Prussia ? I had to put a stop to all
that." She took Dorothea by the arm and more or less dragged
her to a sofa. But hardly had she turned to address a remark
to her other neighbour than Dorothea had escaped and was
on the move again, continuing her guerrilla warfare. In the end
she left just a few minutes before it was polite to do so, while
Madame de Lieven swore vengefully to herself that this was
the last time she would invite Dorothea to her house.

*   *   *   *   *

One of the main reasons that had made Dorothea prefer
Prussia to France was the seeming stability of the first compared with the constant effervescence and turmoil of the second.
Internationally, Prussia was a loyal member of the so-called
Holy Alliance, pledged to maintain the *status quo* in Europe
and implacably opposed to any kind of liberalism or of constitutional concession. Since the death of her uncle Dorothea's
never very robust liberal beliefs had succumbed to her natural
instincts of conservatism. Now she viewed every political
problem through the eyes of an autocratic Prussian aristocrat,
and to such eyes the ends of the Holy Alliance must have
seemed eminently sound.

Internally the Government of Frederick William IV seemed equally respectable in its policies. The king it is true made fitful dabs in the direction of reform but his vanity and feebleness were such that his coterie of ultra-conservative advisers had little difficulty in checking him before anything substantial could be achieved. And yet, in fact, there was greater danger than the king ever imagined, not so much from internal revolt as from the tremendous force of German nationalism which was shortly to shatter the fabric of traditional Germany. In 1847, Prussia seemed an oasis of calm amidst the grumblings of a Europe in travail, but the calm was precarious and only a small, deluded circle around the king were able to persuade themselves that it would last for long.

By the time Dorothea got back to Prussia at the end of 1847 every state in Italy seemed to be on the verge of an uprising. Her first worry was for Bacourt who had just been sent as Ambassador to Turin. Every day brought new stories of murder and atrocity : " I know that the Diplomatic Corps is less exposed than most," she wrote to him, " but to have crimes committed all around one even when one is not the victim makes life sad and difficult." But her preoccupations did not stop there. Revolution was contagious and what happened one day in Italy could happen the next in France, in Austria, even in stable, docile Prussia. All over Europe the despots were fidgeting uneasily and the mobs preparing their weapons.

Sicily in January, 1848, ushered in the *annus mirabilis* of revolution. The news passed Dorothea by almost unnoticed ; this remote and unsavoury island seemed to have little to do with the real world of Europe. But the next month brought tidings she could not ignore. On 28th February, the news of the abdication of Louis-Philippe threw Berlin into a frenzy of consternation or liberal enthusiasm. None of the conservative Prussians had thought much of the bourgeois monarch with his uneasy fumblings between reform and repression but at least he had been a more or less dependable figure. Who or what would replace him no one dared imagine.

For the royal family Dorothea felt pity but no very great regret. But, haunted as she always had been by the spectre of the Terror, she wondered with dread what would happen now they had gone. Would her friends be safe, and her children ? Barante was in Paris ; Bacourt was by now in Turin and Pauline safely in a village in Normandy but both Alexander and Louis were in Paris and the latter closely associated with the régime. Already her ever-fertile facility for foreseeing disaster was invoked and she seemed to hear the tumbrils rumbling through the streets once more.

Her panic did not last for long. Within a few days she was writing to her children urging them not to emigrate ; the danger that might threaten them if they stayed seemed to her inconsiderable compared with the temptation which an impecunious Government would feel to confiscate their property if they fled the country. Some of Dorothea's confidence came from the news that the régime had fallen with little bloodshed, but she probably drew still more strength from comforting the obviously exaggerated fears of her friend the Princess of Prussia. The princess, whose dearly loved cousin the Duchess of Orleans was in the thick of the trouble, was convinced that riot and mass-murder would shortly sweep away the ruling classes of all Europe. Dorothea was as capable as anyone of predicting woe but the intemperate clamour of the Princess of Prussia was too much even for her and she refound her own sense of proportion in seeking to still the other's alarm.

The flames of revolution spread eastwards. On 13th March, the students of Vienna were in arms, and Metternich chased from power. Ten days later Venice and Milan had driven out their Austrian garrisons. There was trouble at Cassel and rioting in Baden. Prussia could not stand out alone. Already the murmuring for constitutional reform was growing louder. "The best chance here," wrote Dorothea to Bacourt, "is openly and promptly to adopt the constitutional forms ; if there is delay, hesitation or trickery, then we are going to have a quite incalculable crisis." She was right, a few concessions and perhaps a national crusade for the liberation of Poland from the Russians could still have rallied the Prussians behind the Crown. But openness and promptness were not in Frederick William's repertoire. For the few vital days he did nothing at all or made a few grudging concessions which whetted the appetites of the liberals without satisfying any of their demands. By 18th March, when he finally summoned the Diet and made vague promises of future federal reform for Germany, it was too late. The liberal middle-classes might have been satisfied but the mob was out of hand. For a week rioting raged across Prussia and even when the worst was over the country still remained shaken and without real Government.

*   *   *   *   *

Dorothea was at Sagan for the worst of the troubles. The crowd attacked the town hall and the barracks and it says much for the owner that the castle, easily the most tempting target, was left untouched. Her presence, so she told Bacourt, seemed to have a calming effect on the people. Indeed, she had made herself very popular during her years at the castle and the prosperity which she had brought was not forgotten in the moment of upheaval. But even though she had confidence in the loyalty or at least the tolerance of her neighbours, Sagan was dangerously close to the Russian frontier. All Silesia was in confusion and straggling marauders made life a constant peril. To stay in the country was to invite trouble. Once the risk of rioting had died down there was not much left for her to do and, besides, at Berlin she would find Lichnowsky. Without her guidance and, if necessary, restraining hand she had good reason to believe that he would get himself into one sort of trouble or another.

It was certainly high time she got back. Lichnowsky was playing a typically double game of the kind which might have seemed cunning and dangerous to the uninitiated but to those who knew him betrayed only complete uncertainty as to what he hoped to achieve and how he hoped to achieve it. His sole preoccupation seemed to be to stir up disorder in the vague hope that he would be able to pick up some benefit from the debris. Associated as he was with the liberal camp, he imagined that any breakdown of monarchal rule would work to his advantage and never stopped to consider whether it might not instead lead to his destruction. Bismarck described him during the rioting as alternately haunting the royal apartments where he spread alarming rumours about the weakness of the troops, and sallying out to the barricades to egg on the rioters, urging them now in Polish and now in German to stand firm. His courage, energy and enthusiasm were rarely more clearly demonstrated, but equally evident were the irresponsibility and fundamental silliness which marred everything he did.

In spite of his best efforts, the insurrection in Berlin was never a very formidable affair and only the feebleness of the king prevented its being stamped out without more ado. By the time Dorothea returned an uneasy peace had been restored. The Diet had duly met, passed its electoral law and dissolved itself. Attention turned to Frankfurt where the first Federal Assembly was shortly to meet. " Berlin is dead," wrote Dorothea. " If it was not for occasional disturbance in the streets and groups of people reading the abominable posters, one would think that plague had swept the city." The worst danger seemed to have passed but she feared that it might at any moment return. She had money and diamonds sewn into her clothes and all her plans were ready for a possible escape. Courageous when actually faced by real danger, she was always quick to imagine it when it was not there. At Sagan, with a dangerous mob roaming the town, she had been unperturbed. Now, when the stolid citizens of Berlin were congratulating themselves on achieving victory at so small a cost, she told herself that murder lurked in every heart and bloody disorder around every corner.

In May, Lichnowsky left Berlin for the meeting of the Federal Assembly. Ostensibly he was a champion of the liberals but in fact he was already discontented at the little appreciation shown him by his colleagues and his aristocratic disdain was quickened by their cautious ways and middle-class manners. His volatile nature was preparing itself for a return to the right ; spurred on in the *volte-face* by the knowledge that Dorothea, at least, would think him justified.

With her lover gone and the countryside around Sagan pacified, Dorothea saw no reason to linger further in the uneasy city. She returned to Sagan and awaited gloomily the further blows of fate. No good would come of the Frankfurt Assembly, of that she was sure. With its dreams of a greater Germany and pretensions towards democracy it seemed to encourage all the unsettling influences which she most loathed and feared. What else could be expected of an assembly which was " feebly led and filled with ignorant and uncouth elements. It is impossible to imagine what sort of building such workmen will construct. It will be a house without stairs, without cellar, without roof : four walls which the first wind will bring down. Or so I fear, at least. At Frankfurt they are hoping to raise the temple of Solomon ; instead they are going to open the Tower of Babel." " Patriotic, ambitious, laborious," wrote H. A. L. Fisher[2] of the Frankfurt Assembly. " It contained some of the finest characters and noblest minds in Germany." Given the different points of view of the observers, the two comments perhaps add up to very much the same thing.

As she brooded at Sagan, news, little by little, arrived to comfort Dorothea. First she learned that Prince Windischgrätz had crushed the Bohemian rebellion at Prague, then, still more gratifying, that General Cavaignac had quelled the mob in Paris, leaving ten thousand casualties on the barricades. Dorothea was fiercely satisfied by the news. The rebellions of 1848 had disturbed her deeply and, in particular, the unrest in Prussia, the country which she had chosen for its stability, seemed to her a personal betrayal. She was stirred to a quite unwonted belligerency, convinced that the popular movements must be repressed at once and ruthlessly. " I am surprised to find that I would welcome a fierce struggle rather than the gradual degeneration which will rot our whole system ! "

Personally benevolent and disliking violence, Dorothea at the age of fifty-six was nevertheless an out-and-out reactionary. She believed blindly and passionately in the social order, the preordained and immutable hierarchical system laid down by the Almighty and interpreted as need arose by the more responsible elements of the Church and the aristocracy. Only by accepting this order and seeking to better his own and others' lots within it could a man fulfil his duty. To attack it was an offence against mankind and against God. Her indignation against those who would not accept this fundamental social order, her eagerness to see the Berlin mob crushed as harshly as that of Paris, was not inspired by fears for her own wealth or safety but by a fervour as pure and as disinterested as any which lent fury to the excesses of religious persecution. For Dorothea, the defence of the established order against the assaults of the discontented was not an expedient measure of self-protection but a crusade against the ungodly.

*   *   *   *   *

By July things had quietened down sufficiently to make travelling once more practicable without too much danger and discomfort. First Dorothea went to take the waters at Teplitz ; her journey across the devastated countryside saddened and depressed her and the town itself, with only a handful of aged paralytics who had been too ill to run away, did little to restore her spirits. From thence she went on to perform another duty which compassion and loyalty made necessary. Unlike the King and Queen of France, who had taken refuge in England, the Duchess of Orleans had fled to Eisenach in Western Germany. Save at the very first, Dorothea had never felt that she was worthy of her husband, but this new catastrophe had made her resolve to go at the first opportunity and give what comfort she could.

She found the duchess ill with worry and living in what for her was painful poverty. Dorothea came prepared to pity ; she was completely conquered by the resignation and dignity in distress which she found : " so calm, so serene, so lucid . . . so strong for truth on every subject, in a word so admirable in every way . . . She stands aloof from every intrigue ; she neither deludes herself nor allows herself to become discouraged ; she is completely free of bitterness, rancour or passion—there is only gentleness, reason and balanced judgment." Most admirable of all, Dorothea found the duchess quite well disposed to the idea of a reconciliation with the Bourbons and perhaps a marriage between the two exiled lines. Her enthusiasm might have been modified if she could have foreseen the long history of stubborn vanity which was for so many years to prevent any fusion of the two lines and in which the Duchess of Orleans was to play as guilty a role as anyone.

By September, Dorothea was back in Sagan. The indecision of the king had allowed disorder to grow again and only the

presence of a well-trained civil guard made it possible for her
to live there at all. But it was the news from Frankfurt which
gave Dorothea most cause for disquiet. Lichnowsky had finally
deserted the liberal party and for that there was reason to be
grateful. But, intemperate in treason as in every other field
of life, he brandished his new loyalty with a vehemence which
made him the man in all Germany most hated by the left.
Not content with proclaiming himself the champion of the old
German nobility, Lichnowsky took a savage pleasure in
harrying and—still worse—mocking his former associates.
Karl Vogt, zoologist, philosopher and professional atheist, was
caricatured by Lichnowsky as Nebuchadnezzar, crouched on
the ground stuffing his mouth with hay. The cruel drawing was
passed around the assembly and enjoyed much success. Karl
Vogt, who could have forgiven anything save that of being
made the object of ridicule, promised himself revenge and
Karl Vogt was only one of many.

Circourt, the representative of the new French Republic,
warned Lichnowsky that he was going the right way to get
himself murdered. Whatever his faults, Lichnowsky was no
coward. " What do you want me to do ? " he asked. " If I
have to, I am ready to be a martyr in the right cause, but I
shall never desert it. I shall never allow anyone in Parliament
to insult with impunity the cockade of Prussia or the arms of
our ancient chivalry." They were brave words and it would
not have been in his nature to answer otherwise even though
he had known what gruesome fate awaited him.

On the 16th of September, after a particularly stormy
session at the assembly, the left decided that the time had
come for recourse to violence. On the 18th riots broke out and
the barricades went up. The Prussian and Austrian troops on
the spot proved inadequate to clear the town and reinforce-
ments were sent for. Unarmed and without an escort, Lichnowsky and General Auerswald set out to meet them. Fool-
hardiness met its usual fate. At the gates of the city the couple
were recognised and attacked by a group of rioters. The
general was killed on the spot by blows from a cudgel,
Lichnowsky was literally torn to pieces by the mob. What was
left of his shattered body was picked up a little later by royal

troops; a whisper of life still lingered but before the day was ended he had died in agony.

Dorothea was still at Sagan. It does not need much imagination to conceive the agony of mind into which the macabre fate of her lover must have thrown her. Alone in her great house, tired, ageing, uncertain of the future, she saw thus brutally extinguished the last flame which had served to warm her life and to comfort her for the fading of her beauty. It was not just the death itself but the manner of it which must have caused her suffering. That Lichnowsky should have died nobly, leading his troops into battle or defending some stronghold of the royal cause, would have been tragic enough. But to have been torn apart by a pack of peasants in a gutter of Frankfurt, to die in a pointless scuffle provoked by his own folly and hot-headedness; what a pitiable end was there for a hero.

Mercifully for Dorothea the rapidly worsening situation all over Prussia prevented her brooding lengthily on her lover's end. The loyalty of the army itself seemed in question and all over Silesia there was disorder with looting, burning and murder a commonplace event. One night there were explosions near the castle and everyone thought that an attack was imminent; a few days later came the news that the neighbouring castle of the Prince of Hatzfeldt had been attacked and four of his farms burnt to the ground. "We have taken our precautions," wrote Dorothea to Bacourt, "my army has been organised for defence and, if we have to die, at least we will not do so without a struggle. I shall not run away and have no fear so far as I am concerned because I am completely indifferent as to what happens to me."

On this occasion there can be no doubt that she meant what she said. She did not exaggerate her indifference, rather she would have welcomed death as saving her the grey years of pain which seemed to lie ahead. At this moment it must have seemed that Lichnowsky had provided all that made life pleasurable and exciting, all, almost, that made it tolerable. Yet, though his death had made her indifferent to her own safety, her sense of duty was far too strong to allow her to be equally indifferent to that of other people. The knowledge that the welfare, perhaps even the lives of many others might depend on her steadfastness forced her to take an interest in what was being done for her own defence.

The future seemed to depend on what happened in Vienna. Dorothea had too little faith in the Prussian army and the strength of mind of the king to believe that revolution in Berlin could long be held in check if the imperial house of Austria had been overthrown. Every day conflicting reports seemed to come in ; now the royal army had re-established complete control, now all was said to be in disorder and the city lost. It was not till the very end of October that it became clear that Windischgrätz had crushed the liberals of Vienna as effectively as he had the Czechs some months before. The way was clear for Prince Felix Schwarzenberg to lead Austria back to predominance in the old German Federation and to put himself for ever among the most doughty protagonists of reaction and repression.

Even the example of Vienna could not immediately inspire Frederick William to decisive action. But on 3rd November he plucked up all his courage ; changed his ministers, dispersed his Parliament and dissolved the civil guard. He found the opposition pitifully unable to withstand him. " If I can believe my latest letters from Berlin," wrote Dorothea, " we are about to enter a new era. I admit I am still incredulous and fear that I will remain so for a long time." She could have had more faith ; at last the king meant business. Soon there were thirty thousand royal troops sweeping across Silesia. By the end of 1848 the wave of liberal resurgence seemed to have been spent before it had even begun to achieve its ends. Only time was to show how fatally and finally it had shaken the prestigious structure of European aristocracy in whose resilience and strength the Duchess of Sagan seemed now to have such good cause to rejoice.

*   *   *   *   *

Rebellion flickered out and Dorothea was left in peace to lament the dead. In none of her letters which survive did she speak directly of her loss. Lichnowsky seemed to have been blotted out without trace ; if it had not been that he had left everything to Dorothea in his will one might have wondered whether the whole relationship had not been a picturesque romance thought up by gossips unwilling that the legend of the duchess's passions should fade. Impassively she continued with her life. One visit to Gratz to pray at the tomb of Lichnowsky was her tribute to the past; with a stoicism which to some seemed cold-blooded indifference she turned her face towards the future and concentrated on what still remained between the present and the grave.

One part of her life had ended; the most turbulent, the most tormented, but also the most vivid and the most rewarding. Dorothea had found tranquillity, but in it there was also apathy. With Lichnowsky gone, there remained to her only the ties of family and of old, familiar friendships; never again would she feel the fierce, nagging claims of passion. Though in years she could not say what might not lie before her; in living she knew that her course was nearly run. The climax of her life had come and gone; now it remained only to write the epilogue.

" There remain in me no desires, no hopes, no fears, no discontent," she told Barante. " Only profound gratitude to God for those few friends who are still left to me. What is there left better for us to do than tenderly to kiss the cross, however bloody it may be ? " Too often in Dorothea's moments of self-abnegation one seems to sense the facile humility of a small spirit striving to achieve nobility. At this moment of her life it is impossible to doubt her complete sincerity.

15

The pattern of Dorothea's life in the years that followed the catastrophes of 1848 was prudent, unambitious and, on the whole, not disagreeable. Most of the year was spent at Sagan which she had grown to love as she had loved no other home except Rochecotte.

" It has cost me too much in effort and too many sacrifices not to have acquired value in my eyes. And then, I have done some good there, brought life back to the countryside and given new vigour and movement to the population. All my surplus energies have found a use there. I have some reasons to believe that they think well of me there, indeed that they fear my death as the end of the world—or rather the end of this so tiny, almost imperceptible point in the world . . . I have the poor ; it is so good to love and to cherish them, precisely because the individuals themselves have nothing to do with the interest which they inspire. One is conscious of neither their failings nor their qualities but only sees in them the tortured limbs of He who took upon Himself all the sins of the world."

Expressed like that, Dorothea's philanthropy sounds chilly and impersonal, almost inhuman. If Dorothea had made it clear to the poor whom she succoured how little she cared for them as individuals, her charity would hardly have been well received. If she had even believed thoroughly what she wrote it could hardly have failed to show through and mar her deeds. Yet, in fact, Dorothea was well-loved in Sagan. Her love of children, her sensitive perception of the pains or hardships of others, her personal involvement in the lives of those who depended on her : all these lent sympathy and gentleness to the implacable benevolence which she considered prescribed by the Almighty. Partly Dorothea passed her time in good works as a refuge from her memories, partly from religious conviction, partly from a sense of the responsibilities of a great landowner, but most of all because she cared for those who surrounded her. She could not find happiness or contentment herself unless she knew that they too were happy and contented or at least that, if they were not so, it was through no fault or omission of her own.

But her affection for the royal family and her unquenchable craving to be at the centre of great affairs led her from time to time to Berlin. Each time she would protest her reluctance ; all that she wished was to live out her declining years in solitude and silence, she had lost touch with the world and was ill at ease in society, her health was bad and did not fit her for the cold and discomfort of Berlin drawing-rooms. She was not wholly insincere ; since the death of Lichnowsky she had shunned company and was genuinely better satisfied in her rural isolation. But it could never satisfy her wholly. Up to the moment of her death she was continuing to take a keen interest in European politics and for Dorothea the only satisfactory politics were those in which she participated or at least in which she knew all the participants. She cherished her loyalties and hatreds as eagerly as ever and followed events in Paris and London as closely as she did those in Berlin. The appointment of Palmerston as Prime Minister was greeted with dismay and when he fell she wrote gleefully " my old grudge against him and all my subsequent indignation salute his fall with cries of joy. Let us hope that it will prove final and that this evil firebrand has been extinguished for ever." The parish-pump interests of Sagan were good enough to pass the time, but Dorothea's stage was Europe. So long as she had the strength it was there that she would walk.

By the autumn of 1849 she was already restless and set out on a prolonged tour of Germany. First she went to Hanover. The king, blind, eighty years old and living on a diet of oysters and ices, received her kindly and seated her on his right hand where she had full opportunity to observe his habits and reflect on the miracle of his continued existence. From this triumph of royal survival she continued to Eisenach to mourn the tragedy of royal impermanence. The Duchess of Orleans had collected a court of émigrés around her who were united only in misery and in abuse of all those who had stayed behind in France. Now that the movements of the left had been crushed, Dorothea was perfectly ready to accept the new Government of France. She must have found uncongenial the extremist opposition of the court at Eisenach ; certainly when she left it she had few illusions about its chances of recapturing the throne.

Back in Berlin she noted sadly a ceremony which seemed to her to presage the downfall of another monarchy. On 6th February, 1850, King Frederick William took the oath to respect the new constitution. The powers he retained would seem extravagantly large in the mid-twentieth century but to Dorothea—and indeed to much of the Prussian nobility—the ceremony symbolised the end of proper Government. It was not for this that Dorothea had left the unruly turbulence of France ; with Louis Napoleon firmly President in Paris and gradually unmasking his authoritarian ideas she must have wondered whether she had chosen well. When, a few months later, a former soldier, driven demented by some grievance tried to murder the king, her most lurid fears were confirmed. Readily she believed those who told her that the putative assassin was the tool of one of the " democratic " societies which were plotting the downfall of Germany. " More and more the web is being unveiled," she wrote to Bacourt ". . . It is the good Lord alone who saves us, for certainly we do nothing to help him."

Within a few weeks she was able to pass on her fears to Bacourt in person. In the summer she went with the Princess of Prussia to take the waters at Baden. Bacourt, his never very distinguished diplomatic career finally ended by the fall of the Orleanists, had installed himself there. They had seen little of each other since the death of Talleyrand, almost indeed since the end of the prince's London Embassy. Now they had nearly two months together and found that they still suited each other very well. It was comforting for Dorothea to know that in Bacourt she had at least one friend in

France who was younger than her and on whose loyalty she could rely.

* * * * *

Salzburg, Vienna, Ischl, Augsburg, Munich; Dorothea roamed across Germany seeking distraction. In January, 1851, she was back in Berlin, resolutely determined to be dissatisfied by all that happened to her. Wherever she went, it seemed, she was forced to sit next to the king and entertain him. The compliment was flattering but the duty arduous. The king seemed to have arrived at a premature dotage. Perhaps the first shadows of the madness which was later to overwhelm him were already creeping across his naturally befuddled brain; his company at all events was heavy going and did not add to the pleasures of Berlin society. " My life here is free from shocks and disturbances, but also from anything of great interest. My days are complicated by a thousand little social obligations . . . There are no great festivities or causes for me to feel exhausted but a dreary wearing away of the hours. . . ."

Dorothea was in fact screwing up her courage for a visit to France and the blacker she painted her life in Germany the easier it was to convince herself that the other would not be intolerable. It was only four years since she had been there but she had left behind her children resentful of her Prussian preoccupations. Dorothea longed to see them and her grandchildren again and yet at the same time was frightened at the very thought of the meeting. And then it would be her first visit to France since the fall of the Orleanists. Dorothea and her uncle had been friends and champions of Louis-Philippe; how well received would she now be by Louis Napoleon? Could she bear to be an unwanted guest in a country where once she had been so triumphantly at home?

The first communion of her grandchild, Marie de Castellane, provided the incentive which she needed to defy these spectres. Of all her grandchildren it was only Marie whom she really loved. The child was only eleven years old and it was too early for her grandmother to take her seriously in hand but Dorothea did not fail to note that with a father dead and a mother taking refuge ever deeper in a life of meditation and seclusion, it would depend on her to see that Marie's worldly prospects were not neglected.

Dorothea passed a month in cloistered silence with her daughter Pauline, then moved on to the gaiety and brilliant social life of Valençay. Neither way of life can have pleased her altogether; the one too sombre, the other too frivolous, both in their different ways neglecting what she felt to be the duties of the high aristocracy. Still, it was agreeable to be among her children again and she was welcomed with flattering attention. Paris was a different matter. There she went with the greatest reluctance and only because business made it essential. The experience of Madame de Lieven contained nothing to encourage her; the poor princess had gone out of her way to proclaim her goodwill towards the new régime yet her only response had been a cold rebuff.

In spite of her angry words of a few years before, Madame de Lieven gave a dinner for Dorothea. " She found me stupid," reported Dorothea dryly, " and told me so with such clearness that I have every hope she will say and repeat it in all those letters which have so wide a circulation throughout Europe." But otherwise Paris was not so bad as she had feared. She could not bring herself positively to welcome the man who had usurped the throne of Louis-Philippe but at least she had to admit that Louis Napoleon knew how to deal with a mob in a way which his predecessor had never dared even contemplate. That in itself was a great virtue in Dorothea's eyes.

The *coup* of December, 1851, in which Louis Napoleon seized absolute power seemed to Dorothea to presage a new era for France and perhaps for Europe. " If the President has a proper understanding of his mission he will crush the reds for ever. It is the best, indeed the only way to keep himself in power for by it he will earn the gratitude of all Europe." The future emperor also put in a claim for Dorothea's affection when he arrested Adolphe Thiers. The step was, perhaps, hardly an essential part of crushing the reds and the arrest lasted for a disappointingly short time but it seemed to her to show sound judgment.

The visit to France was enough of a success for Dorothea to

repeat it. She decided to pass the following winter at Nice where the climate suited her, where she was well known, where there were no court duties and where, though the factor was not of importance except in her imagination, life was relatively cheap. There she met Bacourt and together they continued the work of sifting through the great mass of papers which Talleyrand had left behind him. She had no plans for publication— Talleyrand had left careful instructions as to the fit moment to give his memoirs to the world—but she conceived it her duty to see that all was in order so that the correct story would later be available to all who wished to know it. Bacourt was the ideal sub-editor for her purposes ; conscientious, discreet, knowledgeable and sufficiently pliable to be brought to see that any given document did not conform to an acceptable and proper pattern of history and so had better be suppressed.

To Nice also, came her children, to spend the winter with her and at last it seemed that family life had been re-established on a basis of lasting warmth and affection. On 26th February —St. Dorothy's Day—1853, she was just about to go to bed when there was a knocking at her door. A crowd of her relations and closest friends poured in on her carrying bouquets, presents and verses in her honour. The lights were turned on in the ballroom and she found that her grandchildren had wreathed it with flowers and that a band had secretly been installed in a corner. The old Marquis of Negro had composed a hymn for St. Dorothy's Day which he proceeded to declaim and the party went on till late into the night.

* * * * *

After many years of effort Dorothea seemed to have struck the balance between Germany and France which she had so long aimed at. She did not find it difficult to remake contact with all who were left of her former friends in France ; with most of them, indeed, she had kept up a more or less assiduous correspondence over the intervening years. Molé, Barante, Guizot, Dupanloup ; she saw them all and was touched and delighted by the pleasure with which they greeted her. But her friends never forgot that she was a visitor whose real life lay elsewhere. Prosper Barante went to Orleans to meet her and spend a few days in her company. " She is marvellously unchanged," he wrote to Guizot, " and has grown no older. She prefers her princely and feudal life at Sagan to her stays in France, and, to tell the truth, there is nothing surprising in that."

To tell the truth there was not. In France she was still a figure of great distinction but her grandeur lay mainly in the past. In Prussia her position was unique and unchallenged ; she ranked second only to the royal family and even by them was treated on terms of intimacy and equality. This reason alone was enough to give her German life an overriding importance in her eyes.

She was anxious that the privileges and status which she enjoyed should be inherited by some at least from among her descendants. Alexander had disappeared to fight in the Crimean War and there was nothing to be done for any of his family. Louis, and after him Boson, would eventually succeed to the Princedom of Sagan ; their immortality was already assured. Pauline lived a life of prayer and seclusion at Rochecotte and would have viewed the splendours of Sagan with distaste. But for Marie de Castellane, Dorothea's favourite grandchild, it was a different matter.

In 1855 Marie was fifteen years old ; quite old enough for well-wishers to be thinking about her marriage. She was young for her age and unusually unsophisticated, pretty though far from beautiful, blonde with seraphic blue eyes, intelligent, kindly and with expectations of inheriting a fortune both from her mother and her grandmother. It had already been tentatively suggested that she might marry the respectable but not very distinguished son of the Duke of Lorges. Dorothea would hear nothing of it. The idea of the match was dropped and Pauline tacitly accepted that her mother would charge herself with Marie's future. The decision came as a relief to her. If she had been forced to, Pauline would have been ready to venture back into French society in search of a husband for her daughter but the thought filled her with dismay and she happily resigned the task to Dorothea.

Dorothea was equally happy to accept the charge. Her life was full but not so full that from time to time she did not have cause to say, "*j'ai failli m'ennuyer.*" The planning of another's future was work which she relished. From this time onwards the marriage of her granddaughter and Marie's safe installation in a place of honour in German society became the principal preoccupation of Dorothea's life.

She had already made up her mind where to look for a husband. Prince William Radziwill, friend of her childhood and son of her godmother Princess Louise of Prussia, had an eldest son, Antoine, who by every standard of birth, wealth, looks, brains and amiability, seemed worthy of Marie. Prince William was quite as alive to the advantages of the match as Dorothea and welcomed it warmly. Antoine was properly docile and ready to take whatever was offered him. There remained only Marie.

In September, 1855, Prince William and his son arrived at Paris to visit the Universal Exhibition which was then drawing all Europe to its doors. After a brief stay they moved on to Rochecotte. Antoine, aged twenty-two and very much a man of the world, looked forward with little enthusiasm to his first meeting with his putative child bride but, when it came, noted with relief that she seemed both pretty and good-natured. Marie was tentatively approving and it was felt that she only needed a little encouragement to be thoroughly in love. The meeting was deemed a success and, though no engagement was officially announced, it was generally agreed that the match was made.

But apart from her successes in this field, the winter of 1855 was a gloomy one for Dorothea. For one thing, she was perpetually worried for her younger son. Alexander, Duke of Dino, had proved himself a contumacious and ungrateful child, but she still cared more for him than for that respectable stick, Louis de Valençay. Alexander wrote rarely to his mother and during the protracted and savage fighting around Sebastopol she was often left without news for three or four weeks at a time. She had every reason to fear for his safety ; his irresponsibility disqualified him for any serious work on the staff and his personal bravery made it certain that he would always be well to the fore in battle. It is only surprising that he survived the campaign. Dorothea wrote to him faithfully by every post. Charles Bocher, a close friend of the Duke of Dino's, tells in his memoirs how they and another friend would always gather in Alexander's tent when the letters arrived so as to exchange titbits of gossip: " The news which the Duchess of Sagan used to send her son on the politics of every Cabinet in Europe was always of the utmost interest."

Alexander's wife, left behind in Paris, diverted herself by running into debt on a scale which even her father-in-law would have found impressive. Prosper Mérimée records a scandal which probably relates to this period. Valentine de Dino was supposed to have taken some diamonds from Bapst the jeweller on the pretext that she wanted to try them on. Being short of money, she then proceeded to pawn them. Bapst threatened to go to law and it ended with the unfortunate Dorothea paying out twenty thousand francs to save the family name. The story may not be true but there was nothing in Valentine's character to make it inherently improbable.

Then, in November, while Dorothea was at Nice, she received the news that Molé had been struck down by an apoplectic fit in the middle of dinner and had died three hours later. Only a month before she had visited him at Champlatreux and he had talked to her wistfully of his loneliness and of the pleasure it gave him to see her again. He was vain, he was egotistical, he was ungrateful, but in spite of it all Dorothea had been fond of him and had recognised his charms and his qualities even when she was most profoundly irritated by his behaviour. She had known him for so long that his death was doubly painful. " He was one of those," she wrote to Bacourt, " who watched me when I made my entry into society. Now I know none of them who is left."

She did not find much to console her when she called on the Duchess of Istria who was then staying in Talleyrand's old house in the Rue St. Florentin. She had expected to have old memories revived but one memory which she had no wish to disturb was rudely awakened when she found herself confronted by Adolphe Thiers. She had not met him since they had quarrelled so violently after Talleyrand's death and since then had followed his career with persistent animosity. But pot-bellied, effervescent, little Monsieur Thiers was not in the least embarrassed. Possibly he felt that it would be better at least to act as if they were still friends, more probably it had simply never occurred to him that Dorothea might bear him a grudge. At all events, he rushed across the room to meet her with hands effusively outstretched and greeted her as if she were his dearest friend. Dorothea was left feeling rather silly. She longed to be rude to him and yet did not wish to make a scene in front of a lot of strangers. In the end she greeted him coolly but politely and Monsieur Thiers was probably left in the complacent belief that his charm had worked as effectively as ever.

*   *   *   *   *

Eighteen fifty-six saw the return visit of Pauline and Marie to Germany. Dorothea came to Berlin to meet them and make sure that they penetrated into the Radziwill Palace. Marie was delighted by the relaxed, friendly atmosphere of the great house and its mob of noisy children. She could not help contrasting it with the bleak severity of life at Rochecotte and feeling no doubt as to which would make her happier. Antoine Radziwill came on to stay with her grandmother at Sagan. It was not long before the kindly but none the less firm pressure of her relations completed what her inclinations had begun. In August, at Teplitz, the engagement was officially announced and in October of the year following they were married in immense pomp in the church of Sagan.

Her granddaughter safely married and become a Prussian, Dorothea's next object was to introduce her to society and establish her impregnably in a position of distinction. She planned to pass on her own political influence and connections in the same spirit as a fond father might ensure that his favourite possessions passed inviolate to his son. First the young Princess Radziwill was presented to King Frederick William IV. "Taking me by the hand," wrote Marie in her memoirs, "he said that he was very happy to see in me the granddaughter of his dearest friend, the Duchess of Sagan. The queen," Marie noted, "was not so forthcoming and, while wishing to be gracious, was none the less cold."

But Frederick William was a sick man and he had no heir.

The future lay with the Prince and Princess of Prussia and Augusta, Princess of Prussia, later to be Queen of Prussia and Empress of Germany, was still Dorothea's most intimate friend and ally. Dorothea was determined that Marie should share this friendship and eventually take her own place at the side of the future queen. She constantly used Marie as an intermediary between herself and the princess. But she never encouraged Marie to the point of indiscretion. " My child," she would always say to her, " the more you become intimate with the princess, the less the public must perceive it. Fix all your conduct by this rule . . . listen much . . . remember all you can . . . and, if that is possible, never speak of it to a soul."

Augusta took to the child at once. She would have been well-disposed to any grandchild of Dorothea but Marie, with her charm, intelligence and unfeigned affection and respect for the princess, was well equipped to step into the role assigned her. Soon she was accepted as a confidante and though she could never hope to take over her grandmother's influence, she still gave Dorothea the satisfaction of knowing that she was placed at court in a position which few others could hope to achieve.

But it did not all go as smoothly as this. A new generation was growing up and the son of the Princess of Prussia, young Frederick William, was ready for a wife. To Dorothea it seemed only proper that, whoever he might marry, his bride should find her most intimate friend and counsellor in Marie Radziwill. When she heard that Princess Victoria of England had been chosen she was a little doubtful about the wisdom of the match but had no doubt at all of the part that Marie should play in its development.

The royal marriage took place in London ; there was some feeling in Berlin that the wedding should be in Prussia but Queen Victoria soon put paid to that idea : " Whatever may be the usual practice of Prussian princes—it is not every day that one marries the eldest daughter of the Queen of England. The matter therefore must be considered as settled and closed."[1] The future Empress Frederick William was almost exactly the same age as Princess Radziwill. She was about to venture into an alien court and Marie, as another exile, had strong claims to her fellow-feeling. It would have been an excellent and wholly natural thing if the two had become friends. Instead they became bitter and notorious enemies. Princess Catherine Radziwill puts the blame wholly on Dorothea. " The Duchess of Curland (sic) disliked the Crown Princess Victoria from the first day she saw her, taking offence at some imagined lack of attention. The truth of the matter was that the Crown Princess had been scared by various things she had heard concerning the Duchess of Sagan and possibly treated her more coldly than was necessary. Dorothea of Curland was not one to forgive a supposed slight. She never forgave the Crown Princess. So long as she lived she pursued her with a disguised but bitter animosity and, after her death, her granddaughter applied herself to discredit the unfortunate Victoria."

The relentless harrying of this little princess is not wholly incompatible with Dorothea's character ; she did resent slights and she did harbour grudges. But she did also preserve some sense of proportion in her dislikes. The persecution of an already unhappy girl would have offered little interest. She seems to have felt for the Princess Victoria the same irritation and discomfort as the latter contrived to provoke throughout all Prussian society. She met her for the first time at a luncheon given by the Princess of Prussia in honour of Queen Victoria and the Prince Consort when they visited Berlin. Queen Victoria went out of her way to be charming ; reminding Dorothea of visits which she and Pauline had paid to Kensington Palace a quarter of a century before, chatting gaily and flattering the duchess with her assumption of intimacy. The crown princess did not make such a strong impression but the report of the luncheon which Dorothea sent to Bacourt a few days later was positively benevolent in tone. " The daughter is taller than the mother but still has less of a royal air. She pleases her husband and has all the marks of a good child-bearer, so that at least she fulfils the two paramount conditions. What is more, she has a frank and natural air . . ."

The crown princess, at first at any rate, found the effort

required to assimilate herself to her new surroundings altogether beyond her powers. She surrounded herself with English friends and looked to London for comfort and advice. When she was about to have her first child she even sent to London for an English doctor. The Prussians were naturally offended and, when the baby was born with a broken arm, their sympathy for the father was mingled with indignation against the mother. " Princess Victoria," wrote Dorothea to Marie, " should forget her English habits and customs. A woman ought to belong body and soul to the fatherland of her husband and children ; otherwise she will make herself and others unhappy, will become disagreeable to them and be a burden to herself."

The comment was aimed as much at Marie as at Princess Victoria, but perhaps even more it reflected on her own unrooted life. Even now she could not feel herself to be at home in Berlin, still less in Paris. The lack of real roots had perhaps contributed more than anything else to the uncertainty and instability which had run through all her life. If her own example and that of the unfortunate Princess Victoria could combine to spare Marie some pain in the future then she would not feel that they had been entirely wasted.

*　　　*　　　*　　　*　　　*

The court into which she had thrust her granddaughter was not an agreeable place to be at the end of the 1850s. Frederick William IV had been struck down by apoplexy in October, 1857. Physically he made a fair recovery but his memory had gone for ever. In 1858 he was packed off to Rome to recuperate. The Prince of Prussia, very conscious that he was already sixty-one years old and egged on by his ambitious wife, insisted on the trappings as well as the substance of power. He was named Regent and celebrated his promotion by changing his Government within a few days of the king's departure from Berlin. Dorothea was doubtful of his political judgment but could not help feeling pleasure that at last her dear friend Augusta was on the point of achieving all she desired.

Frederick William came back to Berlin but it was a poor, broken hulk whom Dorothea, tiptoeing on to the terrace at

Sans Souci, watched mumbling and muttering to himself in the final stages of physical and mental degradation. At the beginning of 1861 the last flicker of life was finally extinguished. Dorothea mourned the loss of her " royal protector " but could not be sorry that something so near a living corpse had at last been laid to rest. At the death-bed of the king, Princess Alexandrine flung herself into the arms of her brother, the Prince of Prussia, now King William and, weeping bitterly, implored him not to trust his wife because " she was an intriguer who would try to meddle with the affairs of state and place her own friends in important positions." It is possible that William would have liked to follow this amiable advice but Augusta was quite as strong a personality as her husband and had her own ideas. It was to be no fault of hers if the queen did not become the most important figure in the land.

It was in anticipation of this moment that Dorothea had worked so hard to ingratiate Marie with the Princess of Prussia and had so assiduously built up the young girl's place at court. Now she had done all she could. From the time of the old king's death, even, indeed, from the time that he fell seriously ill, Dorothea appeared more and more rarely at the palace ; not because she cared any less for the royal family or had any less concern for their well-being, but because she felt herself too old and tired to face the grinding ritual of court life. Seclusion and retirement were more and more what she sought. Her interest in the outside world was never to die but she now relied for her news of it on a few trusted inter- mediaries ; to go out and seek it herself grew increasingly beyond her powers.

Dorothea was old. For twenty years she had written and spoken of herself as ill, failing and tired of life but at the back of her mind had always been the comfortable knowledge that she still had a lot of life in her. Now she suddenly realised that time had caught up with her and she found the discovery hard to bear. In a letter to Bacourt she quoted the words of Madame de Maintenon, " Only death can finally put an end to the troubles of life." " However troublesome life may be," she went on, " no one can like the door by which one escapes it. There comes a time, alas, when one has no more pleasure in living and yet is scared of death. To some extent at least, that is my case."

To be tired of living and scared of dying is not unusual as a state of mind and it takes a very perfect faith to remain entirely unmoved by the growing weaknesses of age and the menace of the unknown. Dorothea, too, was in frequent pain from her recurrent liver trouble. She was not yet ready to withdraw altogether from life but she was in retreat. " Still beautiful at sixty-five," wrote Guizot enthusiastically after meeting her again in 1859, " the same eyes, the same figure ; still Circe. And the same spirit: always free, firm, flexible and understanding. How sad it is that once more she has become a German *grande dame* . . ." But Circe was finding her powers of enchantment ever more painful to sustain ; little by little Dorothea allowed herself to drift to the background of the scene in which for so long she had played a leading role. She knew that the moment of her final exit was coming near and neither wished nor intended to be taken unaware. When the traditional autumn hunting-party met at Sagan it was Boson, Prince of Sagan, eldest son of Louis de Valençay, who met the guests and did the honours as host. Dorothea kept her room. She feared solitude and wished always to be surrounded by those she loved but her taste for a life in society was dead. For fifty years it had excited, tormented and diverted her ; now its powers to dismay or please had faded.

At the end of June, 1861, Dorothea was on the road from Günthersdorf to Sagan. She was caught by a violent storm, " without any exaggeration, the hailstones were as big as billiard balls." The horses bolted and tipped the carriage into the ditch ; only the presence of mind of the coachman in cutting the traces prevented them dashing it to pieces in their panic. Badly bruised and shocked, Dorothea crawled from the wreck. For an hour and a half while the horses were caught and brought back she lay exposed to the batterings of the hail and the remorseless rain. When she got home to Sagan, soaked to the skin and bleeding from the blows of the hail, she was running a high fever. She took to her bed and for several days was despaired of by the doctors. Her tired body made one last effort and pulled her through but never did she imagine that it was a real or lasting recovery, never did her extreme sufferings ease sufficiently to give her a respite from the constant knowledge of approaching death.

By the beginning of 1862 she was little better. As she watched from her window life seep back into the winter landscape, so she felt her own life seeping away, leaving only a pain-racked body to greet the spring. On 1st May, she wrote to Bacourt, " So once again here is this loveliest month with its sunshine, its blossoms and its scents. For me it is nothing but a mockery, for all that the sun shines on is my suffering which seems cruelly to wax at every instant. I have hardly a moment of real rest. For two days now I have gone out, but yesterday, after a drive round the park, I returned only to be seized by an agonising pain which now has just gripped me again . . ." Dorothea still forced herself to maintain her interest in the outside world but it became ever more difficult to raise herself from the slough of pain in which she felt herself sinking and in which, in the end, she knew she was bound to drown.

As a last resort the doctors recommended visits to the waters at Ems and Schlagenbad. The journey gave her much pain and weakened her still further. The treatment did her no good at all. When she came back to Sagan in August she knew that all she had to do was wait and that the wait would not be long. The doctors blandly insisted that her life was not in danger. " God be praised," wrote Pauline, " but what remorseless, crucifying suffering ! " Dorothea praised God too, but it was because she knew that the doctors were wrong and that the end was near.

Her family drew around her as the autumn wore on. Pauline, herself an invalid, was forced to stay at Rochecotte and Alexander was sunning himself at Nice but Louis de Valençay was there, Boson, his son, Marie Radziwill and others among the grandchildren. Calmly and affectionately she took her leave of them. Bacourt was there, faithful to the last, and to him she entrusted the papers which Talleyrand had left in her care. To Guizot she scrawled a painful note in pencil whose every word betrayed the effort which the writing cost her. Her last duties thus done she resigned herself to her solitary struggle with agonising death. Already she had receded voluntarily to the background ; it was as much according to her will that she slipped almost imperceptibly from the stage on the 19th September, 1862.

" I find it almost impossible," wrote Guizot, " to convince myself that I shall never more see those eyes, by turn so brilliant and so profound ; that I shall never more enjoy that conversation, rich and yet simple, which concealed strength in its very grace and which always left more to be understood than was actually said. When a brilliant light suddenly goes out, for some time afterwards one seems to see it shining ; one does not pass at once into the darkness . . ."

*   *   *   *   *

When she knew that death was approaching, Dorothea wrote that she often dreamed of a chateau in which she would reunite everyone she had loved. " Now the evening of my life is wearing on and not even the first stone of my chateau has been laid. I can have no hope but for a reunion in eternity." It is not idle to speculate who might have found a welcome in this spectral home. Her friends were all important in Dorothea's life, it might almost be said that she lived through their lives and expressed herself fully only in their doings. The habits of the age and the stranglehold of aristocratic conformity effectively prevented her from following the sort of life which would best have suited her. As a man she would have made a formidable soldier, ambassador or politician ; as a woman she had to seek in others the capacities which lay latent in herself. In the roll-call of her friends may be read the careers which she would so dearly have loved to call her own.

Certainly, there would have been few women within the walls of her dream chateau : Madame de Lieven, perhaps—as ambitious as herself—and Madame Adélaïde, who was so loyal a friend ; Pauline and Marie from her family. But the men would have more than made up the deficiency. There would have been Adam Czartoryski, hero of the Polish fight for liberation, and Vitrolles, the loyal, tenacious servant of the Bourbons. Clam, the dashing Austrian, later to become field-marshal and aide-de-camp to his Emperor, would have brought with him disturbing memories of Vienna. Molé, the distinguished, charming Molé would have been there ; the austere Royer Collard ; Barante, the historian and diplomat ; Guizot the statesman, for sheer intelligence probably the equal of anyone of his age. Adolphe Thiers could hardly have been omitted for once they had been very close to each other ; Thiers the brilliant, Thiers the irrepressible. The Duke of Orleans, the hope of France cut short, would have graced the assembly with his presence. Lichnowsky, the flamboyant demagogue, would have added a touch of irresponsibility to a group that might otherwise have been almost over-serious. Only Piscatory, that romantic diversion, would have added a flavour of talent unfulfilled ; only Bacourt, the faithful, diligent Bacourt would have filled a place, beyond appeal, in the ranks of the second-rate.

Are there common elements in all these men which, isolated, will betray the pattern of Dorothea's ambitions and her scale of values ? Intelligence—undoubtedly. Nobility of birth— in almost every case. Hunger for power—even Royer Collard was not so remote from worldly affairs as to disdain the lure of office. Courage. Serious purpose. A fineness of mind and delicacy of manner. All these—and yet such categorising is futile for her image of the figure of her age existed in flesh and blood and was never absent from her memory. Much though she cared for her friends and lovers, they could all have been swept from her life and still the dream chateau would not have been empty so long as through the deserted halls had dragged the club-foot of Prince Talleyrand.

When Talleyrand first became to Dorothea more than a distant and rather intimidating uncle by marriage her life had hardly begun to take its shape. She was an uneasy, arrogant, suspicious little girl, craving for love and finding it nowhere, tied to a man for whom she could feel neither affection nor respect, possessed by a vague dissatisfaction yet not even sure enough of herself to have any idea of what it was she wanted. When he died some twenty-five years later the pattern of her life had set hard about her and all that remained was to allow it to run its course. And during this quarter of a century, though he had not been able to satisfy every want, he had played in her life a role incomparably more important than that of any other. By imitation, by reaction, even sometimes by revulsion, Dorothea had built up a personality which complemented the strengths and redressed the weaknesses of her uncle. Only when the old tree came crashing to the ground did it become clear that what had grown up in its shadow was not a dependent creeper but another tree, strong and flourishing in its own right.

If any judgment is to be passed on Dorothea, it is on her life with Talleyrand that it should be based. Certainly it is thus that she would have wished it. He gave her much. He taught her the arts to shine in society and take the lead in great events from the sanctuary of a salon; he taught her prudence, discrimination, when to speak and when to listen, when to rush forward and when to hold back. But far more than that, he showed her what it was to be wanted and needed, he gave her the sense of security and significance that can only come from knowing that one's being is indispensable to another. That was Talleyrand's greatest gift: not that he taught her to be a great political hostess, not even that he loved her and earned her love but that he let her see that he could no more do without her than she without him, that at last her life had a real and valid purpose for another beside herself.

That she honoured the debt in full, no one can deny. Those last years of dedicated service, when she urged him into a retirement which suited so ill her own age and inclinations, when she stoically endured the tempers, the sulks, the black depression of an old man resenting his pain and his failing powers, when she worked so devotedly in the face of constant discouragement to reconcile him with the Church which he had so repeatedly defied: those years present a picture of courage, loyalty and self-sacrifice whose worth no one can fairly denigrate.

" Heartless," Dorothea was often called; " implacable," " malicious," " immoral "; all such epithets, from time to tine, she may have merited. But in the supreme test of her life she did not fail. Her relationship with Prince Talleyrand, rooted though it may have been in ambition on the one side and unattractive passion on the other, matured into singular purity and beauty. Where Dorothea is remembered to-day it is not as Princess of Courland, not as Countess Edmond de Périgord, not as Duchess of Sagan but as Dorothea of Dino, niece and inseparable companion of Prince Talleyrand; friend, servant, comforter and inspirer of that most exacting and discriminating of statesmen. It is on this ground that her life must be judged and on this ground she need have little cause to fear the final judgment.

Bibliography

This book draws almost exclusively on printed sources. The author has been shown a few manuscript letters by or relating to the Duchess of Dino but none was of more than trivial importance. The duchess took with her to her castle of Sagan in Eastern Germany almost all her private papers including many hundreds of letters exchanged between her and Talleyrand and received from Adolphe de Bacourt. All these vanished during the war. Some papers turned up recently at a sale in West Germany which it seemed might have come from the archives of Sagan but, on investigation, the Duke of Talleyrand was satisfied that they were of minor importance and came from another source.

There has only been one full-length study of the Duchess of Dino ; *Le Dernier Amour de Talleyrand* by Françoise de Bernardy (Paris, 1956). She has also been treated at some length in *Talleyrands Nichte* by Maria von Bunsen (Berlin, 1925). The essay by Etienne Lamy, *L'enfance d'une Grande Dame* (Rouen, 1908) is little more than a summary of her own *Souvenirs*, and Lacour-Gayet's essay *La Duchesse de Dino* in the *Revue de Paris* of December, 1922 contains virtually nothing which is not to be found in her *Memoirs*.

Far and away the best source on the Duchess of Dino is her own writings. Her *Souvenirs* (Paris, 1908) cover her life until her marriage in 1809. The so-called *Memoirs* (London, 1909) edited by Princess Radziwill are largely based on bowdlerised versions of her letters to Bacourt. They run from 1831 to her death in 1862. The other work published under her name is her essay on the Chateau of Valençay : *Notice sur Valençay* (Paris, 1848). In addition to this, several collections of her letters exist. The most important of these consists of her letters to Barante (*Souvenirs de Barante*, Paris, 1901). Others are to Madame Adélaïde (*Nouvelle Revue rétrospective*, Paris, 1901 and 1902) ; to Count Molé (*Revue d'Histoire diplomatique*, Paris, 1947) ; to Thiers (*Revue de Paris*, July-August, 1923) and to Vitrolles (edited by Louis Royer, *La Duchesse de Dino et le Baron de Vitrolles*, Grenoble, 1937). Other isolated letters survive and are referred to either in the text or in these notes.

Books about Talleyrand are almost as important for a life of Dorothea as books about the duchess herself. Lacour-Gayet's *Talleyrand* (Paris,

1928-31) is by far the most comprehensive. Duff Cooper's brilliant stud (London, 1932) is of equal value but should be balanced by Loui Madelin's very hostile biography (Paris, 1944). Of less importance but o value for a work on the Duchess of Dino are Lady Blennerhasset' biography of *Talleyrand* (London, 1894) and Joseph McCabe's *Talleyrand a Biographical Study* (London, 1906).

The Duchess of Dino's relations with Talleyrand were such that the figured prominently in all the more-or-less gossipy studies of Talleyrand which have accumulated over the years. Of these, the most valuable i probably *Le Coeur Secret de Talleyrand* by Michel Missoffe (Paris, 1956) Others of considerable use are *La Vie Privée de Talleyrand* by Bernard d Lacombe (Paris, 1903) and *La Vie Privée de Talleyrand* by Jacques Viven (Paris, 1940). The *Souvenirs Intimes sur Monsieur de Talleyrand* by Amédée Pichot (Paris, 1870) is a collection of anecdotes, a few of which are of value. The *Reminiscences of Prince Talleyrand* by Colmache (London, 1848) also adds a little of interest.

Talleyrand's own memoirs, particularly supplemented by many documents in the new Plon edition of the first two volumes (Paul-Louis and Jean-Paul Couchoud—Paris, 1957), are essential to any study of the Duchess of Dino. So also are certain collections of his letters, in particular those to Caulaincourt (*Revue des Deux Mondes*, 1935) and to the Duchess of Courland (*Talleyrand Intime d'après sa correspondance avec la Duchesse de Courlande*, Paris, 1891). As with the Duchess of Dino's letters, certain isolated letters are referred to in the text or in these notes.

Over the next pages the author identifies the principal sources drawn on for each chapter or section of the book. As far as possible the source of quotations is identified in the text but where it seems essential there are references to the text to identify a particular quotation or give fuller details as to the origin of a fact or story.

CHAPTER I

For this, as for the following two chapters, the *Souvenirs* of the duchess are by far the best source and the narrative follows them closely. M. Etienne Lamy's essay provides a useful summary. Next in importance to those come the *Mémoires de Vitrolles* (Paris, 1947). *The Empress Catherine* by Gina Kaus (New York, 1935), the *Memoirs of Prince Adam Czartoryski* (Paris, 1887) and the *Memoirs of the Duchesse d'Abrantès*

Paris, 1831) all provide useful background. Arrigon's life of the Duchess of Courland, *Une Amie de Talleyrand* (Paris, 1946), is of particular value. Nesselrode's *Lettres et Papiers* (Paris, 1908) are also relevant.

1. *Emile* by Jean Jacques Rousseau (1762)
2. Quoted by Christopher Herold in his life of Mme de Staël (London 1959)
3. For a full and flattering account of the Duchess of Courland's salon life, see Hildebrand, *La Societé de Berlin de 1789 à 1815* (*Revue des Deux Mondes*, March, 1870)
4. The letters to Piattoli were published as an annex to the duchess's *Souvenirs*

CHAPTER II

The sources for this chapter are very much as for Chapter I. In addition *Louise de Prusse* by Albert Sorel (Paris, 1937) adds useful background as also do Princess Louise's memoirs, *Quarante cinq ans de ma vie* (Paris, 1911).

1. *Mémoires sur Napoléon*, Countess Kielmannsegge (Paris, 1928)
2. The text of this letter is at Annex VI to the *Souvenirs*

CHAPTER III

The *Souvenirs* of the Duchess of Dino and Arrigon's life of the Duchess of Courland, are still the most useful sources. The *Memoirs of Talleyrand* are very relevant and also the *Mémoires du général de Caulaincourt* (Paris, 1933) and Talleyrand's letters to Caulaincourt published in the *Revue des Deux Mondes*, October-November, 1935. The *Mémoires du chancelier Pasquier* (Paris, 1893-95) and N. K. Schilder's *L'Empereur Alexandre 1er* (St. Petersburg, 1897) are of some use.

1. The peregrinations of Batowski are carefully traced in Missoffe's *Le Coeur Secret de Talleyrand*
2. This conversation, like all others in the book, is as recorded by the Duchess of Dino—in this case in her *Souvenirs*

CHAPTER IV

With the ending of the *Souvenirs* at the time of her marriage there is no substantial account of events by the Duchess of Dino herself until the *Memoirs* begin in 1831. The *Memoirs* of Talleyrand, his letters to the

Duchess of Courland and to Caulaincourt and the *Memoirs* of Countess Kielmannsegge are all of the first importance. Other relevant works not already cited are the *Mémoires de la Comtesse de Boigne* (Paris, 1908), *Le Comte Molé, sa Vie, ses Mémoires* (Paris, 1922-30), *Trois Mois à Paris Lors du Mariage de Napoléon*, by Prince Clary und Aldringen (Paris, 1914), *Napoléon et Talleyrand* and *Dans l'Entourage de l'Empereur* by Emile Dard (Paris, 1935 and 1940), *Histoire des Salons de Paris* by the Duchess d'Abrantès and the *Mémoires du duc de Rovigo* (Paris, 1900).

1. *Correspondance de M. de Rémusat* (Paris, 1884-86)
2. *Réminiscences*, J. J. Coulmann (Paris, 1862)
3. *The Reminiscences and Recollections of Captain Gronow* (London 1862)
4. See the tributes to him in the *Mémoires* of Colonel Combe (Paris, 1853)

CHAPTER V

It is difficult to know how much to include in the bibliography of a book of this nature. Obviously it would be folly to write a chapter dealing principally with the Congress of Vienna without first consulting such works as Sir Harold Nicolson's *Congress of Vienna, 1812-22* (London, 1946) or Albert Sorel's essay *Talleyrand au Congrés de Vienne* in his *Essays* (Paris, 1895) but equally to cite them suggests historical pretensions beyond anything to which this work can lay claim. The most valuable direct sources of material are *Fêtes et Souvenirs du Congrés de Vienne* by the Comte de la Garde-Chambonas (Paris, 1901) and *Les Dessous du Congrés de Vienne* by Commandant Weil (Paris, 1917). This latter draws very heavily on Austrian police reports. *Le Coeur Secret de Talleyrand* by Michel Missoffe is of particular value for its study of the Duchess of Sagan. The *Memoirs of* Friedrich von Gentz (Leipzig, 1873) are useful and *Reconstruction : Talleyrand à Vienne* by Gugliemo Ferrero (Paris, 1940) of general background interest.

1. This incident is exhaustively treated by Michel Missoffe in an essay in the *Miroir de l'Histoire* for April, 1954
2. *Memoirs of Prince Metternich*, translated by Mrs. Napier (London, 1880)
3. Villemain. *Souvenirs contemporains* (Paris, 1864)
4. The story comes from Prince Koslowski

Bibliography

CHAPTER VI

In this chapter, and indeed up to the July Revolution in 1830, the most important single source is the *Souvenirs* of Prosper de Barante (Paris, 1901). As well as letters from the Duchess of Dino, this collection contains many other letters relevant to her life and doings. Other important sources are the *Memoirs* of Molé and of Vitrolles and the Duchess of Dino's letters to Vitrolles edited by Louis Royer. The Memoirs of Aimée de Coigny (Paris, 1902), the *Correspondance de M. de Rémusat* (Paris, 1884), Pasquier's *Histoire de mon temps* (Paris, 1893-95), the *Memoirs of the Comte de Villèle*, and *Memoirs of the court of Louis XVIII* by *A Lady* all add useful detail. The *Mémoires d'Outre-Tombe* of Chateaubriand (Paris, 1848) are essential background for any work on the period.

1. There is another account of this incident in *The Diary of Frances, Lady Shelley* (London, 1913), which suggests that the cause of the duel was not generally known
2. This letter was published in *L'Amateur d'autographes* (Paris, 1909)
3. *Ibid*
4. See the Duchess of Dino's *Notice sur Valençay*
5. Lacour-Gayet's *Talleyrand*, Vol. 3
6. The diaries of Sylvester Douglas, Lord Glenbervie (London, 1928)

CHAPTER VII

The sources for this chapter are much as for Chapter VI. In addition one must mention *Personal Recollections of the duc de Broglie* translated by de Beaufort (London, 1887), the *Journal of Comte Rodolphe Apponyi* (Paris, 1913-26), *Le beau Montrond* by Henri Malo (Paris, 1926), the letters between Talleyrand and Royer Collard published by the Société des Bibliophiles Français (Paris, 1903), Lucas-Dubreton's *Monsieur Thiers* (Paris, 1948) and *Conversations avec M. Thiers* by Henri de Lacombe (*Le Correspondant*, September, 1922).

1. Quoted by permission of the Marquess of Lansdowne
2. Sainte-Beuve. *Nouveaux Lundis* No. 11
3. Quoted by Lacour-Gayet from the Catalogue Nöel Charavay
4. Duchess of Dino *Notice sur Valençay*
5. Diaries of Sylvester Douglas, Lord Glenbervie (London, 1928)
6. The Journal of Henry Edmond Fox (London, 1923)

7. For a flattering account of Piscatory's war effort, see the letter o the Duchess of Broglie (Paris 1896) of 18th October, 1825

8. Letter from Stendhal to Sutton Sharpe of April, 1830 (*Correspondance*, Paris, 1933)

9. For a thoroughly inconclusive examination of this story see the essay by M. Davin (*Le Fureteur*, 1955)

10. Letter to Barante of 1st September, 1824

11. Letter to Mme de Mollien of 20th June, 1827

12. *The French Nation*, D. W. Brogan (London, 1957)

CHAPTER VIII

From now on the *Memoirs* of the Duchess of Dino are the best source of material. Almost all quotations, unless otherwise stated, come from this source. Nearly all the better-known English diarists of the period contribute something : in particular *The Creevey Papers* (London, 1903), *Croker's Correspondence and Diaries* (London, 1885), *The Greville Memoirs* (London, 1885-87) and *A portion of the Journal kept by Thomas Raikes from 1831 to 1847* (London, 1857). *The Letters of Lady Holland to her Son* (London, 1946) and the letters of Lady Harriet Granville (London, 1894) both contain much of value. Dorothea's own letters to Thiers (*Revue de Paris*, July-August, 1923), to Molé and to Madame Adélaïde (*Nouvelle Revue rétrospective*, Paris, 1901 and 1902) are all of importance. Madame de Lieven is an invaluable source of material, particularly in her correspondence with Lord Grey (London, 1890), in the general collection of her letters edited by L. G. Robinson (London, 1902) and, to a lesser degree, in *The Unpublished Diary and Political Sketches of Princess Lieven* (London, 1925). Montgomery Hyde's *Princess Lieven* (London, 1938) is also of value.

Other useful works include G. Pallain's *L'Ambassade de Talleyrand à Londres* (Paris, 1891), the *Correspondence* of M. de Rémusat, the *Souvenirs* of the Duc de Broglie, and Mlle de Bernardy's Life of Count Flahaut : *Son of Talleyrand* (translated by Lucy Norton, London, 1956).

1. Bertin de Veaux's letter to Molé of 18th October, 1830 is quoted in Molé's memoirs.

2. Count Flahaut, quoted by permission of the Marquess of Lansdowne

3. This letter, from the archives of Adolphe de Bacourt, was quoted by Michel Missoffe in his *Coeur Secret de Talleyrand*

4. Prosper Mérimée *Sept Lettres à Stendhal* (Paris, 1898)

Bibliography

CHAPTER IX

This chapter draws on the same sources as the preceding.

1. *Monsieur de Bacourt et la Duchesse de Dino* by G. Monod in the *Mémoires de la Societé des Science Morales, des Lettres et des Arts de Seine-et-Oise,* 1894

CHAPTER X

The *Memoirs of Guizot* (London, 1858) and the *Lettres de M. Guizot à sa Famille et à ses Amis* (Paris, 1884) are of increasing importance over the last third of the Duchess of Dino's life. The *Memoirs* of the Duchess d'Abrantès, of the Countess de Boigne, Barante, Molé, Count Apponyi, the Duke of Broglie and Lady Harriet Granville are again all of value. Of works not previously cited the letters of the Duke of Orleans (Paris, 1889), the Lieven-Palmerston correspondence edited by Lord Sudley (London, 1943) and the *Journal du Maréchal de Castellane* (Paris, 1895-97) are of use. Stendhal's *Lucien Leuwen* provides a far more vivid picture of Orleanist Paris than any memoirs or histories have ever done.

1. From *The Mistress or Love Verses* by Abraham Cowley
2. This is Apponyi's version

CHAPTER XI

Talleyrand's last months have been lavishly treated by the biographers. The Duchess of Dino's own account *Le Retour de Talleyrand à la réligion. Lettre de Mme La Duchesse de Talleyrand à l'abbé Dupanloup* was edited by Princess Radziwill (Paris, 1908). Other important accounts include *La conversion et la mort de M. de Talleyrand,* the *récit* of Barante edited by his grandson Baron de Nervo (Paris, 1910); *La fin de Talleyrand* by Guyot (*Feuilles d'Histoire ;* August, 1909) and Arrigon's *La Duchesse de Dino et la fin de Talleyrand* (*Revue des Deux Mondes,* March-April, 1955). A more prejudiced account is that of Sainte-Beuve (*Nouveaux Lundis,* vol. 12) and there is useful information in the *Vie de Mgr. Dupanloup* by the Abbé Lagrange.

Bibliography

CHAPTER XII

The Duchess of Dino's *Memoirs* and her letters to Molé and Barante are still the most important source. Count Apponyi's Memoirs are also of particular value for this part of her life.

CHAPTER XIII

In addition to the various memoirs and collections of letters already cited the *Souvenirs of the Comte de Sainte-Aulaire* (Paris, 1926) contain some useful material as also does the Journal of Princess Mélanie de Metternich.
1. *Souvenirs* of Princess Antoine Radziwill (Paris, 1931)
2. *Lettres de Prosper Mérimée à la Comtesse de Montijo* (Paris, 1930)

CHAPTER XIV

The Souvenirs of Prince Felix Lichnowsky (Paris, 1844), even though they relate to a period earlier than this chapter, are nevertheless of particular importance and relevance. Bismarck's *Mémoires* (Paris, 1889) contain some useful material, as also do the *Souvenirs d'une Mission à Berlin* of Count Circourt (Paris, 1908).
1. *Mémoires* by Charles Bocher (Paris, 1906)
2. From H. A. L. Fisher's *History of Europe*

CHAPTER XV

Guizot's memoirs, his letters to his family and to Mme Laure de Gasparin (Paris, 1934) are all of importance. *Men and Things of My Time*, by the Marquis de Castellane (translated by Alexander de Mattos, London, 1911) is useful for the light it sheds on the author's mother, Pauline de Castellane, at this period. The *Souvenirs* of Princess Antoine Radziwill (Paris, 1931) are valuable and *The Empress Frederick* by Princess Catherine Radziwill contains interesting, if somewhat unreliable, information.
1. Queen Victoria to the Earl of Clarendon, 25th October, 1857

Index

For the sake of brevity the
Duchess of Dino is referred to throughout as D